Modern Lusts

MODERN LUSTS

ERNEST BORNEMAN—
JAZZ CRITIC, FILMMAKER, SEXOLOGIST

DETLEF SIEGFRIED

Translated by Noah Harley and Jennifer Neuheiser

berghahn

NEW YORK · OXFORD
www.berghahnbooks.com

Published in 2020 by
Berghahn Books
www.berghahnbooks.com

Originally published in German as
Moderne Lüste: Ernest Borneman - Jazzkritiker, Filmemacher, Sexforscher

The translation of this work was funded by Geisteswissenschaften International –
Translation Funding for Humanities and Social Sciences from Germany, a joint
initiative of the Fritz Thyssen Foundation, the German Federal Foreign Office, the
collecting society VG WORT, and the Börsenverein des Deutschen Buchhandels
(German Publishers & Booksellers Association).

Library of Congress Cataloging-in-Publication Data

A C.I.P. cataloging record is available from the Library of Congress
Library of Congress Cataloging in Publication Control Number:
2020937015

British Library Cataloguing in Publication Data

A catalogue record for this book is available from the British Library

EU GPSR Authorized Representative

LOGOS EUROPE, 9 rue Nicolas Poussin, 17000, LA ROCHELLE, France
Email: Contact@logoseurope.eu

ISBN 978-1-78920-288-5 hardback
ISBN 978-1-80758-031-5 paperback
ISBN 978-1-80758-633-1 epub
ISBN 978-1-78920-289-2 web pdf

https://doi.org/10.3167/9781789202885

My worldview isn't Platonic, it's Epicurean.
Ernest Borneman

CONTENTS

ILLUSTRATIONS

Abbreviations

AdK	Akademie der Künste (Academy of Arts), Berlin
AFBF	American Folk Blues Festival
AFN	American Forces Network
AIDS	Acquired Immune Deficiency Syndrome
ARD	Arbeitsgemeinschaft der Rundfunkanstalten Deutschlands (Working Group of Public Broadcasters)
BAK	Bundesarchiv, Koblenz
BBA	Bertolt Brecht Archiv
BBC	British Broadcasting Corporation
BC	*Beat-Club*
BDI	Bundesverband der Deutschen Industrie (Federation of German Industries)
BFI	British Film Institute
CBS	Columbia Broadcasting System
CDU	Christlich Demokratische Union Deutschlands (Christian Democratic Union of Germany)
DEFA	Deutsche Film Aktiengesellschaft
DFF	Deutscher Fernsehfunk (East German television)
DGfS	Deutsche Gesellschaft für Sexualforschung (German Society for Sexual Research)
DGSS	Deutsche Gesellschaft für sozialwissenschaftliche Sexualforschung (German Society for Social-Scientific Sexuality Research)
EBA	Ernest Borneman Archiv
EHA	Elisabeth Hauptmann Archiv
FAZ	*Frankfurter Allgemeine Zeitung*

FDJ	Freie Deutsche Jugend (Free German Youth)
FDP	Freie Demokratische Partei
FFG	Freies Fernsehen Gesellschaft
FR	*Frankfurter Rundschau*
GDR	German Democratic Republic (Deutsche Demokratische Republik)
GFSS	Gesellschaft zur Förderung Sozialwissenschaftlicher Sexualforschung (Society for the Advancement of Social-Scientific Sexuality Research)
HIV	Human Immunodeficiency Virus
HR	Hessischer Rundfunk (Hesse Broadcasting)
HWA	Helene Weigel Archiv
IASB	International African Service Bureau
ITV	Independent Television
KPD	Kommunistische Partei Deutschlands (Communist Party of Germany)
KPÖ	Kommunistische Partei Österreichs (Communist Party of Austria)
LAC	Library and Archives Canada
LRM	Lippman+Rau Musikarchiv
NA	National Archives
NAACP	National Association for the Advancement of Colored People
NDR	Norddeutscher Rundfunk (Northern German Broadcasting)
NFB	National Film Board of Canada
NR	*Neue Revue*
NUL	Northwestern University Library
NWDR	Nordwestdeutscher Rundfunk (Northwest German Broadcasting)
NWRV	Nord- und Westdeutscher Rundfunkverband (North and West German Broadcasting Federation)
ÖGS	Österreichische Gesellschaft für Sexualforschung (Austrian Society for Sexual Research)
ORF	Österreichischer Rundfunk (Austrian Broadcasting)
RB	Radio Bremen

R & B   Rhythm and Blues

SA   Sturmabteilung (Stormtroopers)

SDS   Sozialistischer Deutscher Studentenbund (Socialist German Student League)

SED   Sozialistische Einheitspartei Deutschlands (Socialist Unity Party of Germany)

SFB   Sender Freies Berlin (Radio Free Berlin)

SPD   Sozialdemokratische Partei Deutschlands (Social Democratic Party of Germany)

SPÖ   Sozialdemokratische Partei Österreichs (Social Democratic Party of Austria)

SSB   Sozialistischer Schülerbund (Socialist High School Students Association)

StBB   Staatsbibliothek zu Berlin

StDK   Stiftung Deutsche Kinemathek

SWF   Südwestfunk (Southwest Broadcasting)

SWR   Südwestrundfunk (Southwest Broadcasting)

SZ   *Süddeutsche Zeitung*

UN   United Nations

UNESCO   United Nations Educational, Scientific and Cultural Organization

WDR   Westdeutscher Rundfunk (West German Broadcasting)

ZDF   Zweites Deutsches Fernsehen

INTRODUCTION

I stumbled across the name Ernest Borneman while researching another project. In the archives of Radio Bremen, I discovered that he had been the man behind the famous *Beat-Club*—the first German show to bring beat and pop music to television. The discovery lent a sudden and unexpected historical and political depth to a pop culture phenomenon of the 1960s. Borneman's name rang a bell; I vaguely remembered him as a proponent of sexual emancipation back in the 1980s. I was struck by the alliance of jazz, film, and sex on display in Borneman's biography—each a vital element of modern culture in the twentieth century in its own right, but which came together in his person in a way that seemed rather unusual. Jazz, film, and sex may play an important role in many people's everyday lives, but seldom appear in combination as the object of intensive, scholarly research. A common focal point that allows them to be meaningfully set in relation to one another is rare to come by.

There are other hurdles, too, involving the tension between poetry and truth. Ernest Borneman has always been a polarizing figure, celebrated as an early advocate of jazz and emancipated sexuality by some but seen as a pretentious self-promoter and swindler by others. The fodder for these divergent opinions came from his wide-ranging journalistic activities, his work in film and television, and his mass media presence. Borneman was an untiring autodidact who never earned a conventional academic degree, because he fled Germany in 1933, shortly before completing his Abitur (the equivalent to a high-school diploma, and required for admission to universities in Germany). His years of exile in England and Canada marked a turning point in his life—a place outside the confines of a normal German existence, a setting for his political, cultural, and academic socialization, and a projective surface and realm of fantasy after the fact. He worked diligently at crafting his own biography, piecing together fragments of reality and fiction to form a "biographical illusion" (Pierre Bourdieu) of a life lived as an outsider, bolstering his credibility in the process, and especially his authority as an unconventional scholar. At the same time, doubts as to the veracity of this image have also influenced public perception of him. Writing a biography of Borneman, then, has meant constantly tussling with these autobiographical constructions by correlating them to other contemporary sources. Nevertheless, in what follows, readers should not expect to find the final word on these matters; new sources may come to light that would once again change the picture. What this book has to offer is more a preliminary account, written from a specific perspective.

How is one to approach a biography that immediately communicates such breadth, is so rich in its connections to the politics, society, and art of the twentieth century? Any number of broader perspectives are possible and may further prove highly insightful for future projects: the lasting influence of Borneman's emigration, his journalistic work, the significance of his Jewish background, or how autobiographical constructions function as a form of strategic remembrance. As mentioned above, I have chosen to focus first and foremost on Borneman's interest in cultural products of modernity that were at the time considered to be the epitome of progress and were assigned a special place in society's self-reflection and self-interpretation: jazz—the most avant-garde and popular music style over the first half of the century; film—the most ambitious expression of visual culture in the twentieth century; and the "sexual revolution"—the most extensive transformation of intimate bodily practices and discourses. Given that each of these processes of modernization was particularly effective in raising emotions, it is surprising that Borneman came to them through his own, equally avant-garde self-identification as a Marxist, one moreover in the vein of a "new objectivity" (*neue Sachlichkeit*) as represented by Bertolt Brecht, which advocated processing highly emotional topics in a rationally controlled way. Borneman, however, was anything but a distanced observer. While he succumbed to these modern lusts himself, he also sought to understand them theoretically and shape them practically. This resulted in a kind of tension between pleasure and discipline that was not entirely unusual for a certain type of intellectual in the twentieth century.

It strikes one that Borneman's opinion of himself, one shared by friends and acquaintances but also the public, was of a sensual person, a hedonist who knew how to enjoy the pleasures of life.

And this despite repeated claims of working fourteen to sixteen hours a day, without taking time off on the weekends or for vacations. This self-image of an unremitting Sisyphus was contradicted by other statements and practices—tales of escapades in the bars of London, Paris, and Frankfurt or the handmade leather suitcase with room for two bottles (whiskey and water) and two glasses that was a constant companion in his later years, not to mention the frank accounts of his active sex life and his close relationships with jazz and film stars. In and of themselves, the topics that garnered Borneman's attention were forms of sensory perception specific to twentieth-century modernity. Here modernity is intended in the sense of a "high modernity" as Ulrich Herbert has periodized it, beginning in the last third of the nineteenth century and ending around 1990—a period that coincides almost exactly with the heyday of film, jazz, and the ideal of sexual liberation.[1]

Just like politics or economics, desires and the senses that provide the physiological bases for them have a history. It is not only the ways in which people see, hear, smell, taste, and touch—the "sensory mentality" (Martin Jay)—that have changed over time, but also the interpretation of these senses.[2] The battles fought time and again over these sensory mentalities provide insight into contemporaries' self-images and ideals. Jazz, film, and the sexual revolution may be highly disparate topics, but they do share one thing in common: each represents a specific form of the production of sensuality and sensory perception in the twentieth century. In addition to new fundamental lines of development in society and politics (industrialization, urbanization, rationalization, and individualization), modernity also generated new forms of art that reflected these transformations. The modern novel, modern painting, and photography dealt with the changing times differently than their predecessors; they were more fragmented, more abstract, and closer to everyday life. Some forms of art, such as records, talking films, radio, and television, first emerged during the modern era thanks to new technical discoveries, and came to play a key role in modern society's self-perception. As technical media, they not only changed the auditory and visual landscapes of the twentieth century, they changed sensory perceptions. Two of Borneman's central interests, namely jazz and film, were seen as typical expressions of modernity, ways of perceiving and processing that were well suited to the societal and political changes underway and held the power to alter emotions. Borneman's early involvement with both jazz and film meant he played a role in their development.

In the world of music, jazz figured as one of the most prominent forms of artistic expression in the twentieth century. Although perceived from an early point on as "modern music," according to Ingrid Monson it was not until after World War I that jazz became the "most complex and interesting musical language of the 20th century."[3] For historian and jazz aficionado Eric Hobsbawm, jazz was the most noteworthy cultural phenomenon of the century because it reflected the transformation of society in a comprehensive way, not simply in terms of musical preferences, but also in terms of "race" and class relations, economics, and politics.[4] At the same time, jazz witnessed a struggle over its interpretation that oscillated between the poles of art and popular culture, a debate that played out in similar fashion in film. While individual people could also listen to jazz, its interpretation was primarily a collective act; the level of bodily expression appropriate to the music, for example, was one disputed aspect.

Within the Western tradition, sight has been the most important sense for helping people to conceptualize their world. While photographs were upheld over and against painting as laying greater claim to authenticity, from the end of the nineteenth century on it was the moving images presented in film that gave a stronger impression of reality. At the same time, film became an art form as well as an ideal medium for entertainment via fictive stories, in turn calling into question the postulate of "the victory of the rational eye in modernity."[5] The tension between the pretension of representing reality and the narration of made-up stories played a significant role in the history of film, although a handful of astute observers recognized the constructed nature of documentaries early on as well. At first on the big screen and then later on televisions all over the world, film was the most significant visual media of high modernity.

The sense of touch—often considered to be less important—experienced a renaissance in the twentieth century. After Sigmund Freud, sexuality was no longer viewed simply as a driving force behind human behavior, but also the creation of culture, by way of sublimation. This stood in opposition to an understanding of sexuality often advanced by the state and the church that focused on the dangers of intimate touching and called for the suppression of the sexual drives. Reform movements in the Weimar Republic that had taken aim at sexual liberation and were cut short by National Socialism ultimately experienced a revival in West Germany after the war in the late 1950s. The pill, commercialization, mediatization, and the idea of the "sexual revolution" as espoused by the counterculture of the sixty-eighters in Germany eroded traditional norms and increased tolerance for all kinds of inclinations and practices, while also setting new boundaries for sexual liberation.

It is therefore all the more interesting and telling that Ernest Borneman should of all things select jazz, film, and sexuality as subjects for intensive research and analysis. He was deeply rooted in the sensory world of the twentieth century, which he sought both to understand and mold from a specific perspective. It must also be borne in mind that these disparate fields hardly conflicted with one another, just as Borneman's relentless work habits somehow harmonized with a hedonistic disposition. For this reason, it seemed to make sense to approach a biography of Ernest Borneman from the perspective of the senses, which were not only a source of attraction for Borneman, but also opened up paths to insight and changing the world. This book therefore looks at Borneman's interpretations of jazz, film, and sexuality, how he positioned himself vis-à-vis competing interpretations, and the extent to which he influenced his contemporaries in their own thinking on these subjects. Borneman is not treated exclusively in terms of his self-will, then; his biography also functions as a way of exploring a world of perceptions and emotions that in recent years has piqued the interest of German historiography, not least regarding the history of images, sounds, and bodies. Such an approach means Borneman's biography cannot be reconstructed in consistently linear fashion even if the book does follow a basic chronology, and while any number of biographical ramifications do appear within this context, it goes without saying they should not be viewed from this one perspective.

By the same token, in what follows, "modernity" is dealt with as a social and aesthetic but also political concept, in which the idea of democratization played a significant role. As a Marxist, Borneman strove for equality not only in the sense of representative democracy but in every aspect of society, in particular in social life. This was quite clear from his programmatic goals while involved with the National Film Board of Canada and his work as a jazz critic, but also from his efforts as a sexologist and gender researcher, where he lent emphatic support to the cause of women's emancipation—to the intermittent dismay of those he championed. At the same time, Borneman's appreciation for precursors to modernity gave him a broader frame of reference and sense of orientation. In a letter to his then girlfriend and future wife Eva, for example, Borneman drew similarities between their mutual sources of inspiration, "odd as that collection must appear to outsiders. Joyce-Hemingway-Blues-Elizabethan folksongs-medieval love lyrics-Büchner-Brecht-de Coster—it's really one line of affinity."[6]

All of this cannot be read one-dimensionally as one chapter in the story of progress, as Borneman's work on the place of jazz in African American culture and his sex research both make clear. The African American experience—slavery, racial segregation, exploitation, and political oppression—revealed the dark side of modernity, as did the struggle against exclusion based on ethnic criteria, one that also took place at an aesthetic level. In the realm of sexuality too, a special "dialectic of sexual enlightenment," as sexologist Sophinette Becker has deemed it, justified "sexual liberation" as an ideal, but one whose absolute quality also—against Borneman's will and to his great dismay—ensured its failure.[7]

* * *

There is no particular egotism involved in keeping materials that bear witness to your own life such as letters, memorabilia, or one's own writing. Borneman was a collector when it came to his work, but also to his private life. From the very beginning, he kept everything he either produced himself or that concerned him. That was not all, however. He routinely made carbon copies of his own letters to other people, which means that the correspondence from both sides—and not just the letters that he received—were kept in his archives. What's more, he would sometimes ask recipients to return a handwritten letter if he thought that its contents were particularly valuable and something he wanted to use again. His estate includes letters to Eva, his wife (which he kept after her death), but also letters to his parents, which he must have asked to have back after the war. He sorted everything according to type—letters filed by correspondent in alphabetical order—and stored everything in file folders for easy access. Quite clearly, this was the work not simply of a manic encyclopedist, but of a giant ego. Moreover, as a freelancer, Borneman was his own office. He did not have a secretary, so he had to make sure that he could find the materials that he needed quickly, especially professional correspondence and manuscripts. After his death, even with his large collection of materials on jazz already stored in the archive of the Akademie der Künste (Academy of Arts, AdK), seventy large moving boxes of additional files still went to Berlin, not counting his books. Despite the files' internal organization, this is a tremendous amount of material that is difficult to assess, especially since it has only been sorted roughly, with the exception of the sources on jazz.[8] It has all yet to be cataloged properly in detail. I have sifted through the majority of these sources and consulted further archives in Europe and North America where Borneman left traces, partially in order to fill in gaps (despite the great mass of materials), but more importantly to broaden the range of sources and better reconstruct how he was seen by those around him. Similarly, the collection of Borneman's personal papers contains only a small portion of his many publications, another gap that cannot be filled by his estate alone. This owes in part to the fact that Borneman's enormous library, including his own books and copies of his articles that were published in edited volumes and journal issues, were given to the Chamber of Labor (Arbeiterkammer) in Vienna, where they were not kept as a separate collection but rather incorporated into the library's general collection. Although manuscripts in different version can be found within Borneman's collection at the archives, the publications themselves had to be located separately because the manuscripts were not always sufficient. Thus despite the overwhelming amount of materials, neither the files nor the following account can claim to be complete; a more systematic and targeted analysis of various aspects can only be brought about once the archives are organized and cataloged. Therefore, although a detailed reconstruction of his life may be possible in parts, this biography can only offer an incomplete picture.[9]

* * *

I have benefited greatly from the knowledge and eager assistance of many individuals in writing this book, as well as the generosity of a number of institutions. I would like to thank Werner Grünzweig, the head of the music department at the Akademie der Künste archives for his invaluable help with Borneman's collection of personal papers. I would also like to thank Dagmar Herzog, Michael Rauhut, and Susanne Regener for reading portions of the manuscript and providing critical and encouraging feedback alike. I am grateful for the collegial cooperation of Rolf Aurich and Wolfgang Jacobsen from the Stiftung Deutsche Kinemathek and for discussions with Ulrike Heider. I am indebted to Stephen Borneman for a long afternoon in Vienna, during which I learned a lot about his parents, and who let me use his large collection of photographs, and to Franz Altrichter, Reinhard Lorenz, and Irmi Novak for information and materials. Sarah Gottschalk, Klara Gade Thomsen, and Søren Pedersen provided valuable assistance in archival research and assembling the bibliography. I am also indebted to Hanna Leitgeb, Stefanie Mürbe, and Thedel von Wallmoden for helping to turn a manuscript into a book and to Noah Harley and Jennifer Neuheiser for translating it into English. I am grateful for the financial support provided for research travel by the Department of English, German and Romance Studies at the University of Copenhagen, the Center for Modern European Studies in the Humanities Department of the University of Copenhagen, and the Herbert-Weichmann-Stiftung in Hamburg. Finally, in October 2016 this book received a Geisteswissenschaften International translation award from the Börsenverein des Deutschen Buchhandels, the Fritz Thyssen Foundation, VG Wort, and the Foreign Office, making its translation into English possible. My thanks go to these institutions for their support.

Notes

1. Herbert, *Geschichte Deutschlands im 20. Jahrhundert.*
2. Jütte, *Geschichte der Sinne*; Classen, "The Senses"; Smith, *Sensory History*; Jay, "In the Realm of the Senses." See for instance, Morat, "Die Stadt und die Sinne."
3. Monson, *Saying Something*, 19.
4. Hobsbawm, *The Jazz Scene*, 1.
5. Smith, *Sensory History*, 21.
6. Ernest to Eva, 13 March 1942.
7. Becker, "Pädophilie zwischen Dämonisierung und Verharmlosung."
8. The sources mentioned in the endnotes can be found in this collection (AdK) unless otherwise noted. All of the sources that are not from Borneman's papers in the archive of the Akademie der Künste are identified by an archival abbreviation and corresponding file numbers.
9. Since almost all of Borneman's private correspondence between 1933 and 1960 was written in English, many of the quotes used in this book were originally in English. They were translated by the author into German for the original German edition of this book in order to improve readability but have been faithfully restored to the original English for this translation.

Chapter 1

"In Me You Have Someone on Whom There Is No Relying"
Constants and Constructs

Ernest Borneman (born Ernst Bornemann) began writing at a young age. His first manuscript, drafted at the age of seventeen, still exists—at 264 pages long, it is surprisingly well written for such a young author.[1] *Fahrt ohne Ziel* (A Trip without a Destination) chronicles the author's trip to Sweden in the summer of 1932 with Herbert Louis Steinthal, a friend and the son of the Berlin correspondent for Copenhagen's left-liberal daily newspaper *Politiken.* The book begins by introducing the protagonists, giving an indication of the author's self-perception as a young man: "We—that is Louis, seventeen years old, a Danish national who has been living for more than ten years in Berlin, medium height, slim, unbelievably polite . . . and me, Ernst Bornemann, called Mac, Mackie, or—using my scout name—Schlentiger. I am sixteen years old, a German national, and I live sometimes (when I am not traveling) in the great city of Berlin. I have two passions: traipsing about and singing Negro songs." The self-assigned nickname reveals an affinity for Brecht, while travel and jazz would remain lifelong passions. As the novel progresses, the picture emerges of a young mind marked by an interest in modern movements in architecture, music, and film that matures as the protagonist travels from Norrköping to Stockholm, Göteborg, and Copenhagen, absorbing Scandinavian functionalism on the way. Upon encountering this architectural style he writes, for example, of having found "at long last, New Objectivity [*Neue Sachlichkeit*] expressed in bricks, something I have been trying to find for so long; the Chilehaus in Hamburg was really just a temporary solution." "Nowhere," Borneman continues, "does the decorative ornamentation of the fin-de-siècle style offend the eye of the beholder." For him, Stockholm was "the real manifestation of a *Metropolis* fantasy à la Fritz Lang," and he praised the "Americanized touch" of the city's urban landscape. This trip was also much like a "farewell to his youth"—his parents were under the impression they would have to give up their children's clothing store at Kaiserdamm 116 in the Charlottenburg neighborhood of Berlin for financial reasons. Ernst was supposed to leave school and earn money by working for a printer in Stettin. Things turned out differently.

Ernst Bornemann, born 12 April 1915 in Berlin as the only child of Curt and Hertha Bornemann (née Blochert), attended the Karl Marx School until the summer of 1933. Led by Fritz Karsen, the reformed school was coed, nondenominational, and socially integrative in its approach; its experiments with new pedagogical methods included project-based learning, polytechnic instruction, and flexible age groupings. Young Ernst loved the school, which proved to be his saving grace, as he had already twice been expelled from other schools for his political activities.[2] He was a member of the Socialist High School Students Association (Sozialistischer Schülerbund, SSB), which held close ties to the German Communist Party (KPD) and whose newspaper, *Schulkampf*, he edited.[3] The Karl Marx School was a bastion of the SSB, with a teaching staff that included leftist theoreticians such as Karl Korsch, Siegfried Bernfeld, and KPD education policy maker Edwin Hoernle.[4] In retrospect, Borneman saw his socialization in the SSB as the decisive factor in the development of his own political views. The discussions between the different Socialist-Communist camps, he noted, "were among the most interesting, most lively, and most informative experiences of

Figure 1.1. Art class during Carnival celebrations at the Karl Marx School. Borneman is in the back row, third from right. Courtesy AdK.

my youth."[5] Later in life, he would say of himself and his friends that "we had matured early: sexually at 14, politically at 15, and intellectually between 14 and 16."[6]

Just weeks before completing his Abitur (akin to a high-school graduation exam) Ernst Bornemann (upon emigrating to England he dropped the second "n" from his family name and added an "e" to his given name) left Germany on 5 July 1933, making his way to London as part of a youth transport. In his 1977 autobiography he gives the reason for his flight as the risk posed by the seizure of "membership lists" from Wilhelm Reich's sexual clinics by the paramilitary wing of the Nazi Party (Sturmabteilung, or SA).[7] Earlier sources from the immediate postwar period pertaining to the possibility of material restitution, however, do not mention this but instead offer a less specific account: "If my memory serves, what happened was this: I received warning that I was already on the Gestapo's list, and I tried to get out of Germany through a school exchange program, because the civil servant in charge of the list of selected students was a Social Democrat and he added my name to the list at the last minute."[8] Wilhelm Reich is not mentioned at all in a correspondence between Borneman and his father weighing possible arguments, although there is talk of a general threat. His father wrote:

> I can testify that you were subject to persecution. You often came home late because you were ambushed by the upper school students from other schools and the older Hitler Youth boys who tried to beat you up. But the most important argument proving that the Gestapo had already set its sights on you was this: in the fall of 1933 . . . two huge Gestapo men came into our shop to arrest you. Because fortunately you were not there at the time but already in London, they asked about everything you had been doing for the last few years in detail, and they actually took the chance to claim that you were in Soviet Russia. A half year later, another civil servant came to find out where you were.[9]

His parents' letters from the summer of 1933 also clearly show that they tried to encourage their son to return home. His mother wrote him: "After all, you don't necessarily have to flee Germany as so many others do now."[10] His father thought that he could probably find an internship at a newspaper without having his Abitur, but that he would have to make concessions in light of the political situation: "You would just have to learn how to write apolitically."[11] Although the eighteen-year-old felt at home in London, there were points at which he toyed with the idea of moving on—New York and Brazil were mentioned—but he never considered returning to Berlin.[12] Whether this was all actually motivated by political considerations, a desire for adventure, or some combination of the two is difficult to say. When he briefly considered returning to Germany in spring 1934, his parents urgently advised him against it—especially his mother, who viewed the situation more realistically than his father. When one of his relatives, Ernst Levinsohn, left Berlin in 1938, Borneman's Aunt Erna told him about Levinsohn's interrogation by the Gestapo, which had found Borneman's address in Levinsohn's notebook. "Hopefully this won't cause you trouble," she wrote. "He had to go down to the Gestapo station and let them interrogate him up and down for four hours, then finally he had to sign an agreement to leave Germany by the fall. They told him very clearly that you had attended the Karl Marx School, and they wanted to know how often he had met with you; I'm told he said as often as relatives usually meet up."[13]

When Borneman received orders to report for enlistment in the German army in 1935, he did not show up.[14] In 1936 he signed up at the German consulate "to fulfill his active service and work service requirements" and was transferred to the Ersatzreserve II, a military reserve unit. The document bore the signature of the consul, but the field where Borneman had to sign was left blank. Nor did he turn up for duty, upon which his German citizenship was rescinded.[15] He was not naturalized in Great Britain before the war, and after receiving Canadian citizenship in 1945 Borneman regularly switched his country of residence, but also his nationality. He finally became a British subject in 1959; in 1961 the West German authorities recognized his German citizenship; in 1976 he was naturalized in Austria. Regardless, it was emigration that saved him. As he soberly wrote to his girlfriend Eva in 1942, in the middle of the war, "If I had stayed home nine years ago I'd have a fair chance of being in my grave now."[16]

Eva

Eva Geisel was born into a Jewish family on 16 June 1912 in Barnes, England, making her three years older than Ernest.[17] Her mother was English, her father German. After completing her Abitur in Berlin in 1931, she pursued university courses in German, English, and journalism in Freiburg and Berlin. She then moved to London in 1933, where she worked as a film and theater critic at the *New Statesman* and at Fenner Brockway's *New Leader*. In 1937 she began working in the press department at Columbia Pictures.[18] After the antisemitic pogroms of 1938, her parents followed in her steps, immigrating to England. Eva Geisel was politically active during the war; she supported Jewish refugees, lent her voice to the BBC propaganda broadcasts directed at German women, worked for the Free German Youth organization (Freie Deutsche Jugend, or FDJ), and applied to the Political Intelligence Service of the Foreign Office (although it is unclear whether she was actually hired).[19] In 1943 she relocated to Canada, where she married Ernest that same year. The couple's only child, Stephen, was born on 16 July 1947. In Ottawa she worked, like her husband, first at the National Film Board in the information department, before moving on to the Information Service of the Canadian government in 1946. After returning to London in 1950, she again found work at various publishing houses, eventually becoming the head of the public relations department of Oxford University Press in 1960.[20] Eva Borneman's German-English parentage meant she had grown up bilingual, and shortly after moving to Frankfurt in 1962 she took up as a freelance translator from English to German and vice versa. In 1964 she took over for several years as editor of *Übersetzer*, the monthly magazine of the Association of German-Speaking Translators of Literary and Academic Works (Verband deutschsprachiger Übersetzer literarischer und wissenschaftlicher Werke). The magazine later became the mouthpiece of the translator' division at the German Writers' Association (Verband deutscher Schriftsteller), which belonged to the union for the publishing and printing industries, IG Druck und Papier. She translated numerous literary and academic books, including Anaïs Nin's *Das Delta der Venus* (original English title: *Delta of Venus*) and works by Erica Jong, Joyce Carol Oates, and John Fowles, as well as nonfiction books on sexuality, the Marquis de Sade, Scandinavia, psychology, and psychoanalysis. She was also active writing articles on matters of literary translation and attending numerous international conferences about the profession, and published a few shorter works of her own, including *Canadian Image* and *The Arts in Canada and the Film* while in Canada and *Liebesrezepte—ein Kochbuch für Liebende und Verliebte* (Recipes for Love—A Cookbook for Lovers and Those in Love) in Germany in 1967.

Eva and Ernest met at a party in London in 1933 and, after some back and forth, became a couple. Their correspondence, which was particularly prolific over the many years in which they lived apart, points to an intimate, loving relationship on both sides. Their relationship rested notably on a common interest in leftist politics and modern aesthetics—literature, film, music, and art—although they by no means always shared the same opinion when it came to the details. Eva, whose "intellectual acuity was always on par" with that of her husband, took care of everything during his long periods of absence in Canada, Paris, or Frankfurt and also managed his business affairs.[21] This fits a well-known pattern; without his wife's help, Borneman would never have been able to work as efficiently or market himself as he was able to. It is all the more remarkable that she also pursued her own successful career.

What Is True? Life in Uncertain Times

Borneman aroused controversy everywhere he went. In the world of jazz, US writer Calder Willingham questioned the integrity of Borneman's arguments, holding him to be an egomaniacal swindler and maligning him aggressively; in the world of German television, he was regarded as "un-German." Fellow sex researchers turned their noses up at his involvement with mass media, while the women's movement considered him an arrogant patriarch.[22] Beyond any objections to his theories, there was also the vexing matter that Borneman's qualifications could not be clearly pieced together, not to mention the fact that some of the events he describes in his semi-autobiography *Die Ur-Szene* (The Primal Scene) seem quite implausible. It would have been impossible to fit it all into a single lifetime. When I began writing this book, the psychologist and sex therapist Helmut Kentler warned me not to believe everything Borneman claimed, an opinion I would subsequently encounter in written sources as well. When he first met his future wife in 1933, people were already whispering about the "eighteen-year-old swindler," and Ernest's own father criticized his tendency to "bluff." And in fact, as revealed itself over the course of my research, many of the biographical constructs that he relied on at different points in his life belonged to the realm of myth. His claims, for example, that he was "of mixed Norwegian and Canadian descent," that he "had lived and worked for many years in the USA, South America, and Spain," and that he "had once won the Hollywood Oscar for best short film of the year" were nothing but tall tales.[23] These inventions were in part wishful thinking, but most were tactical moves, as is sometimes quite evident. Shortly after returning to Germany as the head of programming for Freies Fernsehen in 1960, for instance, it made sense for him to state that he had emigrated to England not for political reasons, but because "my father sent me to study in London,"[24] an untruthful claim intended to clear him of the accusation of being a traitorous emigrant, while also suggesting that he had acquired academic training abroad. When he later claimed the opposite—having embraced a political mission at Freies Fernsehen as the "socialist Goebbels"—it was because the times had changed; the shifting zeitgeist had given him a chance to break free from the subaltern position that circumstances had forced upon him, letting him go on the offensive in his work as a German television manager. The story that he told in 1960 had allowed him to survive in a hostile environment; the one he advanced in the 1970s lay closer to his true political socialization, albeit with a deliberate exaggeration of the facts. There is much to speak for the idea that he took the job at Freies Fernsehen not for political reasons, but for the prospect of advancing his own career—one with political side effects.

Borneman's claims regarding his academic bona fides served as a form of self-protection in a system that only recognized formal qualifications, which precluded autodidacts. Borneman repeatedly mentioned or suggested that he had completed a degree at Cambridge, going so far as to state that he had received his PhD there or somewhere else.[25] One CV from 1957 reads: "diverse schools in Geneva, Paris, Berlin and Stockholm (father a diplomat and constantly traveling)." He named various universities he had attended, listing "B.A., M.A., Ph.D."[26] Another CV of his claims that he studied comparative musicology at the University of Berlin between 1929 and 1933, that is, between the ages of fourteen and eighteen, and submitted a thesis in 1933 before completing "post-graduate work at Cambridge" in 1934–35.[27] In conversations with African American studies pioneer Melville J. Herskovits, he postdated his year of birth to 1913, in order to make it more plausible that he had finished his university studies in 1933.[28] As Borneman's personnel file at UNESCO in Paris makes clear, he also had no qualms about making false or misleading statements on official papers. In the field "College or University" on the application form for the organization, he entered: "University in Berlin 1930–1933, University of London 1933–1935, Emmanuel College, Cambridge, 1935–1936."[29] Under "Degrees, Diplomas, or other similar qualifications," he noted: "State exams (BA) 1933"—there is no mention of a PhD here, at any rate. If, as he claimed, he had studied with well-known academics such as the ethnomusicologist Erich von Hornbostel in Berlin, the anthropologist Bronislaw Malinowski in London, the Marxist archaeologist and pre-historian Vere Gordon Childe in Edinburgh, Herskovits in Evanston, and the sex researcher Helena Wright in London, at most it had been as a guest in lectures or in private conversation—in any case primarily in an autodidactic sense and not as a formally enrolled student. In 1977, in *Die Ur-Szene*, Borneman first openly admitted that he had never been able to pursue a proper degree because he had not finished his Abitur. He continued to maintain, however, that he had "audited" "thirteen semesters" with the scholars listed above.[30] By 1990 the story had changed again: he had now "sat in" on lectures given by Helena Wright, yet his short biography in the same book still claims many years of "university study" with the same experts.[31] The fact that Borneman did not name the universities attended, as would have been normal for a curriculum vitae, but listed only the names of noted professors indicates that what he had really "studied" was the works of these scholars. Borneman called attention to his personal relationships with most of these professors, yet his personal estate (which, admittedly, has not been cataloged completely) has yielded no corroborating correspondence to date for the alleged connections. Working from the opposite direction, the large collection of Malinowski's papers contains no correspondence with Borneman. Likewise, any letters he may have exchanged with Childe and Helena Wright have not been preserved, as far as is known. Herskovits's estate, however, contains a highly revealing exchange of letters. While the content of this correspondence is itself fascinating, these letters also show it to be highly improbable that Borneman studied from 1951 to 1953 at Northwestern University. An intensive exchange took place between 1940 and 1942, followed by a short episode in 1947, but nothing else after. Such a silence would not have made any sense had Borneman actually moved to Illinois in 1951 to study with his great mentor and supporter. Nor did he have any time for such an endeavor; in the early 1950s he was fully occupied in England, crafting scripts, producing a movie, and reporting on the British jazz scene for the *Melody Maker*. Moreover, all of Borneman's correspondence from this period was posted from and addressed to London, leaving no doubt as to the fact that he was not in the United States, but in the British capital.

It strikes one that Borneman's self-representation in CVs and biographies refers exclusively to studies in comparative musicology from an early point until late into the 1960s.[32] Not until then does he mention studying with Malinowski, Childe, and Wright, as well as training analysis with Géza Róheim, and no longer speaks of musicology.[33] All of this suggests that Borneman continually reframed his qualifications to suit his current needs. The degree to which his interactions with most of these renowned scholars were anything more than fleeting encounters remains unclear. Nor are such autobiographical revisions for a set aim unusual, it is just that they usually rest on actual facts that are then emphasized or played down, depending on the context. As Willi Winkler recently remarked in relation to a biography of the literary theorist Paul de Man, such posturing is common practice in academia as well—perhaps especially so, as a field in which sensitivity to these issues runs particularly high.[34] Borneman wound up in this predicament after he admitted openly in *Die Ur-Szene* that he hadn't been able to study at a university because he had never finished his Abitur. This admission, of course, automatically cast doubt on his claim of having studied elsewhere. This not only provided the basis for doubts raised about his qualifications by sexologists such as Helmut Kentler and Volkmar Sigusch, but also for attacks made by authoritarian or conservative opponents to any kind of sexual liberation, particularly those from Martin Humer, in whose case they also carried an anti-intellectual aspect.

Into the 1970s, the majority of Borneman's autobiographical fictions pertained to his academic qualifications. This had relevant reasons owing to the fact of his emigration; a letter sent to his father from Canada in 1948 hints at why he was so free with this particular autobiographical detail. In the letter Borneman asks his father not to mention the fact that he did not study at a university to a colleague from the National Film Board (NFB) who was planning to visit the elder Borneman in Berlin. A completed degree was required to work at the NFB; without expressly claiming it, Borneman had led people there to believe that he had studied musicology long ago in Berlin.[35] While his inability to attend university may have motivated him all the more to read books and study outside the formal boundaries of academia—in the British Library and other libraries, and not least in "real life"—it was only much later, after he had published numerous books and formerly elitist institutions of higher education began to open their doors more widely, that Borneman eventually received the chance to complete a PhD despite holding no bachelor's degree. Not until after 1975 did he begin more openly to address his lack of formal academic qualifications. He who earned his credits outside the academic world still lacked the right pedigree however, something that would continue to haunt him. The *Frankfurter Rundschau* spoke of "the strong pressure to contend" to which Borneman had been exposed since coming to West Germany, "which in turn continually drove him to hold his ground in new, often campaign style counterattacks."[36]

Borneman's reason for embellishing his academic laurels finally dissipated upon receiving his doctorate, although this did not mean that he now generally refrained from doing so. Objectively speaking, such artificial claims had not been necessary for a while; by that point Borneman had already written substantial manuscripts, a number of which undoubtedly met academic standards. Throughout his life Borneman harbored a second complex: a clear penchant for implying professional or personal associations with famous people. The line of jazz musicians, film and TV luminaries, writers, and academics that parades through his autobiography seems without end. Unlike with his academic embellishments, most of the stories that Borneman tells of this kind in *Die Ur-Szene*, and which scarcely seem possible in such concentration, can in fact be verified by contemporary sources or statements made by other people. These include his friendships with black revolutionaries from the "Third World" who were ascending to the top of postcolonial states in Africa and Latin America; his acquaintance with countless jazz greats and his internationally renowned role as a jazz critic; his success as an author; his work as a documentary filmmaker in Canada; his collaboration with Orson Welles in Rome and North Africa; his friendship with French intellectuals such as Charles Delauney and Boris Vian while working at UNESCO in Paris; the invention of Radio Bremen's *Beat-Club*, etc. It hardly surprises in this case that he would throw his weight around a bit, choosing to emphasize this or that facet of his life and his role as a pioneer. Still, his self-assigned place at the forefront of progress was not always accurate—claims of forging himself into a political visionary who, to give one example, was "the first" to have "systematically developed the idea of the people's front," of having "the absolute longest experience with TV of any living German," and of coining the term "beat music" were all exaggerations, to put it mildly.[37] At times, these self-embellishments earned him harsh criticism. Others dealt differently with Borneman's exaggeration, such as Hans Krieger in his review of *Die Ur-Szene*, who responded to the patent presumption connected with Borneman's self-perception of always being "the first" with a shrug: "So what?"[38] Still, the question remains: did other reasons for Borneman's autobiographical inventions exist?

The interwar period gave excellent reason for adopting concealment and deception as general codes of conduct, a state that did not fundamentally alter in the years to come. During this period Borneman's great role model, Bertolt Brecht, provided a framework for the young Berliner's aesthetics and work: extensive collection of material, a penchant for precise empirical work, cool and objective depictions, concrete and unadorned language, a distanced perspective, and an interest in foreign cultures as well as colloquial language. Borneman also shared the experience of living in exile. His autobiographical inventions may therefore not only speak to the expectations of employers or a pathological condition, but also be an understandable reaction to life in uncertain times. Brecht himself had conceded in his poem "Of Poor B.B." that "in me you have someone on whom there is no relying." While addressed to his female conquests, the statement undoubtedly carries a much larger meaning. Anticipating a postmodern attitude, Brecht espoused an anti-essentialist view of humanity that was followed by others who took an equally inventive approach to biographical detail, such as Bob Dylan. Yet Borneman's autobiographical constructions did not arise purely from a distinct awareness of the fleeting nature of his current life circumstances, be they place of residence, job, or personal relationships, but were also part of a strategy for survival in a world that often seemed hostile—or at least proved to be different than it appeared. In a letter with autobiographical touches to a friend, Borneman praised the "stimuli that grew" out of life in the Jewish Diaspora: "the provocation inflicted by a hostile environment on the brain of an uprooted individual who is not bound to one country, nation, or 'race.'"[39] For him, the "greatness of the Jewish people" lay in its "response to expulsion." Likewise, he considered the *Stories of Mr. Keuner*, Brecht's "amazing collection of parables," an excellent source of advice for life in dangerous times: "Yielding is time and time again depicted as the duty of those who wish to survive. The urge of self-subjugation thus reverses itself and appears rationally as its opposite."[40] Masquerades were unavoidable, but there was no reason to feel guilty about them. He also advised others to "invent experience" when applying for jobs in order to bolster their claims to certain qualifications.[41] Borneman was by no means an unreliable worker—quite to the contrary in fact. It would also be unfair in matters of love to simply brand him "unfaithful" and leave it at that. When it came to politics, he was not a party man, but a lifelong Marxist faithful to a political stance to the left of social democracy, or "left and free," as Willy Brandt once put it.

The Face on the Cutting-Room Floor

Borneman's ruses went deeper. Nowhere is this revealed more clearly than in his first novel, *The Face on the Cutting-Room Floor*, which contains a great deal of introspection about existential insecurity in modernity. The novel indicates that even as a twenty-year-old, Borneman was entirely conscious of the fact that authenticity and self-determination were impossible in uncertain times. Written between November 1935 and August 1936, the text was intended from the outset to serve as the basis for a film, and its style reflects this accordingly.[42] "This novel constitutes an attempt to apply the methods of modern cinema technique to those of the traditional novel. It does not develop gradually as the normal novel does, but abruptly like a shooting script in which the continuity is built up by a succession of carefully picked high spots of action and dialogue."[43] Borneman first tried to turn the script into a film in 1939, then again in 1950 and the 1960s. Different story outlines appear in his personal papers, but none was ever realized. Nevertheless the book was a great literary success, selling long after its original publication in 1937. In fact, it was "by far the most successful English-language novel written by an exile author in Great Britain."[44] By 1940 it had already sold thirty-six thousand copies; new editions were issued in 1974 and 1986, with numerous reprints.[45] The literary world was enthralled; crime fiction author Julian Symons described *The Face on the Cutting-Room Floor* as a "detective story to end detective stories" and "a dazzling . . . box of tricks," while fifty years after its original publication John Archer regarded the book as "still one of the most interesting detective stories ever written."[46]

Written as an exercise to learn English, as Borneman himself stated, the novel takes the form of a classic detective novel, only to break quickly with the conventional attribution of roles—victim, perpetrator, and detective—and dissolve into a deliberate confusion in which nothing seems certain any longer.[47] Even the question of the novel's author was couched in mystery—intending to disguise his status as an exile, Borneman invented the pseudonym "Cameron McCabe," an anagram composed of the letters in his last name and his nickname, Mac. It took nearly forty years for London publisher (and Borneman's friend) Frederic J. Warburg to clarify the matter when a new edition of the book was published in 1974. The novel takes place in the London film world and turns on the tension between extremely detailed depictions of the topography and environment of the setting on the one hand and the characters' opaque constructions of identity on the other. In the end it is not just the integrity of the characters themselves that turns out be flawed, but also the morality of British society, with a legal system that shows no interest in discovering the truth.

It is not just that the case is never solved. The lines between good and evil are just as difficult to distinguish as those between right and wrong. Literally nothing is what it appears to be, and nothing lives up to the expectations of the reader, who is instead left to his own devices and thrown back on his own capacity to judge. Even in this early text, one of the foundations of Borneman's aesthetic takes definite shape: the reader can only try to approach the reality of the situation by considering all that is left unsaid. The meta-reflection of the literary figure Dr. Müller functions as a "dialectic method"; "things are first built up in order to be torn down again: new evidence is discovered in one instance, only to be recognized as worthless in the next."[48] Very much in keeping with Brecht's notion of realism, which employs breaks in narration and other types of alienating effects, expectations are deconstructed in order to trigger processes in consciousness that should lead to a critical attitude toward claims of authenticity. Its inclusion of things not present, deviation from a linear narrative, open ending, continual self-reflection, and persistent deconstruction all make *The Face on the Cutting-Room Floor* a forerunner to the experimental nouveau roman of the 1950s and 1960s, as well as postmodern literature.[49] At the same time, the book kept within Brecht's tradition, whom Borneman rightly considered to be a master of the invisible hand: "Almost nothing Brecht says can be taken at face value; almost everything has a secondary and tertiary meaning."[50] Ernest Hemingway and James Joyce were also important role models whose works Borneman engaged with extensively; the novel itself alludes to both at multiple points in order to account for its character development and literary form. In Borneman's eyes, Joyce and Hemingway were successful due to their "close affinity to their age: the same complexity of structure, the same dialectic of pattern, the same method of multifariousness to reproduce the instability of postwar life."[51]

The character Dr. Müller summarizes the *condition humaine* common to the novel of contemporary man, whose existence is framed by "uncertainty and instability": "Nothing is firmly fixed, nothing steadfast, nothing solidly established. Everything is in the process of change, demolition, destruction, decay: an exact picture of the man and his age. McCabe, morally uprooted, is fascinated by everything unstable, uncertain, ambiguous, equivocal, multifarious."[52]

With respect to the chosen format of crime fiction, Borneman drew on the new realism represented in Dashiell Hammett's magazine *Black Mask*, published in the 1920s and early 1930s. He credits Hemingway and Hammett with having the greatest influence on *The Face on the Cutting-Room Floor*.[53] In keeping with this tradition and in contrast to Raymond Chandler and the British school of crime novels, Borneman did not view the detective in a positive light. Instead, *Black Mask*—in a tendency Borneman would pick up on—was characterized by an unconcealed amorality: "It is a world in which there can be no triumph for the virtuous and no victory

Figure 1.2. A reflective moment while reading, England, 1950s. Courtesy AdK.

for the just."[54] According to Borneman, Hammett had learned from Hemingway, who in turn had taken inspiration from Joyce and occasionally referenced Hammett, thereby bringing it all full circle. *Black Mask*, he noted, revealed "the impact of the most advanced upon the most popular of contemporary fiction."

The Face on the Cutting-Room Floor reflects Borneman's position as an exile not only in its underlying theme of existential insecurity, but also in the author's decision to set his characters within the world of international film and assign them transnational biographies. Brecht's description of an emigrant's life—changing countries more often than shoes—would become a biographical constant for Borneman, one connected time and again to nationals' mistrust of immigrants. Borneman himself felt the pains associated with his status keenly, particularly his separation from Eva, but also valued his experiences with the foreign and his encounters with people from all over the world. To a certain extent this set him apart from friends such as Hannes Hiller, who focused on the problematic side of exile life, writing, "I have come to believe that insecurity is the cancer that eats away at our life, and you have had more than your share of it."[55] Borneman, however, saw it less as a deadly tumor than a kind of lifeblood; one reply to Hiller came from Paris in 1948, after a tour through several countries: "I hate stability, and I want to see a lot more of the world before I am too old to travel."[56]

Borneman's play with autobiographical facts meant withdrawing from a cultural system that only acknowledged the validity of formal qualifications and prominent figures. This involved questions of power, and certain groups in society from which power was withheld: members of the underprivileged social classes who were denied access to secondary education, which in Borneman's view meant especially people from the working class, blacks, Jews, and other minority groups. The lack of an Abitur by no means diminished his self-confidence—to the contrary, in fact. The notion that anything like "identity" or "authenticity" could exist appeared dubious in the extreme. Folk culture did in fact play a major role in Borneman's ethnological work, and he made an effort to portray and describe it. Still, he remained convinced that pure forms had never existed, but only hybrids, combinations of the most varied sources that were to a large degree constructs. The idea that "reality" could be captured in film, as the principles of documentary film with which he engaged intensively in Canada would have it, was a fiction for him. As his first novel—written at the very beginning of his career—makes unmistakably clear, Borneman was anything but naive. He had a keen eye for social inequalities, interests, and hierarchies as well as the self-contradictory complexity of life; he did not believe any claims to authenticity. How could his own existence have been different—pure, true, identarian?

Brecht as a Model

Bertolt Brecht remained a central figure for Borneman throughout his life; he admired Brecht's aesthetics but also valued his discussion of "objectivity." Borneman met Brecht in the summer of 1930 at the age of fifteen, during rehearsals for the didactic play *Der Jasager* (*He Said Yes*) to which members of Berlin school choirs had been invited. Declared a "school opera" and thus one that had to maintain a "simplicity and naturalness" as Kurt Weill put it, the piece revolves around the sacrifice of a young man who has fallen ill while traveling in a group; he agrees to his own death in order to avoid endangering the success of the expedition, which is devoted to a grand life-or-death cause.[57] When asked whether the actions in the play were credible, the students in attendance answered no. Excerpts from their arguments are reprinted in a volume entitled *Versuche*, or "experiments." Brecht took some of their responses seriously, for example those suggesting that the young man hesitate before agreeing to die, in order to avoid lionizing blind obedience. He actually revised the play and wrote an alternative version in which the young man refuses to agree, *Der Neinsager* (*He Said No*).[58] Borneman said that he had learned a lot from this process, and not just about tactics.[59] Afterward, he and a few other students were invited to Brecht's apartment, where he was particularly impressed by the presence of German heavyweight boxing champion Paul Samson-Körner. Borneman's fascination with the boxer also informed his opinion of Brecht; he wrote, "A poet who is on a first-name basis with boxers has to be taken seriously."[60] Three years later, in the summer of

1933, Brecht rehearsed the play *Die Rundköpfe und die Spitzköpfe* (*Round Heads and Pointed Heads*) with students at the Karl Marx School, including Borneman. In November and December 1934, Brecht and Borneman again worked together on two projects in London. Borneman helped Brecht with a new translation of the *Threepenny Novel*, which appeared in London and New York in 1937 and 1938; in return, Brecht helped Borneman write his first play, *The Windows of Heaven*.[61]

Decades later, with nothing known of the collaboration during these years of exile apart from Borneman's claims, the coeditor of the first handbook of German exile literature, Wilhelm Sternberg, looked into the matter. He received word from Helene Weigel's office that there was nothing in Brecht's papers pointing to any collaborative efforts, nor was mention of Mr. Borneman's name anywhere to be found. Brecht's employee Elisabeth Hauptmann, however, thought it was entirely possible that Borneman had worked on the rough draft of the *Threepenny Novel* with the playwright while Brecht was in London in 1934–35. Borneman did in any event, make Hauptmann a gift of his edited copy of the draft with Brecht's comments when the Berlin Ensemble made a guest appearance in London in 1956.[62] This manuscript is not in the Bertolt Brecht Archive or in the papers of Elisabeth Hauptmann, but a note kept in the Brecht Archive confirms beyond doubt that the two men worked together on the translation. A small piece of paper that must have originally been attached to a manuscript with a paper clip (the rusty contours are easy to make out) bears a short note in Brecht's handwriting: "3penny novel from Bornemann!"[63] Back in Berlin, Hauptmann asked Borneman to write a contribution for a special issue of the East German literature magazine *Sinn und Form* that was planned following Brecht's death. Borneman pursued a collaboration with Hauptmann with two notions of his own: translating and producing *Galileo* for his British television company and filming the *Threepenny Novel* for the official East German film company (Deutsche Film Aktiengesellschaft, commonly known as DEFA).[64] Elisabeth Hauptmann passed Borneman's inquiry about the film project onto Helene Weigel, with a note assuming that Weigel would remember the link between the two men: "You know," she wrote, "Borneman, former student from the Karl Marx School, *He Said Yes*, now in England."[65] *Sinn und Form* published Borneman's article, while contributions from others such as Hans Henny Jahn or Arnold Zweig were not included in the issue. In the mid-1960s Borneman tried once again to launch a project with DEFA and pushed for a translation of his books in East Germany, this time through a friend he met after immigrating to London, the Jewish Communist and later president of the writers' association PEN (Poets Essayists Novelists) in East Germany, Heinz Kamnitzer. Unfortunately, Kamnitzer told him, after reading *The Compromisers* and *Tomorrow Is Now*, that East Germans did not have "much of a sense for the human understanding of erotic, especially when esoteric," so it was still too early to think about a translation.[66] The film projects—a jazz piece for DEFA and a film version of his Thomas Müntzer play for East German television (Deutscher Fernsehfunk, DFF)—never came to fruition.

The Brecht Archive also holds a copy of the manuscript "The Windows of Heaven—A Play in Three Acts by Ernest Borneman." Borneman had given this play, set during the time of the German Peasants' War, to Elisabeth Hauptmann when she was in London in the hope that the Berlin Ensemble might stage it.[67] Arno Reinfrank began a German translation of this piece in the late 1950s, but it was never finished.[68] Borneman also used his earlier collaboration with the famous playwright to try and sell the play, describing it years later to the head of the television play department at Norddeutscher Rundfunk (Northern German Broadcasting, NDR): "Today it reads as if the later Brecht had written a piece in the style of *Baal*, *Trommeln in der Nacht* [*Drums in the Night*], or *Im Dickicht der Städte* [*In the Jungle of Cities*]: its mentality is more like *Mutter Courage* [*Mother Courage*], but its style resembles that of *Baal*."[69] In East Berlin, the reviewer at the Henschel press, to whom Kamnitzer had sent the manuscript to manage the rights issues, waxed ecstatic about the piece. He compared it to Friedrich Wolf's Müntzer play, noting:

> For the most part Borneman's play seems much more realistic, yet it also effects a greater poetic power. Borneman . . . has chosen Old English and the language of the Bible in order to due full justice to the period of the sixteenth century, and especially the religiosity of the time. And he does this well. It is truly remarkable and admirable how beautiful Borneman's language sounds and how he, a former German, has come to such a command of English and, in this case, Old English vocabulary. His images are lyrical but are not undermined by any kind of sentimental emotionality, rather they are powerful and vivid. . . . The figure of Müntzer, who is painted in broad strokes and comes across as somewhat unrealistic in Wolf's play, has been portrayed with more humanity and to greater natural effect by Borneman.[70]

The publisher was skeptical, however, as to whether the play would wind up on stage in the near future, as the public's interest in the topic of the Peasants' War had waned in the wake of several other recent productions on the subject.[71] Nonetheless, they wanted to retain the manuscript to be able to revisit the project at a later date. In 1970, Ernest and Eva Borneman were yet again involved in a matter related to Brecht, preparing a new English translation of *Lux in Tenebris*, one of Brecht's early plays, for a collection of selected plays edited by John Willett.[72]

Brecht and Borneman's 1934 meeting in person ended in disaster, when on a visit with Eva to the poet and his wife, the young man compared Brecht to Hemingway, rousing the ire of his host. Brecht purportedly cried out, "Hemingway! Impossible! Get out!" He received reinforcement from Helene Weigel, who came storming out of the kitchen with a frying pan in her hand: "If Brecht bellows," she said, "you're wrong!"[73] This brought an end to the collaboration between the two men, although not to Borneman's reverence for Brecht. He wrote extensively on Brecht in the wake of the playwright's death in late summer 1956, in several texts that were published between 1957 and 1960.[74] His father provided him with the German literature that he needed from Berlin, sending his son everything he could find by and about Brecht.[75] Beyond merely rehashing the different stages of collaboration between the two men, the writings reveal an extraordinary knowledge of Brecht's lyrical and dramatic productions, as well as his theories of theater. Here too, Borneman took occasion to emphasize the ambiguity he himself considered so important, writing of Brecht that "ambiguity was the formal principle in his work, the key to its magic, the secret of his success."[76] He praised Brecht's aversion to sentimentality as well as his "social" emotionality—his efforts on behalf of the weak. By the same token he admired Brecht's enthusiasm for epic theater, or the attempt to produce in audience members a distanced perspective that would forestall empathy or identification and encourage their active engagement. The same held true for the alienating effects used in Brecht's school: sparse stages, banners and projections, commentary from choirs, music, songs, and direct addresses to the audience. Borneman was fascinated with Brecht's objective style, his rejection of embellishments and metaphysics. In another description of Brecht, Borneman wrote that "he detested philosophy that rhymed: he believed that in literature, just like in mathematics, a beautiful portrayal is one that is brief. When a complete portrayal could be given using an uncommonly small number of words, then it was poetry." Borneman also rightly emphasized Brecht's fascination with the "other," which stemmed not from any kind of romantic longing but from his theory of the theater, in order to effect a "conscious de-romanticization of a consciously chosen romantic backdrop."[77] He was captivated by Brecht's functional personal style: unembellished, decidedly simple clothing, his plain glasses, short hair, brown leather jacket like those often worn by chauffeurs or motorcyclists, the lack of luxury in his private surroundings, the ragged newspaper clippings on the wall, his preference for the color gray. Borneman remained a follower of the avant-garde for his entire life; he was not interested in the "bourgeois democratic legacy" as it was upheld in East Germany, and he criticized attempts to accuse Brecht of formalism. The tragedy in all of this, according to Borneman, was that Brecht's theater ultimately attracted those Brecht actually rejected—poets, intellectuals, and the West—while he was not able to win over the public that he desired, namely the working class, the Party, and the East.[78]

Wilhelm Sternberg's inquiry to Elisabeth Hauptmann concerning Brecht and Borneman's collaboration touched on a basic question for exiles: who could be considered an exiled writer? Borneman's name is not mentioned in the first 1962 edition of the *Bio-Bibliographie* of German exile literature; the second 1970 edition, however, devotes a detailed section to him.[79] As the publisher explained, the book had been "greatly expanded" after a wave of new discoveries had followed in the wake of its publication—but also because there were many authors who felt they had been overlooked. Four hundred new entries were added to the fifteen hundred original. In 1968 Borneman contacted the organization responsible for the publication, the German Academy for Language and Literature (Deutsche Akademie für Sprache und

Dichtung), to ask whether only those exiles who continued to publish in German would be considered for the volume, but not those writing in the language of their place of exile.[80] He argued that it was not only already established authors who belonged in a handbook of German exile literature, but also people such as himself, exiles who did not publish in German but in the language of their host country.[81]

As for all writers, the problem of language was of fundamental importance to Borneman. What language should he write in while in Great Britain? *Fahrt ohne Ziel* was already finished—although unpublished—and was written in German. Had he not been forced out of Germany, he surely would have continued to write in his native language. In London, however, he quickly switched over to English and systematically practiced writing in English, even speaking English rather than German with his girlfriend Eva, who was raised bilingual. After his expulsion, Borneman avoided the German language. He spoke and wrote almost exclusively in English, even communicating with his parents in English in his later years of exile. National Socialism turned what was already an existing aversion to German into complete refusal. From an early point on he developed "a distaste for the language" of his time, considering only sixteenth- and seventeenth-century German worth reading—especially Grimmelshausen's picaresque novel *Simplicissimus*. He disliked German writers' propensity for philosophy, the striving for intellectual depth and finesse that made it impossible to tell a simple story and constituted a kind of national arrogance—the conviction that German "culture" was superior to Western "civilization." In Borneman's eyes, it was both possible and preferable to write intelligently and amusingly at the same time, but there were essentially no role models for this in Germany. He deplored the fact that the art of language in his fatherland consisted only in "rhyming" or "narrative thinking," leaving no room for colloquial language or simple storytelling. Accordingly, he claimed, "There was no German equivalent to writers such as Kipling, Mark Twain or Hemingway." Brecht, he wrote, was the first to develop a simple, concrete language that included a wide array of elements or, as he put it, "everyday words, slang, colloquialisms and the drabbest of drab official language, peppered here and there with foreign words."[82] Anglicisms or other exoticisms, Borneman noted, were Germanized, but in a consciously clumsy way; the effect was both impactful and difficult to comprehend at the same time: "something that sounded vaguely familiar, like the language of a vagrant poet or the way of speaking in a place that none of us had ever visited." Brecht was the first to have shown him the possibilities for the German language beyond high culture and its great remove from reality. "My confidence in the ability of the language to find itself once again," he recalled in his autobiography, "did not exist until I met Brecht and he referred me to Büchner. Even today, Büchner and Brecht are among the few German-speaking authors in the post-Baroque era that I can read without feeling physically ill. I hardly dare even write down what I feel when I read Thomas Mann."[83]

Borneman described his own writing style, which unmistakably resembles Brecht and Hemingway, as follows: "I write as frugally and with as little embellishment as possible. No adjectives, no adverbs, only the shortest possible statements."[84] Hemingway, whom he first read in 1933 and 1934, made "the strongest literary impression on me since Brecht."[85] Numerous passages in Borneman's correspondence and many of his articles reflect an intensive, but not uncritical reading of Hemingway. He told a friend about his own second novel, "I wrecked 'Love Story' trying to do a Hemingway and I didn't get away with it. Nor did anyone else."[86] Borneman's occasional claims, however, to a friendship with Hemingway are likely untrue. Two days after Hemingway's death on 2 July 1961, the *Frankfurter Rundschau* ran an obituary written by Borneman in which the latter claimed to have met the deceased during the Spanish Civil War and to have visited him often in Cuba and Key West.[87] In 1962 he made a similar assertion, this time adding that he had "worked as a camera man during the Spanish Civil War."[88] There are no independent sources corroborating Borneman's involvement in the Spanish Civil War or trips to Cuba or Florida, not to mention a meeting of any kind with Hemingway. Moreover, in his own biography, Borneman only mentions Hemingway in brief and from a distance, and he never repeated the above-mentioned claims, further suggesting there was little more to the story than a close reading of Hemingway's work. Finally, no correspondence between the two men exists in the extensive collection of Hemingway's letters in his estate at the John F. Kennedy Presidential Library and Museum in Boston, nor in Borneman's own papers; the episode can almost certainly be filed under wishful thinking.

"I Am a Jew in This Sense": Praise for the Diaspora

Borneman held an ambivalent relationship with Judaism. He was not religious, but was naturally attuned to the Jewish cultural tradition in which he had grown up through his mother and her family. In London, he benefited from the aid of Jewish institutions and became a member of the Jewish Refugee Committee in 1935, which organized assistance for Jews in Great Britain who had fled Germany. When Eva—herself an atheist and a skeptic—and Ernest got married on 23 May 1943 in Ottawa, they did so according to Jewish tradition, with "Rabbi, Reception and all."[89] In the early 1960s, Borneman produced a three-part radio program on Jewish folk music. As part of his research he contacted Theodor W. Adorno, whose musicology work was quite well known, to request tips about additional materials as well as a meeting in person.[90] The professor readily agreed to discuss the subject with him.[91]

Zionism did very little for Borneman, which often landed him in disputes with many an old and new friend alike. In one case this led to conflict with German publicist Henryk M. Broder, who had left for Israel in 1981 because of antisemitic tendencies within the German Left. Borneman wrote him, noting that "after all the sad experiences in Jewish history, it was a mistake to now freely enter a ghetto where one could be slaughtered." He could not "let go of the nightmare that one day, all the Jews who had fled to Israel would be murdered. That is why I am truly convinced that we Jews (I am one in this sense) should not imitate the nationality craze of the goyim. The Diaspora is not only our fate, it is also a chance to survive."[92] Shortly before Eva's death, Broder had written her one of his "burning with zeal for the land of my fathers" letters, as Borneman described it to a friend. "Eva and I were outraged. I cannot understand how someone who criticized the Germans so astutely could be such an idiot when it came to accepting reactionary politics in Israel."[93] Borneman's views on Israel also repeatedly came up for discussion in his long-standing correspondence with childhood friend Andreas Marck. Marck, a Socialist and kibbutz activist, was the son of the philosopher Siegfried Marck and the women's rights activist Lola Landau; his stepfather was the pacifist travel author Armin T. Wegner, an important figure for Borneman. For Borneman, the Diaspora was not simply a refuge for the Jewish people, but also a fountain of youth. In 1988 he wrote Marck: "I am probably romanticizing the Jews, but it seems to me that this enormously intelligent people owes a good portion of its intelligence to the Diaspora. By that I mean an ability to recognize even from a distance that coming to identify as a nation has unleashed the usual process of stultification on display in so many nations among the petty bourgeois and the nationalists."[94] His views on Israel, however, did nothing to protect him from being the repeated target of antisemitic attacks in German-speaking countries, as came with particular vehemence in the reactions to his public appearances as a sexologist on Austrian television.

As it was, Borneman's relationship with his Jewish heritage provides a key to understanding his life and work. For him exile not only offered refuge, but also opened up all kinds of possibilities. It may have demanded all his strength, but it also provided unexpected opportunities for growth—at least for someone like him, who was just coming of age and at the start of his career. The Diaspora was also an uncertain place, nor was the mid-twentieth century an era of truth and beauty, as was plain to see. Constantly on guard, he observed the world with his eyes open wide, holding unguarded candor to be dangerous.

Notes

1. Ernst Bornemann, *Fahrt ohne Ziel: Epitaph der Jugend*, n.d. The quotes that follow come, in order of appearance, on the following pages: 3, 43, 47, 56, 262.
2. Borneman, *Die Ur-Szene*, 17–22; father and mother to Ernest, 9 May 1934.
3. Sessler, "Parallele Lebensstränge."
4. Ibid.; *Underground* 3 (1970): 23–25; Borneman, *Die Ur-Szene*, 16–21. On the SSB, see also Andresen, "Kommunistische Politik an höheren Schulen."
5. Borneman, *Die Ur-Szene*, 18.
6. Afterword, in Borneman, *The Face on the Cutting-Room Floor*, 260–61.
7. Borneman, *Die Ur-Szene*, 26.
8. Borneman to his father, 28 October 1954.
9. Curt to Ernest, 23 October 1954.
10. Mother to Ernest, 31 July 1933.
11. Father to Ernest, 23 July 1933.
12. Father to Ernest, 17 August 1933.
13. Erna Blochert to Ernest Borneman, 13 August 1938.

14. Mother to Ernest, 15 May 1935.

15. "Ausweis über die Anmeldung im Ausland zur Erfüllung der aktiven Dienstpflicht und Arbeitsdienstpflicht," London, 28 January 1937; afterword in Borneman, *The Face on the Cutting-Room Floor*, 256.

16. Ernest to Eva, 19 April 1942.

17. This information, as well as what follows was taken from two curriculum vitae of Eva Borneman in AdK, EBA.

18. Eva to Ernest, 27 August 1935 and 10 November 1937.

19. Eva to Ernest, 16 June 1941.

20. Borneman to Schmidt, 27 December 1960, BAK, B 263/109.

21. Quoted in Aigner, "Ohne Liebe kein Leben," 10.

22. Willingham to James Higgins, 11 March 1947.

23. *TV Times*, 31 May 1957; [self-published short biography], May 1957; Borneman to Kraemer, 28 November 1960, BAK, B 263/42.

24. *Tele*, 15 October 1960, 5.

25. For example, Borneman to Bob Thiele, 28 January 1944; to Katherine Dunham, 21 February 1949; to Werner Riemer, 25 October 1954.

26. Borneman, "Lebenslauf," 23 January 1957.

27. Production Credits, n.d.

28. Borneman to Herskovits, 18 April 1940, NUL, 35/6/4/5.

29. UNESCO Application for Employment [Ernest Borneman], 18 June 1947, UNESCO Archives, PER/REC 1/79.

30. Borneman, *Die Ur-Szene*, 116.

31. As in the introduction to Borneman, *Ausgewählte Texte*, 7, 201–2.

32. See, for example, his curriculum vitae [1962], RB, *BC*, 1, and the attachment to the letter from Borneman to Heinz Kamnitzer, 28 April 1965, StBB, 375/852.

33. See, for example, his "Wissenschaftlicher Werdegang in tabellarischer Form" [1985].

34. *Süddeutsche Zeitung*, 28 April 2014.

35. Letter dated 14 February 1948.

36. *Frankfurter Rundschau*, 9 August 1977.

37. Borneman, *Die Ur-Szene*, 58; Borneman to Wolf Hanke, Editor-in-Chief of the HR, 17 December 1973; letter without return address to Heinz Kerneck, draft, n.d.; Nordemann to Segger, 21 March 1966.

38. *Die Zeit*, 11 November 1977.

39. Borneman to Andreas Marck, 10 December 1976, printed in Standow, *Ein lüderliches Leben*, 329.

40. Borneman, "Two Brechtians," 483.

41. With respect to a Canadian friend, see, e.g., Ernest to Eva, 7 January 1948.

42. Borneman to Heino Held, 25 November 1935.

43. "'The Law,' Synopsis of Screen Story based on a novel by the author of *The Face on the Cutting-Room Floor* to be published in autumn by Martin Secker & Warburg," n.d. See the references to the screen elements in the novel itself: Borneman, *The Face on the Cutting-Room Floor*, 187–88.

44. Strickhausen, "Englische Romane von Exilautoren," 209.

45. A newspaper story mentions nineteen: *Sonntags-Zeitung*, 28 March 1993.

46. Symons, *Bloody Murder*, 226–28; *The Listener*, 26 March 1987. Additional reviews in Borneman, *The Face on the Cutting-Room Floor*, 248–49.

47. Borneman, *Die Ur-Szene*, 352.

48. Ibid., 160.

49. Ritchie, *German Exiles*, 252; Wiemann, *Exilliteratur in Großbritannien*, 356; Brunnhuber, *The Faces of Janus*, 54–55.

50. Borneman, "Two Brechtians," 479.

51. Borneman, *Face*, 205.

52. Ibid., 204.

53. Borneman, *Die Ur-Szene*, 288.

54. Borneman, "The Black Mask," 65–66.

55. Rudolf Hans Hiller to Ernest, 16 July 1949.

56. Ernest to his father, 14 February 1948.

57. On *Der Jasager* and *Der Neinsager*, see the commentaries in Bertolt Brecht, *Stücke 3*, quotation 420; Knopf, *Brecht-Handbuch*, 88–92.

58. Brecht, *Versuche 1–12*, 319–21.

59. Interview in Borneman, *The Face on the Cutting-Room Floor*, 267.

60. Borneman, *Die Ur-Szene*, 343.

61. Ibid.

62. Borneman to Kamnitzer, 8 October 1965, StBB, Nachlass 375/852; Helene Brecht-Weigel (Secretary: Knauf) to Sternfeld, 1 July 1968, AdK, HWA 4513. Borneman's letter to Sternfeld, which was the reason behind the inquiry: Borneman to Sternfeld, 5 June 1968, AdK, BBA 3.

63. Transcribed handwritten notes by Brecht, Nr. 328/56, AdK, BBA 1, 11451.

64. Borneman to his parents, 23 February 1957.

65. Elisabeth Hauptmann to Helene Weigel, 1 July 1957, AdK, EHA, 672.

66. Kamnitzer to Borneman, 4 August 1965, StBB, Nachlass 375/852.

67. BBA, IKA 969; Borneman (Granada TV) to Hauptmann, 12 September 1956, AdK, EHA 1375; Borneman to Kamnitzer, 8 October 1965, StBB, Nachlass 375/852. Earlier attempts to bring it to West Germany had failed. Borneman to Günter Boas, 16 October1954. The play's early genesis and continued editing by Borneman is confirmed in a letter Borneman wrote in 1940 to Eva, asking her to send him the play "The Sword of Gideon," which was its original title (Ernest to Eva, 20 August 1940).

68. Reinfrank, "The Windows of Heaven."

69. Borneman to Dieter Meichsner, 20 March 1977.

70. [Gutachten zu Windows of Heaven von Ernest Borneman], AdK, BBA, IKA, 263; Kamnitzer to Borneman, 4 May 1965, StBB, Nachlass 375/852.

71. Henschel Verlag to Elisabeth Hauptmann, 3 Jan 1957, AdK, BBA, IKA, 263.

72. Willett, *Collected Plays, Volume 1: 1918–1923*.

73. Borneman, *Die Ur-Szene*, 343; *Abendzeitung* (Munich), October/November 1973. Hans Hiller confirmed this scene in a letter written shortly thereafter; Hiller to Borneman, 10 December 1944.

74. Borneman, "Ein Epitaph für Bertolt Brecht"; Borneman, "The Real Brecht"; Borneman, "Credo Quia Absurdum"; Borneman, "Two Brechtians."

75. Father to Ernest, 11 September 1956 and 16 June 1957.

76. Borneman, "The Real Brecht," 24.

77. Borneman, "Ein Epitaph für Bertolt Brecht," 146; Borneman, "Credo Quia Absurdum," 180.

78. Borneman, "The Real Brecht," 33.

79. Sternfeld, *Deutsche Exil-Literatur 1933–1945*, 67.

80. Ernest Borneman to Deutsche Akademie für Sprache und Dichtung, 27 May 1968, AdK, BBA 3.

81. Borneman, "Vom freiwilligen Exil."

82. Borneman, "Ein Epitaph für Bertolt Brecht," 142–43.

83. Borneman, *Die Ur-Szene*, 311–12.

84. Borneman to Jean-Jacques Kroeber, 22 October 1990.

85. Borneman, *Die Ur-Szene*, 288.

86. Borneman to an unnamed addressee [presumably Hans Hiller], 3 May 1944.

87. *Frankfurter Rundschau*, 4 July 1961.

88. Borneman to Ernst Schnabel, 20 February 1962.

89. Judith Geisel to Eva, 5 July 1943.

90. Borneman to Adorno, 28 October 1963.

91. Note, n.d. [1964].

92. Borneman to Broder, 3 October 1987.

93. Borneman to Marck, 18 January 1988.

94. Borneman to Marck, 28 July 1988.

Chapter 2

HEARING
THE ETHNOLOGY OF JAZZ

By the mid 1940s, Ernest Borneman was considered to be one of the "world's foremost jazz critics and scholars."[1] When he stopped writing about jazz in the 1970s, the British *Jazz Journal* noted that his voice would be missed and that his "loss to jazz writing in this country is severe."[2] For Werner Grünzweig, Borneman was the first person with a "'European' background to analyze the phenomenon of jazz scientifically, and the only German to do so in North America at a point when many of the early jazz musicians were still alive and some were still playing."[3] Moreover, Grünzweig went on, hardly any other jazz critic—and certainly not a German—had managed to establish such a far-reaching international network at such an early stage, or engaged so intensively with the jazz scenes in Canada, the United States, Great Britain, France, and West Germany. Borneman gained recognition as a jazz journalist in the mid-1940s with a series of articles called "The Anthropologist Looks at Jazz," while in the 1950s the broad readership of his column for *Melody Maker* quickly brought him international repute as a jazz ethnologist. His growing reputation prompted other jazz critics who later became friends such as Joachim-Ernst Berendt and Siegfried Schmidt-Joos to contact him or seek him out in London, where he settled down again in 1949. The late 1960s and early 1970s saw the publication of final, longer works on jazz, which took up the debate over how "race" and "class" related to one another as factors in structuring culture. He later lamented the "manic addiction to music, almost bordering on the compulsive-neurotic, that I have suffered from my entire life," choosing instead to distance himself from it in order to avoid succumbing to its temptations; "I know," he wrote, "that once I start playing the music that I love, I won't be able to stop."[4]

From his youth until well into his fifties, Borneman did not simply succumb to this "danger" as a listener however, but reflected deeply on African American music and its sociocultural underpinnings. As an autodidact, Borneman was one of the first to approach jazz not as a separate sphere—an aesthetic form created by individual genius or "races"—but ultimately as a product of the societal conditions in which it came about. While he pursued an anti-essentialist perspective, he was also interested in the cultural components of jazz, in the links connecting various components that had developed in different contexts under concrete circumstances. Such an angle meant his ethnological perspective rested on a topic that had not yet made its way into academic circles when he began his research.

Jazz has always been more than just a style of music. As John Gennari put it, it was a source for modernity's cultural imagination, an archive of mythological images, and an aesthetic model for new forms of writing, seeing, and moving.[5] Jazz critics set themselves the task of translating this new sensual experience into words, and thereby loading it with meaning. Reflecting on his role as a critic (he did not like the label, given to him by Max Jones), Borneman saw it as facilitating the breakthrough of those musicians he thought were deserving.[6] He sought to influence the opinions of his readers, and consequently their actions. For him, it was the critic who first produced jazz; the history of jazz was written not only by the different styles of musicians, but also by the interpretations of critics. Looking back, he recalled the nearly complete lack of scholarly literature on jazz when he first began to write about it.

> The few of us who started probing into jazz history during the early thirties had the infinitely rewarding experience, which few critics and historians have had, to see their opinions becoming public coin during their own lifetime—among musicians as much as among listeners. The distinction between New Orleans jazz, swing music and all the other variants of jazz was wholly the work of the critics, not of the musicians.[7]

The same applied to the jazz and blues revivals and the growing influence of Latin American styles in the 1950s and 1960s. Borneman believed that the public would steer jazz in the right direction, because "I have faith in human beings." The task of the critic, he claimed, was to "sense the direction of the public will, to articulate it, to oppose it where it is of social and aesthetic evil, and to support it where it does the most good." In his eyes, critics were not just naive observers, reporters, or commentators; they also fashioned social and aesthetic experiences according to their own standards.

Borneman's role in developing this aesthetic force of modernity amounted to more than just his work on the origins and various cultural traditions present in jazz music. His writings on the "cult of jazz" and the "myth of jazz" also described it as a comprehensive social phenomenon that was in no way limited only to sound and hearing. Instead, the group settings in which this music was often experienced— through activities such as dancing, collecting, and archiving—and its associations with a shared language, clothing style, and search for "authenticity" all played an important role. Jazz was a cultural practice in a broad sense, whose interpreters were engaged in negotiating how to create a form of musical expression suited to modern society. Identifying its point of departure in preceding forms regarded as "premodern" was a part of the story.

Black London: A Transcultural Experience

Ernest Borneman grew up in a musical household. His father played the piano, his mother the violin, and discussions about music formed a part of everyday life, albeit under the common motto of "art as duty," as Borneman himself described it. This notion of art as a duty, labor, and task within the context of a bourgeois upbringing ended up scaring many young people off music. Borneman was no different, but fled to jazz because it offered the exact opposite: immediacy, lightness, exuberance, and "a complete absence of theory."[8] He listened to jazz music for the first time at fifteen, at the encouragement of music ethnologist Erich von Hornbostel, a relative of Borneman's who allowed young Ernest to attend his course lectures. Together with his teacher Carl Stumpf, in 1904 Hornbostel had founded the Berlin Phonogram Archive—a unique ethnological collection of sound recordings from around the world—which he continued to head until he emigrated in 1933. It was Hornbostel who played Borneman a New Orleans jazz record in 1930; "it's the real link between improvisation and composition," he told him, between "folk music and art music, the polyphonic age and the modern tradition. It's jazz music!"[9] Three days later, on a summer evening, Hornbostel took the teenager and a few of his students with him to Haus Vaterland to see Sidney Bechet play. According to Borneman, the professor explained that he had been to many jazz concerts all over Europe. "This, he said, was true devotion to the tough academic tradition of relentless intellectual pursuit. He reminded us, especially, of the great physical strain and the sacrifice of quiet study that was involved in these long and tiresome journeys. We sympathized and were sent by Sidney Bechet and the blues. This, I suppose, was my initiation into the secret cult of the faithful." It was not until living as an exile in Britain, however, that Borneman would truly come to know the many facets of a flourishing jazz scene in a Western European metropolis. Borneman's discovery of jazz in a political context—amid the rising radicalism of the Pan-African movement in the 1930s from its heart in London and later, with escalating calls for decolonization within the literary and philosophical Négritude movement of late 1940s Paris—would leave a lasting impression on his perspective as a jazz critic. Borneman kept company with the black intellectuals at the helm of these movements, whose Pan-Africanism proved to be both the "real ideology" behind the decolonization of Africa and the foundation for the radical African American civil rights movement in the 1960s.[10] The movements' protagonists saw jazz as a means of expressing a new, African self-consciousness.

Arrived in London on 8 July 1933, Borneman began to frequent the jazz clubs Nest and Shim Sham, also joining the recently established No. 1 Rhythm Club. He partially earned his keep with occasional performances as a jazz musician, initially as a pianist and then as a bass player.[11] While he would later recall having shared the stage with Louis Armstrong, Cab Calloway, Duke Ellington, and other jazz greats of the era, it is doubtful whether this was truly the case.[12] From time to time he would concede in interviews that he was actually a bad musician who had given up playing at the end of the 1930s; other texts speak of concerts with famous musicians while in Canada.[13] When one author suggested forming a band composed of jazz critics in 1959, Borneman was included alongside other towering figures such as Max Jones, Albert McCarthy, and Paul Oliver, although he was entrusted with only a minor role on the bongo drums.[14] Every now and then Borneman crafted blues poems, a few of which were published. A Canadian jazz band also set them to music for the radio, though he stood no chance of making any money with them.[15]

As a young exile, Borneman's first jazz concert in London was a benefit for the Scottsboro Boys, a group of young African Americans who had been falsely accused of, then sentenced for, raping a white woman in 1931. In addition to African American organizations, the Communist parties in the United States and Europe also organized campaigns to protest their convictions.[16] "So happy!!!" the eighteen-year-old Borneman wrote after spending his first few days and nights in London partying, going to jazz clubs, and distributing flyers.[17] It was not just the music that fascinated him; it was his entire experience of the black community and its expressivity. From this perspective, the jazz played by African Americans was no longer inferior or in need of refinement by white musicians, as older experts had deemed it, but was itself the standard, the original form of jazz. In the end it was not blacks who should adopt European culture, but rather whites who should look to a culture of African American origin. Autobiographical materials from the time leave little doubt as to just how enthralled Borneman was by the variety of London's nightlife—"all the languages, colors, classes, criminals, reporters, hookers, sailors," as he described the mix of people in Blue Café.[18] More than anything, however, he was fascinated by his interactions with black people. He gained access to this world through Nancy Cunard, a left-wing journalist and publisher at home in various bohemian circles in London and Paris who lived together with the black jazz pianist Henry Crowder and spoke out against racism. Eva Geisel's earliest memory of her eventual husband was at a dance at the League of Africans in 1933 with Nancy Cunard, who "jangled past with huge bracelets made of ivory."[19] Borneman later interpreted his association with Cunard, who kept regular company with black Communists, in a political context, as a commitment to the revolution.[20]

Borneman's first years in London were in fact shaped by a small group of black revolutionaries from British colonies in the Caribbean and Africa, who in Pan-Africanism were in the process of developing a common political consciousness.[21] He was strongly influenced by C. L. R. James, a historian and political activist from Trinidad fourteen years his senior who had come to England one year before Borneman. In early 1934 James settled down in London, where he would eventually become a leading Trotskyist intellectual. By the time of his move to the United States in 1938, James had written books about the Communist International's transformation into an organization in support of the Soviet Union's national interests; the only successful slave revolt, led by Toussaint L'Ouverture in Haiti; the popular title *History of*

Negro Revolt, a play and a novel—and this all in addition to countless political essays and newspaper articles about the British national sport, cricket. Like Borneman, his publications spanned a variety of topics. The two men did not always write about the same things, but they shared an interest in jazz and their Marxist perspective, with the older James encouraging the younger Borneman's development on three accounts: politically, a receptivity to the non-Stalinist radical Left; culturally, an interest in Africa and the Caribbean (not in opposition to, but in interaction with European culture); and regarding his working methods, an empirical, encyclopedic approach that encompassed a broad spectrum of topics and styles.

London was a center for Socialist activism of all stripes in the early 1930s, with blacks from the Commonwealth playing a major role. As the Communist International switched to its popular front policy and cut back on anti-colonial efforts, many black Communists turned toward Pan-Africanism. This movement continued to pursue an anti-imperialist agenda, calling for the unity and freedom of all Africans—a decolonized Africa, and freedom from racial oppression for the descendants of the African slaves who had been carted off to the New World. As the author of anti-colonial writings and cofounder of the International African Service Bureau (IASB), established in 1937 in London to support the cause of national independence in Africa, James became a towering figure in the radical Pan-African movement. He associated with many intellectuals and artists in London, including the African American blues singer Paul Robeson, the French anarchist Daniel Guerin, and the German emigré Communist theorist Karl Korsch.

James—also known as "Nello"—lived in different shared flats in London; he formed the first one, nicknamed the Hermitage, with Ernest Borneman and German teacher Ernst Perl. Borneman had met James, along with other students from the Commonwealth, at the international Student Movement House on Russell Square, where the two became friends.[22] The three men rented a three-room flat in Bloomsbury at 9 Heathcote Street, where Borneman lived from December 1933 to December 1937. Their home became a meeting place for black intellectuals, who, as Borneman recalled, discussed politics and art all day and all night, touching on topics such as factional struggles within international communism between the Stalinists and Trotskyists, but also the concept of a left-wing black movement independent of the white-dominated parties and unions.[23] As the file on James in the National Archives in London reveals, the British secret service agencies kept watch on the flat, tracking mail and telephone calls while planting agents at the meetings held there in order to contain any revolutionary subversion.[24] Regulars at the flat included Jomo Kenyatta, who studied in London from 1934 to 1938 and later became the first president of Kenya, and Eric Williams, who wrote a dissertation that was strongly influenced by James on the dissolution of the slave trade in the West Indies at Oxford, and who later became the first prime minister of Trinidad and Tobago. Another frequent visitor was George Padmore from Trinidad, a friend from James's youth who had been chosen by the Communist International to head the International Trade

Union Committee of Negro Workers in Hamburg and who had studied alongside Kenyatta in Moscow for a spell before he was ousted from the Soviet and British Communist parties for criticizing the popular front. Borneman later claimed to have met Padmore in Hamburg shortly before he emigrated, and to have met with him almost daily in London, beginning in 1935.[25] Other occasional visitors included I. T. A. Wallace-Johnson, the former editor of the Communist *Negro Worker* and general secretary of the IASB since 1937; the left-wing publisher Fred Warburg; Fenner Brockway, the chairman of the Independent Labour Party; and Rajani Palme Dutt, the British Communist Party's chief theorist. While leftist critics of the Communist Party attacked the Moscow Trials and the Soviet Union's turn from world revolution, Communist Party supporters lambasted black organizations as a form of "racism" that stood in the way of a popular front. Borneman later repeatedly returned to the issues that had been discussed at the flat, especially the political debates about the character of the Soviet Union, albeit with a much more skeptical attitude than directly after his immigration to London; he spoke of "the great disillusionment at the Hermitage."[26]

Such was Borneman's political context as a young Marxist in his London exile. In light of the formative impulses he received there and his studies with Hornbostel, it is hardly surprising that Borneman showed an interest in the social foundations of jazz, the everyday music of this postcolonial, revolutionary world. Ernest and Eva Borneman's memories of this time were often euphoric; Eva raved about the "stormy chaps from the Hermitage," and the "most Puritan and moral young man that I knew."[27] The first years of exile spent at the Hermitage doubtless had a great impact on Borneman. As an older man, he wrote, "This house has been burned in my brain with hot coals. Nothing prior to it and nothing after it really exists. That was the life that I wanted to lead, but it will never happen."[28] "All of us," he later wrote in reference to the communal attitude at the Hermitage, "were nearly penniless, all of us were in exile, but we did not have the slightest doubt that we were going to change the face of the globe."[29] Almost nothing of what he had once thought out while studying with Hornbostel "could withstand the test of the Negro movement struggling for control of whole continents. I had to scrap almost everything I had worked out till then, and I had to give up once and for all the idea that music can be conceived as something developing on its own—something but slightly influenced by the hot breath of social struggle."[30]

Borneman's mother worried throughout the first few weeks of her son's London exile that he was ensconced "so fully in Negro circles" and about the age difference with his new friends.[31] After visiting at the end of 1933, however, she wrote him that she was happy to know "the kind of people that are around you." She took a special liking to his flatmates Perl and James, writing, "Both of them are worthy people, although they might be difficult for you and your kind. But these two . . . are the best company to keep you under control and look to polish off your rough edges."[32] While he had already published some articles in English, she advised him to follow

Figure 2.1. Listening to records on Ernest's bed in "The Hermitage," 1937. Courtesy AdK.

James's advice and write a book. "Then you will have something to show for yourself," she wrote, "and you will keep busy, working on something that makes you happy."[33] Conversations with James were also important for the precocious German from a political perspective, as the two shared a Marxist-Leninist worldview. Borneman admired James, commenting on the latter's 1937 *World Revolution* that it was "a pure Trotskyist encyclopedia. Excellent. To my mind the best thing since Marx, Engels, Lenin, Trotsky."[34] Since returning to England James had been an active member of the Independent Labour Party (ILP), a left-wing group that had split off from the Labour Party. According to government records, he visited Moscow in 1936, where he attended one of the Moscow Trials, and had since become a committed Trotskyist and leader of the leftist Marxists within the ILP.[35] Borneman became familiar with Trotsky through James but never became a Trotskyist himself; in this respect the two men were "on very different wavelengths."[36] Borneman still stood firmly on the side of the Soviet Union during his first years in London, although he did appreciate the value of the radical, activist side of communism, that is, the "practice of Marxism rather than theory," bringing him closer to James.[37] Borneman attended Socialist and Communist assemblies in London, though it is very unlikely that he ever traveled to the Soviet Union, as the British intelligence agency MI5 claimed.[38] True, the Gestapo had said the same thing to Borneman's father, but there is no further evidence to support the claims. More importantly, the otherwise garrulous Borneman never mentioned such a trip. Decades later, in 1983, Borneman stated that he had "left the CP," "nearly 50 years ago," which meant in the mid-1930s.[39] This is the most direct evidence in support of the idea that Borneman had belonged to the Communist Party—it is also the only. As for many Communists, the German-Soviet Nonaggression Pact in 1939 triggered a crisis of identity for Borneman. In a letter, he wrote of his "great disillusion," although he also insisted that "it was only partial disillusion: the basic creed that the world could be improved remained. That it should be improved had never been doubted."[40]

When James left for the United States in 1938, the two men parted ways. It was Eva who first met up with James again in New York in 1944, after which the Bornemans made more of an effort to keep in touch.[41] Ernest and Nello began corresponding again in 1946, with James likely seeking to exert political influence in Canada. For his part, Borneman cautioned James against harboring any illusions that he might drum up any support, writing that he knew only three people who "sympathized."[42] Borneman suggested meeting in New York, in part to resume a number of discussions from the days at the Hermitage that still bore contemporary relevance. The families saw each other for the last time in the 1950s, when James and his wife visited London, but the two men continued to correspond about Borneman's career prospects working in film policy for countries such as Trinidad and Ghana, both of which were now run by mutual friends from their days in London.[43]

As a young emigré, Borneman visited the British Library almost every day to work on his articles, novels, and plays. He also started work on his *Bibliography of American Negro Music*, later adding material from the Schomburg Library in Harlem in 1946. Borneman's work on jazz as folk music bore visible traces of James's influence, especially the latter's convictions that the masses were a motivating force in history and that cultural elements of the Caribbean such as calypso music were an expression of the emerging West Indian nation.[44] Kenyatta may likewise have influenced Borneman's interest in cultural anthropology. Borneman claimed to have attended lectures given by Bronislaw Malinowski at the London School of Economics with

Kenyatta and to have studied African languages in the reading rooms at the British Museum and the School of Oriental and African Studies.[45]

A History of American Negro Music

Throughout his early years in London, Borneman looked to make a name for himself in film. In this case, too, the black milieu and socialization he underwent played a key role. An outline for an early, formally avant-garde film gives a sign of the subjects and approach that were to appear in more refined form in later projects. A black man straggles wearily into a nightclub, where he is carried away by the rhythm of the jazz music. Plied with alcohol by the (white) guests and shot to death at the end, his last breath becomes "a heartbeat . . . that dully thuds, involuntarily, in the images of his dreams, where it becomes the rhythm of the slave songs of his ancestors," but also "the beat of the dance music of the emancipated Negros with which they begin to conquer the world that they have lost." The beat of the rhythm coming from the "jungle drums of African negros" lifts "the audience to an unthinkable level of ecstasy," and through the combination of sound and picture set to rhythm, they "become conscious of it . . . hammered into their BRAIN." "All of this takes places in a strange state somewhere between reality and dream, in which the valves of the controlling consciousness break open and the pressure within the sub-consciousness from the long pent-up and perpetually repressed masses slackens." The treatment draws a direct connection between sensual impressions and rational processes and also contains a political message: by raising awareness of the history of black suffering, the film would become "a battering ram that can be used to storm and break down all the walls of human stupidity, idleness, and weakness."[46] Borneman thus presents jazz as a medium for the self-emancipation of black people.

Directly before his internment as an "enemy alien" in the summer of 1940, Borneman had been on the verge of breaking out as a jazz connoisseur. A few weeks earlier the BBC had finally caved to pressure from the jazz clubs, lifting a ban on jazz that had been on the books since 1935 and broadcasting its first program on jazz, a three-part series called *Outlaw Ballads*, at the end of April and the beginning of May. Borneman was ready and waiting; that same spring he had taken part in a radio discussion entitled "Jazz for Moderns." While the interest of the white British public in "jazz" as performed by local orchestras at dances had waned since the end of the 1920s, the popularity of "hot jazz" played by small African American bands had grown. In scholarly literature on jazz, the year 1932, when the New Dixieland Band toured England and Louis Armstrong played in London, is cited as the beginning of the revival of jazz in its traditional form.[47] Within a year, other jazz greats such as Coleman Hawkins, Cab Calloway, and Duke Ellington were on tours of their own. Borneman thus encountered an erupting jazz scene that had a tremendous need for press coverage and publicity. Borneman's circle of friends included a number of jazz experts, many of whom emerged as specialists on various aspects of jazz by the end of the war. Journalists such as Max Jones, Denis Preston, and Charles Wilford Smith all devoted themselves intensively to the subject of jazz, researching, publishing, and in some cases making it their life's work. The role such specialists held in England was all the more important because, apart from a handful of exceptions, in the early 1930s very few of the music's African American protagonists could be seen playing live; the isolationist stance adopted by the British musicians' union to protect national interests in the face of US competition had made it difficult to contract African American performers. British jazz fans who wanted to hear the original versions therefore had no other choice but to turn to records. Borneman had already acquired an enormous amount of cultural capital in this regard, in the form of 250 to 300 records that he had collected since his youth, which he owned until his internment in 1940.[48] After the war, he used his position as a critic at different music magazines to access new recordings. In 1955 alone, the record company Decca sent him records for review valued at a total of 30,000 British pounds, not to mention those he received from other companies.[49] The value of this capital grew in proportion to its scarcity; especially in the 1930s and 1940s, it was no simple matter to come across a longed-for record. Researching and then hunting for titles in the few record shops around town or at the Caledonian market both required and generated a strong network of contacts; connections were then further strengthened in jazz clubs and magazines, the latter of which offered more than just an intellectual forum of exchange. True experts knew the serial numbers of the record companies by heart, both for the originals and the new editions. For these hunter-gatherers, the records became more important than the music.

Jazz clubs provided an ideal setting for up-and-coming critics; members would cull through their collections for a new record or to find material about a set topic, then bring it in to share and provide commentary before the ensuing discussion.[50] Generally speaking, these listener communities were kept separate from the live jazz music scene; concerts, while undoubtedly offering a more complete experience, made it difficult to hold a conversation, given the volume, and difficult to study anything in depth, since the music was gone once it was played. What was more, jazz aficionados were essentially forced to seek out such quasi-academic listening and discussion events by virtue of the fact that there were hardly any live performances by African Americans in Great Britain. At their weekly meetings, as Borneman recalled in a highly entertaining depiction of London's "jazz cult" in the 1930s, "one critic after another cultivated his public image by laying his favorite record on the big gramophone, expecting the other members to nod in agreement with the row of adverbs and adjectives that formed the basis of his commentary."[51] In this case, a self-image of the jazz critic as scholar developed. Many came from a highly educated background, as Borneman sketched in another description of his first years in England: a helpful flatmate in Cambridge had introduced him to the "three hallmarks of English undergraduate society, namely grey flannel trousers, a checked tweed jacket, and a portable H.M.V. Record player with some Parlophone new-rhythm-style records"—new

British editions of American classics.[52] In one letter written to his father after the war addressing two articles of his on the "jazz cult" that appeared in *Harper's Magazine*, Borneman makes clear just how important jazz records were as the material basis for a professional career, noting triumphantly that the money from the articles "should pay for all the old records that you used to say that I was wasting my money on when I was younger."[53] In Canada, where the conditions were much better than in London, he continued to build up his collection with stacks of old blues records purchased all over the North American continent. Bessie Smith, Ma Rainey, Bessie Jackson, Lead-belly and Joe Turner were particular favorites. He defined his field of interest as "all kinds of blues, from vocals to boogie, work songs, original spirituals and authentic Latin American and West Indian Negro music."[54]

At the same time, British fans' enthusiasm for collecting knowledge and records alike favored a traditionalist vein in jazz, as their chief interest lay in older recordings. There existed no general consensus on the African American origins of jazz among new jazz listeners, especially as Europeans were cut off from live performances by African Americans, and familiar only with white dance combos. It was commonly asserted that jazz was "white" music, making Borneman's research on the roots of jazz all the more important.[55] Indeed, it was only a historical and ethnological perspective that could truly clarify the origins of jazz. Borneman himself dated the beginnings

Figure 2.2. Listening and discussing: shaping and forming opinions at the Rhythm Club Nr. 1 in London, 1957. Borneman is seated fourth from left. Courtesy AdK.

of his study of African American music back to his work with Hornbostel around 1930, when he allegedly chose the subject as a potential dissertation topic (temporarily putting aside doubts as to whether he could have been so task-oriented at the tender age of fifteen). He goes on to state that he continued collecting and cataloging additional materials until 1939, ultimately revising and rewriting the entire piece.[56] Three manuscripts exist today, a draft of a dissertation on musicology, a short draft of an application for a research project, and a draft of a nonacademic book entitled "The History of American Negro Folk Music." Professor Joseph Hirst wrote an expert review of this last manuscript, noting that "this is one of those pioneer works which are bound to become standard text books of musicology. . . . These are the discoveries of a music-detective, and, indeed, the book has the thrills and the fascination of a detective thriller without ever losing the thoroughly annotated and carefully referenced character of sound academic research."[57] The manuscript was accepted for publication by Allen & Unwin in London, in cooperation with E. P. Dutton in New York, but the project was postponed in December 1939 due to paper shortages brought about from the war. Borneman's attempt to locate another New York publisher failed. In 1941, shortly after Borneman was released from internment in Canada, Eva waxed optimistic about the project in the hope that Constant Lambert would bring out the book on jazz: "We now need money and fame to get things going, and your book on jazz music will surely find an audience, here and over there as well."[58] Borneman sent out the manuscript to acquaintances and kept telling friends and colleagues that it would come out, through Harvard University Press among others;[59] he had already announced his "History of American Negro Music" in 1939, for example, in an *Esquire* article.[60] The book was never published, however, nor were any of the later manuscript versions. The same proved true for the 214-page "Bibliography of American Negro Music," which included about one thousand titles and was written around the same time.[61]

Borneman repeatedly applied for funded research projects in order to lend his arguments academic weight, but to no avail.[62] In early 1940 he approached Melville J. Herskovits at Northwestern University in Chicago, seeking advice about possible scholarships to support field research in the United States.[63] He sent the famous anthropologist, who had just published his path-breaking book *The Myth of the Negro Past*, a bibliography and synopsis. In doing so, Borneman initially drew on an indirect contact from 1938, when Borneman's friend J. C. Trevor, a lecturer at Cambridge and erstwhile student of Herskovits, had told his mentor about his friend's research. Herskovits, who had helped many European refugees, gave Borneman cause for hope about the possibility of publishing his bibliography. He also indicated a willingness to help find the young emigré some scholarship possibilities but asked for proof that Borneman had taught for two years at the university level, something that Borneman obviously could not provide.[64] The young man explained that the papers confirming his academic training had been lost in the move to America. Herskovits nevertheless managed to get Borneman, now interned in Canada, considered for a scholarship at his university.[65] In the end nothing came of the affair; the professor made it clear that another persecuted student of his with whom he had been working closely for a few years now took precedence, Jewish anthropologist Mieczyslaw Kolinski, whose life was at risk living in occupied Belgium.[66] Yet Herskovits still did what he could to help Borneman find a scholarship that would allow him to immigrate to the United States, corresponding with a number of organizations, such as the Institute of International Education and the American Council of Learned Societies, and sending books to Borneman at his internment camp.[67] When Borneman once again applied for a scholarship in 1947, Herskovits wrote in his letter of recommendation to the Guggenheim Foundation that he was very excited about the project and was convinced Borneman would succeed. He also noted that he had been impressed with Borneman's character when the two had met for the first time the year before.[68] Later on, when his protégé applied to work for UNESCO, Herskovits wrote another positive letter of recommendation. He described the applicant as a man of "great competence" and "high character," also mentioning that he was "most cooperative."[69] In this last case Borneman got the job, but he never set foot inside the walls of academia during these years. No evidence could be found to confirm, as he claims in *Die Ur-Szene*, that he studied with Herskovits for two semesters between jobs at the National Film Board of Canada and UNESCO. Society had been unfair to Borneman, Charles Wilford Smith once commented in a letter to his friend, in not allowing him to complete his basic studies.[70]

Borneman's German background lent the whole matter a particular urgency that was not shared by American or British jazz initiates. In his first letter to Herskovits from 1940, he explained:

> Those of us who were forced, by the political events in Germany, to face the question of racial versus social influences in the development of cultural patterns, had to make clear-cut decisions as to whether the transmission of folk-lore occurred through direct inheritance or rather through post-natal contact between parent and child. There were few fields of study which enabled a more productive inquiry into these principles than that of African-American music.[71]

Borneman's intensive preoccupation with jazz also changed the way he as a researcher approached his subject, however. In 1945–46, looking to tell the story of the transformation of a character searching for his roots in black music, Borneman reflected on his own development. For the most part, he noted, it was much like what Norman Mailer would describe in "The White Negro" a few years later:

> I am only too well aware of this peculiar psychological drama because it is largely my own story as a European middle-class student in search of American Negro music: I sought for purely academic knowledge and found, instead, a most profound change of character, caused, no doubt,

by my gradual identification with the Negro musicians whose lives and experiences I came to share in my search for the origins of their music."[72]

His work on jazz essentially focused on two topics: first, the link between African American folk music and present-day modern dance music, and second the reciprocal relationships between social background and popular culture. In both respects, Borneman went well beyond prevailing notions at the time, which held jazz first and foremost to be a purely musical phenomenon—a rhythmic innovation—to be judged according to the criteria of taste.[73] Borneman's exploration of jazz within its historical context led him to emphasize its transformation over time and to view it as a construction, a "cult" and a "myth," which he described time and again in great detail. In doing so, he often vexed jazz lovers such as the American writer Calder Willingham, who was hopping mad over Borneman's claim that his notion of the timelessness of beautiful music was utter nonsense; in 1946 Borneman wrote to Willingham, asserting that New Orleans jazz was unfortunately "dead music" now.[74]

In addition to a number of shorter publications on his ideas about jazz, Borneman also produced two more substantial texts: an unpublished manuscript from 1940, and a pamphlet entitled *A Critic Looks at Jazz* from 1946. Borneman's estate contains a 580-page manuscript entitled "Swing Music: An Encyclopedia of Jazz," which was likely the draft of his dissertation. Following introductory sections on the history of American art music, slavery, and emancipation, the manuscript reconstructs the history of African American "folk music" in different parts of the United States. A second part describes the local backdrop in US capitals for jazz, such as New Orleans, Chicago, and New York, and explores jazz in Europe through the lens of different national scenes and their clubs. A third part, a chapter entitled "What Is Jazz?" explores its musical and linguistic characteristics.

While Borneman had originally envisioned the work as an encyclopedic study of developments in American music since World War I, he eventually narrowed the topic down to African American music and jazz in particular, and gave the work a sociological orientation. The project did not lose its empirical character despite this shift in focus; Borneman once told the African American writer Richard Wright that he was no fan of grand theories, be they from Herskovits or someone else. The more he learned about music, he reflected, the less faith he had in them. By the same token, he also maintained that if there was any purpose to anthropology, it was as field research and empirical science.[75] Borneman was not referring to the biological science of anthropology in this case, but cultural anthropology as it was understood in North America at the time—empirical cultural studies that dealt with the habits and practices of everyday life in different cultures. Exploring jazz from the perspective of cultural anthropology, as Borneman did, meant taking an interest in culture broadly conceived, its origin in changing social practices and in interaction with other cultures, rather than the idea that culture existed separately, in and of itself. When considering the origins of jazz among African slaves brought to America, he therefore posed questions like "Is culture race-bound? Is it bound to district and climate? Will it survive transplantation to a different culture, a different country, a different race, a different form of social organization?" His study was guided by the premise that all forms of human activity, music included, had to be understood as "mere sublimations and elaborations of the elementary needs of human society."[76] As with film, for Borneman jazz was a form of art that sprang from a differentiated social organization encompassing great masses of people, as it had in the United States:

> Jazz music is a more highly socialized form of art than any other form of music—more, in fact, than any form of art except Cinema which, like Jazz music, came to existence at a time when human society had developed a structure of such complexity that almost every human being took part, in one way or another, in the production of almost every product produced by any other human being at any other spot where human beings lived. It is no accident that both Jazz and Cinema should have developed in that excellent melting pot of peoples and races which is America. Here the process of international and intersocial penetration reached its height in the form of a merchant civilization which commercialized all forms of art at a rate which left Europe dazzled and agape.[77]

Borneman's study posed the question of how social development in the United States had influenced jazz and, inversely, how jazz influenced society. Essentially, it revolved around the problem of how art should be analyzed, not as a preconceived aesthetic norm, but as a product of the context in which it emerged. Jazz could not be fully comprehended via social factors, he contended, because as a form of art it exhibited a certain degree of autonomy. Borneman explained that, as a Marxist, he considered the relationship between economy and aesthetics similar to that between the base and its superstructure.[78] Yet he also postulated that jazz not only had been shaped by American society, but had in fact shaped American society itself. The relationship between the base and the superstructure was thus set on early Marxist footing, rather than a crude—and wonted—materialist vision of a lopsided relationship of dependence. In its historical perspective, Borneman's theoretical framework relied heavily on Bertolt Brecht's notion of a "theater of the scientific age," which was intended to expose social laws in an experimental way by assuming a distanced position, with history and the coming "scientific age" constituting the ideal observation towers. Like Brecht, Borneman also worked with the temporal axis of past–present–future, which enabled a distanced perspective and thus a critical position: "The theories and the critical standards of art which are based on an aesthetic analysis of existing works of art are totally untenable: they must be replaced by a theory that is flexible enough to stretch not only from the past to the present, but also beyond the present to the future."[79] This theory was indeed Marxist, albeit not in the form of a partisan dogmatism, but rather a "leftist divergence" that afforded noneconomic factors, including art, a relatively autonomous position.[80] To Borneman's mind, this historical approach demonstrated that social relationships could be altered—the past from the point of view of the present, the present from the point of view of utopia. Borneman made the future of jazz dependent on the development of society: "A good society produces good music, a bad one bad music."[81] Jazz, he contended, had reached a dead end "from which there is only one way out: a social change that liberates it from nightclubs and turns it back to folk music." This statement reveals one of Borneman's basic premises, namely that jazz should not seek its deliverance in pop music or in its elevation by associating with the European music tradition, but should rather be preserved as folk music. "In order to make such an advance possible," Borneman wrote, "Jazz must drop the commercialism of Tin Pan Alley and of Broadway, the lulling saccharine of 'sweet Jazz,' the cheaply aphrodisiacal 'Jitterbug Jazz'—all those elements of social and sexual dope which are now associated with the functions that Jazz is forced to fulfill in the modern nightclub."[82] Ultimately, the future belonged to jazz because it was not necessarily associated with a particular social class; opera and classical symphony music, on the other hand, were doomed to failure as preferences of the ruling class.[83] Borneman's subsequent role in establishing the blues in Great Britain after the war, moreover, was rooted in this same idea of jazz as folk music.

If music were influenced by the needs of society, as Borneman maintained, what role did one's membership in a "race" play? Not a particularly important one, came the reply. The descendants of the slaves brought in from West Africa did not simply reproduce "African" music, but combined the few elements of West African traditions that had been carried over from their ancestors (Borneman termed this "secondary Africanism") with diverse cultural influences from the plethora of ethnic or national traditions represented in the melting pot of the United States. All of these elements, Borneman argued, fed into "a new music that had very little resemblance with original African music. It was no longer Negro music at all, nor was it Negro-music-diluted-by-the-music-of-the-white-red-and-yellow-races-of-America; it was simply no longer racial music at all. In fact, it had never been racial music."[84] Writing in reference to Hornbostel, Borneman explained further that if the West Africans had been brought not to the United States but to China, they would have made Chinese-style music: "Music is formed by the social structure of society and not by its racial structure. . . . The difference between African and European music is not the difference between two different races but the difference between two different forms of social organisation." Likewise taking up with Melville J. Herskovits, whose famous book *The Myth of the Negro Past* he had read while working for the National Film Board of Canada with an eye toward its application in ethnographic documentaries,[85] he asserted that "the musical customs in America changed—not through the impact of another race but through the impact of another people with a different musical custom which was the result of a different social system." This was an unqualified statement that did justice to the influence of African traditions, but without undermining the hybridity of jazz as a combination of different traditions.

One of the people Borneman was able to enlist in support of his book project was Richard Wright, a former Communist and the protagonist of the Harlem Renaissance movement in the 1920s and 1930s whose bestselling book *Native Son* had just been published. The writer considered Borneman's manuscript "epochal," although he did suggest a number of changes. In search of a second opinion, Wright forwarded it to John Hammond, an influential journalist, record producer, and advocate of traditional jazz.[86] In late 1941 Borneman broached the subject with Wright, who had read the galley proofs of Borneman's most recent novel and developed an impression of Borneman's literary talent. Borneman also brought Wright on board at the National Film Board of Canada as a contributor to a project on Afro-Canadians.[87] After revising the manuscript in light of Wright's and Hammond's comments, Borneman turned to Harlem blues musician and author W. C. Handy, who added a great deal of factual material, and to Herskovits, who thought it too Marxist. After 1944, sections of it were finally published as a series in *The Record Changer*.[88] After passing muster in the journal, which purported to bring together "the most critical and best-informed readership on this topic in the world," the series was then published as a monograph, although it did not appear in its entirety or through a major publisher, as had originally been the hope.[89]

"The Anthropologist Looks at Jazz"

In June 1940 Borneman was interned as an "enemy alien" and later deported to Canada, where he took a job with the National Film Board of Canada after his release in June 1941. Outside of work he came to enjoy the nightlife in Ottawa and Toronto and continued to build up his network of jazz contacts now in North America, where it was far simpler to study jazz history than in England.[90] He made frequent trips to the United States and joined the Hot Club Chicago—his membership card is among his papers. Borneman's correspondence with his girlfriend and eventual wife Eva Geisel, who had remained in London, reflects an intensive preoccupation with the jazz scene—not only the music, but also the dances, clothing, and other elements of the "jazz cult." From the very beginning, jazz was more than just a sonic form for Borneman; it was also a social phenomenon whose symbols and rituals formed the basis of a modern lifestyle. Even before the war was over he began to publish regularly on jazz, eventually becoming one of the most internationally renowned jazz critics of his day. The work that made his reputation was "The Anthropologist Looks at Jazz," an eight-part article series that was published from April 1944 to February 1945 in *The Record Changer*, a jazz magazine founded by Gordon Gullickson in 1942. Borneman joined the editorial team as a contributing editor in May 1944, moving up the ranks to associate editor by September 1946 until he was replaced by Nesuhi Ertegün in August 1947, after which he returned to being a contributing editor. Gullickson had hit upon the name for the series; Borneman, at least as he told jazz author Stanley Dance, would never have dared to claim this title for himself "after four years of university studies, but no degree" (itself already an exaggeration of the facts).[91] The magazine appeared monthly, turning from a four-page insider's gazette into a sixty-page magazine with a color cover. In his role as a coeditor, Borneman helped to expand the journal into a multifaceted magazine that intended to serve musicians, academically inclined readers, and music lovers in general, in addition to record collectors.[92] The issues took on a mixed format, with the first half featuring articles on jazz and the second half serving as a marketplace for used records. Borneman's series appeared as a monograph in 1946—the book proved highly influential because, as the publisher Max Jones outlined in his preface, it explored jazz from an academic point of view, more specifically that of a cultural anthropologist and a sociologist, thereby establishing "valid critical standards." Borneman's work at *The Record Changer* also brought him back into contact with some of his old friends in London like Jones and Smith, who read the magazine. Smith reported to Borneman in October 1944 that Jones had read two of Borneman's articles in *The Record Changer* that he thought to be "extremely good" and a further demonstration of the fact that the subtlest jazz criticism came from Europeans.[93] For Albert J. McCarthy, the magazine was "the leading jazz magazine in the States, and probably the finest in the world," and had "brought out more serious articles" in the five years of its existence—citing Borneman's series as an example—than most other magazines combined.[94] The magazine was a platform for traditionalists who scorned bebop, with Barry Ulanov and Leonard Feather leading its defense at the magazine *Metronome*. Despite increasing pressure to take sides on this debate, it was not easy to delineate the respective fronts. Charles Wilford Smith, who prized *The Record Changer*, suggested to Borneman that the magazine reduce its attacks on Feather because they were taking up too much space ("all that Moldy Fig stuff is tiresomely esoteric, and the sarcasm so depressingly heavy").[95] In early 1948, when Bill Grauer took over for Gullickson—Borneman had already left his editorial post—the editorial stance changed; *The Record Changer* now looked to shed its reputation as a "sectarian publication" and reflect a new kind of pluralism by opening up more to bebop.[96]

Many of Borneman's jazz colleagues had become professionally involved in the jazz business in the meantime, figures like Denis Preston, a jazz critic and cousin of Eric Hobsbawm who joined the BBC as a moderator, but also Max Jones, who published Borneman's fifty-three-page pamphlet *A Critic Looks at Jazz* under his Jazz Music Books imprint. Among other things, Jones had worked for *Melody Maker* since 1940 and founded a jazz club aligned with the Communist Party.[97] He shared an interest with Borneman in the social backgrounds of jazz in the United States and was especially intrigued by racism and poverty as conditioning factors in blues music, which he considered to be the essence of jazz. Such topics formed the basis of *Jazz Music*, a magazine Jones founded with Albert McCarthy in 1942 that ran until 1953 and whose Marxist bent—a common approach in the United States, but considered "a radical shift in British jazz writing"—found its basis in Borneman's essays.[98] Folk music, Borneman maintained, could only survive if composers and arrangers were kept away from it.[99] Writing to Borneman at the beginning of 1945, Jones noted that in comparison to mainstream jazz critics, those who thought about jazz in these kinds of "puristic ideals" were "few and scattered and generally incoherent." He and his friends, he commented,

> believe very much in your approach to the subject and don't minimise the strengths of West African survivals in Afro-Am. folk art of all kinds. . . . Like you, I think I can listen by the hour to the good race discs which these Panassians find boring and unimaginative. And to my older paramounts by Blind Lemon J., Elzadie Robinson, Norfolk Jubilee 4 and so on, and some of the fine Lomax albums . . . I can soak up in them but find it difficult to write down just what is so hard and honest and moving about them.[100]

This was precisely what Borneman showed himself capable of, making *A Critic Looks at Jazz* one of the "most authoritative works published on the origins of jazz and the role of blues," at least in the opinion of blues expert Paul Oliver.[101] This quest to trace the roots of the music also came as a revelation to blues musicians themselves, who were not necessarily aware of its history. Mezz Mezzrow, for example, gives a sentimental description in his 1946 autobiography of how he had been completely "bowled over" when Borneman told him that the blues music that he had recorded with Sidney Bechet could be traced back much further than earlier jazz greats, to the ships of the slave trade and the musical traditions of West Africa.[102]

Borneman argued that Kurt Weill and Hanns Eisler connected not to the American disciples of the European music tradition while in exile in the United States, but rather to the music inspired by the African American tradition, which embodied the original elements of American popular music. The only music of significance to come from the American continent was folk music, but it lost its significance when it was no longer made by the people but for the people instead, as with Tin Pan Alley (a synonym for the US music industry named after its geographic center in Manhattan), which Borneman always opposed.[103] The foundation for this unique folk culture, he continued, was the slave trade. Borneman accounted for the institution of slavery, as he did the abolitionist movement, in purely Marxist terms, drawing in particular on C. L. R. James and the Communist historian Herbert Aptheker. Yet Borneman also now refined the answers to the questions he had posed in his "Swing Music" manuscript. While the core of the matter still revolved around the extent to which cultures are "racial achievements," he now focused on the interplay of social and cultural patterns—concretely on the way in which slavery had influenced Afro-American music and, vice versa, the way black music had influenced its surrounding social fabric.[104] The origins of jazz, Borneman argued, could not simply be traced back to "African music," which was much too broad of a category. Rather, drawing on Herskovits's theory, Borneman differentiated between basic song types that would be sung on different occasions, maintaining that with their arrival on the American continent, slaves would only continue to sing songs that also served a purpose in their new context—those related to work, love, weddings, and funerals, for example.[105] Most important, however, was the slaves' appropriation of other cultural traditions from different immigrant groups, which then melted together with the surviving African traditional elements to create a "whole new wealth of Afro-American music."[106] This mutual adoption of new cultural input, a process that could be empirically observed, led Borneman to the conclusion that "the racial element seems to be of amazingly small importance in the determination of musical archetypes. There is no such thing as pure 'Negro music' in America; nor is there any such thing as racial inheritance or racial proclivity in music."[107] Like Herskovits, he argued that there were no correlations between "race" and culture. In his eyes, tradition was not a "racial" inheritance but the result of upbringing, which meant that folk music was tied to environmental factors. Blues had exercised the strongest and most lasting influence on American popular music, symbolizing the ambivalent progress of emancipation from slavery without social recognition. It became the "archetype of jazz" but was also appropriated by white folk singers, thereby becoming, as Borneman put it, "one of the backbones of American folk music."[108] Borneman went on to describe the further development of jazz, noting that its different variations were defined not by their respective structural characteristics in a musical sense, but by their social and political backgrounds.[109] Jazz was the most revolutionary cultural form of modernity because it was democratic and could be practiced by anyone, even those without a musical education. It also bore the volatile freight of long-repressed revolts and the cultural opiate for failure, a substitute for political action. Jazz, Borneman wrote, "at its best, became the American's Negro's music of protest and assertion: Jazz, at its worst, became the white man's music of indolence and escape; more than even movies, it has become the opium of the people. . . . It is up to us, the lovers and critics and collectors of jazz, to decide which of the two we will support and which of the two we shall conquer."[110] He concluded with a critique of commercialized big band jazz, arguing it had opted for arrangement instead of improvisation, and appealed for the rebirth of jazz as a form of folk music that would not be created rationally but intuitively.[111] In a parallel letter to W. C. Handy, Borneman accused him of having, in the process of making blues accessible to white listeners, helped white imitators get a leg up in the music business, who then ousted original interpreters such as Ma Rainey and Bessie Smith. While Rainey and Smith languished in poverty, "the smart Tin Pan Alley boys of this white world write 'symphonic arrangements' on St. Louis Blues in which all remnants of the pain and joy of the race are irrevocably eradicated."[112]

In a later article from 1959 entitled "The Roots of Jazz," Borneman worked through the differences between European and African music, which he located in the insistence on precision and the conscious refutation of it, respectively. In the African tradition, precision and directness were avoided, replaced by implication and circumscription:

> While the whole European tradition strives for regularity—of pitch, of time, of timbre and of vibrato—the African tradition strives precisely for the negation of these elements. In language, the African tradition aims at circumlocution rather than exact definition. The direct statement is considered crude and unimaginative; the veiling of all contents in ever-changing paraphrases is considered the criterion of intelligence and personality. In music, the same tendency towards obliquity and ellipsis is noticeable: no note is attacked straight; the voice or instrument always approaches it from above or below, plays around the implied pitch without ever remaining on it for any length of time, and departs from it without ever having committed itself to a single meaning. The timbre is veiled and paraphrased by constantly changing vibrato, tremolo and overtone effects. The timing and accentuation, finally, are not *stated*, but *implied* or *suggested*. The musician challenges himself to find and hold his orientation while denying or withholding all signposts.[113]

Scholarly literature on the subject has pointed out that in this "deservedly influential essay," Borneman hit on an important point. As Eric Sundquist notes, it was a "a rich statement of the possibilities for reading African American literature, particularly that written at the historical moment when black music takes on its characteristic modern forms, in a context in which the tonalities of a hidden language and the limits of cultural hearing are taken seriously into account."[114]

In response to the wide and overwhelmingly positive reception among readers— the well-known US jazz author Charles Edward Smith referred to Borneman as the "the world's greatest jazz critic"—*The Record Changer* set Borneman up with a "Question and Answers" column.[115] It ran from July 1944 until long after Borneman's "Anthropologist" series had ended, finally coming to a close in June 1947, when Nesuhi Ertegün, later a producer of many jazz greats, took over Borneman's post as an editor at the magazine alongside Gullickson.[116] In retrospect, Borneman identified ten central thematic issues addressed in the five hundred or so letters to the editor. The most important questions dealt with the "racial" character of jazz: "If jazz is a form of Negro folk music, how does it affect white musicians and white listeners?" "Could the theory of the survival of African elements in American Negro music not be interpreted as a form of racism, and is it therefore not objectionable from a social point of view?"[117] Borneman's refusal to discredit popular forms such as New Orleans jazz as inferior also sparked debate, which turned on the tension between democratic and avant-garde art. As for the first set of problems, Borneman distinctly reiterated his point that cultural Africanism was not biologically, but rather socially determined.[118] He returned time and again to the idea that it should not be the task of the jazz critic to judge individual musicians, but rather to describe the social context of their art; if one criticized certain musical forms, he argued, one would have to attack the entire web of conditions that made bad music popular—its commercial context.

Borneman continued work on his major book on jazz, which was "more or less finished" in 1947. Yet he did not want to make the same mistake again and publish the manuscript as a series, he told Ertegün, because it had allowed others to appropriate his arguments.[119] An outline of the manuscript, entitled "A History of American Negro Music: With Special Reference to the Interaction of Social and Cultural Patterns and the Survival of West African Music in the United States of America," focuses on the relationship of social and cultural factors in addition to the mixture of remnants of African tribe culture and European imports in the United States. It recapitulates the African American influence on music, taking a long historical perspective that ranges from the eighteenth century to the present day, and ends with a chapter on first principles entitled "Towards a Sociology of Art."[120] In 1949 Borneman sent a revised version of the large manuscript to Katherine Dunham, who had written an anthropological dissertation in 1938 about dance in Haiti influenced by Herskovits before returning to her career as a dancer and choreographer. He asked her for feedback while the book was being prepared for publication at Oxford University Press.[121] No book, however, ever materialized.

Throughout the height of European jazz in the 1950s Borneman published pieces in countless magazines, including special interest publications like *Jazz Journal* and *DownBeat*, but also major popular magazines such as *Harper's Magazine* and *Variety*. By the second half of the 1940s he was writing on a regular basis for *Melody Maker*, Britain's most important popular music magazine; from 6 May 1950 until 12 December 1953 he held a weekly jazz column, "One Night Stand," writing less frequently thereafter.[122] Borneman's work at the *Melody Maker* was facilitated by Max Jones, who had already made an effort to publish several of Borneman's jazz manuscripts while the latter was interned.[123] Once back in England, Borneman now pitched a column to the magazine's enthusiastic editor that "would cover all aspects of dance music, from jazz to bop, and from show tunes to pop, the whole to be treated in a brief, pungent, humorous and yet not glib manner; something, in short, which would treat the whole field of popular music in the English equivalent to the tone and style which the *New Yorker* magazine uses in talking of movies, theatre, nightclubs, fashion shows and topical affairs."[124] Borneman noted that while he found the *Melody Maker* quite good at the time, he thought it lacked humor and "a certain kind of urbanity," a gap his column would fill. Borneman wrote numerous concert reviews in addition to thoroughgoing articles about present-day jazz, historical developments, the jazz milieu in London and at the BBC, and even commentaries on the police raids in jazz clubs. At the same time, he never lost sight of the continental jazz scene, in particular in Germany. As it turned out, Borneman's writings on jazz propelled developments that would soon make their effects known.

Critics at War: Blues versus Swing and Bebop

Somewhere around 1940 a new direction in jazz music began to emerge in Harlem: bebop (or bop). It developed as a kind of counterpoint to swing, a popular and commercially successful music at the time that was considered by its detractors to be stuck in a routine but also dominated by white musicians like Benny Goodman and Glenn Miller. The protagonists of early "modern jazz" included the trumpet player Dizzie Gillespie, the pianist Thelonious Monk, and the alto saxophonist Charlie Parker. In contrast to big band swing music, the personality of the individual musician played a key role in bop, as expressed in long improvisations with a small supporting band. Fans defended it as an especially topical—that is, "modern"—form because it reflected the tempo and the complexity as well as the contradictions and individualism of contemporary society better than the now outdated New Orleans jazz of the 1920s (also referred to as "Dixieland"). In its fragmentation, numerous solos, and improvisations and complex harmonies, bop did not make for great dance music. Rather, it was deemed largely contemplative in nature, a more abstract, intellectual alternative to popular forms of jazz—certainly one that was less accessible, which meant that it excluded a broader audience. Bop turned jazz into an avant-garde art form, although it must be said that the borders between "art" and "entertainment" were just as flexible for the musicians themselves as for jazz fans, whose preferences were much broader than academic debate led one to believe.[125]

Borneman's central point of contention with bebop was that it lacked a beat. Jazz was first and foremost rhythmic music, he noted, but in bop a regular beat went missing.[126] The perception of bop as an elitist encapsulation of individual genius sparked a counter-movement among jazz fans that harkened back to the popular traditions of jazz and sought to revive simpler forms. At the same time, this search for the original and authentic form of jazz also opposed itself to swing music, which was regarded as a type of commercial alienation. The very fact that Borneman titled his manuscript "Swing Music" in 1940 indicates that at the time, this term was still considered synonymous with jazz. It was not until shortly thereafter that this equivalence was called into doubt, in a dispute surrounding the true nature of jazz conducted almost exclusively by white critics. Borneman himself questioned the interchangeable use of the terms, preferring the more sociologically precise term "African American music." This search for authenticity was supported not least by leftists who detected a bourgeois transformation of the working class in swing and bebop, both of which had become alienated from the ideal of folk music, albeit in different ways. In general, jazz was perceived as anti-fascist, even leftist music, because of its anti-racism and the repression of its fans in fascist countries.[127] Many British jazz associations held close ties to Communists and anarchists. In particular, the British Young Communist League supported the Dixieland movement, which developed rapidly in the 1950s. In the movement's emphasis on the African American roots of jazz, young Communists perceived a revitalization of jazz as the folk music of the working class.[128] That said, Dixieland also provided a point of entry into traditional jazz for a majority of young people because it was better for dancing. The Communist historian—and contemporary witness—Eric Hobsbawm has made a detailed case supporting the idea that jazz was rebellious music in Great Britain.[129] As the New Left began its ascent in the mid-1950s, traditional jazz gained support, providing the background music for the first British antinuclear protests in 1958.

Individual African American musicians also continued to travel to Great Britain throughout the early 1950s, circumventing the prohibitions against their performances by billing themselves as folk singers, who were not considered competition for the entertainment industry. Big Bill Broonzy's two concerts on 22 September 1951 in Kingsway Hall sent shock waves throughout the scene: while the younger US audience already considered him to be old-fashioned, their British counterparts found him to be particularly authentic, the representative of a long tradition of social exclusion, despair, and self-assertion.[130] The US ethnomusicologist Alan Lomax, himself having disappeared to Great Britain for a time in the face of the Red Scare in the United States, moderated and contextualized Broonzy's London performance. Broonzy played during the first concert, but the second was primarily a conversation with Lomax, lending it a particular feeling of authenticity. In Borneman's words, "Both of them were still talking and arguing and asking for news about old friends when they were already on stage—with the result that the audience felt as if they had wandered more or less by accident into one of those fabulous jazz parties of which the books are full."[131] The music press gave a detailed account of the contexts in which the songs emerged, and Broonzy himself tried to match the expectations of the audience by presenting traditional material in a raw style that left listeners believing they had heard how the music of the black rural population in the United States really sounded. This seemed to establish a musical point of reference that countered the "alienation" stemming from commercialization or polished technology with authenticity. Blues was simple, socially relevant music. Borneman contended that it was "one of the least well-attended concerts of the last few years, but the best and most memorable as far as this writer is concerned."[132] Broonzy's appearances had such astounding impact because the last live performances given by an African American artist in Great Britain had taken place almost twenty years prior. Hence the quality of surprise and deep feeling that authenticity would come to develop as its trademarks, despite its being a construction. That which was understood to be "authentic" was seen as "serious," anti-commercial, and raw (the adjective "primitive" was sometimes used)—early on, this was country blues from the US South; urban blues were already considered a modern variation of the original. Anything that was not largely focused on making a big profit was considered credible; this was and remained another important characteristic of authenticity. As the rise of rhythm and blues would soon show, however, "genuine" and "commercial" were not complete opposites.

Coming from the field of cultural anthropology and developed during the heyday of swing while bebop was just emerging, Borneman's arguments were significant for the battle between jazz critics because they inquired into the roots of jazz while attacking commercialization and intellectualization in equal measure, and sought to qualify an emotionally charged debate driven by judgments of taste. The fight between "traditionalists" and "modernists" would plague the jazz world well into the 1960s and became laced with a noticeable amount of bitterness, despite only a minority of jazz fans gravitating to the extreme ends of the spectrum—the great majority could, in fact, take something from both sides. Borneman sought a role as a mediator in the dispute, for a time getting himself caught in the crossfire. While he made little secret of his skepticism toward bebop, he was also critical of the idea of reviving a rural music tradition in the industrial, urban setting of the contemporary

"Thus we conclude a round-table discussion on the subject, 'Early New Orleans Jazz Compared to Modern Hot Music'."

Figure 2.3. The battle lines as caricatured in *The Record Changer*, July 1946.

world. This was consistent with Borneman's thought in general, since he saw music as expressive of social relationships' development throughout history. The idea of revitalizing New Orleans jazz as advocated by Rudi Blesh and others, he wrote, "is not only naive and essentially romantic, but also dangerous because it can only be done with the help of the slick financial and promotional methods which were the original cause of the decline of the music."[133] Many unionists in the United States—Borneman singled out Jim Higgins—might have been modern in a political sense, but in terms of aesthetics they were stuck in the bourgeois Romantic Age. This explains his remark that "I'm opposed to Blesh for the same reasons that the USSR is." He was arguing not as a liberal but "as a Socialist," he continued, not only repudiating Blesh but also "the whole gang of Bourgeois romantics around Peggy Guggenheim and Virgil Thomson and the defunct 'Modern Music' clique." Borneman accounted for the fact that he received no less than eighty-six outraged letters written in response to his first article in the "Anthropologist" series in 1944 as follows: he had merely been expressing his preference for early jazz to many of its later forms "because it seemed to have preserved a good deal of the dignity of rural folk music"; the attempt to revive it, however, "seemed to me as funny as the organized revival of folk dancing among the rural citizens of Greenwich Village." "This innocuous piece of logic," he concluded, set him at the "most exposed position between the contending forces of jazz—the Fundamentalists and the Modernists."[134]

Borneman tried repeatedly to mediate between the two sides, or rather to break up the small circles of critics firmly ensconced in their positions.[135] It was easier said than done. The readers' letters, filled alternatively with hate and praise in response to the very same article, demonstrate just how slight a role actual arguments played in the maelstrom.[136] Bernard Gendron's assessment, which reduces Borneman to "one of the few 'moldy figs' . . . to fight systematically and recurrently against bebop," is certainly too one-sided.[137] While Borneman's historical interest in the story of how jazz came to be did bring him closer to the "traditionalists," he regularly pointed out the necessity of developing new, contemporary forms of music. From his perspective, jazz had achieved its rebellious potential during the Nazi occupation of Europe, when any form proved to be "a powerful spring of action."[138] This affinity became all the more clear in the 1950s as the blues revival gained in popularity, a development driven by Borneman's profession that blues lay at the "heart" of jazz.[139]

Borneman distanced himself from the two sides for different reasons. The traditionalists, he felt, harbored romantic motives—they showed too little faith in traditional jazz as a basis for the continued development of popular music. At the same time, he thought that swing and bebop had moved too far away from folk culture— swing by way of commercialization and bebop by way of its artistic ambitions. The individualism of bebop also bothered him; he considered it to be a bad imitation of European art music. This was, of course, in contrast to New Orleans jazz, which could not care less about the European tradition. By Borneman's account, the modernists were not interested in the purpose or content of their preferred style; it was only the novelty value, techniques, and the complexity of the harmony structure that mattered.[140] The slang term "moldy fig," coined by the "modernist" magazine *Metronome* in 1942 to attack the traditionalists, was defamatory in Borneman's mind, especially as used by Leonard Feather. In 1945 Feather had politicized the term, applying it to "the extreme right of jazz," the "reactive element in music," whose categorizations and exclusionary discourses gave it a "fascist" character.[141] Borneman maintained that such boundaries were indeed being put into place, but by the traditionalists (he named Eddie Condon) and the modernists both, not least by Feather himself.

Borneman had friendships with a number of jazz musicians. One was clarinetist Milton "Mezz" Mezzrow, a former "White Negro" who wanted to cross the racial boundary from the white side and who had met Borneman at a concert in Montreal in 1945.[142] Borneman praised Mezzrow's blues book when it was published in 1946, later declaring that he had always valued Mezzrow highly as "one of the few whites who ever tried to live as a Negro, and secondly because he was one of the few musicians who really, like myself, only wanted to play the blues, and considered the rest of jazz kitschy."[143] Borneman also admired the protagonist of his first jazz concert in Berlin, the Creole clarinetist Sidney Bechet, whom he met several times on both sides of the Atlantic and considered far and away the best jazz musician—"He's the only one I never get tired of."[144] Both Mezzrow and Bechet were central figures in the New Orleans revival and for Borneman "most profoundly represent the best that each race and each tradition has contributed to the other"; their work together exhibited "the human quality of great mutual respect."[145] During his Ottawa days Borneman also befriended Rex Stewart, whose European touring in the 1940s led to frequent encounters in Paris. Borneman recounted a few days spent with Stewart in the late fall of 1947 to Eva: "We made some records, played one concert at the Salle Pleyel, and spent two nights at a bar named Barclay's Club"; they were accompanied by Lena Horne, a jazz singer with African American, Indian, and European roots who moved to Europe in 1945 to escape her experience of discrimination in the United States as an African American and for her alleged Communist sympathies.[146] In an unorthodox move, Stewart also played bebop numbers at his concerts and used lyrics written by Leonard Feather—"which must have been agony in the ears of promoter Hugues Panassié," Borneman wrote regarding a concert on 5 December 1948 in Salle Pleyel.[147] Even after their days in Paris, Stewart and Borneman stayed in touch. Another friend of Borneman's was the trumpet player Humphrey Lyttleton, a star of London's New Orleans scene who was also involved in a number of Borneman's projects.

Bebop reached its zenith in 1948, having gained recognition as an art form not only by students of jazz and parts of the jazz press, but by the mass media. It had also achieved commercial success, complete with its own club, the Royal Roost, which dominated New York's jazz scene.[148] Its heyday did not last long; by the middle of 1949 its popularity had diminished, a demise hastened by the crisis in the jazz business and the rise of competing musical styles. Even its stalwart defenders among the

Figure 2.4. With Louis Armstrong in Club Malesherbes, Paris, 2 March 1948.
Courtesy AdK.

jazz magazines, especially *Metronome*, gave up on it. This did not change the fact that many of its stars still had a following and some of their pieces would become classics as time went on, but as a movement bebop was dead. To a certain extent its authority had already been undermined before it actually peaked, not simply by contrary jazz critics, but also by numerous musicians who had turned against it, not least because it had ruined some of the traditional jazz venues on Fifty-Second Street. The guests who frequented these places never developed a taste for the new style, so the bars closed down, only to be replaced by striptease clubs. Countless well-known musicians also voiced their dislike of the bop style, calling it "nervous" or "fake." The criticism coming from contemporary musicians hit a high note when Louis Armstrong came out against bebop. During the first International Jazz Festival in Nice in 1948, initiated and organized by Panassié, Ernest Borneman invited Armstrong and others, including Mezz Mezzrow and Barney Bigard, to a hotel room for an open discussion of the current state of jazz, which was subsequently published by *DownBeat*.[149] More than any other jazz musician, Borneman revered Armstrong. For him, Armstrong had revived jazz, rescuing it from the ruins of ragtime and the brass bands on the one hand, Tin Pan Alley and European entertainment music on the other. In Armstrong, Borneman wrote in an encomium honoring the musician's fiftieth birthday, a person had come as close as was possible to the humanistic ideal of the "universal man."[150] For years, people had tried without success to get a statement out of Louis Armstrong about bebop. It was in Nice, as Borneman wrote to his wife, that Armstrong finally caved in: "That night we broke the ice and I got clearance for it. It's quite a story." He mentioned in passing a night spent drinking in bars, commenting, "Now I know why Hemingway wrote things just that way when he was out here as a young man."[151] After the festival, Borneman went back to Paris with Armstrong for a series of concerts, receptions, and parties. Borneman was in complete agreement with what "Satchmo" had said about bebop on the Côte d'Azur. Armstrong spoke of "weird chords which don't mean nothing," and he predicted that the novelty of bop would soon wear off, "because it's really no good and you got no melody to remember and no beat to dance to." As Armstrong saw it, the alternative was a return to the roots, which always lay at the heart of any jazz revival by necessity: "The legit composers always go back to folk tunes, the simple things, where it all comes from. So they'll come back to us when all the shouting about bop and science is over."[152] Other well-respected jazz musicians voiced different opinions. Duke Ellington, for example, maintained shortly after Armstrong that he did not see bebop only as a matter of technique. For Ellington, at least as Borneman quoted him from an interview in Paris, bebop was "part of the emancipation of the American Negro."[153]

Jazz in Paris

The years Borneman spent in Paris from 1947 to 1949 were a revelation. The German occupation had only further fueled French enthusiasm for jazz; with numerous black musicians coming from the United States and enveloped in the philosophy of existentialism, Paris became the center for both "traditional" and "modern" jazz in Europe. In the 1940s and 1950s the French capital had become a sort of European mecca for African American artists in general, who felt that they faced less racism there than in the United States.[154] Borneman lived in the same city as Richard Wright, James Baldwin, and Sidney Bechet. Throughout 1947 and 1948 Borneman kept contact with countless musicians, promoters, and jazz critics. He wrote for the French jazz magazine *Jazz Hot*, served as the Paris correspondent for *DownBeat* and *Variety*, and also published articles in the new voice of the Négritude movement, a magazine founded in 1947 titled *Présence Africaine*. This magazine looked to serve as an anchor for a Pan-African perspective in Europe, publishing authors such as Léopold Seder Senghor, E. Franklin Frazier, and C. L. R. James.[155] As an African-inspired art form, jazz and blues played a significant role in *Présence Africaine*, where they were discussed by experts such as the French jazz exponent Hugues Panassié, Wright, and Borneman.

Borneman arrived in Paris as a newly minted UNESCO employee, just as a battle between Panassié and his earlier ally Charles Delaunay about the future course of jazz had flared. Borneman was in touch with both men, although he was a friend of Delaunay, who defended bebop against Panassié's traditionalist preferences.[156] In October 1947, shortly after arriving in Paris, Borneman visited the Hot Club de France with Delaunay, where "out of every window comes the well-known sound of bebop intermixed with little cries of '*C'est formidable!*' or '*Comme c'est chaud, mon ami, comme c'est chaud!*'"[157] Commenting on the confrontation between the two camps as it played out on one stage during the summer of 1948, Borneman came to a positive conclusion. It was not only the mood among the enemy camps and the after-show parties full of young women and men that proved the vivacity of jazz in all its forms. It was the "astonishingly high caliber of French jazz, both of the old and the new school"; it had become apparent, firstly, that there was a considerable market for both forms of jazz in Europe and, secondly, that French musicians were about to catch up to the Americans.[158]

Borneman befriended the young jazz musicians Maxim Saury and Claude Bolling; his friend Mezz Mezzrow also found himself in the French metropolis in 1948. One of his new friends was the universal talent Boris Vian, whose plays Borneman enjoyed. Vian, in turn, quoted his "bon ami Borneman" in his popular jazz writings.[159] Vian followed Borneman's work in the international jazz press until his early death. Borneman met Vian as a "minor jazz trumpeter" who had been able to remain independent of the different jazz camps. Borneman was also left totally bewildered by the permissiveness of one of Vian's plays at the Théâtre Verlaine, for which Vian had given him a free ticket.[160] It concerned a black man who had decided to exact revenge for the lynching death of his brother by raping as many white women as possible—an "extremely pornographic play" that depicted every sexual grouping conceivable. One of the highlights of Borneman's nighttime escapades came during Duke Ellington's visit to Paris in July 1948. Borneman accompanied Ellington for three afternoons and evenings, along with Jean Genet, Yves Montand, and Simone Signoret.[161] *DownBeat* received a detailed account; jazz criticism was not only pseudo-scientific, it also had to feed the jazz scene's gossip mill. In early 1950, shortly after returning to London, Borneman sent a good dozen photos of his going-away party in Paris to Jim Godbolt at *Illustrated Jazz*, likely in an effort to shore up his reputation as one of the great critics on the international jazz scene. The party took place in a small jazz club, Bolling's local bar, and the guest list included nothing less than "just about all the better French jazzmen, not to mention Katherine Dunham and most of the Parisien underworld."[162]

Even after the bebop movement waned, the battle between the camps continued in what is described simply as the battle between the traditionalists and the

Figure 2.5. Katherine Dunham and Boris Vian dancing at Borneman's farewell party in Paris, late 1949. Courtesy AdK.

modernists, with the modern styles now described as "progressive" and "cool" jazz. More forcefully than before, Borneman positioned himself outside the battle lines. He continued to defend jazz as a simple form against any ambitious attempts to measure it against classical music, which he believed were always bound to fail. The search for simplicity was in keeping with the times, especially given that the "New Objectivity" (*Neue Sachlichkeit* in German) was still in vogue even after 1945. Originating in the 1920s, the movement was founded on the rejection of all things ornamental and bombastic—in general the importance of appearances under Wilheminism—but also the emphasis of expressionism. The subsequent pathos of National Socialism had only bolstered the legitimacy of the overall movement. For Borneman, jazz was "simple and straightforward and enormously convincing in an age which seemed to have lost the gift of simplicity."[163] It was also dance music and took place where people went to enjoy themselves. In discussions around how to overcome the crisis of jazz around 1950, Borneman criticized the "progressives" as "naive" in their neoclassical ambition and "sterile" in their musical expression. They were, he argued, "'progressive' in name only but not progressive in fact from anything which the old jazzmen on one side and the legitimate modernists on the other have already done better."[164]

Borneman also criticized the traditionalists more forcefully than before. Looking back to the origins of the conflict, he explained that he had shared the same boat with the traditionalists and bebop followers when both turned against big band swing, but he separated himself from the traditionalists when they adopted the slogan "the farther back, the better." In response to a reader's letter asking him how he saw his own position in 1951, he answered as follows: "I stand in spirit on the side of the modernists who are trying to express the real problems of our age in a musical language that best covers them." But, he continued, when they were exhausted from all their finger exercises and tried to sell something as new that was already old hat for the pioneers of the new music, when their music had nothing to say in terms of content, "then men like myself are driven away from modern jazz to the simplicity and good taste of the early Louis on one side and to the complexity and good taste of the late Schönberg and Hindemith on the other."[165] Whenever Borneman spoke of a lack of "content," either here or later on, he meant social relevance. This did not refer to achieving a political goal, but rather "the function of music in the social reality of its listeners."[166] As long as jazz was dancing music, Borneman claimed, it had a concrete social function, but it lost this function the moment that jazz musicians switched to art. Just exactly what Borneman meant with "content"—beyond social relevance that is, which modern styles certainly had as well—remained unclear and, above all, not concrete. On 29 June 1954 he did a show for the BBC series *World of Jazz*, which addressed the question "What's it about?" with reference to the "content of jazz." Borneman called upon jazz fans to go to their favorite musicians and ask them to play their favorite songs, and then to ask, "What do you want to say with this?" Nine out of ten musicians and just as many jazz critics, Borneman said, would be left speechless. Still, the show apparently did not carry a positive message. Maurice Burman, a fellow critic, found it to be "mentally stimulating," but also "illogical and confusing."[167] More recently, Ingrid Monson explored the notion of "saying something" in jazz, highlighting the permanent difficulty inherent in trying to translate a musical idiom into language.[168] As Borneman claimed, trying to sum up in words what jazz "meant" was difficult, but he had not gone far enough by primarily ascribing this problem to the "modernists." In fact, music held a "social function in the reality" of musicians just as it did for listeners, but this could only be determined by reflecting on the respective cultural and political contexts as they appeared in talking and writing about jazz, and not least in what the critics said. Free jazz, for example, was particularly charged with meaning, serving as an apt musical expression of black self-determination. It was the relationship between sound and its social and cultural contexts that was always being brought up by musicians, audiences, and critics, likewise the meaning of improvisation in jazz as a dialogue beyond the narrow framework of music itself.

In his critique of the traditionalists, Borneman took issue with the scientification that had crept into the jazz debate in written form and negatively impacted musicians' feeling toward music. All the literature on jazz written in the 1940s by Panassié, Blesh, Lang, and even himself, Borneman claimed, had not improved the music but only made it worse as musicians began listening to the theories. Rather than improvising, he went on, they were imitating, losing individuality, character, and personality in the process.[169] Borneman directed his ire at the small circle of those who judged what was good or bad, with no tolerance for any deviation from what they had determined to be the pure doctrine of New Orleans jazz. In an article from 1952, he came to a rather surprising conclusion:

> We have little taste for bop, but we find more of a beat, more of the genuine jazz spirit in Charlie Parker than in much of today's New Orleans music, including that by the old men of the Crescent City itself; we think there's more jazz, even from the purist point of view, in Kenny Clarke than in any New Orleans style drummer in this country; and we want to plead with all jazz-lovers to take time out from partisanship, time out from stereotypes, time out to reinvestigate all the old premises with which writers like ourselves nursed the jazz revival into existence.[170]

In doing so, Borneman now emphasized the point that jazz, as the revolutionary music that it had been in its early days, had been consumed by its social acceptance. As he put it, "Yesterday's revolutionaries become today's diehards."[171] Although he contended that present-day jazz needed to change, he considered African American folk music—blues, labor songs, dances, and spirituals—to be an immutable standard worth holding on to.

Borneman even gave practical consideration to the idea of reconciling traditional and modern jazz in order to find a "new sound," organizing a jazz workshop for the BBC on 11 October 1952 as part of its entertainment program. This attempt to prove the unity of jazz met with a mixed response, however; it convinced very few, nor did the instigator defend his position fervently.[172] Instead, it became increasingly clear that blues would form the basis of a revival movement to reach a great mass of people, expanding from its center in Britain to overtake the United States in the 1960s. It was a process in which Borneman's work would play an important role.

Jazz in Film

Jazz continued to play a central role in Borneman's artistic visual work after he returned to London, further proof that it not only spoke to the sense of hearing, but was involved in a more comprehensive mobilization of perceptions. Given that jazz was not only an auditory experience, Borneman sought to find a suitable form of visualization. In an article for *Melody Maker* in 1951, he explored the potential of jazz for film, lamenting that nobody had managed to visualize the subject adequately.[173] Jazz figured in existing productions almost exclusively as entertainment at its very worst, he noted, stuffed full of comical figures and an ever-smiling Uncle Tom.[174] By contrast, Borneman wanted to bring more jazz bands to the big screen and introduce more realistic material.

In the 1950s and early 1960s Borneman wrote a large number of musicals, most in collaboration with composer Malcolm Rayment, though few ever came to the stage. All were set in the sociocultural context of jazz; none followed the usual separation of dialogue, song, and dance—rather, the characters sang and danced throughout the piece. "In our musicals the whole of the action is danced, the whole of it is sung," Borneman wrote. "There is no dialogue without music, no music without dancing, and no songs that stop the action: all songs take the action forward and are part of a continuous flow of music."[175] Nor were they intended as comedies—the usual genre for jazz films, which often relied on racist stereotypes—but as tragedies. Borneman's first attempt included the 1950 made-for-television film *Tremolo*, followed in 1954 by the movie *Face the Music* and the television program *Four O'Clock in the Morning Blues*.[176]

The filming of his murder mystery *Bang! You're Dead!* and a series of projects commissioned by the BBC filled Borneman with hope, as he reported to his parents in Berlin in late 1953: "Finally, the floodgates seem to have opened. For the first time, my life seems to be more full of hope."[177] His first television film for the BBC, *Four O'Clock in the Morning Blues* (forty-five minutes long, with the Johnny Dankworth Orchestra, Cleo Laines, and Frank Holder as singers, and George Carden as the choreographer) was also his first dance film. He wrote the screenplay but also directed the film, which was produced live and aired on 9 March 1954.[178] The story was set in a nightclub, after the party had wound down and the last guests departed, right around four o'clock in the morning. Suddenly, the pianist is inspired and the band returns to the stage to improvise a private jazz session while the two dancers from the club respond to associations from their past—the story of their failed marriage—and the band's female and male singer provide commentary, much like a Greek chorus. The response of the British audience, not yet accustomed to the presence of an independent youth culture on the screen, was split. "It turned into a scandal," Borneman wrote his father. "Thousands of listeners wrote to the BBC in protest—they called it obscene, scandalous, a danger to the youth, a disgrace, decadent, etc."[179] Even the music press was polarized, caught along the fault line dividing popular from avant-garde approaches. *Jazz Journal*, which upheld jazz's reputation as an art form, commented that "as an insight into the lives of a couple of neurotics [the program] was extremely clever and the use of jazz music unusual and very effective, but as an advertisement of jazz music it could not have been more diabolic. No wonder jazz gets a bad name if this kind of thing is sprung upon the public."[180] One reader in the same magazine commented that the show, despite all its faults, was "still the best show on jazz we've ever had on TV." He praised its dirtiness, which he felt represented jazz more conclusively than a highly polished surface, and called for more of its kind on television. Likewise, a nineteen-year-old waiter wrote to the channel that finally, something true about British youth culture had appeared in the media. The BBC, he was sure, was inundated with the protests of older viewers, for whom the dancers and dance musicians were either "comic figures" or symbols of criminality among the youth, "but believe me, Sir, if the word of your younger listeners is worth anything at all to you, you have finally found someone who knows what he is talking about when he talks about us, the young."[181] A *DownBeat* employee on a trip who had watched the show from his hotel also congratulated the BBC for airing the best show that he had ever seen. Whoever wrote and produced it, he claimed, "knew the jazz world, knew America, knew human beings, and knew his television."[182] The less partisan press focused on the cinematic aspects. A review that appeared in several papers read, "I am intrigued. I smell experiment. This programme does not sound as if it will appeal to the majority of viewers."[183] Another paper praised it: "A clever piece, reminiscent of the Avant Garde style of pre-war years, after much practise brought to perfection in Germany at the time of the Weimar Republic."[184] Borneman himself later explained that this "jazz opera," as he now called it, had come close to achieving his "own ideal of what television should be," a realization of something "realistic and stylized, acted and danced, that could be woven together in a way that allowed a new form to emerge."[185]

Borneman explained to a colleague, British director Desmond Davis, why it was that he had favored the jazz milieu in his recent television productions. It was not because he was a jazz lover, but because jazz musicians were "a script writer's vade mecum in this country": they were on the edge of the underworld without being really part of it. Given the absence of the gangster in the United Kingdom, everything a good American screenwriter might express through that social role could be shown by his British colleague through the jazz musician, he explained. He also cited the immense popularity of jazz among the mainstream youth as another reason. Critics thought that *Four O'Clock in the Morning Blues* was awful, Borneman wrote to Davis, but the "listeners panel" thought it was great.[186] This was not entirely correct on multiple accounts—neither his claim of purely professional motivations nor the allegedly unconditional generational divide among audiences. Nonetheless, these distinctions reveal just how much he sidelined questions of taste to focus instead on decidedly cinematic considerations that were grounded in aesthetic arguments. Undoubtedly, they also indicate his awareness of the great potential that the emergence of an independent youth culture, fundamentally different from that of older generations, had for attracting attention. Stylizing his own work as being celebrated by youth and attacked by adults piqued public interest.

His greatest success in this particular genre was *Betty Slow Drag* (1953), a twenty-six-minute short in color that he directed and wrote the screenplay for, in addition to the blues lyrics. Malcolm Rayment wrote the music, Eva Geisel wrote the story; the sketches were done by Ursula Hertz, Russell Quay did the stage design, Lusia Krakowska edited; musicians included Humphrey Lyttelton and a number of other British jazz players.[187] In a synopsis written for the German market, the film was labeled a "satirical dance film, a cinematic joke. The group of young English film technicians, dancers, musicians and painters who filmed it for their own enjoyment, with their own money and on their own free time had nothing else in mind other than trying to create an unconventional film style with as little means as possible."[188] The material is set in a jazz club in New Orleans during the ragtime era around the turn of the century and is presented by a female blues singer, chorus, and jazz band. Here, too, Borneman combined voice, band, and dance into a polarized, alienated structure: "Dinah Kaye . . . sings in a street ballad voice accentuated by jazz. A male choir comments on what happens like a Greek chorus. A ragtime pianola, a Negro marching band and a small blues combo accompany the dancers, who act everything out in a wordless, ironic pantomime." The story tells of "how Betty meets Slow Drag the musician, and declares herself ready to give her heart and her hand to him under one condition: she must first wear a diamond ring on her finger."[189] After Slow Drag murders the jeweler Rosenbloom to get the ring and is sentenced to death, Betty strikes a deal with the devil in order to get her diamond. At the end, she forces him to release Slow Drag as well as Rosenbloom and his diamonds, thus arriving at her goal.

Betty Slow Drag was more experimental than any of Borneman's other productions; anti-commercial in the way it was made and allegedly a spontaneous creation from below, the initiative of a small group of enthusiasts. Eva made a virtue of financial necessity, selling her story as fresh and "avant-garde" despite being well aware of the problematic nature of the term's historical derivation. It all began in the old days, Eva wrote, when the residents of Montmartre, Chelsea, and Greenwich Village could still say the word "avant-garde" without blushing and bearded young men with used cameras in one hand and a well-read copy of Pudovkin's classic *Film Technique* in the other suggested there was hope and promise that one day, there would be noncommercial cinema.[190] This movement, she wrote, was interrupted by the talkies, which drove the costs of filmmaking so high that they could no longer be footed by just one person; only a few exceptions among the filmmakers, such as Cocteau and Welles, were in a position to amass enough money for the occasional experiment with unconventional cinema. Generally however, she continued, the tradition of individual filmmaking had come to an end by the 1920s. The only option for "the third generation of cinéastes" was collective production, even though these projects were plagued by difficulties in acquiring money and establishing consensus. Now the impossible had been realized however, as Eva Borneman's account went—a group of incorrigible optimists had dared to make a music film like no other, one that believed they had to stick close to reality in order to create realistic cinema but saw no reason why realism should determine the logic of every type of film.

It thus only bolstered the credibility of a project styled as avant-garde that it had come about under improvised circumstances and been filmed in five days as a home-grown production on a budget of just 1,600 British pounds, with simple, coarsely done backdrops set up in a small studio in Soho.[191] A London selection committee nominated it as an experimental film for the Edinburgh Film Festival in 1953, obviously making light of the whole affair. There was discord among the event's planners in Edinburgh, however—a fact that paired wonderfully with the film's "avant-garde" pretensions—in contrast to largely positive feedback from the press, they found the film to be too "American," too "sexy." This prompted Borneman to contact John Grierson, who, like several others from the old documentary film movement, sat on the festival's board of directors.[192] Grierson did in fact intervene, leading festival organizers to announce two weeks later that the film would be shown "because of its idea and because of it as an experiment."[193] Borneman himself was highly pleased with the film. Echoing Eva's description, he wrote to his father that it might be "the first to really make a contribution to the history of film." Evidently it was important to him to present something new, something bearing his own signature, and which might represent a new paradigm. "You might find it appalling," he wrote to Berlin, "but at least it is not like any other film that has ever been made anywhere."[194]

For a short film it received a surprisingly large number of write-ups in the press, all of which were positive. The popular music press was similarly enthusiastic. Like *Bandwagon* and others of its kind, the *New Musical Express* printed a large photo series that included "the one and only Borneman," while *Melody Maker* sent a clear, though overlooked signal to the music industry: "'Betty' is box office."[195] The specialist press, designed for more elevated tastes, was more evenhanded. In *Jazz Journal*, Charles Fox reminded readers that the jazz world was waiting on good jazz films, which, apart from Gjon Mili's *Jammin' the Blues* and Norman McLaren's *Begone Dull Care*, were few and far between.[196] Whereas Mili's film broke with Hollywood convention by showing black jazz musicians at work, McLaren's film visually depicted the music of Oscar Peterson with abstract forms and symbols, a project that was similar to but less representational than *Five for Four*, an earlier film for which Borneman had the idea. But what fans really wanted, Fox argued, was a film that described the life of jazz musicians. Turning to Borneman's collaboration, Fox wrote, "Certainly there is a curious mixture of comedy and horror side by side throughout *Betty Slow Drag*. While not at all uncommon in drama or in literature, it is unusual in a film of this genre. And visually it fluctuates between the comic lunacy of the Keystone cops and the intense expressionism of Caligari and 1920's German cinema, a resemblance accentuated by highly stylized backgrounds." This group, Fox noted, had promised to make more jazz films—an agreeable prospect for the eyes and the ears.[197]

Following on its success in Great Britain, *Betty Slow Drag* was the only short film invited to take part in the Fourth International Film Festival in Berlin in June 1954, where it received an award. Manfred Delling, an important voice in visual and musical youth culture, was impressed, calling it "a highly amusing, inventive, and very bold jazz grotesque, made by English 'amateurs,' but truly a little masterpiece as a film."[198] There were others, too, who highlighted the project's freshness and outsider status, using adjectives such as "cheeky," "racy," "totally unconventional," all of which further emphasized the breach in taboo among the youth.[199] Despite all the enthusiasm surrounding the success of this experiment, it should not be forgotten that the film was only shown twice in public, in Edinburgh and Berlin; it was by no means a commercial success.

There followed a more conventional, but also more successful film project, *Face the Music* (84 minutes, directed by Terence Fisher), which aired in the United States as *The Black Glove* on 29 January 1954 and premiered in Great Britain on 22 February 1954; ATV reran it on 8 July 1959 as part of the *Great Movies of Our Time* series. Borneman wrote the story and screenplay for this film, which was set once again in the jazz scene at the edge of London's underworld.[200] An American jazz trumpeter who has just arrived in the city is suspected of having murdered a blues singer. He tries to find the killer, only to fall victim to an attempt on his own life before he is able to unmask the true murderer. The whole film takes place in the milieu of a nightclub, peppered with a love story and a few jazz scenes performed by Kenny Baker's band. One film magazine praised its authentic atmosphere, powerful story, realistic staging, and the overall sophistication of the film.[201] Another wrote, "Effective murder mystery plot, smooth star performance, lively trumpet interludes."[202]

The Beat Is Back: The Blues Revival in Great Britain

While jazz experienced a short-lived renaissance as musical entertainment with Dixieland in the late 1950s, it was rarely thought of as popular music afterward. Yet over the course of that same decade, the blues revival soon brought forth a new kind of popular music from the roots of jazz that came to be known as rhythm and blues, rock 'n' roll, and beat. As Paul Oliver notes, Iain Lang's 1943 argument that all blues was jazz had in fact been taken up by Borneman, who went so far as to say that blues was the "heart" of jazz.[203] Borneman himself was of the opinion that Lang had stolen the argument from him after Eva left his long manuscript with Lang while Borneman was held in internment camp and that Lang had copied the gist of the work.[204] Borneman's insight about the "heart" of jazz "which gave firm recognition of blues" (Oliver) was further underscored by another early classic piece of jazz criticism, Rudi Blesh's *Shining Trumpets*. As "a figure at the vanguard of blues proselytism," Borneman helped to pave the way for the British blues boom of the long 1960s.[205]

Borneman also became politically involved, pressing for years for the British jazz scene, cut off from African American musicians by the protectionism of the British musicians' union, to rejuvenate itself by engaging with its original impulse. He uniformly rejected what he considered a "copy of American jazz." In 1953 he suggested that British jazz musicians should look to the Commonwealth for inspiration. It has been noted in scholarly literature that Borneman had showed "determined ingenuity"

Figure 2.6. Film poster for *Face the Music*, 1954. Courtesy AdK.

in his attempts to understand British jazz as music created within the context of the empire.[206] A perception of "Britishness" in jazz, however, also came from the attributes that were ascribed to the music itself and its forms of expression. By nationalizing New Orleans jazz, for example, British critics and musicians laid the foundation for what would later become the British Sound, which transformed musical roots previously thought of as autochthonous into an idiom of worldwide popularity that came to be known as the "British Invasion" when it conquered the US hit charts.

Borneman regularly took national jazz bands to task for merely copying African American music instead of coming up with anything original. His criticism stemmed from the ideal that the development of musical idioms shaped by unique national characteristics should allow musicians to realize their creative potential. A copy, in his eyes, meant dependency, that is, the opposite of the independence he had in mind. When *Melody Maker* asked him in 1948 to give an outsider's perspective on the British jazz scene from Paris, Borneman pulled no punches. British dance music suffered from isolation and sterility, brought on by the boycott called by the musicians' union. If one thing had caused the downfall of this once powerful musical force, he continued, it was "the gradual alienation of the idiom from the one and only source that can ever revitalize it—the flux of native African-American folk music."[207]

In other regards, too, the conditions for jazz in the postwar period were anything but ideal. In 1951 the BBC aired half as many jazz programs as in 1940, with most of them criticized for lacking imagination.[208] After he returned to London, Borneman continued to rebuke the British jazz scene for its lack of verve in his column "One Night Stand." Indeed, his very first piece addressed the situation directly, criticizing the quality of the bands that he had seen at the competition of the National Federation of British Jazz Organisations. Nothing had changed since the prewar years; New Orleans jazz was still played as close to the original as possible.[209] British jazz musicians were just as talented as their US peers, Borneman argued; it was just that they needed to free themselves from their dependence on the US jazz scene. In doing so they should neither lose touch with nor shy away from making comparisons to African American jazz, because that was the only way for them to improve.[210] The situation in Britain presented a particular study in contrasts to the scene in Paris, where Borneman had recently found that constant contact with African American musicians improved the quality of French jazz immensely.[211] It was not national isolation that would promote domestic talent, but its opposite—complete transparency. That, however, was exactly what the interest groups within the British entertainment industry were fighting. Time and again, Borneman sallied forth against the protectionist politics of the union and the Songwriter's Guild, remarking that "if you believe that art is indivisible and provides the sole field of human enterprise in which the principle of free trade is morally and economically justifiable, you are bound to find yourself in opposition to the policy of a guild or union which divides the world of art into national protectorates."[212] The entire concept of a nation, according to Borneman, was foreign to the mind of an artist. It was not until 1957, after twenty-two years, that the prohibition against live performances by US bands was lifted, with the following boom in concerts in fact playing a key role in the British blues revival.[213] For his part Borneman remained skeptical, continuing to criticize the lack of innovative will. Writing to the American producer Lester Koenig in 1959, he remarked that Great Britain was so overwhelmingly different from Germany, Scandinavia, the Netherlands, Belgium, Russia, and Czechoslovakia that "it makes you wonder why this island hasn't sunk yet. Well, it will one of these days." Borneman considered this, too, to be an expression of the paralysis that had led to the collapse of the British Empire.[214] He was of the opinion that British jazz per se had a much broader cultural horizon than US jazz; one merely needed to begin with the musical roots in the United Kingdom itself in order to create something new. Characteristic forms of African American folk music had also developed within the British colonies in the Caribbean—Jamaica, Trinidad and Tobago, Granada, the Virgin Islands, Barbados, the Bahamas, etc.—which were ideal for a jazz revival.[215] While the decline of the empire following the wave of decolonization around 1945 seemed to push this out of the realm of possibility, Borneman prophesized that one day people would find a new kind of music on its way—a combination of African, West Indian, and European elements that could only be found in Great Britain. His prediction, at least in terms of popular music, proved only partially correct. The actual impulse for renewal came from something for which Borneman had also advocated—the blues revival.

Borneman belonged to what was initially a small circle of critics and experts searching and propagating what they considered original "'pure' jazz" (Paul Oliver). There is much to say for the recent suggestion that in the late 1940s, nobody knew more about blues in Europe than Ernest Borneman.[216] At the time, there was no researcher outside of the United States who would have worked more on the topic. For Borneman, African American folk music had three main currents: work songs, spirituals, and blues. The more jazz fans delved into the subject of Borneman's research, the roots of African American music, the more solidly blues took center stage.[217] One outcome of the individualization that occurred after emancipation from slavery and the end of the plantation system was numerous itinerant black singers who traveled around the United States, performing as blues soloists. They not only connected the wide variety of African American musical traditions, but also helped to connect US Americans from the most diverse ethnic backgrounds by laying the foundation for what would become the first common musical language—jazz. As Borneman put it, "That groundwork was the blues."[218] As time went on, white folk singers also adopted the themes, melodies, and harmonies common to the blues, turning it into one of the main pillars of American folk music per se. This made the blues both a sign and a symbol of the emancipation of African Americans. In Borneman's eyes, blues music was the only type of jazz that was not already outdated or doomed to become passé. "The blues is the heart of jazz," he wrote. "Jazz lives as long as the pulse of the blues beats in its veins. Jazz dies when it says farewell to the blues."[219] Jazz was therefore only jazz when it drew on blues, an argument that set him apart from Panassié, who maintained that improvisation could be applied to any piece. Borneman found Panassié's argument too superficial, because it only addressed form and lacked any real "message." By contrast, Borneman postulated, "jazz is a bluesification of a given piece; it achieves maximum potency only when the piece is itself structured like the blues."[220]

Like many of his friends and allies in the blues establishment, such as Max Jones, Rex Harris, or Paul Oliver, Borneman spread his views on the traditions of jazz in small specialist magazines and major publications alike, as well as lectures on records he gave at the invitation of jazz clubs and radio stations. Educational efforts on the radio were popular with many channels and included many experts—not least because they were lucrative. In a sense, they were a continuation of the earlier listening and discussion groups, albeit now with the help of electronic media, which gave them greater appeal to an already receptive youth culture. Through this kind of programming, young musicians such as Alexis Korner were introduced to the blues and thus became familiar with a tradition, as Borneman noted, "that no British band, no British singer, no British accompanist could have furnished for any amount of money."[221]

While British jazz critics judged blues in its urban, "modern" form as performed by Muddy Waters or John Lee Hooker to be "authentic" and therefore worthy of praise, they were more ambivalent toward the current rhythm and blues (R & B) trend (the name that US record companies switched to using instead of "race records" once the label no longer seemed appropriate). Most of them were also skeptical about the rise of musicians such as Fats Domino, Chuck Berry, and Bo Diddley, who appealed to the teenage market. They found R & B too loud, too fast, and lacking in depth; in short, it was too popular and too commercial.[222] Borneman, however, rated it positively. To him, R & B represented what he had always called for: the adaptation of a tradition to meet the changing needs of society. Rhythm and blues was loved by present-day African American youth, but also broke down the racial barrier by appealing to white youth as well. The upswing in the purchasing power of African American consumers, coupled with the corresponding growth in the number of black-owned radio and television stations, led to a boom in R & B. Borneman celebrated this "sudden rediscovery of the beat" as an expression of the African American community "at long last reasserting its own taste," countering the white critics who had sold as progress what was in fact rhythmic regression.[223] He was skeptical, however, of rock 'n' roll as played by whites, which had its breakthrough in Great Britain with Bill Haley's film *Rock Around the Clock* in 1956, followed by Haley's 1957 tour. In Borneman's opinion, rock 'n' roll was a watered-down form of blues. He also balked at the signal sound of rock 'n' roll, the electric guitar, which had moved from the background to center stage, a position it would only build on with the long solo improvisations to come. Its sound, as he sometimes said, was "a pain in my ear."[224] Nonetheless, unlike the majority of his colleagues, he also defended rock 'n' roll. In doing so, he cited what he saw as a justified response among younger musicians to two fads in music, namely "beatless pop" and "beatless bop," neither of which satisfied the central need of youth to dance.[225] In general he did not believe in mourning and mooning over the music of the past, which after all was a product of its times. It was more important to make life worth living in the present, which might result in a new urban folk music that, if not jazz, was still pleasing to the ears.[226]

Rock 'n' roll, however, was not the only type of music contributing to the great British blues revival that began in 1957. There was a second style, created by devotees of blues and New Orleans jazz, which fanned the flames of independence among

British youth and paved the way for thousands of new bands in its reliance on instruments as simple as a washboard and tea chest bass and how easy it was to play: skiffle. Borneman was also more optimistic about skiffle than the majority of his colleagues. He rightly hoped that the new craze would revive jazz and pop music in Great Britain, all the while fomenting interest in blues.[227] The UK's abandonment of its isolationist policies in 1957, the influx of African American artists, and the spike in immigration from Africa and the Caribbean all quickened the pulse of the nightlife in Great Britain.[228] This wave of immigration, however, generated a mixed reaction. Many a white young man responded with aggression and racist attacks; others were intrigued by what they saw as a more relaxed lifestyle; still other Teddy Boys incorporated both reactions. The close links between the blues-based music styles were plain to see in the ease with which musicians were able to move quickly from traditional jazz to skiffle and then to rock 'n' roll, as in the case of the Shadows, Lonnie Donegan, or Tommy Steele. These young bands would imitate other stars before going on to make their own songs and independent interpretations, making it easy for amateurs to get a start in the business. As Paul McCartney recalled of his Liverpool beginnings with the Quarrymen in 1956, "We started off by imitating Elvis, Buddy Holly, Chuck Berry, Carl Perkins, Gene Vincent, The Coasters, The Drifters—we just copied what they did."[229] As jazz progressed from skiffle to rock 'n' roll, the beat increasingly took center stage, resulting in a driving rhythm that—when combined with a higher volume, flippant attitude, and show elements—raised entertainment value and broadened its social resonance. The pageantry, amusement, corporeality, easy accessibility, and aura of exclusion that still clung to the blues made skiffle and rock 'n' roll ideal musical styles for young people, especially those who were not middle class. At the same time, these styles served as political projective surfaces, abetted by the increased use of textual forms of expression in the 1960s, which also made them interesting to young intellectuals. Consequently, R & B, skiffle, rock 'n' roll, and what came to be called beat music in the early 1960s attracted a socially diverse audience composed of young people from both the working and middle classes.

Borneman observed all this with mixed feelings. On the one hand, he saw it as a way of bringing blues up to date, undoubtedly a positive development. On the other hand, beat and pop had a flattening effect that stemmed from their commercial roots. He reminded Pat Brand, the editor of *Melody Maker*, that he was the only one of the magazine's authors to defend rock 'n' roll, "because I felt in my bones that the kids needed a change after bop."[230] Borneman explained his viewpoint in detail to the jazz musician and author Victor Lewis, noting that the youth were "a beat generation in more senses than one."[231] Long before the music industry had commercialized rock 'n' roll, he contended, the African Americans had given it its start as a form of rhythm and blues—a return to the true heart of jazz. Borneman elaborated:

> It was a rebellion of the Negro public against those Negro musicians who had moved themselves out of the community by catering to European

standards of value. It was a genuine grass roots rebellion against big city fancies like cool jazz, progressive jazz, West Coast jazz. . . . The exaggeration with which the kids now applaud the sledgehammer beat of Rock 'n' Roll is the direct outcome of their frustration—the direct outcome of the beatless years—the years since modern jazz turned away from swing music.[232]

Young people around the world, Borneman insisted, wanted to dance: "Jazz conquered the world because it offered them the ideal beat to dance to. If modern jazz turns itself into concert music, can Vic really be surprised to find the youngsters deserting him and his music for the greener pastures of rock 'n' roll, mambo and chachacha?"[233] In a later text, he put it more forcefully: "The regular beat, one that could be danced to, that jazz had refused to provide, was supplied by these usurpers with an extra strong emphasis and extra volume."[234] Borneman's thesis of the modernist betrayal of dance music, however, failed to recognize that by turning to art music, the protagonists of modern jazz had broken down the assumption that black musicians were always dance musicians. This took part in a struggle for recognition that shared in the general assumptions about the modern artist: African Americans were capable not merely of making entertaining music that was considered "light" or superficial; just like whites, they too could make first-class modern music marked by abstraction, virtuosity, and individualism. Within the context of the civil rights movement in the United States, the insistence on the modern aesthetics of this music acquired a political dimension. The transition to art music was therefore tied to a process of emancipation that called for the equality of African Americans at all levels, even at the level of what was considered "high culture."[235]

Borneman also showed a certain skepticism toward the youth that developed out of general ideas about generational differences. As early as 1956, he observed the political involvement that characterized his own generation was foreign to today's youth, who were "essentially disengaged."[236] Borneman's sixth novel, *The Compromisers*, published in 1962, was dedicated to the themes of rebellion and assimilation, again reflecting on the idealism of youth and its erosion in midlife—this time albeit under the strong influence of the critical young intelligentsia of the late 1950s. In *The Compromisers*, he takes up with the tableau of characters from *Love Story*, his second novel from 1941, to tell the story of four people bound to each other: Joe Banyan, a film producer and the prototype of the angry young man of the 1930s; his friend and later Oxford professor Peter Pickering; Paula, Joe's girlfriend and Pete's wife after his death; and Carole Blanchard, Paula's French lover for many years.

While the publisher's advertising misleadingly marketed the book as an "erotic novel," claiming that it was one of the few convincing lesbian portraits written by a man, at heart the novel was about something else, pieced together from numerous aspects. The form of the novel is also complex; flashbacks and visions of the future break up the chronological narrative and create a sense of suspense, especially the systematic returns—reminiscent of Hemingway's style—to Joe's time spent at the North African front during World War II, where he will be killed by the novel's end. The flashbacks can be read as a continuous commentary on the main narrative of the novel. The once unconventional and rebellious teenagers Pete and Paula have now adjusted to their new circumstances and achieved success and wealth. Taking the distanced perspective of an academic, Pete finds the nonconformist students interesting but naturally dismisses them as nonsensical youth. Though their marriage is a nightmare, Paula gives up her lover for the sake of the children. Left by her lover Paula, it is Carol who reveals the moral of the story: Pete and Paula are "compromisers"—they make compromises with themselves, with each other, and with others, and they raise their children to do the same. They do so, moreover, without criticizing or protesting anything; this too forms a part of the compromise. As such, they are the epitome of the liberal tradition. By contrast, Joe refuses to make compromises and pays for it with his life, sacrificing himself for his comrades in North Africa. The book did not sell well, a fact Borneman could never understand: "It's a mystery to me, I must say, why Graham Greene, who has very similar vices and virtues, should have been a most successful author while I have just managed to get by."[237]

The drafts for jazz and beat music television shows Borneman wrote also reveal a serious and productive engagement with the more modern forms of rhythm and blues. Following the success of the British Invasion and the global breakthrough of pop music in all its different variations, however, Borneman's texts regained some of their former fury. He sided entirely with the most radical of the protesting students, who viewed the whole phenomenon as a prime example of cultural imperialism. While Borneman himself did not publish anything to this effect, his book reviews from the 1970s reflect a conviction that pop music was inferior. Even those who argued along similar lines, such as Siegfried Schmidt-Joos and Helmut Salzinger, were not critical enough in his eyes. He was repeatedly overcome by the feeling, as when reading Schmidt-Joos's *Rock Lexikon* (written with Barry Graves), "that . . . someone has condescended to write about these people just for the sake of the filthy lucre, though he actually despises them."[238] Borneman even castigated Helmut Salzinger's *Rock Power*, an early classic among rock-friendly critiques of the culture industry, admitting, however, that his sympathies lay with the left-wing author "in terms of music (and politics)."[239] He shared Salzinger's view that beat, rock, pop, and underground music were by no means revolutionary but functioned as valves that let energy escape instead of channeling it to change society. "This book," Borneman remarked, "scolds and curses and yells at the moneymakers, the shufflers of millions, who act as if they have something in common with the poor, with every poor fool who spends his last hard earned penny to pay these charlatans, these pied-pipers of Hamelin."[240] But that was all that Borneman agreed with. In the rest of the review he contradicted Salzinger—who was born in 1935, making him twenty years Borneman's junior—with a plausible argument that nonetheless had a certain generational tinge. Borneman criticized Salzinger's discography at the end of the book, one that named bands like the Beatles, the Rolling Stones, Elvis, and the Kinks, writing that "all the white shit is there" but that the black originators were missing. "The fathers of this music shine in their absence," he noted, countering that "Salzinger sees fit to mention all the transvestism that turned music into the playground of those who will never join the fight for a better world, who lack the discipline, fortitude and courage to stand up for anything other than their own sexual orientation. It'll all go to seed." Borneman's critique is not entirely justified. Salzinger absolutely appreciated the African American origins of the music, but as a young European, the leading musicians of his generation who had adapted the blues and popularized it in new forms were equally important. To a large extent, musical socialization is generation-specific. What was in vogue in the 1960s was just as foreign to Borneman as the claims of younger leftists that rock music and revolution necessarily went hand in hand. This did not change the fact, however, that Borneman agreed with other, sometimes even younger authors, who held that these kinds of expectations were illusions, including Salzinger, Wolfgang Harich, Hans G Helms, and Jost Hermand.

As with every other jazz critic, Borneman could not live from this work alone, but had to navigate several areas in different media in order to make ends meet.[241] One area was his continued work in film, which grew more important over the course of the 1950s as private television offered a new source of income. It became so important, in fact, that he was already speaking of his "retirement from the jazz world" in 1957, although this did not yet come to pass.[242] From 1941 to 1949 he held permanent jobs in Ottawa and Paris that ensured regular income but also left him time to study the jazz scenes in Canada, the United States, and the French capital. When he crossed over to freelance work in 1949 while working for Orson Welles, it became much harder for Borneman to keep his head above water, although his financial situation improved somewhat by the mid-1950s. Tax records provide an approximate indication of his sources of income and general financial situation. On his tax return for 1951–52, he stated an income in the amount of 390 British pounds, a whole 282 pounds of which came from his column in *Melody Maker*. This was augmented by Eva's earnings of 152 British pounds, about 80 percent of which came from her translation work for the Foreign Office.[243] With this income, Borneman complained, he was just about able to stay afloat, but not much else.[244] The situation took a turn for the better by 1953–54, when Ernest's work in film and television brought in more money. In sum, the stated income for this tax year amounted to 1,510 British pounds. Nonetheless, given that this had to be enough—combined with Eva's income, of course, for which information is lacking for this year—to feed a family and support his father in Berlin, the Bornemans had to manage their affairs prudently. While Ernest and Eva often thought of returning to Canada, they also frequently mention going back to Germany. Ernest's father, Curt Bornemann, still had contacts to Berlin's cultural life, and Enno Neumann, the son of the elder Borneman's girlfriend, was a young actor who also tried to find a publisher for Ernest's manuscripts. As Ernest wrote home, "All I need is a reputation to be built in Germany."[245] The best chance, it seemed, would be in film and television, but the results of Curt's inquiries were depressing: given the lack of capital, there were "2000 film people out on the street." Curt had managed to speak with Thea von Harbou, a famous screenplay writer (*Metropolis* and *M* among others) and the wife of Fritz Lang, who had reestablished the German filmmakers' association. Initially she showed some interest in a number of Ernest's manuscripts and planned to put in a good word for him.[246] Soon, however, she got cold feet. "It seems she has hardened up some," wrote Curt's girlfriend, Erna Neumann. "Now she thinks your stuff is too risky and that German producers can't afford such experiments."[247] Borneman thus remained in London for a while, not least because he was able to get a foot in the door with the private television channels—a new market that Germany had no inkling of yet.

Jazz in Germany

The collapse of the Nazi regime in 1945 brought an end to its antisemitic extermination campaign; this did not mean that racism had come to an end in Germany. Beneath the show of cosmopolitanism and tolerance, cultural difference was still often determined on the basis of bodily characteristics such as skin color, hair color, or figure type, some of which still bore negative connotations, although attempts were made to see them in a positive light as time went on. Young, modern-minded intellectuals who rejected the Third Reich and cultural traditionalism took an increasing interest in African American culture, viewing it as a medium of emancipation. Musical styles such as jazz and blues potentially offered an emotional way for these circles to distance themselves from racist ideals and to embrace a broader, multi-ethnic world. African Americans were also seen as modeling how to live in existentially insecure times, as they had developed patterns of behavior allowing them to survive a history that was full of exploitation and discrimination. Norman Mailer's concept of the "white negro"—a white nonconformist who took on the manner of black Americans—provided a prime example of these kinds of ideas. The West German jazz propagandist Joachim-Ernst Berendt introduced Mailer's concept to West Germany in 1962, and in retrospect, he saw in Mailer's idea "the whole of the 1960s in a nutshell."[248] Still, even these notions of "black" characteristics rested on racial stereotypes. Blacks were seen as spontaneous, corporeal, virile, and emotional, thus standing directly opposite the prevailing German ideal: the disciplined man of technocratic modernity, driven by reason. Initially a largely cultural phenomenon, the "racial glorification of black men"[249] took on a political aspect with the Black Panthers, a black organization known for its radical politics, reinforcing yet another racial stereotype.

The tenacious racism still prevalent in many places charged these processes of exchange, in which black music, black rebellion, and leading black figures were imported to Europe and West Germany, with particularly explosive freight. That said, as a period of pronounced material and cultural upheaval, the lines of demarcation between the "self" and the "other" became increasingly unclear during the 1950s and 1960s. West German modernity had to resituate itself against the backdrop of the lost war and in light of a need to deal with the Nazi past in a self-critical way, not to mention the trends in globalization and a veritable media explosion. This relatively open situation allowed more room to absorb inspiration coming from African Americans, who seemed all the more "authentic" the more "alienated" one's own world appeared to be. As a part of aesthetic modernity that also embodied a critique of modernity with ties to Black Power, the anti-colonial movement, and the upward re-valuation of African cultural heritage, African and African American traditions were particularly well suited as sources of inspiration for what Paul Gilroy has termed the "counterculture of modernity."[250]

Despite his skepticism toward the mentality and politics of the population to the east of the Rhine, Borneman kept an interest in the cultural landscape in West Germany, including the jazz scene. Even without any contact to the jazz world of postwar Germany, his recognized status as an authority in international jazz criticism drew attention. In 1948 Hans Blüthner, the head of the Berlin Hot Club, contacted Borneman's father after getting a hold of *A Critic Looks at Jazz*; he wanted to get to know the son.[251] At the beginning of the 1950s a live wire stretched between London and the greats of the German jazz scene; Borneman corresponded with concert organizer Horst Lippmann, who wanted to set up some jazz programs on Hessischer Rundfunk, the public broadcaster in Hesse.[252] After reading Borneman's articles in *Melody Maker*, the jazz editor for the southwestern German broadcaster, Joachim-Ernst Berendt, similarly sought out a London audience with Borneman in the early 1950s,[253] marking the beginning of a lifelong friendship between the two men. The pianist and jazz journalist Günter Boas and his wife also visited the Bornemans in 1954,[254] while others, music journalist Siegfried Schmidt-Joos and the writer Hans G Helms among them, contacted Borneman once they became aware of him through articles and radio broadcasts of his that aired in Germany.[255] Academics, too, turned to him as an authority in the field of African American music: in the course of his dissertation work at the time, Alfons M. Dauer, the music ethnologist and later professor of African American studies in Graz, asked Borneman for material.[256] Borneman therefore served as a direct link between the German scene and the goings-on in the all-important English-speaking world. At the same time, he proved an ideal candidate for publicizing German jazz, especially because he could speak the native language. His biography gave him an essential role in winning the battle for the legitimacy of jazz in Germany and ensuring German culture's increased openness to inspiration from the West.

On all his trips east of the Rhine, Borneman made a study of German jazz clubs, frequently reporting on what he had seen and heard in the music press and on BBC radio programs. A first flyby visit to Berlin in 1948 found him not only with film-makers from East and West, but also with underground musicians and activists from the local Hot Club. He wrote about the re-education efforts of the US military government for *DownBeat*—which even included a Rex Stewart concert in the Delphi Palast—and the difficulties facing the emerging jazz scene. The economic troubles resulting from currency reform, the constant power cuts, and the aggressive rejection of jazz by the majority of the population did not exactly make for fertile ground. Taking into account the long period of prohibition, however, the Berlin jazz scene was not doing all that bad for itself. A number of the wind players and pianists were actually able to keep up with American standards, while others, given the unfortunate circumstances, deserved praise simply because they were able to play any jazz at all.[257] After returning from one trip to West Germany in 1953, Borneman told *Melody Maker* readers that the standard for modern jazz was exceptionally high, especially compared to more traditional styles.[258] He suggested that this discrepancy stemmed from the fact that African American music was even less well known in Germany than in Great Britain, and the sound of cool jazz shared more in common with the German symphonic tradition. Borneman had made a careful study of the scene and for the most part was full of praise in particular descriptions of its best musicians and bands—Kurt Edelhagen, Erwin Lehn, Hans Koller, Jutta Hipp, Joki Freund, and Paul Kuhn. He did, however, detect the persistence of one German trait, namely a tendency toward perfectionism and accuracy that at times left little room for the unexpected, or for proper "swing."

Borneman was also suspicious of the pretentious philosophical assertions of the German jazz press, which was not least concerned with gaining a level of respectability in the musical life of a country that set great stock in its tradition of classical music—especially after the collapse of the Third Reich, which had put the legitimacy of German culture in general in doubt.[259] Not only Goethe and Schiller, but also Mozart, Bach, and Wagner were and were to remain guarantors of the superiority of German culture. Jazz, therefore, was certainly not German to many of these critics, but rather "American yammering" and "negro music." The more jazz was considered to be an art form and therefore highbrow, the more likely it was to be accepted by the German public, especially its dominant classes. To Western observers, the arrangement must have seemed absurd. Indeed, Borneman made light of Berendt's first book *Der Jazz*, published in 1950, which bore the simple subtitle *A Contemporary Critical Study*. It is, he wrote,

> so Germanic as to be practically parody . . . there is hardly a word about jazz, music or any other stable pivot of jazz history, jazz criticism or jazz discography. Instead, we find the word jazz used as a jumping-off point for a series of philosophical considerations. . . . I doubt whether there is any modern philosopher, psychiatrist, painter, author or higher mathematician of importance who is not mentioned in the text. What they are doing in a book entitled *Der Jazz* neither they or I shall ever know, but as a kind of mental hurdle race—a sort of intellectual gymkhana—the book can't be beaten.[260]

Borneman met again with jazz journalists and musicians such as Dietrich Schulz-Köhn, Dieter Zimmerle, and Günter Boas on a trip through West Germany in the summer of 1954, also visiting jazz clubs and doing radio shows for Northwest German Broadcasting (Nordwestdeutscher Rundfunk, NWDR) and American Forces Network (AFN).[261] Borneman's radio appearances had in fact already made him somewhat famous in Germany, even outside circles in the know. Much like the newspaper *Bild*'s coverage of the visit of the Iranian royal couple Reza Pahlevi and Soraya, the magazine *Jazz Podium* announced the visit of the "English jazz critic and writer" and his wife to Germany in July and August 1958; the paper made sure to mention that every inch of the "racy sport car" the couple drove was filled with records and recordings.[262]

Anything rejected by a German population that was in large part still nationalist and antisemitic was sure to find favor with the younger generations, as Borneman noted in a 1959 BBC program analyzing the state of jazz in Germany from an anthropological perspective. The rapid and radical Americanization then under way, he argued, stemmed from the lack of an acceptable tradition of folk music:

> Young German jazzmen became spiritual Americans, displaced persons whose musical home was the United States. Compare this with British dance musicians who had a tradition of their own to fall back on . . . it took years before they could shake off these shackles. But the young Germans had nothing to lose. Completely uprooted and despising everything in their own country, they offered a clean sheet to the American pen. The result is a music almost indistinguishable from stateside jazz.[263]

There is much right about this assessment, but it still seems one-sided. He ignored other traditions that played a significant role in shaping the musical preferences of the young German intelligentsia for example, such as French chanson—Georges Brassens, Jacques Brel, and Juliette Gréco—or the leftist song material of the Weimar Republic—Bertolt Brecht, Hanns Eisler, and Ernst Busch.

Borneman's thesis about the radical Americanization of German jazz did not improve his opinion of the music. Ten years after the report in *Melody Maker* mentioned above, his opinion of the active German jazz musicians had not changed for the better. To the contrary, as he told Jeffrey Kruger, the owner of the Flamingo Jazz Club in Soho, "the German musicians are not really very good. They're accurate and some have fine musicianship, but if you hear them as often as I do now, you realise that there's very little originality, very little creative drive, and—worst of all—no depth."[264] Unlike their American counterparts, European bands were in general not able to swing, develop any kind of warmth, or even just make dance music, he continued. In short, European jazz—German jazz included—was "clever, imitative, cold and swingless."[265]

Meanwhile, little had changed in terms of Borneman's approach to jazz or his emotional attitude toward it. In the early 1960s, Joachim-Ernst Berendt made a renewed effort at reconciling Borneman to present-day modern jazz by introducing him to one of its superstars. Borneman, as Berendt recalled, still "favored the older styles of jazz. It seemed to make sense to introduce him to the newer ones. So, I invited him to a concert by the great saxophonist John Coltrane in Frankfurt. Ernest—who sat next to me wriggling with unease—didn't know what to do with the music."[266] For Borneman, music was not only a matter of taste—it was bound up in its sociopolitical function, which he still found lacking in modern jazz. Nonetheless, he showed a willingness to learn and remain self-critical. Years later, Borneman admitted to Berendt that the latter "had been right when it came to most musical questions." "Much of what used to be abhorrent to me (or that I could only listen to narcissistically) has prevailed and seems even conservative to me today," he told Berendt. "You had a better sense of the times in music than I."[267]

The Spanish Tinge: Creole Jazz

Within the broad spectrum of African American music that spread throughout the 1940s and 1950s, developing a following among fans on all rungs of the social ladder, Borneman popularized a particular variety that had garnered very little attention from other jazz authors before him—Creole jazz from the Caribbean. Borneman cited an academic interest in Creole jazz, in the early 1950s calling into question one myth in jazz research, namely the assumption that jazz had gotten its start in 1895 with the New Orleans band founded by its leader, Buddy Bolden. Admitting his role in the initial construction and dissemination of the myth, he now revised his position, asking what had preceded Buddy Bolden. While scholars knew something about the music that was sung and played on the "Place Congo," the traditional meeting point of African slaves in New Orleans, there was still a missing link between this music and jazz. Borneman identified an original impulse for New Orleans jazz in the admixture of African, French, and Spanish influences in the Caribbean and regions of the North American continent under periodic European control, including the initially French, then Spanish colony of Louisiana, with its capital in New Orleans.[268] Borneman argued that the combination of African with Catholic southern European elements—the Creole tradition—had a prehistory, one which began in Europe. Arabian music, he contended, had been strongly influenced by Africans, which meant that the Moors had brought African elements into European music when they ruled over parts of southwest Europe from 711 to 1492. In this line of thinking, the West African slaves who were brought to the Caribbean were to a certain degree already acquainted with the music of the French and Spanish colonists, who had been influenced by their own ancestors. In contrast to many other jazz historians, Borneman relativized the supposed absolute opposition between "African" and "European" music. In his eyes, jazz was "not a form of musical argumentation between two enemy worlds, but rather it was, to the contrary, a reunification of what had once been identical musical elements."[269] The fusion of the African, Spanish, and French traditions in Caribbean jazz were for Borneman a "second symbiosis" of African and European music, and thus represented a counterbalance to the oft-studied fusion of African and British/northern European influences. It was Jelly Roll Morton, a jazz pioneer with a francophone background, who coined the phrase "the Spanish tinge," believing it to be this influence that first gave jazz the spice it needed. This "tinge" had temporarily gone missing in the migration from New Orleans to Chicago, Borneman noted, only to return in stronger form after Puerto Rico's annexation to the United States in 1917, which prompted both a wave of immigration from the Caribbean and a nascent interest among white audiences. Borneman developed the thesis that the origins of jazz went back well before Buddy Bolden to French and Spanish Creole music with its African heritage, which culminated in the Afro-Cuban trend of the present day in the 1950s. The Afro-Cuban movement in modern jazz, he maintained, "has been deemed by some traditionalists to be a sign of decay—a fashion streak similar to rock 'n' roll or skiffle, introduced by thrill seekers merely for the purposes of their own self-enrichment. This is of course total nonsense; jazz began as a Latin-American form of music—the popular music of New Orleans, a city that was populated by people of Spanish, French and African descent." This Spanish tinge was lost as jazz moved north, but counted among the origins of jazz, or as he put it, "Thus the true spirit of jazz might nearly have died out had not a new group of musicians from Puerto Rico, Cuba and the Dominican Republic conquered Harlem in the 1940s. These men did not play jazz, but a sort of ancestral form of jazz so that when U.S. jazz musicians heard the mix of Spanish with African melodies for the first time, they recalled the legacy that had gone missing in their own music during the emigration from New Orleans to New York."[270] Borneman pointed to a lineage in evidence among musicians coming directly from the Creole tradition such as Sidney Bechet, Kid Ory, or Jelly Roll Morton. But he also saw evidence of a Spanish tinge in the music of Duke Ellington and Louis Armstrong, as well as Dizzy Gillespie and Charlie Parker, who sought to ground their music in the roots of the jazz tradition.[271] To this extent, the "imitation of European music" of which the "traditionalists" accused modern jazz (Borneman included) had not begun with Gillespie or Dave Brubeck, but rather with Buddy Bolden and Jelly Roll Morton. According to Borneman:

> This music was never "pure" in the racist sense of the word. On the contrary, the fascination of jazz, and the ease with which it conquered the entire globe, was precisely due to the fact that it was a musical *hybrid* in which more complex aspects of African and European music had been modified sufficiently to provide a common denominator not only for Europeans and Africans but for all races. Jazz, in effect, was the first musical *lingua franca* which mankind had produced.[272]

Borneman believed it was this "Spanish tinge" that could foster a revival of jazz. Early intimations of such a process were already apparent in Great Britain, where a strong and influential group of West Indian musicians were collaborating with their white counterparts. As he saw it, Latin American jazz, unlike skiffle and rock 'n' roll, had not been commercially tainted but came from a traditional source. It had reintroduced dance to jazz but most importantly countered the content and significance of "empty and formalistic art." "Creole music," he wrote, "always has something to tell. It is never abstract. Whenever jazz has turned to its Creole roots, it regained some of its power, some of its affirmation of life, some of its lyrical joy in the good things in this world, which it had lost on the long path from Congo Square to Carnegie Hall."[273]

Borneman dealt extensively with the topic, composing the three-part BBC series *Folk Music of Cuba* in 1953, in addition to British and West German radio programs in the 1950s and early 1960s with titles such as *Creole Echoes, Der Mond über Trinidad* (The Moon over Trinidad), and *Rohrzucker, Tabak und Trommeln* (Cane Sugar, Tobacco and Drums). From 1953 to 1957, he wrote a column for *Melody Maker,* "Tropicana," which was unique in the British music press in its exclusive focus on Latin American music. Other columns, "The Latin Touch" and "Exotica," followed in 1955 for *Gramophone Record Review*. His efforts did not resonate as widely as hoped, however. *Melody Maker* discontinued his column "Tropicana" as part of a streamlining effort in 1957 when it did not seem to attract enough readers.[274] Borneman was nonetheless convinced that Latin American music's influence would continue to grow and that it would win over a larger audience. Calypso, he claimed, would become greater than rock 'n' roll.[275] He had grown less enthusiastic by the end of the 1950s but still took encouragement from the preferences of younger jazz listeners. It was not only the music press that had hindered the Latin wave, he contended, but also the major record companies. In their ignorance, as he put it, it was only at the "dogged insistence of a lot of little teenage girls in pencil skirts" that an out-of-touch group of bosses had been forced to climb out of their ivory towers.[276] At the same time, he continued, the forces of commercialization had led the genuine innovative power of Latin American music astray into banality. Still, he wrote in a radio manuscript in 1959, "we stand today at the beginning of a music revolution resembling that of World War I. Just like when jazz began to conquer the world back then, Cuban folk music has now started to become the international music of the teenagers, the younger generation of all nations. All over the world, young people are turning away from jazz and rock 'n' roll to Twist, Pachanga, Mambo, and Chachacha."[277]

At the time, Borneman's ideas about the "Spanish tinge" were well received and widely read. The theory of jazz's origins in the African rhythmic roots of French and Spanish Creoles and the recent Afro-Cuban trend in jazz only representing a full circle was "interesting and possibly very true," fellow critic Maurice Burman commented.[278] Joachim-Ernst Berendt maintained that "to my knowledge, Ernest Borneman is the only one to date to refer to the 'Creole world' as a musical unity."[279] That said, Borneman's work on this topic was not uncontroversial. In stark contrast to his idea of himself as "far and away the best informed person within my small, specialized field in England," Borneman's contemporary and Latino specialist Derick

Armstrong thought him entertaining, but no expert on Latin American music.[280] Gunther Schuller, an authority on early jazz, considered Borneman's idea about a strong, early African influence within Spanish music that had subsequently been taken back up by West African slaves to be untenable.[281] Current research has also criticized Borneman's thesis on the Creole origins of New Orleans jazz and its later turn against those origins for being too "shortsighted," as it overlooked the diversity of the city's music scene. Nonetheless, present-day scholars have praised Borneman for some of his "valuable insights."[282] As Borneman himself duly noted in his autobiography, the attention he paid to Latin American music was based on the assumption that it "would blend with jazz into a new music form," but this perspective had later "proven to be false."[283] In the late 1950s he still credited himself with a "sixth sense" for coming trends, but this was to be the last time.[284] Even in retrospect he overlooked the fact that an actual revival had taken place in other areas he had delved into, namely the West African influences on African American music, in which the blues took center stage. His vision was obscured in this respect by his persistent anti-commercialism, which did not want to concede the blues revival any kind of emancipatory implications. As soon as big business got involved, Borneman was convinced, listeners became mere puppets. He did not see that listeners had taken to rock and pop independently, based on their own needs and predilections. Nevertheless, he tried constantly to give contemporary youth culture a place in the media.

Sound and Vision: Beat on Television

Borneman had experimented with talking film ever since his work with Hornbostel, in particular through the interplay of visual and musical sequences. His work at the National Film Board of Canada included ethnological sketches and the use of jazz music as a rhythmic basis for animated films and, later in the 1950s, work on an adequate representation of jazz in film. He focused especially, however, on musical movies as an international medium that transcended the language barrier. In all of his experiments, he sought to achieve the same authenticity and spontaneity that he saw to be the ideals of jazz. This same idea would inform a TV series on youth music he produced that caused quite a stir in West Germany in the 1960s.

He had advocated for this last project—a youth music program that would bring present-day trends in pop music to German television—since 1961. As the plan became a reality, however, Borneman's potential for innovation, as well as its limits, were put on full display. Despite his best efforts, the series *Hit & Hot*, envisioned for the West German TV station Freies Fernsehen, never came to fruition. A note from his early days at the station illustrates his ideas for tapping into present-day youth culture. He tried to locate a producer who "was at home in all the youth organizations, teenagers clubs, beer bars and other youth meeting points, so that he could pick up amateurs and beginners in every artistic field, assess them, and bring them to us"—an ethnologist, in other words, who knew the ins and outs of his target audience.[285] It would be the ethnologist's job to figure out the preferred styles within the set environment and then prepare them for television. A short while later, Borneman sent Walter Hilpert, the head of North German Broadcasting (Norddeutscher Rundfunk, NDR), an outline for a music program called *Tempo 61*.[286] Borneman's proposal was apparently about as unpopular as red lips and blue fingernails had been previously with the programming advisory council at Freies Fernsehen. Three years later, however, Radio Bremen, the smallest broadcaster within the Working Group of Public Broadcasters (Arbeitsgemeinschaft der Rundfunkanstalten Deutschlands, ARD), responded positively to a number of proposals, all of which were designed to carve out a space for the new youth culture on German television.[287] In his outline for a series titled *Jazz Club*, Borneman developed a concept for a music program created exclusively for young people. Substantial elements of the program would later appear almost unaltered in the *Beat-Club* series, launched in 1965. Borneman envisioned Saturday afternoons as "Teen Age" day at Freies Fernsehen, a slot that *Beat-Club* would in fact occupy later on the ARD.[288] It was a daring, but also logical concept in that it wrecked the ideal of Saturday afternoons as a family hour. As it was, the notion of a broadcasting slot devoted to watching television together with one's trusted family circle had in theory existed only since the traditionalist program *Der blaue Bock* (The Blue Goat) had occupied the slot. In the proposal that Radio Bremen reviewed in June 1964, Borneman sketched out a decidedly unfettered concept for new forms of music entertainment on television based on what he had already started in Great Britain. He tried to claim the copyright for *Six-Five Special*, a jazz program that aired on the BBC starting in 1957 and marked a turning point in the presentation of pop music on British television.[289] Borneman purported that he had "proposed" this program, which was produced by Jack Good, to the BBC. He cited passages from his concept outline, which revolved around the idea of providing a platform for new music styles such as rock 'n' roll, skiffle, and mambo on television in order to satisfy "the public craving for a return of beat."[290]

Six-Five Special was designed as a show "*by* young people *for* young people" that was all about spontaneity and improvisation.[291] Approximately one hundred teenagers took part as guests, dancing as they wished, talking to each other, or otherwise behaving freely. The intent was to give an authentic effect—"it was just like a crowded jazz bar, and it produced amazing, tightly-packed close-ups of sweating dancers and hypnotized faces."[292] Borneman attributed the success of *Six-Five Special*—chiefly among teenagers, but also some adults—to the "intimacy that was entirely without precedent." The progression of the show was also geared entirely toward authenticity; one music band or soloist followed after another, with a minimal amount of moderation from a young man and a young woman who were supposed to combine a ready wit with an inside scoop and to appeal to viewers by creating the impression of a "half-amorous, half-ironic relationship."[293] Borneman had not directed the show himself, he explained, because he was working at another broadcaster at the time. Over time the program lost some of its appeal and was overtaken in the ratings by other shows. For Borneman, the chief function of the German version was to develop and encourage the musical potential of German youth. By directly addressing the public in this way, Borneman wanted to foster German talent, in the hope of being able to counter hit songs he thought artificial by encouraging young people to create their own, genuine music. He had no problem if this were all in English, which young people tended to love, unlike older Germans.

Borneman's contact to the broadcaster was facilitated by Siegfried Schmidt-Joos, who had been the jazz editor at Radio Bremen since 1959. The two knew each other from Schmidt-Joos's visit to Borneman in London; the former was considered a protégé of Berendt's and a well-known, influential music journalist in his own right.[294] Borneman had already been in touch with Radio Bremen, but only with its radio programming department, so Schmidt-Joos took it upon himself to forward Borneman's ideas for two television series on to programming director Hans Abich, putting his own weight behind them.[295] While the head of television film and entertainment, Hans Bachmüller, had doubts about whether "we in Germany have as many good bands as we would need" and whether jazz really needed to be made to "suit everyone's tastes," editor Michael Leckebusch was enthusiastic. "I had the idea of a jazz club once before," he commented. "It will be a ton of work, but it might be a great series, unlike any before it in Germany."[296] Borneman ultimately put together a proposal for *Beat-Club* as a further elaboration of the "jazz club" idea: live productions, no recordings, moving cameras among the dancers, a bare-bones stage setting, and spur-of-the-moment dialogue. All in all, it was to be an "unstaged, seemingly natural show in which we are not trying to hide anything."[297] The show was supposed to offer a broad spectrum of strongly rhythmic music: jazz, twist, rock 'n' roll, R & B, and beat. In the end, Borneman was contracted to write the screenplay for the new series and direct it; Leckebusch was put in charge of editing the program.[298]

Radio Bremen advertised the new project during its news service, with reference to the success of *Six-Five Special* and Jack Good's ITV series *Oh Boy!* in Great Britain. The advertisement also noted that "the jazz and beat expert Ernest Borneman" had come on board as its director, "bringing with him years of experience in British television."[299] Borneman, however, never actually took the director's chair for the series. During preparations for the show's premier, the intended head of the show ended up at such cross purposes with his editor that Bachmüller rescinded Borneman's contract and handed the screenplay and direction over to Leckebusch instead.[300] As Bachmüller put it, the reasons for the split had to do with "interpretive differences" when it came to the concept of the show, combined with a generational competition.[301] The dissonance had grown quite apparent after Borneman's four-day visit to Bremen in August 1965.[302] Leckebusch saw himself as a young outsider without much backing, but full of fresh ideas, whom Borneman—a fifty-year-old internationally renowned TV man (who furthermore had been brought on board by "some kind of executive channel")—was trying to sell on something new for a young audience. He also claimed that Borneman was a "master of staging things" in the studio, while he himself was all about spontaneity.[303] Borneman's screenplay did in fact set all kinds of specific language in the mouths of the moderators, such as announcing plans for a club structure codified by membership and creating a "new German sound." Nothing like this was to be found in the screenplay later used to produce the show, which was written by Leckebusch.[304]

Nonetheless, it was still Borneman's idea of a quasi-documentary show for young people about beat and its authentic aura that was broadcast in the end. For this reason, Borneman later spoke of Leckebusch's *Beat-Club* as "plagiarism," for which, after settling with Radio Bremen, he received a lump sum amount and a payment after each show until the program was reformed in 1967, something Schmidt-Joos referred to as "severance pay."[305] *Beat-Club* would never have been born without Borneman's efforts, but the transformation of the basic format into an internationally successful television phenomenon was entirely Leckebusch's work. Once again, Borneman had started something innovative, only to hit a limit. Leckebusch was just twenty-eight years old and, in many respects, held closer connections to the scene that was supposed to be served by the show. Borneman could not understand how he, someone with greater experience, could be replaced by a beginner "who had yet to prove himself at all in the field."[306] It was not the last time he would be forced to recognize the fact that he was no longer young. When it came to such a target audience, it was not experience but proximity that mattered.

Black Light, White Shadow: Free Jazz and Black Nationalism

Speaking with US music critic Ralph Gleason in 1959, Borneman justified his interest in the "Spanish tinge" by citing his aversion to the "dreary conformism that rules jazz theory these days" and the now canonical narrative of progress running from New Orleans to Chicago to New York.[307] He wanted to challenge the well-known arguments, whether traditionalist or modernist, by asking new questions. Borneman declared a particular interest in the origins and actors of "white blues," and did in fact turn again in the 1960s to the question of whether there was a racial component to jazz and blues. This took place, moreover, within the context of a potent political movement that emerged both in the United States and on the African continent. This movement was accompanied by new and forceful currents within African American music—free jazz and the blues revival—that partially confirmed Borneman's assumptions and partially called his legitimacy as a white jazz critic into question.

US musicologist Ingrid Monson recently made a convincing case for the close connection in the 1960s between jazz's development as African American–inspired music on the one hand and concurrent political events on the other. The advent of decolonization in Africa in the first few years of the decade in tandem with the expanding civil rights movement in the United States led to an increased self-awareness among African American musicians that fueled the debate on the extent to which music was a "racially" determined cultural product. In the black power movement, for example, free jazz was celebrated as the highest musical embodiment of black culture and a source of black pride.[308] Since the end of World War II, jazz musicians had perpetually been surrounded by an aura of taboo breaking, nonconformism, self-determination, and social criticism, attracting public admiration in the process.[309] Not surprisingly, even before the black power movement there was often a strong affinity for jazz among leftist circles in particular. The radical new claim laid out in the 1960s—the movement's self-awareness as being of a black minority with a legitimate right to respect and direct say—also influenced liberal and leftist critics, who now more readily took their cues from it. More than ever before, great numbers of young people in the United States and Europe came to embrace African American music and culture as a standard for their own aesthetic, moral, and political actions. Many of them even wanted to "become black" symbolically in order to take part in the supposed superiority of African American culture and legitimate their own conduct. This not quite selfless love of African American culture, dubbed "Afroamerikanophilie" (Afro-Americanophilism) by Moritz Ege, was particularly apparent in the field of music—in jazz, blues, and soul, as well as the social practices associated with these styles.[310] Among the student protesters of the late 1960s, African Americans' engagement was seen as an important part of a global revolt, a revolutionary strike at the heart of the beast.

In this context, whoever had not already confronted the political aspects of jazz or taken a position now had to do so. Borneman was better prepared for this process of politicization than other jazz critics, as he had been highly politicized himself since his teenage days and come of age in London within the Pan-African movement that was now celebrating its victory. Furthermore, from the very beginning of his career as a jazz critic Borneman had considered the ethnic aspects of jazz; African American culture always served as a major point of reference regarding not only his own aesthetic preferences, but also his research into the history of jazz. As early as 1948 he anticipated the way forward for the eventual blues revival of the 1960s, noting that African Americans were the original source to whom musicians should look—not to imitate them, but rather to create something of their own.[311] This, of course, tapped into the overarching question of whether to strive for racial equality. In the late 1950s Borneman found himself on one side of the fence when Leonard Feather spoke out in favor of eliminating the criterion of race altogether and assuming complete racial equality, while Borneman argued for the exact opposite. Their dispute represented a broader discursive shift within the jazz community, from the ideology of color blindness—that is, all races are equal—to a positive awareness of the autonomy of African American culture. Whereas Feather was more closely aligned with the aesthetic preferences of the black power movement for free jazz, Borneman was closer to the movement when it came to asserting the legitimacy of a separate black cultural awareness. Before escalating in the early 1960s with the rise of black nationalism, this debate was carried out on the pages of *Jazz Monthly* in 1958–59 between the two critics and others. The topic was complex—the legal equality of African Americans demanded by the civil rights movement was undisputed in the jazz scene for example, while the question of whether whites could or should play jazz or blues remained controversial. Feather, who believed blues to be a remnant of the cultural subjection of blacks, contended that the distinction between "Negro jazz" and "white jazz" had outlived its purpose, as modern jazz had allowed blacks to overcome the "Uncle Tom" stereotype and anchored their legacy in everyday American life.[312] Borneman, by contrast, saw this as a strategy to reinforce white supremacy. Whites can play jazz just as well as blacks? The notion sought to push black people out of the business in order to make room for whites, who had achieved their success mostly through imitation rather than any originality. For Borneman, African Americans' leading role had not been predetermined by any racial faculty—cultural characteristics were not inheritable but acquired in socialization. What was more, these were empirically identifiable: in any type of jazz, blacks were the leaders and whites were the followers. In Borneman's view, Feather's concept would create conformity. The specific cultural contributions of African Americans to the great American melting pot would get lost in the race to make everyone equal, damaging their pride and making survival impossible.[313] This argument gave credence to the growing self-confidence of African American musicians and their rejection of white culture. The black civil rights movement identified with Miles Davis and John Coltrane, as each represented the dignity and extraordinary quality of black culture. When James Brown proclaimed, "I'm black and I'm proud," to the world in 1968, it was explicitly this sort of self-confidence that Borneman had supported ten years previous. As Borneman noted, the ancestors of the blacks had been abducted from Africa and enslaved by the ancestors of the whites for generations. The only way to ensure survival, to develop trust and self-respect, was for blacks to adopt an attitude along the lines of "You owe us apologies and reparations for the damage you've done us. Although you've bullied and urged and tempted us to accept your ways of life, we still think ours are better." To Borneman, legal equality for black people was a prerequisite for the development of variety, whereas Feather's notion of equality was incompatible with the idea of variety, sounding the death knell of human civilization. As also becomes clear from Borneman's argument, however, the opposition between racial equality and liberal positions on the one side and the insistence on cultural self-determination and rebellion on the other did not have to correspond with aesthetic preferences: Borneman may have criticized free jazz, but he still asserted the achievements of African American culture.

In 1965, with the blues boom spurring on intensive academic engagement with the subject, Borneman resumed work on his "History of American Negro Music." He dreamed of being able to "one day become a professor in America thanks to this book (despite my lack of a university degree)."[314] There was no chance of this happening in Germany, though he did later have hopes of becoming a professor at the University of Music and Performing Arts in Graz, whose jazz institute "was a pioneering school in the field," and which wanted to hire Borneman as a professor of African American musical studies.[315] The process of establishing the position dragged on, however, and it was eventually awarded to the musicologist and ethnologist Alfons M. Dauer in 1976. By that point Borneman had long since turned his attention to a different field, earning his PhD in psychology at the University of Bremen that same year.

It became increasingly clear to Borneman that the time had come to make a change in 1960—twenty years after he had written his long manuscript on jazz—with the appearance of Paul Oliver's classic study *Blues Fell This Morning*. A thoroughly researched, sociohistorical exploration of the content of blues in light of the context from which it emerged, the book also featured a preface by Richard Wright, whom Borneman had tried to get to write an endorsement for his own book manuscript. Oliver's achievement provided the sort of foundation that Borneman had always tried to establish but never managed to bring into existence.[316] There were two reasons for this. First, Borneman had not managed to concentrate on this one project. Rather, he had tried to do everything all at once—especially with his music journalism and many projects in fiction, film, and television—and not for financial reasons alone, but also because he became bored easily and would then move on to something new. Second, since 1953 he had concentrated more heavily on the Caribbean aspects of jazz, which while relevant were marginal at best when it came to the preoccupation of the contemporary British music world—the blues revival, with young people only showing an interest in something Borneman himself had identified as the core of African American music. Borneman would return to his old subject once more, after his stint at Freies Fernsehen in Germany ended in failure and his new job at an advertising agency proved unfulfilling. Commenting on the project in a letter to Frank Kofsky, he wrote, "It will be a great book, but it is slow, slow going—two more years maybe, until I'm finished." He fully intended the book to pick up with his old approach, representing "a proper dialectic study of the interrelation between economics, social life and art."[317]

The explicit anti-racism of the jazz and blues scene was as welcome a development as it was problematic. Most jazz critics of the 1950s and 1960s agreed among themselves that blues, as Max Jones put it, was "essentially folk-music possessing pronounced racial characteristics," which meant that it could only be played and sung adequately by African Americans.[318] All this changed over the course of the 1960s with the success of an increasing number of white blues musicians, a phenomenon that prompted the question "Can whites play (or sing) the blues?"[319] Answering this question meant navigating the relationship between music, race, and power via the notion of authenticity. According to critics as well as fellow black musicians, white blues musicians such as Eric Burdon, John Mayall, and Eric Clapton could play blues in a technical sense just as well as their black counterparts. It remained questionable, however, whether they could sing just as well. The commercially successful adaption of African American material also raised the question of whether white blues musicians had "stolen" the music from blacks.[320] There was no doubt that popular white bands such as Cream or Led Zeppelin were profiting significantly more from the blues boom than were the music's original black players, while at the same time the former credited themselves with having revived and carried on the blues tradition and helped a number of black musicians achieve a new popularity. Yet there is no doubt that European blues musicians and talents lived under completely different social and cultural conditions than their African American predecessors. Similar to the student activists, the West German jazz "pope," Joachim-Ernst Berendt, regarded the success of the blues at the end of the 1960 as a boon, although he recognized that its commercial success often benefited its white interpreters rather than its black creators. Norman Mailer's idea regarding the transmission of specifically black mannerisms to young whites had essentially come to pass; it was no longer blacks who were crossing the "racial Maginot line," but rather masses of whites.[321] This had, in turn, changed their view of the world, as well as their behavior: If, as Berendt put it, "young people today think more differently than ever before, this has something to do with the fact that they have black music and black messages in their souls."[322]

While young Europeans, especially men, had a fascination with black people, this by no means meant that ethnic prejudices or feelings of superiority had disappeared. Discrimination was in part projected onto other groups, and even the positive turn in the perception of black people was laden with ambiguity. The Lippmann and Rau concert agency for example, which organized the American Folk Blues Festival (AFBF) from 1962 onward, was criticized by African Americans for having only presented a very specific image of black artists—that of older "archaic types" (Fritz Rau)—in order to provide the authenticity that white young people in Europe so desired.[323] Put more bluntly, it was the image of a blues artist as ideally an old, poor, somewhat strange figure from a rural background that appealed to young whites and was presented at the AFBF in the form of an "authentic documentation."[324] Once upon a time the musician had been a success, only to disappear from public view before being rescued from his miserable existence by Horst Lippmann & Co., who reintroduced him to the stage. This romanticized and patronizing image of blues singers was also on display in AFBF brochures, which were produced every year but always depicted blacks as sage representatives of a suppressed race from which something could be learned.[325] The concerts themselves gave the same kind of impression, as Charles Keil reported; he referred to the AFBF guest performance in London as a "a third rate minstrel show." Keil also claimed that if the show were performed for a black audience in Chicago, it would go down in scorn and ridicule. Yet in London, he wrote, thousands of young Brits had listened in awestruck silence: "The more ludicrous the performance, the more thunderous the applause at its conclusion."[326]

Like many jazz critics (and not just those in Germany), Berendt harbored a romantic, essentialist view of black culture, albeit with an anti-racist thrust.[327] For him, blacks were the bearers of positive cultural attributes from which whites only had something to learn. In the end, he thought that ideally the contrasts between the races would disappear entirely. In a book on the blues from 1970 summarizing his work to date and pointing to new directions in light of the blues boom, Berendt argued that while white bands could never totally achieve the "authenticity" of black blues, they still carried "the black 'message'" more deeply in their white souls than their predecessors, that is, Elvis and the Beatles.[328] The originals, however, were still B. B. King and John Lee Hooker, not Clapton and Mayall. Blues remained black music at heart despite its success among white young people, an important fact because it retained its power of inspiration within the white world. At the same time, he pointed out, the black power movement had for the first time taken the monopoly on the jazz discourse out of the hands of white Afro-Americanophiles, forcing them to "face up to challenges in dialogue."[329] Defensive positions thus dominated the narrative. In this respect, Berendt cited an accusation popularized by LeRoi Jones (who later gave himself the name Amiri Baraka) that whites had stolen black music in order to get rich. Helmut Salzinger also rejected Jones's construction as undifferentiated "black racism" whose "objective was just as idiotic as that of white racism."[330] By means of such interpretations, German commentators were able to rescue the appropriation of black music by whites without destroying the authentic character of the originals. Werner Sollors, later a professor of African American studies at Harvard, and Bernd Weyergraf took a more radical approach; as the translators of Amiri Baraka's *Blues People* into German, which appeared in 1969 for the underground Melzer Verlag, they placed the political role of the black population at the center of their interpretation.[331] In their afterword they treated blues as folklore in a condescending sense, as an aesthetic phenomenon that may well have made mention of the black proletariat, but by no means mobilized it.

They criticized Baraka for really addressing "the educated minority of a black and white middle class that tended to use artistic language to suppress conflicts that actually needed to be addressed."[332] They did magnanimously concede, however, that Baraka had "not yet come to terms with assimilation and alienation" and that this "contradiction" made the book "honest and readable." The authors castigated his "bourgeois ideas of harmony" and his "folklorist's interest in cultural nationalism," calling instead for a "revolutionary black nationalism" that would supersede racial boundaries and take on capitalists of all skin colors. In his 1981 preface, Manfred Miller also argued that the author, who declared black culture to be progressive per se, had taken a "racial" position for failing to criticize the black bourgeoisie from a class-conscious perspective but rather for its "assimilation to white culture," thereby ignoring the fact that pauperized whites in the US South also played "authentic blues."[333] Radical Germans countered the "race" issue as had been put front and center by the black power movement by focusing on "class" instead, thereby claiming solidarity with rebellious-minded blacks.

In effect, the myth of the "noble savage" experienced a resurrection: it was not whites who elevated blacks to the level of Western culture, but rather blacks who indicted the technocratic modernity of and division of labor in the white world by imparting fundamental human experiences that had been lost to the West. The goal was to provide whites with the material they needed to create their own identities, after which they should be able to reflect critically on their own society while developing arguments and cultural tools to understand and change the present. Young African Americans, on the other hand, generally saw old blues musicians as the heroes of yesterday. They preferred to listen to soul, which blended blues and gospel into dance music and had been dismissed by white blues fans—especially from leftist-radical circles—as a commercial, mass consumer product. One flyer circulating within the anarchist underground of West Berlin came from a subculture that identified itself as "The Blues"; bearing the title "Pigs Are Not Always Pink!," the article below referred to the "godfather of soul" James Brown as a "black pig" for purportedly siding with the black power movement for commercial reasons.[334] Here one sees how the ambivalence of ethnically codified attraction and rejection that had always determined white perceptions of blacks could also be observed within milieus that considered themselves decidedly anti-racist. Writing for the *Frankfurter Rundschau* in 1968 with reference to the musicians Lippmann and Rau brought to the stage, Wolfgang Vogel quipped, "The blues don't need these people any more. There is no place for dinosaurs. Sorry, don't mean to be rude, but the standards today are being set by others, and their names are Clapton, Winwood, etc. and not something else."[335] White blues interpreters, he claimed, "could do blues better," and they were sending black American artists "back into the annals of blues history." Yet all of this, he maintained, "had less to do with race than with the perspective of the interpreters." Alexis Korner wrote in a similar vein, "It is no longer a question of race or skin color; it is a question of attitude."[336] From this perspective, one quite similar to Feather's, blues had shed its ethnic ties—whites could play it just as well, if not better, and their critiques of African American blues were all the more legitimate for not stemming from racist views. Yet this topic too was controversial, with many critics continuing to detect a difference between "black" and "white" blues. Joachim-Ernst Berendt maintained, for example, that the "authenticity" of white blues bands was "astonishing, but still relative."[337]

Although Borneman had been one of the instigators of this debate in the early and mid-1960s, by this point he was no longer involved. Nonetheless, the debate itself shows that essential questions concerning ethnicity, politics, and power came up in conversations around musical style—with jazz as with popular music. When Borneman did finally distance himself from the idea of writing a fully developed account of African American music, his decision primarily had to do with the self-empowerment of African Americans, who were then questioning the privileged position white critics held in the past. He gave the following reasons: first, it was more than one person could accomplish; second, the trend in ethnomusicology had shifted toward detailed studies rather than broad overviews; third, and perhaps most importantly, the predominant attitude in the black power movement was that whites were not in a position to express an opinion about black music. "As a non-Negro musicologist," Borneman wrote, "you can therefore still write on selected aspects of American folk music in which the Negro has played a part. But to single him out as a creative force, as a cultural entity with a clear profile, has become inadvisable to the extent that the Negro himself, who is to be the beneficiary of any such research, feels that the harm of it outweighs the benefits."[338] For this reason, Borneman's articles in the early 1970s no longer focused on the history of African music's legacy in the new world, but on the history of social tensions and their influence on African American music. These writings did go beyond what he had originally planned in one respect: they began to integrate the reactions of blacks to white perceptions of black music.

Between 1970 and 1972, the journal *Jazzforschung/Jazz Research* published "Black Light and White Shadow: Notes for a History of American Negro Music," a two-part article by Borneman that contained a few brief excerpts from the original work. Planned initially as a three-volume set and containing more than twenty chapters, it was never to appear as a book. The collection of manuscripts and published fragments that begins in 1940—and which ends in 1972 with his final major publication on the impact of the black power movement—gives a relatively cohesive, defined image, while still reflecting the changes that occurred over a period lasting more than thirty years.[339] Although Paul Oliver encouraged Borneman to publish a smaller book on the subject in his series "Blues Paperbacks," the project never materialized.[340]

In the late 1950s, Borneman wrote to Ralph Gleason about wanting to publish something on the perpetual "mealy-mouthed talk about 'race' that goes on among jazz critics, the jazz crowd, the 'progressives,' and even the NAACP."[341] At the second international conference on jazz research in April 1972 in Strobl (Austria), Borneman reflected on the reverberations of the black power movement within jazz research. Given that the decisive positions within the record industry and jazz criticism were occupied by whites (almost exclusively men), he noted, the conviction with which many a black jazz musician and the handful of black jazz critics with ties to black power protested this hegemony was understandable. This remained true despite the fact that there were some "white exceptions" among jazz critics who were not simply open to black culture but even promoted it among the broader public.[342] Ernest Borneman's interpretation differed from the latter in that he argued from the vantage point of the black power movement, but without banishing the element of "race" in favor of "class." To the contrary, he believed it was important to step out of the ivory tower and express solidarity while also trying to convince the black power movement to distance itself from its own racism toward whites. Because jazz research could no longer be "impartial,"[343] he wrote,

> it seems to me that it is my duty as a student of Afro-American music to support the maker of Afro-American music in his struggle for liberation, just as I consider it my duty to fight against all attempts to push jazz into a ghetto. The black freedom movement, with all its childhood troubles and inner dissensions, still remains one of the few hopeful, creative developments on the American horizon today. We cannot afford to dissociate ourselves from it. But we cannot afford either, to keep silent out of mistaken tact when we see our black brothers stumble innocently into the

same errors which have already cost us a good many battles in our own struggle for liberation.[344]

As for Lenin, who Borneman is referencing here, these "childhood troubles" resulted from a radically exaggerated understanding of a problem, in this case ongoing racial discrimination, which Borneman sought to explain to his readers in a historical account that was extended as it was lucid. Once again, the text itself was actually a chapter from a book on African American music that had been in the works for thirty years, but now only appeared in fragments. Part of his purpose in the chapter was also to explain why the black community had adopted the cultural chauvinism of the day instead of rejecting it.

This critique implicitly took aim at Amiri Baraka, who had forcefully criticized Borneman shortly before the appearance of his famous book *Blues People*. Baraka drew on Borneman in his own work to prove that African music was not inferior, despite the contrary claims of many contemporaries.[345] Scholars have rightly noted Baraka's use of Borneman to support his arguments about resistance in black culture.[346] Both authors shared an anthropological perspective on the topic as well as a Marxist-dialectical approach to their analyses; they differed in their estimation of current trends in jazz. Baraka affirmed that he valued Borneman's writings greatly but disagreed with Borneman's critical attitude toward the young jazz avant-garde. He spoke in reference to an article from the first issue of the new magazine *Jazz* in early 1963 in which Borneman, in the role of contributing editor, sought to debunk a number of the era's current "jazz myths." One of these myths was the idea that present-day jazz had to distance itself from traditional "Uncle Tom music" in the name of progress.[347] Borneman once again criticized modern forms of jazz as interpreted by artists like Dizzie Gillespie and Henry Rollins, who were considered revolutionary and celebrated within the emerging black nationalist movement as talking the language of liberation. For Borneman, if the tension between form and content that creates art is lost because the focus has come to rest exclusively with form, then the resulting art—now deprived of content—will be nothing but ornamentation: "Most jazz music is musical ornamentation—high class doodling. Or intellectual doodling."[348] The abstraction so praised by the jazz avant-garde, he contended, brought nothing of value to jazz or the present day. "If you want to judge a jazz musician's work, ask yourself not only how well he plays his instrument, how original he is (how different from others), but also what he has to *say*. Ask the unfashionable question: 'What is he *expressing*? What's the *subject matter*? What is it *about*?' And you will find that the accepted jazz hierarchy falls into a complete new order."[349] In response to all this Baraka suspected not only Borneman of conservatism, but also the makers of the magazine (he himself sat on the editorial board). The editors denied his claim, arguing that the magazine sought to report on all directions in jazz, regardless of any respective individual preferences.[350] Baraka viewed Borneman as an "aging liberal" and called him out, writing, "Mr. Borneman, listen to what you want to, and leave off with the diatribes, already. They're very unbecoming from a man who has contributed so much in the way of intelligent writing about the music."[351] The reactions to Borneman's article were mixed, but Amiri Baraka's response came as a particular source of disappointment for the then 48-year-old Borneman and may have been part of the reason that he gave up on jazz journalism for a time in the mid-1960s, "with a certain resignation," as Berendt noted.[352] In a letter to Dan Morgenstern, the editor of the magazine, Borneman wrote bitterly that "Mr. Jones is doing me an injustice if he thinks that I am haranguing him or anybody else, or that I'm trying to convince anybody of anything. I'm too old to be a missionary. But I'm still young enough to be curious. I really want to know."[353]

While Baraka charged Borneman with "conservatism," the line between traditionalist and progressive was not as easy to draw as it seems at first glance. Where Borneman recognized the real potential of jazz in the folk music of the blues tradition, Jones, much like Feather, saw an outdated, passive form of "Uncle Tom" music vanquished by wild, modern jazz. Yet as Borneman clearly pointed out in his reply, it was in fact blues that had appealed to young people in Great Britain, sparking the British blues wave of the 1960s. On the one hand, there was the avant-garde of intelligent and technically brilliant jazz musicians, whose highly artificial language spoke to a small, elite audience; on the other, the legacy of rhythm and blues, rock 'n' roll, twist, and beat, music that had a huge following and also harmonized completely with the interest of music producers. "Here, as in the old days, you don't have to explain anything."[354] Borneman believed that in jazz, as with painting, the ideal of abstraction was in essence just a kind of formalistic game without much content. He described his alternative as follows: "Music, if it has to have any justification at all, must say something human and concrete, something that widens our understanding of our own nature and that of the world around us—something, ultimately, that helps us to make the world better." The conflict between the artistic revolutionaries and the folklorist-traditionalists was not in fact irresolvable. It underwent a historical transformation instead, as displayed in the magazine in which the war between the two was waged. The division between the two camps by no means ran along an age line, as Baraka had suggested; quite a few of the younger musicians as well as critics moved from jazz to blues and then on to pop, just like the magazine *Jazz* itself, which reported more and more on folk and rock music after 1966 and renamed itself *Jazz-Pop* in 1967.

Borneman later expanded his critique of Amiri Baraka; the latter had drawn on Borneman's research but then denied Borneman's right to even deal with the topic. This is how Borneman viewed the matter, at least, in "Black Light and White Shadow." "Those of us who have spent three or four decades studying black music and preaching its virtues to blacks who did not want to be reminded that they were black, are now being told by the children of those whom we taught that black was beautiful, to shut up and cultivate our own white garden." According to Borneman,

Baraka's point that whites could not understand jazz and blues and should therefore only tackle their own cultural products was not dialectic, and might even be termed "fascistic,"[355] with his belief in race as the definitive cultural line of separation running parallel to European racial ideologies and apartheid in South Africa. Taking a sociocultural tack, Borneman highlighted more complex realities, including class differences within the black community, or the fact that a black Marxist sociologist like E. Franklin Frazier denied the significance of racial factors and traced back any differences to social factors instead, while white anthropologists like Melville J. Herskovits saw black culture as superior. Society was by no means based solely on skin color, Borneman contended; at the very least it was the interplay between race and class that mattered, not to mention the difference between the sexes. He would return to this final distinction in his critique of the male chauvinism present within the "rightist" Muslim wing of black power in anticipation of his large study on patriarchy from 1975. Borneman also reflected on the antisemitism in this camp, which had even attacked Jewish representatives of the liberal establishment who had strongly advocated for black equality. The black radicals saw these liberals as particularly dangerous because they propagated the idea of racial equality rather than embracing separatism. "Black" and "white"—categories as coarse as these distracted from the fact that both designated groups showed such great internal variation and such a vast number of intermediate forms as to make them useless for all intents and purposes.

"I Would Really Like to Be a Negro"

Given jazz critics' privileged access to black culture, a tension can often be observed between openness and enthusiasm on the one hand and a tendency toward racial mysticism stemming from overidentification on the other. It is not easy, as John Gennari rightly points out, to do justice to the emotional complexity that results from this tension.[356] "I would really like to be a Negro"—this confession, coming on 12 July 1933 from then eighteen-year-old Ernest Borneman four days after his arrival in London, speaks to the spontaneous fascination triggered by his intensive contact with black people, their forms of musical expression and political views.[357] After all, James, Padmore, and Kenyatta were going to "change the face of the globe." While such romantic sentiment may have mixed with a criticism of the specific forms of behavior and views of concrete black figures, Borneman still found it difficult to tamp down his emotional identification with black politics and culture. He sought to overcome these romantic projections by adopting an analytic, scientific approach. Unlike many jazz fans, Borneman thought that racial characteristics had nothing to do with the musical quality of jazz. Rather, what mattered was the particular mix of different cultural traditions in the Caribbean and the United States, where the rhythms of West Africa had played an important role, and which could be examined on an empirical basis. Essentializing interpretations of blackness appear occasionally in Borneman's works, but they did not define his approach, which was decidedly anti-essentialist. It

was taken for granted that racial discrimination must be abolished and that segregation as a political reality needed to be opposed. But since "race" was not a particularly
relevant category in his work in general, his goal was not to sublate its supposed
oppositions into some kind of a higher entity. Instead, he demonstrated repeatedly
how cultural fusions were created from a multiplicity of traditions. Ethnicity did play
a certain role, but this was as a culturally defining element, not a genetic factor. Jazz
music was, at its core, what he defined as "folk music": "music of the American mix
of whites, negroes, Indians, and others."[358] As opposed to the European symphonic
tradition, jazz was essentially devoid of race and class—a music that belonged to the
future.

By no means did this make ethnicity irrelevant to Borneman. He was not color
blind. Ethnic differences were indeed relevant, though not for racist motives—quite
the contrary in fact. After lunch with his friend Denis Preston and his South African
wife, Helen Nontando Jabavu, Borneman wrote to Eva, "Some old talk about cultural patterns and some old insistence that Negroes are 'just like' white folks."[359] A
year earlier, he had commented after lunch with the same couple, "How they all want
to be good white bourgeois citizens!"[360] When Richard Wright visited Borneman in
1944, he had tried to convince his host "that American Negroes have no culture and
that my whole work on the survival of Africanisms is just European romanticism."
At the same time, Borneman faulted the writer for suffering, like the anthropologist Frazier, "from that well-known racial masochism which I have already noticed
among Jews to a similar extent." Borneman was duly impressed by *Black Metropolis*,
a book about the South Side of Chicago published in 1945 that Wright had worked
on with others and that quickly became a classic in urban sociology. Yet he also criticized its "peculiar kind of social behaviourism," which reminded him of the "'emancipated European Jews" whom he had met in the internment camps—"all of them
still desperately trying to prove that Jews never had any culture or anything else of
their own . . . and that if Jews could only merge with the gentiles and be just like
them the whole 'Jewish problem' could be solved."[361] The same "wishful thinking"
and *Selbsthass* (he used the German word for self-hate) could also be found among
African Americans and was particularly depressing in its Marxist version, where the
exclusively economic explanation of societal phenomena separated social from cultural factors. Borneman hoped that his study of jazz had shown Wright that "your
people have a hell of great tradition to remember and to be proud of."[362] Studies like
Black Metropolis could be much more effective, he continued, if they did not only
try to list factors that reduced the "races" to their lowest common denominator, that
is, social aspects. Borneman criticized Wright for underestimating the achievements
of African American culture and his goal of achieving cultural equality with whites,
but he also rejected Wright's insistence on the racial foundation of African American
culture. As Borneman noted, Wright was prepared to write for the *Record Changer*,
"but this damned mania of his makes all his writing on Negro music sound as if it
were written by Gobineau," referring to the nineteenth-century French racial theorist

who insisted on the inequality of the races, rejected race mixing, and provided the ideological foundation for the ethno-nationalist (*völkisch*) movement in Germany.[363] Like many Pan-Africanists, Wright was motivated by a "feeling of racial solidarity" that rested on the belief in a fundamental difference between races and placed the essence of black identity in Africa.[364] Senghor himself, the founder of the Négritude movement, had in fact drawn directly on Gobineau in order to argue that "le nègre" was not only more emotional, but also more energetic than a European.[365] Imanuel Geiss has pointed out the theoretical similarities between the "majority irrational, romantic tendency in the Pan-African movement" and the German *völkisch* movement, whose roots lay in the romanticization of the German *Volk* and folk culture. Such was the ideological minefield Borneman tread upon—difficult terrain to navigate effectively while avoiding essentialist ideas of what constituted a "race." Borneman also considered "the people" to be the bearers of culture, but this was on a social, not an ethnic basis. It was small wonder, then, that he rejected the idea put forth by Gobineau and his followers that race created culture, especially given Borneman's experience with the Holocaust, his Jewish heritage, and his Marxist outlook. It should be noted, however, in light of his close connections with and admiration for Pan-African intellectuals, that the line separating the legitimate appreciation of unrecognized cultural achievement and its racial justification was very thin. In contrast to many postwar German intellectuals who were quick to trot out the notion of "black racism," whether from a feeling of being put at a disadvantage or a preconceived notion of what was correct, Borneman took the question of how race and culture related to one another as the premise for his own scholarship. He doubted the notion that there was a "racial entity" called "Negro jazz."[366] This put him at odds with many other jazz critics and musicians who had revived the romantic image of the "noble savage," one that had only been strengthened by the idealized self-image projected by the Négritude movement itself. The fact that Borneman was not color blind did not prevent his disappointment at exclusionary trends within black nationalism that were based on skin color. In the early 1970s he also rejected the idea of an ethnically based revolutionary movement:

> If blacks want to gain rights, a feeling of self-worth, dignity, and livelihoods, they can only do so as part of a social, not racial movement. Those of us in Europe who have survived the experience of a racist or "national" socialism have learned its pitfalls, but a black radical stumbles right into them when he follows the call to do to his own thing—his own racial, ethnic, national thing. But Black Nationalism, when compared to nationalism as a whole, is just as reactionary a concept as Hitler's racial thing.[367]

From the mid-1970s onward Borneman distanced himself from jazz criticism and even from jazz itself; he no longer wanted to be subject to its "addictiveness," as he put it, but he had also lost his ability to see it as a present-day phenomenon. Occasionally, however, he was still posed musical questions. Shortly before his death, for example, a jazz researcher approached him hoping to glean some information about Sidney Bechet's performances in Berlin in the early 1930s. Borneman brushed the inquiry aside, explaining, "I am too old, too tired, and too politically disappointed to be able to answer any music questions sensibly."[368] His answer itself, however, was quite revealing: it made clear that music was still more than just sound to him—it was something with social and political dimensions.

Several years ago, in his critique of Bernard Gendron's book on the relationship between pop music and the avant-garde—one in which Gendron firmly took the side of the "modernists" and deplored Borneman as an aggressive "moldy fig"—the well-known American music critic Robert Christgau remarked that Borneman actually "seems pretty smart even though he was wrong," then posing the question "Is his writing of, pardon me, lasting value?"[369] A good question, and one that is not easy to answer. Hundreds of books about jazz have been written since Borneman first started working on the subject that have since expanded our knowledge, but also added layers of nuance. Many of the details and facts that Borneman worked out have surely been revised in the process, and many of his assessments and expectations have also proved false. His approach, however, still seems largely applicable. Apart from revisionist positions that seek to play up the significance of "white" cultural elements in jazz and fight the windmills of a supposed "political correctness," in many respects Borneman's approach resembles the way in which scholars from any number of disciplines study jazz today: not only as a matter of sound, but as a form of music embedded in a social context and laden with symbolic meanings that connects it to its producers and listeners alike. Researchers explore these elements, but they also look to the role played by community building and socialization, discourse, dance, reading, even clothing. They do so from an anthropological perspective that does not judge cultural achievements according to pre-existing hierarchies, but examines each on its own terms, seeking to identify the factors at work in a particular case. Casting about beyond acknowledged "high brow culture," they stress the legitimacy of popular culture as embraced and expressed by the masses. Such work also remains sensitive to issues of political power and hierarchies. Expressing solidarity with and respect for the achievements and opinions of a suppressed minority, it acknowledges the claim of such groups to articulate their rights at a political level. Scholars work from a broad geographical perspective that moves beyond national restrictions or "the West" to take a global approach, with a particular interest in the "black Atlantic," or the transfer and acculturation of African musical traditions on the American continent. Like Borneman, such an approach rests on the assumption that culture is never "pure" but exists only in hybrid form, as a mix of different elements. And like Borneman, some of this research is also still ahead of the times, in the way it considers the relationship between sounds and visions, or rather the visualization of jazz. Indeed, one of Borneman's greatest achievements from the early days, when hardly anyone had addressed jazz from an academic perspective, was to have established intersubjective, verifiable standards of analysis that moved the discourse on jazz away from questions of taste to a higher, more objective level. Borneman did this moreover as an autodidact whose talent was never recognized by academia, just like many of the African American scholars he so admired. Paul Oliver considered him "probably the most diversely talented historian jazz ever had, able to draw on a wide range of references to support his arguments."[370] In West Germany, too, the breadth of his intellectual horizon was praised, with Ulrich Olshausen of the *Frankfurter Allgemeine Zeitung* lauding his "magnificent, wide-ranging historical perspective."[371] In many respects then, although most of his work has long been forgotten, Ernest Borneman ranks among the classic thinkers in international jazz research.

Notes

1. Hentoff and McCarthy, *Jazz: New Perspectives on the History of Jazz*.
2. *Jazz Journal*, no. 29, 1976. The secondary literature on Ernest Borneman's significance as a "jazz critic" is not extensive; see Grünzweig, "Not Just a 'One Night Stand'"; Schaal, "Der vergessene Jazzkritiker."
3. Grünzweig, "Not Just a 'One Night Stand,'" 113.
4. Borneman, *Die Ur-Szene*, 355, 370.
5. Gennari, *Blowin' Hot and Cool*, 4.
6. Borneman to Leon Wolff, n.d.
7. This and the following quotes in *Jazz Monthly*, February 1957, 32.
8. *Jazz Monthly*, December 1957, 32.
9. This and the following in Borneman, "The Jazz Cult, I," 142.
10. Geiss, *Panafrikanismus*, 11.
11. Ernest Borneman, "Curriculum vitae," RB, *BC* 1.
12. Borneman, *Die Ur-Szene*, 361; interview in Borneman, *The Face on the Cutting-Room Floor*, 265.
13. Ibid.; Borneman, "Rezension John F. Sweed," 64; Borneman, *Die Ur-Szene*, 366.
14. Boatfield, "From the Sidelines," 68.
15. As presented by Derrick Stewart-Baxter in *Jazz Journal* 6/3, March 1953, 4, and April 1953, 16. Borneman to Eva, 18 November 1941 and to Erich Themmel, 15 December 1982. In retrospect the number had grown to "close to a hundred." "Many of them have become classics, now considered 'traditional,'" he noted. "Aside from me, I don't think that any other white person has ever written verses that speak the idiom of classic blues so well."
16. Borneman, *Die Ur-Szene*, 357–59.
17. See Borneman's diary-like notes from 11 and 12 July 1933 on untitled papers in AdK, EBA.
18. "Seltsamer Abend mit Rusche," n.d.
19. Eva to Ernest, 14 April 1942.
20. Ernest to Eva, 14 June 1941.
21. For more detailed information on the group and its London context, see Fryer, *Staying Power*, 334–51. See also Robinson, *Black Marxism*, 241–86; Buhle, *C. L. R. James*, 38–56.
22. Student Movement House Appeal (Mary Trevelyan) to Under Secretary of State, Home Office, 18 July 1941.
23. Dhondy, *C. L. R. James*, 55; Worcester, *C. L. R. James*, xv. See also the firsthand account in Held, "Geschichte einer Freundschaft."
24. C. L. R. James, [1936]; Metropolitan Police, Special Branch, Cyril Lionel Robert James, 3 March 1937; C. L. R. James, 30 March 1937, both files in NA, KV2/1824.
25. Borneman, *Die Ur-Szene*, 301.
26. Borneman to Geisel, 20 September 1942; Borneman to unnamed (Presumably Rudolf Hans Hiller), 3 May 1944. His recollections were similar in a letter to Eva dated 22 October 1947.

27. Eva to Ernest, 26 October 1942.

28. Borneman, *Die Ur-Szene*, 309.

29. This and the following quote in Borneman, "Black Light and White Shadow: Notes for a History of American Negro Music," 27.

30. Ibid.

31. Hertha to Ernest, 3 August 1933.

32. Hertha to Ernest, 29 January 1934.

33. Hertha to Ernest, 7 February 1934.

34. Ernest Borneman, *London Belated News*, 13 April 1937. See also Borneman, "Black Light and White Shadow: Notes for a History of American Negro Music," 26.

35. Vernon Kell to General MacBrian, 23 December 1936; Metropolitan Police, Special Branch, Cyril Lionel Robert James, 3 March 1937, both in NA, KV2/1824.

36. Borneman, *Die Ur-Szene*, 298. See also "Korrupte SPÖ, Gott-Vater Kreisky & sexfeindliche Eminenzen."

37. As he wrote appreciatively about the ideas of a Communist waiter who had worked all over the world before landing in a London club ("Seltsamer Abend mit Rusche," n.d.).

38. Copy of extracts from report on Ernst Bornemann, associate of James, 9 May 1939, NA, KV2/1824; Held, "Geschichte einer Freundschaft," 58.

39. Borneman to Andreas Marck, 27 June 1983, as reprinted in Standow, *Ein lüderliches Leben*, 343.

40. Ernest to Eva, 20 September 1942.

41. Eva Borneman to Richard Wright, 8 November 1945, YUBL, Richard Wright Papers, 94/1225; Address book of Eva Borneman, n.d. (Canada years).

42. Borneman to James, 20 August 1946.

43. Eva to Ernest, 19 September 1941; Borneman to James, 2 January 1958 and 27 November 1958; Borneman, *Die Ur-Szene*, 300.

44. Worcester, *C. L. R. James*, xii–xiii.

45. Borneman, *Die Ur-Szene*, 304, 306. Kenyatta actually figures as the character Joe Banyan in Borneman's novels *A Love Story* and *The Compromisers*.

46. Ernest Borneman, "Tonfilmversuche, Nr. 3, Eine kleine Nachtmusik: Gegenwartsvariationen über ein Mozartsches Thema," n.d.

47. Schwartz, *How Britain Got the Blues*, 7–8.

48. Eva to Ernest, 29 July 1941.

49. F. E. Attwood (Decca) to Borneman, 3 April 1956.

50. Schwartz, *How Britain Got the Blues*, 10–16.

51. Borneman, "Jazz Cult, I," 145–46. Reprinted with part II in Condon and Gehman, *Eddie Condon's Treasury of Jazz*.

52. Ibid., 143.

53. Ernest to Curt, 5 January 1947.

54. Borneman to Howard E. Penny, 4 August 1944; Borneman to Bob Thiele, 28 January 1944. See Borneman, "Boogie Woogie."

55. See Schwartz, *How Britain Got the Blues*, 16.

56. See, for example, Borneman to Wright, 30 January 1942; and Ernest Borneman, "American Negro Music," n.d.; both located in YUBL, Richard Wright Papers, 94/1225. The earliest memos to be found in his estate papers date back to 1935 (Borneman, "American Negro Music," 1; Ernest to Eva, 6 November 1935). In 1945, Borneman sent a manuscript to Max Jones supposedly written around 1935, which was "immature and now terribly outdated," but "still about thirty percent ahead of mainstream jazz sociology today as it was back then, too" (Borneman to Jones, 16 March 1945).

57. Ernest Borneman to the editors of *Downbeat*, 9 November 1939 (draft).

58. Eva to Ernest, 28 July 1941.

59. See, for example, Ernest Borneman to Max Jones, 16 March 1945; and Borneman to Bob Thiele, 21 March 1945.

60. Mahlon J. Rentschler to Borneman, 28 November 1939.

61. Ernest Jules Borneman, "A Bibliography of American Negro Music with a short introduction on African Native Music intended as a supplement to D. H. Varley's Royal Empire Society Bibliography No. 8" (Ms.), 13 February 1940, AdK, EBA 115.

62. Ernest Borneman, "American Negro Music: A Preliminary Inquiry into the Origin of Ring Shouts, Spirituals, Work Songs, Blues, Minstrelsy, Ragtime, Jazz and Swing Music," n.d., AdK, EBA 3.

63. Borneman to Herskovits, 18 April 1940, NUL, 35/6/4/5.

64. See the correspondence in NUL 35/6 and Eva to Ernest, 8 June 1940; Ernest to Eva, 8 November 1940.

65. Borneman to Herskovits, 22 December 1940, NUL, 35/6/4/5.

66. Herskovits to Borneman, 21 October 1940; Herskovits to Edgar J. Fisher, 25 November 1940; both in NUL, 35/6/4/5.

67. Herskovits to Lillian C. Lehman, NUL, 35/6/4/5.

68. Herskovits to Guggenheim Foundation, 8 January 1947, NUL, 35/6/37/21.

69. UNESCO, Application for Employment [Ernest Borneman], 18 June 1947, UNESCO Archives, PER/REC 1/79.

70. Smith to Borneman, 30 June 1940.

71. Borneman to Herskovits, 18 April 1940, NUL, 35/6/4/5.

72. Ernest Borneman (National Film Board), "A Draft Prospectus on American Negro Film Production: Finance and Story Aspects," n.d.

73. Gabbard, ed., *Representing Jazz*.

74. Borneman to Willingham, 15 June 1946.

75. Borneman to Wright, 30 January 1942, YUBL, Richard Wright Papers, 94/1225.

76. Borneman, "Swing Music: An Encyclopedia of Jazz," n.d., 24.

77. Ibid.

78. Borneman to Jim Higgins, 13 February 1947.

79. Borneman, "Swing Music," 519; following quote 552.

80. According to Brecht in Müller, *Die Funktion der Geschichte im Werk Bertolt Brechts*.

81. This and the following in Borneman, "Swing Music," 545–46.

82. Ibid., 546.

83. Ibid., 550.

84. Ibid., 565–68

85. Excerpts from Herskovits, *The Myth of the Negro Past*. On Herskovits, see Gershenhorn, *Melville J. Herskovits and the Racial Politics of Knowledge*.

86. Ernest to Eva, 18 November 1941 and 7 February 1942.

87. Borneman to Wright, 30 January 1942, YUBL, Richard Wright Papers, 94/1225. On Wright at the NFB see Ellis, *John Grierson*, 142.

88. Borneman to Wright, 28 April 1945, YUBL, Richard Wright Papers, 94/1225.

89. Ibid.

90. Ernest to Eva, 21 February 1942.

91. Borneman to Dance, 16 August 1962.

92. Borneman to Gullickson, 15 September 1944.

93. Smith to Borneman, 24 October 1944.

94. McCarthy, "The Literature of Jazz," 174.

95. Smith to Borneman, 6 February 1946.

96. Editorial in the *Record Changer*, February 1948.

97. Smith to Borneman, 30 June 1940.

98. Schwartz, *How Britain Got the Blues*, 24.

99. Borneman to W. C. Handy, 30 January 1945.

100. Max Jones to Borneman, 13 March 1945.

101. Oliver, "Taking the Measure of the Blues," 32. Bob Groom also acknowledged Borneman as an early blues researcher; see Groom, *The Blues Revival*, 89.

102. Mezzrow and Wolfe, *Really the Blues*, 332.

103. Borneman, *A Critic Looks at Jazz*, 25.

104. Ibid., 28.

105. Counter to Borneman, find a stronger continuity in Roberts, *Black Music of Two Worlds*, 57–58, 71. See Gennari, *Blowin' Hot and Cool*, 16.

106. Borneman, *A Critic Looks at Jazz*, 32.

107. Ibid., 36.

108. Ibid., 38.

109. Ibid., 44.

110. Ibid., 47.

111. Ibid., 53.

112. Borneman to Handy, 30 January 1945.

113. Borneman, "The Roots of Jazz," 17 (slightly different version in *Past and Future*).

114. Sundquist, *To Wake the Nations*, 322.

115. Gullickson to Borneman, 23 February 1946; see also Ertegun to Borneman, 9 June 1947.

116. Ertegun was in complete agreement, Gullilckson assured Borneman, "that you have provided the *Record Changer* with the best jazz-writing ever printed in any jazz magazine and that he was anxious for you to continue contributions" (Gullickson to Borneman, 22 May 1947). A selection of letters to the editor can be found as an enclosure with the letter in Borneman to Wright, 28 April 1945, YUBL, Richard Wright Papers, 94/1225. A debate with Roger Pryor Dodge is printed in Dodge, *Hot Jazz and Jazz Dance*, 126–39.

117. *Record Changer*, August 1947, 6.

118. Borneman, "The Anthropologist Looks Back." It is here he took issue with Rudi Blesh's book *Shining Trumpets* (New York: Knopf, 1949).

119. Borneman to Ertegun, 7 June 1947.

120. Ernest Borneman, "A History of American Negro Music," n.d., YUBL, Richard Wright Papers, 89/1087b.

121. Borneman to Dunham, 21 February 1949; Borneman, *Die Ur-Szene*, 367.

122. Clippings in AdK, EBA 34 and at the Jazz Institute in Darmstadt.

123. Max Jones to Borneman, 22 December 1945.

124. Borneman to Pat Brand, [April 1950].

125. Gendron, *Between Montmartre and the Mudd Club*.

126. *Melody Maker*, 8 November 1952.

127. Borneman's position in *Melody Maker*, 23 September 1950.

128. Schwartz, *How Britain Got the Blues*, 18–19.

129. Hobsbawm, *The Jazz Scene*, 252–69.

130. See Schwartz, *How Britain Got the Blues*, 39–44.

131. *Melody Maker*, 29 September 1951.

132. Ibid.

133. Borneman to Jim Higgins, 13 February 1947.

134. Borneman, "The Jazz Cult, II," 261.

135. *DownBeat*, 30 July 1947.

136. Borneman, "The Jazz Cult, II," 273.

137. Gendron, *Between Montmartre and the Mudd Club*, 150.

138. Borneman, "The Jazz Cult, II," 272.

139. Graves, "Zur Geschichte des Blues," 7.

140. He covers this in detail in his two-part article "Both Schools of Critics Wrong" in *DownBeat*, 30 July and 13 August 1947.

141. Quoted in Gendron, *Between Montmartre and the Mudd Club*, 136.

142. *Record Changer*, January 1946, 8.

143. Borneman, *Die Ur-Szene*, 366.

144. Borneman to Jim [Moynahan], 15 June 1945.

145. Borneman, "King Jazz," 9.

146. Ernest to Eva, 9 December 1947.

147. *DownBeat*, 14 January 1948.

148. Periodization according to Gendron, *Between Montmartre and the Mudd Club*, 151–55.

149. Borneman's report on the festival in *DownBeat*, 24 March 1948.

150. *Melody Maker*, 15 July 1950.

151. Borneman to Eva, 7 March 1948.

152. *DownBeat*, 7 April 1948, reprinted in Berrett, *The Louis Armstrong Companion*, 144–51, here 147, 151. See Borneman, *Die Ur-Szene*, 366.

153. *DownBeat*, 8 September 1948.

154. Campbell, *Exiled in Paris*.

155. Borneman, "Les racines de la musique Américaine Noire." See Rowley, *Richard Wright*, 363–64.

156. Ernest to Pete Davis, 14 February 1948.

157. Ernest to Eva, 26 October 1947.

158. *DownBeat*, 16 June 1948.

159. Borneman, letter to unknown addressee (presumably Hiller), 29 May 1948. Quote from Boris Vian in *Jazz Hot*, no. 23 (May 1948), in Vian, *Oeuvres*, 169. See Miles Kington's introduction in Zwerin, *Round About Close to Midnight*.

160. Ernest to Eva, 29 May 1948.

161. Borneman, letter to unknown addressee (presumably Hiller), 24 July 1948; articles in *DownBeat*, 25 August and 8 September 1948. See Borneman, *Die Ur-Szene*, 366.

162. Borneman to Godbolt, 10 February 1950.

163. *Melody Maker*, 10 June 1950.

164. *Melody Maker*, 1 September 1951.

165. *Melody Maker*, 8 September 1951. Critique by Steve Race in *Melody Maker*, 15 September 1951.

166. Borneman, "Zur Frage einer wertfreien Jazzforschung."

167. *Melody Maker*, 31 July 1954.

168. Monson, *Saying Something*. On the perspective of musicians see esp. Porter, *What Is this Thing Called Jazz?*

169. *Melody Maker*, 5 April 1952.

170. Ibid.

171. *Melody Maker*, 24 May 1952.

172. *New Musical Express (NME)*, 17 October 1952; *Melody Maker*, 25 October 1952, *Daily Herald*, 11 October 1952.

173. Melody Maker, 16 June 1951.

174. Melody Maker, 27 March 1954.

175. Untitled, n.d.

176. "The Midnight Memories: An Original TV Musical by Ernest Borneman."

177. Ernest to his parents, 11 November 1953.

178. *Four O'Clock in the Morning Blues: A Dance Play*, written and directed by Ernest Borneman.

179. Ernest to his father, 20 March 1954.

180. *Jazz Journal*, no. 4 (April 1954).

181. Art Darton to Chief Producer, BBC Television Service, 10 March 1954.

182. Ted Hallock (*DownBeat*) to Head of BBC Television, 9 March 1954.

183. *Daily Dispatch*, 23 February 1954.

184. *Birmingham Gazette*, undated clipping.

185. Borneman, *Die Ur-Szene*, 369–70. See also the interview in Borneman, *The Face on the Cutting-Room Floor*, 265.

186. Borneman to Desmond Davis, 15 March 1954.

187. Synopsis of *Betty Slow Drag*, n.d.

188. German synopsis of *Betty Slow Drag*, n.d.

189. Ibid.

190. Eva Geisel, "Betty Slow Drag," n.d.

191. Untitled, n.d.

192. Borneman to John Grierson, 21 July 1953, University of Stirling, John Grierson Archive.

193. Grierson to [illegible addressee], 24 January 1953; Edinburgh Film Festival [illegible signature], 4 August 1953, both at the University of Sterling, John Grierson Archive. See also Borneman's version in his letter to Isador Caplan, 9 February 1955.

194. Ernest to father and Erna Neumann, 20 March 1953.

195. *New Musical Express* (*NME*), 21 February 1953; *Melody Maker*, 12 September 1953.

196. On Mili's film, see Knight, "Jammin' the Blues, or the Sight of Jazz, 1944."

197. *Jazz Journal*, August 1953, 15. For more on the resonance in the press, see Borneman's letter to John Grierson, 21 July 1953, University of Stirling, John Grierson Archive.

198. Printed in several newspapers, including *Hamburger Anzeiger*, 24 June 1954.

199. Quotes from the press review: *Betty Slow Drag*, press reports, n.d.

200. A master script of *Trumpet Story* has been preserved in Borneman's papers.

201. *Kinematograph Weekly*, 4 February 1954.

202. [Overview of press resonance], n.d.

203. Oliver, *Songsters and Saints*, 5; Lang, *The Background of the Blues*; Borneman, *A Critic Looks at Jazz*, 40.

204. Borneman to Max Jones, 5 January 1946.

205. Schwartz, "Preaching the Gospel of the Blues," 147. In the midst of the boom in British blues, Borneman clearly reaffirmed his affinity for the blues in 1963 in Borneman, "Some Jazz Myths Questioned."

206. Moore, *Inside British Jazz*, 65.

207. *Melody Maker*, 14 February 1948.

208. *Melody Maker*, 27 May 1950, 13 January 1951, 5 January 1952, and 30 August 1952.

209. *Melody Maker*, 6 May 1950.

210. *Melody Maker*, 26 May 1951.

211. *DownBeat*, 16 June 1948.

212. *Melody Maker*, 2 June 1951. See also 3 March 1951 and 31 January 1953.

213. Schwartz, *How Britain Got the Blues*, 8–9.

214. Borneman to Lester Koenig, 2 January 1959.

215. *Melody Maker*, 8 November 1952 and 22 August 1953. See Moore, *Inside British Jazz*, 65.

216. Schwartz, *How Britain Got the Blues*, 20.

217. Borneman, *A Critic Looks at Jazz*, 38–39.

218. Borneman, "The Blues: A Study in Ambiguity," 76.

219. Ibid., 91.

220. Borneman, *Die Ur-Szene*, 357.

221. *Melody Maker*, 30 August 1952. On the development of blues from a subgenre of jazz to an idiom of pop culture, see the overview in Oliver, "Blue-Eyed Blues."

222. See Schwartz, *How Britain Got the Blues*, 52–53.

223. *Melody Maker*, 4 April 1953.

224. *Melody Maker*, 17 October 1953.

225. Ernest Borneman to Pat Brand, 19 February 1957; and "Don't Knock the Rock: An Answer to Vic Lewis by Ernest Borneman," n.d. [1958].

226. Borneman to Higgins, 3 May 1947.

227. Schwartz, *How Britain Got the Blues*, 68.

228. Cf. Osgerby, *Youth in Britain since 1945*, 119–20.

229. As quoted in Marwick, *The Sixties*, 68.

230. Borneman to Pat Brand, 19 February 1957.

231. Manuscript "Don't Knock the Rock: An Answer to Vic Lewis by Ernest Borneman," n.d. [1958].

232. Ibid.

233. Ibid.

234. Ernest Borneman, "Zur Frage einer wertfreien Jazzforschung," n.d. (late 1970s).

235. Monson, *Freedom Sounds.*

236. Borneman to Stanley Dance, 20 September 1956.

237. Borneman to José Shelley, 4 November 1942.

238. In *Jazzforschung/Jazz Research* 8 (1976): 233. He was even more dramatic when dismantling a book by Werner Faulstich in *Jahrbuch für Volksliedforschung* 25 (1980): 147–48.

239. In *Jazzforschung/Jazz Research* 5 (1973): 186–87, here 186.

240. Ibid.

241. See Gennari, *Blowin' Hot and Cool,* 7–8.

242. *Jazz Monthly*, December 1957, 32.

243. Borneman's tax returns are held in the collection Sammlung Borneman, StDK.

244. Ernest to father, 12 March 1951.

245. Ernest to father, 2 November 1950.

246. Father to Ernest, 14 December 1950; father to Ernest, 18 January 1951.

247. Erna to Eva, 8 July 1951.

248. Berendt, *Ein Fenster aus Jazz*, 259. See Siegfried, *Time is on my Side*, 359–61. In general, see Gilroy, *The Black Atlantic.*

249. Marx, "The White Negro."

250. Gilroy, *The Black Atlantic.*

251. Curt to Ernest, 6 August 1948.

252. Borneman to Günter Boas, 25 August 1954, LRM.

253. Berendt, *Ein Fenster aus Jazz*, 20; Berendt, "Ernest Borneman und die weiblichen Stimmen," 116.

254. Correspondence in LRM.

255. Helms to Borneman, 15 January 1954.

256. Dauer to Borneman, 13 December 1954.

257. *DownBeat*, 6 October 1948.

258. *Melody Maker*, 17 October 1953.

259. Monod, *Settling Scores.*

260. *Melody Maker*, 3 May 1952.

261. Borneman, 1954 calender.

262. *Jazz Podium* 7/9 (September 1958): 180.

263. Ernest Borneman, "Jazz on the Continent": [No. 1] Germany (manuscript of a BBC program in 1959).

264. Borneman to Jeffrey Kruger, London, 25 June 1963.

265. Borneman, "Ninth German Jazz Festival."

266. Berendt, "Ernest Borneman und die weiblichen Stimmen," 117.

267. Borneman to Berendt, 23 July 1987.

268. Borneman developed his thesis on the "Spanish tinge" in jazz in greater detail in an article that was published several times, "Creole Echoes." A forty-four-page undated manuscript, "The African Rebound," presumably from the late 1950s or early 1960s, is based on these texts, some of which he further expounds upon. It was possibly intended as a chapter in a longer work on jazz.

269. Ernst Borneman, "Congo Square: Eine Neudeutung der Jazzgeschichte, Teil eins: Die afro-europäische Tradition," n.d., unnumbered pages.

270. Ernest Borneman, "The Spanish Tinge (Die Spanische Färbung)," handwritten note: RIAS 1958.

271. Borneman, "Jazz und die kreolische Volksmusik," n.d.; Borneman, "Jazz and the Creole Tradition."

272. Ernest Borneman, "The African Rebound," 41–42, n.d.

273. Borneman, "Creole Echoes," 70.

274. Pat Brand to Borneman, 18 February 1957 and 21 February 1957.

275. Borneman to Pat Brand, 19 February 1957.

276. According to Latino expert Derick Armstrong, as cited in Borneman, "The Record Companies," 27.

277. Ernest Borneman, Die kubanische Volksmusik, Bremen, April 1959.

278. *Melody Maker*, 30 July 1955.

279. Berendt, *Ein Fenster aus Jazz*, 20.

280. Borneman to Ms. Chavez (Decca), London, 12 March 1957; Armstrong, "Cuban Music—A Reply."
281. Schuller, *Early Jazz*, 14–15.
282. Raeburn, "Beyond the 'Spanish Tinge,'" 26.
283. Borneman, *Die Ur-Szene*, 368.
284. Borneman to Michael Frostick, 28 May 1959.
285. Borneman to Huber, 7 July 1960, BAK, B 263/110.
286. Borneman to Hilpert, 12 September 1961
287. More in Siegfried, *Time is on my Side*, 332–54.
288. Borneman to Gladenbeck and Schmidt, 5 April 1960, BAK, B 263/42.
289. For more detail, see Hill, "Television and Pop."
290. "Jazz Club: Ein Programmvorschlag von Ernest Borneman," 8 June 1964, RB, *BC* 1.
291. Ibid.
292. Ibid.
293. Ibid.
294. See Schmidt-Joos, *My Back Pages*, 11–17.
295. Borneman, *Die Ur-Szene*, 368; Schmidt-Joos to Abich, 25 May 1964, RB, *BC* 1.
296. [File note Bachmüller], 15 June 1964, RB, Folder GEMA-Meldungen und Mitwirkende; Leckebusch's handwritten note on the proposal "Altona Ramblers," 15 June 1964, RB, *BC* 1.
297. "Beat-Klub: Ein Fernsehprogramm von Ernest Borneman," n.d.
298. Leckebusch to Programming Director, 16 June 1965, RB, *BC* 1; Announcement text for 25 September 1965, RB, *BC* 1.
299. B. to K., 30 July 1965, RB, *BC* 1.
300. Leckebusch to S., 1 December 1965, RB, *BC* 1.
301. Letter to Heinz Kerneck, draft, n.d., no sender.
302. See the entries in his calendar from 1965.
303. According to talks with the writer on 23 January 1998.
304. Both versions in RB, *BC* 1.
305. Attorneys Dr. Salander et al. to attorney Dr. Klaus Gätjen, 18 July 1968; Schmidt-Joos, *My Back Pages*, 11.
306. Borneman to attorney Friedrich Fromm, 25 September 1965.
307. Borneman to Gleason, 21 May 1959.
308. Kofsky, *Black Nationalism and the Revolution in Music*; Floyd, *The Power of Black Music*.
309. Monson, *Freedom Sounds*, 5, 15.
310. Ege, *Schwarz werden*.
311. *Melody Maker*, 14 February 1948.
312. Feather, "Not Ashamed of the Blues."
313. Borneman, "Ashamed of Race"; "Ashamed of Race II." The foundation for this argument had appeared in his very first article for the *Record Changer* in April 1944, p. 5.
314. Ernest to Curt and Erna, 15 September 1965.
315. Ernest to Curt, 25 March 1971. Quote: Grünzweig, "Not Just a 'One Night Stand,'" 114.
316. It was evident that Borneman valued Oliver's work from a review he wrote of one of Oliver's later books, in *Jazzforschung* 3/4 (1971–72): 256.
317. Borneman to his father, 17 September 1965; Borneman to Frank Kofsky, 22 May 1965.
318. L. Jones, *Blues People*, 86.
319. Garon, *Blues and the Poetic Spirit*, 61.
320. Cf. Schwartz, *How Britain Got the Blues*, 231–37.
321. Berendt, *Blues*, no page numbers, with reference to Eldridge Cleaver. This point is reinforced again in Berendt, *Das große Jazzbuch*, 178–80.
322. Berendt, *Blues*, no page numbers.
323. See also Rau's self-critical reflections in Brigl and Schmidt-Joos, *Fritz Rau*, 149. There were also early observations that the AFBF was more like a "zoo" or an "ethnographic museum." See, for example, Zimmer, "Der Blues ist überall," 232. For more recent scholarship, see Adelt, *Blues Music in the Sixties*, 78-82.

324. Keil, *Urban Blues*, 34–37.

325. See Siegfried, *Time is on my Side*, 369–72.

326. Keil, *Urban Blues*, 34–37. See also Groom's *The Blues Revival*, in which he argues that Keil's exaggerated depiction was an unjustified attack on the musicians and audience (86).

327. Hurley, *The Return of Jazz*, 60–63.

328. Berendt, *Blues*. Some passages in the book came from an article he published in *Jazz Podium*, no. 10 (1968).

329. Ege, *Schwarz werden*, 72.

330. Salzinger, *Rock Power oder Wie musikalisch ist die Revolution?*, 20.

331. As Baraka turned away from "Black Nationalism" to embrace Maoism, Sollors published an analysis of his work from a biographical perspective in Sollors, *Amiri Baraka/LeRoi Jones*.

332. Sollors and Weyergraf, "Nachwort," 299–300. On the following, see p. 301, 308–10.

333. Miller, "Vorwort."

334. Schwarze Zelle Neukölln/Kreuzberg, "White Panther, Schweine sind nicht immer rosa!," in the "APO und soziale Bewegungen" archive of the faculty of political and social sciences at the Freie Universität Berlin, Anarchisten Berlin, Flugblätter. See Ege, *Schwarz werden*, 34.

335. *Frankfurter Rundschau*, 17 October 1969.

336. As quoted in Schwartz, *How Britain Got the Blues*, 236.

337. Berendt, "The Blues got white—got he?," 316.

338. Borneman, "Black Light and White Shadow: Notes for a History of American Negro Music," 30.

339. In 1954, for example, *Das Internationale Podium* (no. 3, 11–13; no. 4, 12–13.) published a two-part article based on a section of the book translated by Berendt: "Sklaverei und die Wurzeln der Negermusik in Amerika."

340. Oliver to Borneman, 15 December 1970. Borneman's review of the series in *Jazzforschung/Jazz Research* 2 (1970): 192–93.

341. Borneman to Gleason, 21 May 1959.

342. Gennari, *Blowin' Hot and Cool*, 9.

343. Ernest Borneman, "Black Light and White Shadow: After Black Power, What?," n.d.

344. Ibid., 34.

345. Quotes from Borneman's "The Roots of Jazz," which appeared in 1959, in L. Jones, *Blues People*, 24–25, 31, 42.

346. Radano, *New Musical Figurations*, 26.

347. Borneman, "Some Jazz Myths Questioned."

348. Ibid., 7.

349. Ibid., 8.

350. *Jazz* 2 (February 1963): 3.

351. Ibid., 23.

352. Berendt, *Ein Fenster aus Jazz*, 201. Other letters to the editor about Borneman's pieces, which according to the editorial staff would have sufficed for an entire issue of the magazine, were printed in the March issue.

353. Borneman to the Editor of *Jazz*, 13 March 1963. He reaffirmed his position in an additional statement and a later answer to Jones in the December 1965 issue of the same magazine (Ernest Borneman's answer to "Will Jazz Survive the Century?," in *Jazz* [March 1963]: 22, and in Borneman, "Form and Content in Jazz").

354. For this quote and the following, see Borneman, "Form and Content in Jazz," 22, 30.

355. Borneman, Black Light and White Shadow," 13–14.

356. Gennari, *Blowin' Hot and Cool*, 8.

357. Note, 12 July 1933.

358. Ernest to Eva, 6 November 1935.

359. Ernest to Eva, 4 January 1949.

360. Ernest to Eva, 30 December 1947.

361. Borneman to Wright, 14 December 1945, YUBL, Richard Wright Papers, 94/1225.

362. Ibid.

363. Borneman to Gullickson, 16 August 1944.

364. Geiss, *Panafrikanismus*, 9.

365. This and the following in ibid., 249 and 427, note 65.

366. Borneman, "Some Jazz Myths Questioned," 6.

367. Borneman, "Rezension von John F. Sweed."

368. Borneman to Hans Pehl, 17 February 1995.

369. *Bookforum*, June 2002, http://www.robertchristgau.com/xg/bkrev/gendron-02.php (accessed 14 January 2014).

370. Oliver, "That Certain Feeling," 14.

371. *FAZ*, April 17, 1971.

Chapter 3

SEEING
LIFE ON THE BIG SCREEN

It was not only in the world of sound that Ernest Borneman immersed himself in theoretical questions, but also that of images. Ultimately, however, he dug even further into practicalities. He once remarked in retrospect that his interest in cinema had come from the films of Germany's Weimar Republic. "Nothing has left a stronger mark on my memory than the first impressions left behind by *Metropolis, Spione, Die Frau im Mond* and *M.*"[1] Once in London, his initial interest was largely in film. Many of Borneman's earliest friends from his days in the British capital—Jack Chambers, Jack Sheerboom, Jim Harris, Pete Davis, and Jim Turner—were film enthusiasts and members of the Socialist-Communist film group Kino. It was in this milieu that the young emigrant Borneman set out to "achieve something."[2] His friend Rudolph "Hannes" Hiller recalled an early conversation about the topic at the Hermitage: "It was all about how to gatecrash into the film business. I remember you saying that the main thing was to get your foot in the door," regardless of whether it was as a cameraman or a janitor.[3] Borneman's first journalistic piece dealt with film, which he also began writing a book about under the working title "The Mechanized Muse."[4]

Borneman's technical interest in film was readily apparent from his early studies of sound recording, the relationship between sound and image, and film cutting techniques. He also made repeated reference to his collaboration with Erich von Hornbostel, who had constructed a device to record and analyze the "so-called 'significant tone' and other overtone and timbre effects in African folk music" on thirty-five-millimeter film that used the entire width of the film to record sound, rather than the customary narrow sound strip.[5] Using a selenium cell, an optical image of music could be created to determine exactly "when a singer or an instrument started up, how high or low each note was, which vibrato was being used, and which waves were blending to create the timbres." This led to a series of experiments with synthetic sound. Hornbostel not only worked with special optical effects, Borneman noted, but also "extensively with the corresponding effects on the acoustic side—synthetic sound, pre-recorded sound, electronic instruments etc."

Borneman's first longer text on the topic, "Sound Rhythm and the Film," was published in 1934 in the British film magazine *Sight and Sound*. The piece described the latest experiments with talking films, which took up with the pioneering work of Edmund Meisel. Meisel, who had composed the music for *Battleship Potemkin* and *October* (dir. Sergei Eisenstein) as well as *Berlin—Symphony of a Metropolis* (dir. Walter Ruttmann) and had collaborated with Bertolt Brecht and Erwin Piscator, wanted to prove that assembling a film followed the same rules as a musical composition. Writing in the first person plural, Borneman described experiments at a German film institute in Berlin that began with Meisel's work but went a step further by cutting visual and sound materials in parallel. The goal was to investigate the idea of "visual music," in which sound and vision complement one another. What these experiments showed, Borneman wrote, was that only instrumental music strengthened the impact of the images; vocal music by contrast distracted the audience, dividing its attention between sound and image. Nowhere in the article did Borneman clarify who the "we" was of whom he spoke; it is only suggested that the author was part of a team working on scientific questions about talking film. Borneman was presumably referring to his work under Hornbostel, which sought to visualize the differences in the breadth and frequency of vibrato, timbre, and pitch with the help of thirty-five-millimeter film. In a later source he clarifies the situation somewhat: while working on the experiments with Hornbostel, Meisel had contacted him about the idea of using the device to develop "synthetic sounds" for film.[6]

Other jobs similarly mentioned in passing include work as a sound assistant for various record companies and film production companies.[7] Borneman found his first permanent post in 1935–36 at Criterion Films, led by Douglas Fairbanks Jr. As a "film editor," he summarized and reviewed books, screenplays, and stage plays. None of his assignments ever became films in their own right, but he was involved in four company productions, including *The Amateur Gentleman* (1936) and *Crime over London* (1936).[8] As television emerged, Borneman joined the newly established television branch of the BBC as an intern, later detailing his enthusiasm for electronic cameras and the possibilities of live television and describing his role in the famous early live broadcasts of the BBC, such as the coronation procession of King George VI in 1937, the boat race from Oxford to Cambridge in 1939, and the derby that same year.[9] Apart from ex post facto statements, no independent sources corroborate any of this, leaving the truth of such claims somewhat dubious. Borneman was most likely in contact with people working for British documentary filmmaker John Grierson in the 1930s; his personal papers at any rate include a friend's invitation to attend an event with Raymond Spottiswoode—whom Borneman surely knew—at the Student Movement House, which Borneman often frequented.[10] Even before the war broke out, Borneman worked for the film department of the British ministry of intelligence, assuming the role of technical advisor for a film production company at London's Ealing Studios directly after.[11] Borneman's literary works reflect the fact that he had actually gotten his foot in the door in the film industry, most clearly in his first novel *The Face on the Cutting-Room Floor* (1937), which vividly describes the atmosphere of a film studio through the people working there, filming conditions, editing techniques, and special effects. Indeed, he later claimed everything that happened in the book had been taken directly from his own life story while earning a living at Criterion Films.[12] Set against the backdrop of "the clapping of the scissors and the rustle of the celluloid and the rotating of the winder," the story is told convincingly, peppered with film business jargon and detailed descriptions.[13]

Borneman's work in film and television can be divided into three stages: first, his work at the National Film Board of Canada (NFB) in the 1940s; second, his freelance work on a number of films and television productions in the 1950s; and finally, his management work at Freies Fernsehen in West Germany at the beginning of the 1960s.

The National Film Board of Canada

On 17 May 1940 Borneman was sent to an internment camp, a fate that met many Germans living in Great Britain who were deemed to be "enemy aliens" in the wake of the seemingly unstoppable German offensive in Europe. The particular reason for the young Berliner's internment, as it later came out, was his proximity to Communist circles during his early years in London and the fact that he had roomed with C. L. R. James, who had aroused the suspicions of the British government as an internationally active Trotskyist of West Indian descent. Borneman was detained not as a Nazi, but as a purportedly active Communist.[14] He was initially held at Kempton Park on the outskirts of London and then transferred to Huyton near Liverpool before he was shipped off to Canada with a number of other internees just a few weeks later, on 3 July.[15]

About a year later John Grierson, the British documentary film pioneer, secured Borneman's release from the camp in order to hire him for the state-run National Film Board of Canada (NFB), which Grierson had set up in 1939.[16] Borneman's release was facilitated by Alexander Paterson, the head of the Prison Commission at the British Home Office, who liked Borneman and had been his "sponsor" back when he was in London.[17] The two men knew each other from when Borneman had translated for a delegation from the German Ministry of Justice during a 1934 visit to Great Britain. A prison reformer, Paterson had already put in a good word for Borneman when the latter had sought naturalization as a British citizen. He commented on Borneman's work for the ministry, noting that it was quite clear that Borneman's sympathies were "strongly anti-Nazi," and he recommended him as a "man of considerable ability and marked originality."[18] As it became clear to the Canadian government that it had not been sent the "Nazis" it was expecting, but rather refugees from Germany, it petitioned the British government to assist in finding a solution to the problem, which in turn identified Paterson as the right man for the job. Paterson helped to secure the release of many internees or facilitated their return to England.[19] In Borneman's case it was Paterson who told his friend Grierson, then searching for suitable personnel for the NFB, about Borneman's character and skills. After the immigration authorities signed off on his case, on 10 June 1941 the "enemy alien" Borneman was released from Camp N near Sherbrooke in Québec, from where he traveled to Ottawa to take up his new position at the NFB. He was joined at the NFB by other internees, at least one of whom Borneman had brought on board.[20] As is often recounted, a number of Jewish refugees and other foreigners found a home in Grierson's institute after being thoroughly vetted by the British and Canadian security offices.[21] They made up a very small number on the whole, however; records indicate that only 5 percent of the employees were foreign-born.[22] "We had great luck in getting Ernest released in Canada," Paterson told Borneman's girlfriend Eva not long after his release, as the British Army Headquarters had refused to agree to the release of the supposed Communist for quite some time.[23] One of Borneman's friends in the camp was the composer Fritz Grundland (aka Freddy Grant), who similarly considered Borneman's release as facilitated by the post at the NFB to be "a chance in a million."[24]

Borneman thus became one of the first employees of the NFB, whose ranks numbered sixty-three in August and grew only slightly through the fall of 1941, but had swelled to almost two hundred a year later.[25] Originally, Borneman was supposed to work as a "research man," but by mid-July had already sent in his first screenplay (working title: *Stamp Out Hitler*), to the delight of Grierson and his team, and translated the German films *Sieg im Westen* (*Victory in the West*) and *Feuertaufe* (*Baptism by Fire*).[26] The screenplay focused on special-issue stamps for the war effort (presumably released in 1941 under the title *Want to Buy a Bomb?*). His first foray into film production came in the form of a trip north with US anthropologist and ethnomusicologist Laura Bolton to shoot ethnological films about the life, work, and traditions of the indigenous peoples of Canada.[27] This first project was followed by a second joint effort between the two in the same year.[28] Borneman was already familiar with recording non-European music from his time working with Hornbostel, a skill he would continue to find good use for later in ethnomusicology studies about Africa. He was happy—he had finally gotten his foot in the door: "After years on the outside I'm finally on the inside of the movies, with responsibility and freedom and a chance to put at least part of my theories into practice."[29] On the other hand, he also missed his girlfriend, especially in the first few weeks—a situation that actually benefited his work. "I use work as dope," he wrote Eva. "What else can I do?" Even this did not take away from the deep satisfaction he felt with life at the time: "I cannot even appreciate the incredible luck of my present life—the freedom, the security, the job I always longed for, the continent I always strove at, the astonishing food of French Canada, the breathtaking elegance and chic of the French women, the magnificent coffee—none of it means as much as my mind tells me it should."[30]

Now in Canada, John Grierson was no longer an aesthete when it came to his documentary films but a social reformer. Grierson viewed documentaries as a political instrument ideally suited to influence social development, a means of education to enlighten the masses, and an instrument of propaganda to mobilize them.[31] As the most widespread audiovisual medium available for reaching great masses before the advent of television—especially young, less formally educated men and women—film was an incredibly effective instrument of propaganda. Although the NFB was financed by the government and was not revolutionary, but rather intended as a means of social reform, its political approach strengthened the appeal that documentary film held for the young leftists, "with a sprinkling of Communists," who found themselves working together at the NFB in Canada.[32] The NFB got its start just as World War II broke out, and its stormy early years were largely bound up in the project of turning the former British colony of Canada, first granted independence in 1931, into its own nation. For many who worked at the NFB, these two aspects were interrelated. They wanted to capitalize on the modernizing effect of the war in order to build Canada's future in times of peace. As Borneman put it, the goal was to "turn a backward nation of immense potentiality into a modern, socialist power conscious of its potential strength." Just as the legitimacy of socialism had been bolstered throughout Europe and North America by Germany's invasion of the Soviet Union on 22 June 1941, the Socialist-minded employees of the NFB also saw themselves as all the more justified in their fight against the Nazis and their optimistic hope for a brighter future in a Canadian welfare state. With hundreds of its documentary films distributed well beyond the borders of Canada by United Artists, the NFB quickly rose to become one of the world's top film studios not long after it was founded. Films from its series *World in Action* were shown before the main features at sixty-five hundred cinemas in the United States, reaching a monthly audience of thirty to forty million people worldwide.[33] The soundtrack was recorded in staccato style by "The Voice of Canada" Lorne Greene, the popular newscaster on the country's public radio station. Greene later became famous around the world as Ben Cartwright on the television show *Bonanza.* The increasing demand for NFB productions in both Canada and other countries resulted in a tremendous boom in production in the early 1940s; between January 1943 and June 1945 it put out no less than 432 films.[34] In 1942 Borneman rightly noted that the NFB had become the "pioneer studio on the Western Hemisphere," serving as a source of inspiration for feature films coming from leading US studios.[35]

Studies addressing the content of NFB projects have shown the clear leftist bent of the productions.[36] On the one hand, since 1941, depictions of the war cast the Soviet Union in a sympathetic light, not only as a combatant but also in terms of its political order. Films following suit included *Inside Fighting Russia* (1942) by Stuart Legg and James Beveridge, and Tom Daly's *Our Northern Neighbour* (1944). Borneman's *Zero Hour* (1944) also deserves mention in this context as an example of a film that propagates a national united front as a precondition for defeating fascism.[37] A Socialist baseline can also be detected in the working class's depiction as a value-adding, progressive class that would bring about Canada's future as a welfare state. Borneman

Figure 3.1. A Lancaster bomber approaches the Reich's capital: film poster for *Target Berlin*, 1944. © NFB. Reproduced with permission.

was by no means the only one to treat these kinds of topics in his films, but he made a definite contribution to the general approach taken by the NFB. Indeed, the working class was portrayed as a driving force in the war effort itself. The topic appears in several finished films Borneman worked on, including *Industrial Workers* from 1943 (editing), *Ships and Men* from 1944 (production and editing), and *Mosquito Squad-*

ron from 1944 (production). These films honored, respectively, the contributions of the Canadian steelworkers on the Great Lakes, the seamen of the merchant marines, and the engineers, workers, and crews of Canada's agile mosquito bombers.[38]

Of the propaganda films Borneman worked on that sought to mobilize Canadians for the war against Germany, one stands out in particular, which he also directed: *Target Berlin* from 1944. Made in cooperation with the Canadian Air Force, the film traced the path of the first Lancaster bomber, from the design and production phases to the plane's transfer to England and its first flight over enemy territory. The Canadian military plane was infamous; the largest and most powerful bomber in World War II, it was responsible for an enormous amount of destruction in Germany and an equally large psychological impact. The fifteen-minute film depicts the plane as the result of the joint efforts of the Canadian nation—a giant in airplane production during the war, manufacturing some eight thousand planes—combining documentary film sequences of the plane's production and its flights over Germany with acted scenes expressing the pride of the workers at the factory, for example. Peaceful narrative sections, some of which included theoretical explanations of the mechanisms of mass production, were followed by more dramatic bits underscored by deliberate music cues and unusual camera focal lengths. The end and climax of the film shows one thousand planes attacking Berlin. The offensive, as the Canadian instructor supportively told his flight teams before they took off, was supposed to be just as impactful as the early attack on Hamburg, making a decisive hit to bring down the enemy. The attack is shown from the perspective of the bomber's crew and falls out of focus over time, so that the final minutes are quite abstract. The viewer's attention is drawn almost entirely downward, toward an initially dark expanse illuminated by large, increasingly concentrated points of light, from which more and more structures of the bombed-out city emerge. The film ends with the crews cheering over a direct hit. The reception of the film confirmed that its intended propaganda effect had been achieved. The ministry in charge was very pleased and congratulated everyone involved. "Not without reason," according to the ministry, the film had "greatly impressed our aircraft people."[39] A telegram from a cinema owner in Edmonton suggests just how much the film influenced Canada's perception of itself as a nation at war: "*Target Berlin* was well received by over ten thousand people. It certainly has proven that Canada is really doing bigger things in its war effort than many people realized before seeing this particular series of *Canada Carries On*."[40]

An important theme running through many NFB films was the democratization of society, not least in the workplace. There was a general tendency to play up the influence of the workers while also propagating cooperation between workers and company executives, as had appeared during the war in the form of combined labor-management committees.[41] Treated chiefly in the work of British documentary film pioneer Stanley Hawes, the subject is taken up in the 1942 film *Industrial Workers*, made for the Ministry of Munitions and Supply and directed by Borneman.[42] The film's message was provocative given its comparative perspective, in which it posed the "question of the production committee in comparison with the workers' soviets in the USSR." At the time, the film's director actually feared that the film might have to be revamped for political reasons.[43]

NFB films also offered a vision of the postwar world even while the war was ongoing. The cooperative, coordinated harnessing of the country's strength as revealed in the war effort was supposed to continue after the war and lead the country on toward prosperity for all. *Tomorrow's World* (1943) for example—produced by Raymond Spottiswoode and edited by Ernest Borneman for the series *Canada Carries On*—depicted the boom in North America's industry brought about by the war and suggested the feasibility of a bright future.[44] In the future, the film postulated, the forces awakened during the war would be deployed to secure the peaceful existence of the common citizen. The experiences of the wartime economy were important in this scenario: a planned economy was better able to satisfy the needs of all than was capitalist competition, while the waste of raw materials must be avoided by recycling used material rather than throwing it out. The film propagated the ideal of a world that produced tirelessly for the benefit of all humanity. Generally speaking, the leftist tendency at the NFB was pluralistic and by no means fully in sync with the positions of the respective political parties; the same held true for social engineer Grierson's vision of an eventual future that proceeded from the ideal of a rationally planned society. Borneman described the vision as follows: "My view, if any, would be that we are entering upon a new and interim society which is neither capitalist nor socialist, but in which we can achieve central planning without loss of individual initiative, by the mere process of absorbing initiative in the function of planning."[45] Nonetheless, the activities of the National Film Board—not least because its films were sympathetic to the Soviet Union and offered Socialist visions of the future—seemed increasingly suspicious toward the end of the war and the beginning of the Cold War. As a result, the institution was vetted politically and downsized considerably.

Laocoön Writhing in the Agony of Creation

Like many of his colleagues, Ernest Borneman did not only wear one hat in Ottawa between 1941 and 1945 but was involved in a number of documentary films as an editor, producer, and director. After several years he became the production supervisor for educational film and then, in 1946, the coordinator of International Film Distribution—the third distribution track alongside Canadian cinema and non-cinema distribution—which had seven employees.[46] It is difficult to say just how many films Borneman was involved in, as the NFB's collective working method meant many productions did not list credits, leaving it unclear which employees did what for each film. A list of works that Borneman composed around this time gives him a role in seventeen film titles and cursorily mentions thirty-five other "shorts" he produced for the NFB.[47] In terms of content, his works represent a cross-section of what the NFB produced in the first half of the 1940s: educational films on Canada's war effort designed to mobilize citizens, and documentaries about daily life in Canada that were supposed to shore up a feeling of national unity by embracing the great social and regional variety of the country.[48] If further examples were needed to show how nations are constructed as "imagined communities" and film's use as an instrument of welfare state "engineering," the work of the National Film Board of Canada—produced on behalf of the respective ministries about all kinds of topics in public affairs—provides ample fodder. The films were shown not only in Canadian cinemas, but also in industrial plants, schools, and hospitals, also making their way to some of the country's farthest-flung settlements through a system of traveling film presenters. Commercial distribution channels abroad also ensured that Canadian film made a name for itself beyond the country's borders.

Borneman had already gained some experience with films related to war as a technical advisor for *All Hands*, a thirty-minute film strip from the series *Careless Talk*, which was put out by the British intelligence agency in 1940 to caution the British population against exchanging important war-related information in public. His estate also contains the draft of a screenplay for a film that was supposed to highlight the necessity of blackouts.[49] Borneman's efforts to shoot a film about the propaganda of the Axis powers reveal what a source of motivation, but also agitation, his work on anti-Nazi films was: "I am battling for permission to make a big picture on the

Figure 3.2. Borneman acting out a scene in the "documentary film" *The War for Men's Minds*, 1943. © NFB. Reproduced with permission.

'Strategy of Terror,'" he wrote, "a documentary on 'Psychological Warfare' using German, Italian and Japanese material. Tonight I'm running the first copy of *Triumph des Willens*, and my heart goes off in a triphammer beat at the very idea of it."[50] Given the fragmentary nature of the remaining production documents, it remains unclear just how much Borneman was involved in *The War for Men's Minds* (1943), a film devoted to the subject, which used cuts from Leni Riefenstahl's classic propaganda films. Borneman makes an appearance, at any rate, in two shorter scenes.[51] The forty-minute film, a sprawling narrative that bundles together many NFB themes, exposes Nazi propaganda as a deception conceived of in the interests of an aggressive conception of the *Volk*. At the same time, however, it portrays Allied propaganda as educational in its espousal of civilized values—liberty, equality, fraternity—and propagates the notion that the war was "a people's war for a people's world." Although the existing sources attribute all the relevant functions—screenplay, production, direction, editing—solely to Stuart Legg, this type of information has proved to be quite misleading for other productions. What is certain, however, is that Borneman was already developing this idea at the beginning of 1942, more than a year before *The War for Men's Minds* came out. It is of course plausible that Grierson chose Legg to carry out the project rather than Borneman, but it remains quite clear that Borneman reflected on his work—namely propaganda—not only as part of the NFB collective, but also personally.

As his colleague Graham McInnes recalls, Borneman originally came to the NFB to edit film, a key process in filmmaking in which a narrative emerges from the selection and recombination of otherwise unrelated film clips.[52] He was at his happiest and "in some ways at his best," McInnes commented, "in the cutting room." McInnes also wrote that Borneman's "fanatical capacity for unrelenting hard work" and his encyclopedic knowledge of jazz inevitably brought him in contact with a wide variety of aspects of filmmaking. "A passionate love for film" and gratitude toward Grierson and the NFB for making it possible for him to work in the field, McInnes contends, accounted for Borneman's untiring commitment to his work. Although somewhat stereotypical, the qualities that McInnes attributes to Borneman's personality do not seem to be off the mark. He characterizes Borneman as a manic, yet quick and precise worker who exhibited a "fine mixture of Teutonic exactitude and a Jewish sense of extrovert lyricism," calling him "a Laocoön writhing in the agony of creation." From McInnes's perspective, Borneman may have been a fanatic who devoured and defended facts, but he was never boring.[53]

The inquisitive exile traveled regularly around Canada, planning a series with Grierson about Nova Scotia, mining, and communal agricultural production set to air in the summer of 1942 and accompanying Grierson to New Brunswick as the assistant director on a film about lobsters.[54] For *Niagara Frontier* (1943, production), which looked at Canada's economic foundation of modern agriculture and industrial production, he traveled around the Niagara Falls area with his team, crossing the US border for the first time in his life.[55] He visited Montreal and other places in Québec for several weeks at Grierson's behest in order to study separatism within the

French-speaking province from the perspective of an impartial foreigner.[56] In 1944 he took his first flight with a crew to Vancouver on the Pacific Ocean.[57] He also makes repeated reference to trips to Detroit and Chicago.

Borneman and Grierson

John Grierson had moved to Canada at the end of the 1930s to take over various government film projects. With the National Film Act of 1939, he was tasked with developing and implementing a uniform film policy, under the auspices of which the National Film Board of Canada would go on to become one of the world's largest organizations working in the field of documentary film. Grierson was the uncontested ideological head of the project and its tireless coordinator. He recruited his employees—many of them young intellectuals still in their twenties—wherever he could get a hold of them, even abroad. By no means did they all come from the film business, but their youth and enthusiasm made them quick learners, a process only accelerated by the harried work atmosphere, long hours, relatively high degree of transparency, and independence that prevailed at the NFB. It was a place where "everybody does everything," Borneman noted.[58] There was a lot to do, and it had to get done fast. It also had to be done well, however, because the enemy was a powerful one: the German propaganda machine, whose vehemence and technical modernity had been proved by Riefenstahl's films. Although there were specific areas of responsibility within the organization's leadership, the working methods at the NFB generally produced well-rounded employees who could be put to work in different capacities. This gave all the more cause for employees to adore Grierson, often referring to him as "God" behind his back.[59] Yet the bright light in which they themselves cast their leader tended to overshadow their own contributions to the enterprise. Consequently, much of the existing scholarly literature on the NFB only seldom mentions the individual actors involved in realizing the project alongside Grierson.[60] Ernest Borneman was no exception. He also revered Grierson, commenting that of all the great people that he had met during his life, he admired C. L. R. James and John Grierson the most.[61] Whereas James was also a friend, Grierson remained first and foremost a role model and a teacher for Borneman, although the two men did occasionally meet outside work, attending the many parties hosted by film people in Ottawa, meeting for dinner at Grierson's place, or listening to records at Borneman's apartment. Apart from setting the intellectual context, Grierson served as the guarantor for the project when it came to the Canadian government, creating a material dependency. As Ernest wrote to Eva, "Without Grierson, no film board. Without the film board, no job for me. Without job, no chance to lay a foundation. For our future."[62] Yet Borneman's opinion of the man was not uncritical. He was bothered by the patriarchal aura that surrounded Grierson, one that embodied the dynamic with which he drove the project forward but also proved a stumbling block for many of the younger people working for him, who felt trapped under the authority of their leader. The NFB, as Borneman told Eva at the end of 1942, had become a missionary outpost: "It all reminds me very much of my first movie experience, making films for the SPD and KPD at the old German Film Institute studios, only on a much larger scale, with more money to spend and with less fear of political intervention. But the basic mood is the same: tense, fervent, fanatical and with an almost religious belief in Grierson, the Leader. I'm one of the few outsiders left over."[63] The intellectual differences between the two would soon reveal themselves in a tangle over a film project. Borneman was also skeptical when it came to Grierson's fundamental political stance, observing that Grierson had ingested so much of Marxist dialectic that almost anything that he had said at one point could be countered by something else that he had said in a different situation at a different time.[64]

Borneman was quite happy with *Northland*, a film he finished up in the summer of 1942, which singled out the dangerous work that miners were doing in the north of Canada to ensure the country's supply of electricity. His colleagues and his boss were also duly impressed.[65] *Northland* had gone over so well in fact, Borneman wrote, that "God" put him in charge of assembling a cinema film with the working title of *Wartime Transport*, for the series *Canada Carries On*. He was to put together his own team for the project and assume full responsibility for the program and its budget, which was set to become one of the eight production units in existence at the time. In time these units became increasingly independent in their productions, taking on everything from the negotiations with potential clients in the ministries, the development of scripts, and the creation of the teams to editing and sound recordings.[66] It was only during the final phase that Grierson had to give his "okay." This largely self-determined process proved its worth, not least, as one employee wrote, by developing "individual styles."[67] When Borneman, who to this point had only done short "educationals" for "non-theatrical production," was put in charge of the educational films department for "Unit H," he was bowled over by the trust placed in him: "It is the most generous offer anyone at the Film Board ever received, and it puts me with one dialectic leap to the top of the hierarchy. Now, for the first time, I can do what I please."[68]

Indeed, the "educationals" were considered to be quite important at the NFB. They were supposed to contribute to the education of democratic citizens and to bolster the country's trust in parliamentary democracy.[69] In a similar vein, the goal of *Wartime Transport* was to help develop a sense of Canada as a nation via the communal war effort by depicting a train that traveled for five days from the West to the East Coast to pick up soldiers from all across the country—"a parable of a nation moving to war with a big convoy as climax and conclusion." Borneman was pleased: "I'm set for the thing I've been waiting for ever since I became interested in the movies."[70] Work on the film got off to a good start, and Borneman got his own film crew. His cameraman was Boris Kaufman, the brother of Dziga Vertov and a leading camera specialist at the NFB, and eventually Borneman got his own assistant. He was also initially given a free hand with the film.[71] Things did not stay on track, however; he soon found himself locked in a conflict with Grierson that would expose the two men's different answers to the question of what constituted an appropriate documentary style.

The cracks began to appear just a few days after he had written so euphorically to Eva in the middle of November 1942, when he presented his raw cut of *Wartime Transport*. As Borneman put it while still under shock from the whole event, "My first fight with Grierson."[72] The head of the NFB—who was known for not getting lost in the details when critiquing films shortly before their completion, but rather getting straight to the point and often demanding revisions—asked Borneman to expand on the social significance of some scenes.[73] Borneman objected to the changes, however, arguing that they would disrupt the flow of the film. In principle the conflict was not just about this particular film but the more fundamental question of the relationship between form and content. Borneman wanted to make his own kind of documentary film, which in his eyes meant presenting "reality" according to certain aesthetic standards, not fabricating "illustrated commentaries." Grierson, on the other hand, held it to be "European" and "formalist" to prioritize the aesthetic of a film over its purpose. At the same time, the subtext of what became a rather loud fight played a crucial role, rooted as it was in the tensions between dependency and mutual respect between the counterparts. Borneman maintained that Grierson had not wanted to come down too harshly because he did not want to make Borneman feel ungrateful for having contradicted him; Borneman did, however, think that it was ungrateful to have disagreed with Grierson in the first place. In the end, it appeared that the whole affair had been more of a psychological struggle than a discussion about the matter at hand. "And in the end," Borneman lamented, "I emerged weak as water and equally perspiring."

While this conflict had smoldered, it had never flared up in terms of a concrete production before. Grierson himself put the dissonance to Borneman the following way: "You're concerned with compiling facts on celluloid. I'm concerned with creating attitudes in my audience." This, Borneman wrote, hit the nail on the head. Borneman's aim was to tell stories in a very specific way, namely a matter-of-fact recounting of circumstances, actions, and character dialogues from which viewers were supposed to draw their own conclusions. Grierson, in contrast, wanted to tell people how they were supposed to see things.[74] Given Grierson's "aesthetic of symbolic expression," the discrepancy between the two men's styles is not surprising. Grierson wanted to get at empirical reality in an essentialist sense, while Borneman, according to Grierson, was only scratching the surface.[75] For Grierson, the "aesthetic of symbolic expression" was only a means to an end, while for Borneman it was a layer in its own right—the layer at which the artistic will to form expressed itself.

Earlier on, Borneman had already criticized the fact that art had given way to output at the NFB, and the craft of filmmaking to the speed of production. Others, including Stanley Hawes, shared his view and found the majority of the NFB's films stereotypical and boring; the critical spirit, as it were, suffocated under the dictates of mass production.[76] Grierson, however, defended the benefits of quantity over the aesthetic weaknesses that many of his British protégés purported to find in his films, describing NFB productions as everything from overly direct to vulgar. Grierson responded, "If we bang them out one a fortnight and no misses, instead of sitting six months on our fannies cuddling them to sweet smootheroo, it's because a lot of bravos in Russia and Japan and Germany are banging out things too and we'd maybe better learn how, in time."[77] Efficient propaganda could be fought only with propaganda of greater efficiency, whose more convincing values would ultimately reach the people. The aesthetic limitations that came with limited time were not undesirable, but rather testified to the closeness of NFB productions to reality: "Times press and so must production; and with it must go a harder and more direct style."[78] It was no wonder that Borneman's artistic inclinations had already drawn Grierson's ire by the spring of 1942; to the documentary film pioneer, Borneman's concern for technique and attitude did not seem contemporary so much as a "nineteenth century hangover" and "nostalgia for the Fin de Siècle."[79] With the chronological classification, Grierson was likely not only referring to the collectivism that had replaced individualism in the first half of the twentieth century and which Grierson considered contemporary. In an artistic sense, the reproach took aim at the ideals of realistic painting and photography—in painting at the French realists around Courbet and their attempt to depict reality as faithfully as possible, and at early photography for claiming for itself the ability to create a more satisfactory depiction of the real.

After the war, Borneman related that he had turned to sound film in the 1930s—especially documentary film, which for him represented a "world view"—"in the first place as a technician, not as an intellectual, something I'm very proud of."[80] What precisely Borneman was proud of and what he rejected can scarcely be determined on the basis of such a terse statement. Still, it is clear that technical aspects mattered greatly to him, while potential philosophical or political implications were less relevant. At the same time, the statement sounds an ideal of craft, a notion of the formal quality of one's own work that extends to every field of activity, regardless of whether that was in film, music, or fiction. In the same interview Borneman maintained that his novels were also "documentary." Especially his second book, *A Love Story* (1941), "had a sensational impact given the concrete backdrop of the London underworld, 'a sort of Baedeker of the slums.'" [81]

Technique plays a significant role in Borneman's first novel, *The Face on the Cutting-Room Floor* (1937). It is one that is essential to the dramatization of documentary material: cutting film. The key piece of evidence in this detective story is a sequence filmed by an automatic camera that, when edited differently, "documents" two different versions of the murder. Even before working professionally in the genre, Borneman was clear that the reality to which documentary film laid claim should be approached with caution. At the National Film Board he was eager to learn about every realm of activity—editing, but also animated cartoons, where he was able to study the work of tested forerunners. "I spend almost all my time from early morning

Figure 3.3. Ernest Borneman peering into the small screen of a moviola, a technical aid in film editing that allows for a close view of the material. The attached loudspeaker above replays sound synchronized to the image. In the background his colleague Betty Brunke is editing with a handheld device. © NFB. Reproduced with permission.

till late at night at the studio," he reported back to London, "running old films on the movable, trying to impregnate Legg's cutting tricks in my mind, trying to find out why some cuts work and others don't, why a dissolve seems so rarely perfect, why a fade-out should affect you so differently from a wipe-out."[82]

In Ottawa Borneman gave lectures on the history, concept, and techniques of documentary film, speaking in 1944–45 at the Movie Makers Club, for example, on the topic "Documentary Film in England" and showing the classics *Night Mail* (dir. Harry Watt, Basil Wright, 1936) and *North Sea* (dir. Harry Watt, 1938). At the Film Survey Group of the National Film Society of Canada, he introduced G. W. Pabst's *The Love of Jeanne Ney* (*Die Liebe der Jeanne Ney*, 1927) and Ernö Metzner's *Accident* (*Polizeibericht Überfall*, 1928) as examples of the use of lenses to achieve psychological effects, and Gerhard Lamprecht's *Emil and the Detectives* (*Emil und die Detektive*, 1931) as an example of employing children actors. In 1946 he gave a presentation entitled "Experimental and Unusual Films" for the Film Survey Group, including *Rain* (dir. Joris Ivens, 1929), *At Land* and *Choreography for Camera* (dir. Maja Deren, 1944–45), *Isle of the Dead* (dir. Norman McLaren, 1946), *Granton Trawler* (dir. Edgar Anstey, John Grierson, 1934), and *Rien Que Les Heures* (dir. Alberto Cavalcanti, 1926). In 1946–47 Borneman sat on the board of the National Film Society of Canada.[83]

Shortly after beginning work at the NFB, Borneman wrote that "Grierson likes my first four scripts—animated abstracts à la Fischinger—and I am very happy about it and very hard at work."[84] He also worked on an animated film about the life of Wilfrid Laurier, for the celebrations of what would have been the former French Canadian prime minister's one hundredth birthday in November 1941.[85] From the very beginning Borneman collaborated with Norman McLaren, who Grierson had brought in from New York,[86] for example in *Five for Four: An Exercise in National Rythmetic* (1941), a three-minute animated cartoon for the War Savings Committees that was acclaimed as a pioneering work and for which Borneman had the idea and wrote the script.[87] The film opens with a series of abstract lines and numbers, followed by figures—dollar bills and bags of money—moving in rhythm to an improvised boogie-woogie melody. The film advertised war loans: in McLaren's animation four dollars float to the post office across a three-dimensional but unnaturally colored landscape and return as a war savings certificate that earns a dollar of interest after seven years. Borneman also collaborated with McLaren on several jazz films that used music from Benny Goodman and Oscar Peterson, among others.[88] He set out to develop himself as a film editor from the outset, recutting the documentary film *The Strategy of Metals* and basing one of his first successes, *Northland*, on material that not he but Spottiswoode had already filmed in 1940 and for which Borneman took over the editing.

Borneman's concept of realism can be gauged by his contemporary reaction to Ernest Hemingway's *For Whom the Bell Tolls* and Orson Welles's film *Citizen Kane*, both of which came out in 1941, at the beginning of his time at the NFB. Borneman revered Hemingway and took after him, implicitly shaping character through factual descriptions expressed in terse language, mostly in dialogue. He greeted Eva's enthusiastic review of *For Whom the Bell Tolls* skeptically, replying that "Hemingway's whole strength of stating thoughts and feelings in terms of external description—landscape, weather, location—has disappeared and given way to the method of the hybrid entertainment novel which attempts to *describe* thoughts and sentiments—a job that can't be done."[89] Hemingway wasn't an intellectual author. "By sheer implication he has reached depths of meaning" unreached by greater minds, "but he can't write politics, philosophy, sociology. Don't let him try."[90]

For Borneman, writing was about describing characters in their connection to the real world, "the world as revealed by sense."[91] "The sensuous world is accepted as the real because it is the only world that art can realize." In his search for alternatives to a psychologizing depiction of his characters, Borneman had come across the possibility of "employing sensory impressions as a proxy for other experiences, especially at moments where my protagonists' inability to understand and verbalize their own inner lives meant they could only be characterized through their environment and its effect on their five senses." A precise description of the world was much better suited to eliciting complex emotions than was an analytical method. Borneman explained that he had

> set himself the task of never intervening in events as an omniscient author to explain, of letting all the characters speak for themselves and representing them not through their thoughts but their words, so that the reader could guess what they were hiding and were afraid of based on what they kept silent about and what sort of untruths they advanced. This was a rejection of the philosophical novel and the land of poets and thinkers, for which the poet serves only so long as he thinks.[92]

Later, he would formulate the subtle principle of representation that began in *The Face on the Cutting-Room Floor* and continued in *The Man Who Loved Women* (1968) as follows: the reader "must form an image for himself of what occurs in reality out of all that the narrator *leaves out*, what he does *not* say."[93] Such a discriminating approach could be reconciled to Grierson's propaganda aims only with difficulty.

At the same time, Borneman's assessment of *Citizen Kane* made it clear how fascinated he was by the technical innovations and filmic experiments for which this early icon of US dramatic film became famous: striking low- and high-angle shots to signal the social status of a figure, wide-angle shots to mark the subjective view of the camera, reflections, and cross-fades.

> It is all too damned self-conscious, exhibitionistic, but something survives—an impression of enormous brilliance—vain, self-righteous, adolescent—but courageous in a tough, stubborn manner. Good. The scream of the raped woman in the tent scene when Kane slaps his wife's face. The microphotography of sound and picture in the typewriter sequence. The pan up into the ceiling of the opera house with the girl's voice climbing, climbing—and then the Heineish anti-climax—the thumb and index finger on the stagehands' nose. On the fade-out into the filament of the lamp with the synchronized fade-out of the high-frequency recorder. And all the acting. Supreme. But—the March of Time idea and the Rosebud keystone—how wretchedly poor—the whole "back-to-youth" and "back to the primitives"-solution—oh hell![94]

The clash with Grierson was followed by second, than a third "on this subject of ideology, philosophy and politics in our movie program."[95] Grierson's first biographer, Forsyth Hardy, tells of one fight in which Borneman criticized German idealism and Grierson defended it, albeit with arguments that his counterpart could scarcely have disputed, namely with reference to Marx's sources of inspiration, Hegel and Feuerbach.[96] When it came to film, Borneman felt the priority Grierson attached to politics and propaganda to be an imposition, fearing that *Wartime Transport*, "my best picture, 'sweetly put together' (Legg), will be scrapped in favour of a pan-american geo-political epic."[97] The project was in fact shelved in 1943, with it remaining unclear if this was due exclusively to the fact that Borneman did not want to go along with Grierson. What is certain is that Borneman asked his boss for permission to continue on his own initiative, despite fears that Grierson might react negatively. The extent to which he saw himself as what would later be called a "film auteur" is revealed in his comment to Eva that he no longer wanted to make films "to someone else's policy."[98] Grierson wanted nothing to do with the plan, but the conflict ended in a compromise: Borneman would lose his own production unit but continue to work on "theatricals," or films for the cinema, in a new unit focusing on the topics of reconstruction, raw materials, and natural preservation led by his friend James Beveridge. Some material from *Wartime Transport* would be reused for a new film, *The Battle of Supplies*, which however would not offer the independence that Borneman had in mind. "It's a plagiarism of Legg's style with little or nothing of my own ideas."[99]

Borneman would later again become a "unit producer" (with a salary raise) and was also among the dozen employees for whom Ross McLean secured an exemption from military service on the grounds that their assistance was "essential" for fulfilling the work of the NFB, in particular for the Ministry of Defense.[100] He now made films that more clearly bore his signature, including the already mentioned *Zero Hour: The Storm of the Invasion* (1944), which appeared both in the series *Canada Carries On* as well as *The World in Action*.[101] *Zero Hour* was a particular coup for Borneman, who wrote, cut, and produced the film, as it represented the first visual documentation of the Allied landing on the European mainland, one that he had prepared multiple versions of beginning in February 1944.[102] The first part gives the background story of the invasion and is composed of material from the filming units of the US, British, and Canadian armies, commercial film teams, and captured German material. It details enemy tactics and the preparations and methods among the military groups involved—in particular the *Blitzkrieg* tactic used in Norway and Crete, as well as the countermeasures developed by the Allies. This background was followed in the second part by the actual invasion, for which Norman McLaren animated title cards for thirteen different versions in which the landing played out at potential locations, accompanied by an equal number of commentaries penned by Borneman. The material was drawn from Allied as well as German stock footage and showed fighting or maneuvers along coastlines and beaches, so that a few days after the actual landing an in-depth filmed depiction was ready for release, which, Borneman would later write, "even now looks more convincing than most of the actual film material later shot on the beaches of Normandy."[103] When the first radio reports about the invasion came in early on the morning of 6 June 1944, the Normandy version of the film was inserted and the re-edited commentary recorded with Lorne Greene. The NFB informational material advised theater owners to claim the film was a "top attraction"; on 8 June it ran in nearly ten thousand cinemas in Canada and the United States. The campaign was a knockout; it took US companies ten days to release film reports on an event of true historical global importance.[104] Grierson's pronouncement? "Well, what did I say? It always takes a German to make a war or a war film."[105]

Not only internally within the NFB but also within the press, the film was praised as "most striking," "startlingly realistic," "thrilling," and "unusually dramatic"; the *Montreal Star* held that the merits of the film even brought it within the vicinity of Stuart Legg's *Churchill's Island*, which had won an Oscar in 1941 as the NFB's first production.[106] *Zero Hour* leaves little doubt that Borneman in no way considered documentary film a mere reflection of "reality." In its pre-constructed style the film, after all, was released without a single clip of actual events. Nowhere does it become clearer that the reality depicted as such was imagined. Such deviations, granted, were no longer an exception at the NFB, as the acted-out scenes included in any number of documentary films can attest.

Zero Hour was also an example of how the skills required at the NFB shifted over the course of the war. As less and less material could be filmed by one's own means, there came an increasing reliance on visual material of the most diverse origin, which

Figure 3.4. Preparation before editing: looking over the material. Courtesy AdK.

was then cut together from screenplays prepared in-house.[107] The shaping power in film thus migrated from directors and cameramen to the screenplay writer and the editor, a change that suited Borneman's proclivities. Arising less from conceptual aims than from the global context of contemporary events, the shift raised entirely new questions regarding the criteria for collecting film material, cutting techniques, and crafting the accompanying commentary, for example, and opened up a broad field for artistic creativity. Still, Borneman noted critically, technical or aesthetic consequence was rarely thought through at the NFB. "The style came out of the job," Borneman noted, paraphrasing Grierson—namely from considerations relating to politics or content. The *ex cathedra* commentary of the films stemmed from an intention to give citizens a sense of orientation in order to counteract the confusion about world politics since the Munich Agreement of 1938. If the style of the films came across as harsh and objective, it was because the Wehrmacht itself came across as harsh and tough, which made an objective perspective on the world particularly appropriate. If the tempo of the editing and the films' delivery speed seemed faster than before, it was in order to instill in the minds of Canadians a sense of urgency and the toughness and immediacy necessary to make decisions and take action.[108] There was no time for independent aesthetic considerations, so NFB employees hewed more closely to the foundational body of work that French avant-garde filmmakers and Soviet directors Sergei Eisenstein, Vsevolod Pudovkin, and Alexander Dovzhenko had created over the previous two decades. Legg's juxtaposition of contrasting images was inconceivable without Russian experiments in montage, Borneman argued, and his efforts to connect images by carrying over motion from one take to the next were impossible without the trials of the French avant-garde to achieve similar visual links, albeit with other aesthetic motives.

Content and Form

Academic research describes the aesthetic weave of Grierson and Legg's films in terms of their strong images of people (often workers and soldiers) and objects (often means of transportation), dramatic music, apodictic narration, and assertive commentary—all with the didactic aim of imparting to "simple people" the self-consciousness they needed to take control of their own destiny.[109] This took up with the British school of documentary film as shaped by Grierson since the 1920s, but also with contemporary experiments among innovative leftist filmmakers in Europe, the Soviet Union, and the United States. While an interest in Soviet films' subjects of labor and workers had initially developed via attention to the aesthetic concepts of Soviet filmmakers, in particular their editing, Soviet film policy also offered an example of how film could be used as an instrument of social reform that viewed itself "scientifically" and how the state might form a common-interest group with film producers.[110] For Grierson, the camera was well positioned as a tool to confront the cinema with life itself and a better way of classifying the events of the modern world than dramatic film. To the extent that there was a world to be portrayed, one that existed outside the senses and was empirically ascertainable, this was a naturalistic approach. On the other hand, it was clear that this could not proceed without a shaping influence—to the contrary. Documentary film, Grierson thought, involved "the creative treatment of actuality," in which the "creative" element consisted in the dramatization of nonfiction material.[111] Lifted from "reality," this material had greater power to convince than did its fictional counterpart, although its arrangement within a dramatic narration meant it did not fundamentally differ from dramatic film. For purposes of dramatization Grierson used symbolic allusion, or allegory, as well suited to capture glimpses of levels of reality—ideologies or social structures—hidden behind the immediacy of the images, a principle he termed "symbolic expressionism." Aesthetically impactful material was thus principally subordinate to educational and political goals; even if documentary film did make use of artistic creativity in order to achieve its political ends, the prevailing view during the NFB period considered it an "anti-aesthetic movement" at heart. "The penalty of realism is that it is about reality and has to bother for ever not about being 'beautiful' but about being right."[112] According to one early coworker, aesthetics came as a matter of course for Grierson, who himself had engaged intensively with technique and questions of form.[113] Artistic questions shouldn't be the central focus, however—a conviction of his that only grew stronger in Canada during the war. It was necessary to remove the "mind" out of its "daydreams" precisely because the reality of the war and the new world order demanded it. "In our world it is specially necessary these days to guard against the aesthetic argument."[114] Aesthetes were nevertheless "liked" and "needed." Camerawork, montage, and accompanying commentary were filmic means to work out more abstract connections, just as the very organization of the material that had been recorded itself implied a dramatic narrative. The political and educational function of the filmmaker consisted in this goal—the targeted deployment of such means to develop these same connections. Whether their use was sensible and proper was not a question of aesthetics but expediency. Grierson's coworkers themselves certainly regarded film as a political medium and not a playground for aesthetic experiments.[115] As Borneman's example showed, however, this did not mean that politically effective films could not also satisfy aesthetic pretensions.

Borneman later described the tension between politics and aesthetics in his work, which took an aesthetic turn during the war years albeit within a political frame, in the following terms: "As a politically active scribbler but one who still had literary interests, I wanted on the one hand to win over the largest possible audience for my politics. On the other, I also wanted to write novels, theater pieces, and films that would take new paths in form and style."[116] Concretely, the emphasis in his work fluctuated, shifting first to one side, then the other. His highly successful 1937 novel *The Face on the Cutting-Room Floor*, for example, was formally brilliant but contained no directly political subjects, with a vague political subtext that could be made out only with difficulty.[117] This collided head-on with Grierson's view of things. Looking back, NFB employee Basil Wright concluded that for him and his coworkers it was ultimately about the film and that Grierson had had to tighten the reins. After all, Grierson had hired people who saw themselves as avant-garde and wanted to test out film as an aesthetic medium, to which Grierson had countered: we are doing this within the context of our jobs, for which we receive public funding and whose primary aim is not aesthetic, but social.[118] Grierson used this anti-aesthetic rhetoric not because he denied the aesthetic relevance of documentary film, but in order to discipline his ambitious young team and focus their energies on the National Film Board's central task. Not everybody always set the priorities as the boss demanded. Borneman at any rate commented dryly on his preoccupation with a long-since vanished historical era: "If he had known that I'm not even from the nineteenth century but at the latest from the eighteenth, he never would have hauled me out of the camp"—"at the latest," because during his exile in Britain Borneman had discovered an aesthetic point of reference in English literature of the sixteenth and seventeenth centuries, in Shakespeare, Marlowe, and others, who hadn't written for a small elite but for a socially diverse, mass audience.[119]

At the same time, Grierson's view of the relationship between art and politics was so closely aligned with the concept of realism elaborated by Bertolt Brecht, a figure Borneman idolized beyond all measure, that Borneman's repeated declarations of esteem for his boss in this context were certainly not just a manner of speaking. Grierson's provocative anti-aesthetic statements—whether it was his frequent use of the aphorism that in times of radical change, marching songs were the only type of songs worth writing, or his sympathy for the expression attributed to Hermann Göring that when he heard the word "culture" he undid the safety catch on his Browning—were intended as pointed versions of a position that at the time was widespread.[120] They represented the "cool conduct" that had arisen during the interwar period, as well as the militant bearing taken by both the left and right, one which only radicalized during World War II.[121] Because everything was at stake, decisiveness, drive, and efficiency were the most important standards for political and, at times, aesthetic positions. It is unlikely that Borneman could not or would not follow such a program; he was focused instead on retaining an awareness of aesthetic aspects while preparing propaganda, and not entirely surrendering his own criteria—not least in order to improve it. Documentary film first achieved its truth and aesthetic from its share of reality. Borneman saw his task as "with all its powers of juxtaposition, to take the scraps of reality, the rough with the fine, and bring them to order and significance and therefore to beauty."[122] Especially for an exile such as Borneman, who for biographical reasons alone could no longer bring himself to believe in ideals such as authenticity or individual identity, there was no question that what was at stake was no mere depiction of "reality," but rather a dramatized arrangement of representations of reality with political aims, aided by aesthetic means acquired by whatever method.

Borneman did not leave behind any conclusive aesthetic statement on film. His ideas can nevertheless be approximated on the basis of a text published in 1945 and revised in the early 1970s entitled *Socialist Films for a Capitalist Government*.[123] The dispute surrounding *Wartime Transport* and its eventual fate provides a first inkling. Grierson's acceptance as leader rested not least on his ability to instill a sense of common purpose among employees. Inspired by the political and technical visions articulated by the film commissioner, which mixed with egalitarian ideals and feelings of moral superiority, many employees threw themselves at the never-ending work, prepared to subordinate their own individual efforts to the commonly created product. The NFB policy of discouraging auteurs thus found broad acceptance. For most employees, film work was group work per se, a notion that fit in with the community spirit to which Borneman's colleague Evelyn Cherry explicitly attested. In retrospect it may sound laughable that everyone loved one another, "but it was true. We did love each other. We worked in groups. We recognized cinema as a group thing."[124]

Not everybody shared this collective approach however—in the course of the learning curve set off by the output required of a young and inexperienced team, a high-pressure working environment, and the broad set of practical demands, many a film worker under Grierson and his leadership team developed his or her own ambitions. Communal work also had the effect of laying talent bare, and the production units themselves were firmly in support of individual styles. Borneman, who explicitly did not want to be lost in the anonymous mass of NFB productions but to develop his own profile, saw that this contradicted the ideal of collectivity. Spotting a conflict, he aimed relatively high: "The very achievement of a sort of personal montage-style clashes violently with the Film Board's declassed anonymity of style and policy. I'll now either have to knuckle down and make pictures like the rest or I'll get away with it and put my own stamp on the style and mentality of the whole organization."[125] Such ambitions would necessarily go to pieces when confronted with Grierson's rejection of aesthetic primacy and associated "pleasant vanity."[126]

While Borneman's text on the history of NFB is not at all a theoretical treatment on questions of style in documentary film, it is theoretically informed throughout—on his journey from the internment camp to the NFB, Borneman had already asked Eva to send him books about film by Pudovkin, Balasz, Arnheim, and Richter—and a number of characteristics of what he called his "personal montage-style" emerge.[127] These include a concern for an aspect of film he repeatedly terms "dialectic," meaning the principle of montage, in which cutting together contrasting images à la Eisenstein gives rise to a third layer at which a process of realization occurs. By the middle of the 1930s Borneman had engaged with Eisenstein's notion of "dialectical montage."[128] This principle clearly underlies his 1942 film (script and direction) *Blitzkrieg Tactics*, which Borneman made despite initial reservations ("But Grierson, I'm the most peaceful man in the world, I've never seen a tank in all my life") at the insistence of his boss ("Nonsense, all Germans know how to make war. Go and make a war film").[129] The film itself presents competing concepts of armored warfare based on German and Western technical literature and illustrated with relevant footage. Borneman wrote the film "as a piece of dialectics, the old world arguing tactics with the new," with two commentators representing each of the respective positions—Borneman himself the German perspective, and Lorne Greene that of the West. Used as a military training film in the Canadian army, *Blitzkrieg Tactics* became a "minor classic of its kind" according to Borneman, with the film's "dialectical" arrangement often subsequently copied for similar training films.[130]

That this dialectical principle could not be thought of as simply setting dissimilar elements side by side becomes clear from Borneman's description of montage, in an often cited quote in subsequent research literature that defines the overall impression of the film first in terms of the parallel between image and commentary. The short duration of the films—most were between ten and twenty minutes long—made it necessary to approach their subject in a concentrated fashion, that is, to locate material that offered "the most highly condensed meaning within the shortest possible footage." Because there was no time to cut from long shots to medium shots and close-ups, such a goal could be reached most effectively with takes in which a single shot collapsed all three levels, showing ongoing action in the foreground and background, with the main action occurring simultaneously in the middle ground.[131] Similarly, because there was no time to lose on individual details, the task consisted in balancing out immanent and transcendental values as carefully as possible.

From James Joyce—whose sentences combined "two or three different meanings—two or three different sets of symbols; a single word may combine two or three"—Borneman had learned the principle of palimpsest, or overlaying textual elements and their meanings to fashion a multilayered fabric with an underlying historical structure.[132] He applied this principle to film, a medium that was all the more suitable for its combination of image and sound. For Borneman, the most interesting task consisted in the correspondence between various components, with the intention of synchronizing sensory impressions:

> Since visual, music and effects tracks were running side by side in a highly complex three-part counterpoint, and since the visual by itself constantly skipped from place to place all around the globe, it became doubly important for the commentary to draw the two other tracks and the visual together into a single continuity, and this had to be done in such a manner as to make its points through the subconscious as well as through the conscious mind of the spectator.

Within this context, the most significant innovation consisted in using metaphors and similes projected from a coincidental aspect of the visual onto a coincidental aspect of the commentary, so that the two levels merged together in the subconscious. This technique is illustrated in sequences from various NFB films, including *Labour Front*. The image shows workers streaming out of a factory door as one hears the commentator say, "Of all the revolutions wrought by war, none has been so significant or so irrevocable as that which has swept away the scourge of unemployment and *opened those floodgates of human energy* that are the working capital of the people." Other techniques took aim at not subconscious but cognitive processes, including ironic constellations such as a sequence featuring Mussolini at groundbreaking ceremonies, laying founding stones, kissing babies, and finally in a children's clinic, accompanied by the commentary "Already I control the forces of Politics and those of Economics. Soon I shall even control *the great forces acting in the Nature.*"

Another documentary filmmaker, Grierson's student Edgar Anstey, observed in Stuart Legg's films just how precisely the editing was pegged to the narration: "Maximum commentary impact depended on a very precise relationship between picture and, not only word, but sometimes even syllable."[133] Borneman made little secret of how greatly he valued Legg's abilities, praising his NFB early productions from 1939, which had given Canadian documentary film a first taste of its task as a medium in an industrial nation.[134] This growing awareness came in part from Legg's exploration of the fate of unemployed youth in the slums of an industrial Canadian city and the resulting protest of those who would have preferred to see a positive image of their nation. Commenting on two other 1942 films, Borneman noted that they were the most intelligent treatments of political aspects of film made to date.[135] As Borneman saw it, over the course of two series that looked past individual details and the borders of the nation—*Canada Carries On* (sixty-two films that primarily showed Canadian affairs, often in their interaction with other parts of the world) and *The World in Action* (thirty films dedicated to international events)—Legg had moved past his initial debt to the "human story" of British documentary film to form a technique of political analysis that represented Canada's true contribution to the continued development of documentary film. While initially the central focus had been on mustering forces for the war effort, it had now shifted to shaping the economic, social, and political structures of the postwar world. Borneman's praise for Legg's early Canadian films alone indicates where the former's sympathies lay. He distinguished between "editorials," which proceeded from general principles, and films that treated higher-level problems via a "human story."[136] Among his own films Borneman cited the abstract representation of Canada's industrialization and urbanization in *Industrial Workers* as an example of an editorial, while *Ships and Men*, which similarly delivered an impactful, formal account of ship construction and the development of the Canadian merchant marine via the example of a father and son, stood for the connection of the general with the individual.[137] While the first echoed Legg's later films, the second recalled Stanley Hawes's work, which began with the individual and demonstrated a respect for the workers as people, while avoiding false theatrics or vague phraseology. For the first time since Legg's *Case of Charlie Gordon*, Borneman wrote, with Hawes's films the National Film Board had returned to a humane presentation of the workers' issue.[138] Of course, as was always the case with documentary film, despite the film's focus on the individual, it was not about that specific case per se but about broader issues, as worked out through modern filming techniques. *Ships and Men*—a film that impresses with its camerawork, editing, and music and on which a young Erving Goffman collaborated, among others—depicts the shipyard in Russian fashion.[139]

The scale of the production site is emphasized, with angled shots taken from below (of cranes and docks) or above (of people climbing stairs), while the music of Louis Applebaum, with whom Borneman collaborated on repeated occasion, underscores the value and achievement of shipyard labor through forceful, quick-paced, and dramatic melodies in a style similar to Hanns Eisler's score for *Kuhle Wampe or Who Owns the World?* (1932).[140] Tom Daly later criticized the attempt to create a maximal sensory impression through the combination of tempo and drama in image, music, and narration for stirring the viewer but ultimately leaving him behind, breathless—"it was like having to run to keep up all the time."[141]

As becomes clear from this context as well, Borneman was not the only employee at the National Film Board for whom aesthetic questions were a primary concern. There was no question, for that matter, that he also believed in documentary film as a political project. At a fundamental level Borneman enjoyed the free, unsupervised work and maintaining direct contact with Grierson, "a man of great intellectual acumen who talks my language on every subject." Like anybody, Borneman could arrive when he wanted and work as long as he wanted—a freedom that made him productive. Grierson's new appointment to wartime information chief also benefited the NFB, which grew in importance while its people received even greater independence. He was "truly the only man in this country with enough guts and brains and policy to run the tremendous job of co-coordinating education, propaganda and wartime morale and I'm grateful to be around while the job gets done."[142]

Work and Pleasure

The extent to which Borneman actually perceived himself as an outsider at the NFB, as he wrote to Eva, is not entirely clear.[143] Speaking for an unspecified collective, McInnes supports the notion that Borneman kept his distance from "us" and "we from him."[144] Borneman himself assessed his working environment in one letter as follows: "I get on very well with all of them."[145] Spottiswoode was an exception—a "pain in the neck," arrogant, ill-tempered, and sporting a poor sense of humor. Borneman lived with other colleagues at 42 Stanley Avenue, right around the corner from the NFB office in John Street, and was close friends with his flatmate James Beveridge—nearly the same age as Borneman and "really about the best guy I've met in all these many years"—as well as Norman McLaren. He kept in contact with both in the postwar period.[146] Beveridge had already worked alongside Grierson in London and been selected by the latter to succeed him as Canadian government commissioner for film. McLaren was another early coworker, the head of the NFB animated film studio, who later became one of the best-known specialists for animated film worldwide.[147] Through the NFB Borneman also met the somewhat older Basil Wright, a Cambridge graduate and partner of Grierson's since the late 1920s, who would go on to collaborate with Borneman after the war in Paris and on various film projects in London.

Outside of his circle of colleagues there was only a small group of authors and theater people "amidst the civil servants of Ottawa."[148] This included a married couple at whose house Borneman felt right at home, as he wrote to Eva, among "the sort of thing we are used to—books, paintings, furniture, records—the whole atmosphere of the place is Stockholm or Prague or Paris in the nineteen thirties or a little before. That is pleasant—and also very oddly out of date. A dreamlike chirico-esque quality of nostalgia crystallized into a concrete shape of living."[149] For Borneman the European ambience offered an oasis among the few cultural attractions the drowsy Canadian capital had to offer, or "the complete and utter intellectual emptiness," as he groused. As a melting pot of people from a broad range of national and cultural backgrounds, the National Film Board was sure to cause a stir in the small town of Ottawa, while the widespread skepticism among the local population toward the "arty types" of the NFB, whose ranks had swelled to nearly eight hundred employees by October 1945, only strengthened what was a lively communal life among colleagues.[150] Like many of his coworkers, Borneman busied himself at the city's "Little Theatre," which provided an ideal setting for organizing film and theater. He did this, as he noted, "to help the community."[151] The city's "bohemian element" regularly enjoyed itself at numerous parties that were thrown together.[152] Borneman also made regular social outings to Stanley's, a dance hall located on the other side of the river in the French town of Hull, in order to relax but also explicitly not to isolate himself from other colleagues.[153] On the other hand, full of longing for his girlfriend, who had stayed behind in London, Borneman at times grew so fed up with all the parties that he gave into old fantasies, writing, "Comes the revolution, commissar B. will sign a little order for the liquidation of all parties, mainly wedding parties, but the rest too."[154]

Whenever there was an opportunity, Borneman took advantage of the country's larger cities, Montreal and Toronto, and the nightlife they had to offer. He gave Eva a full account of one weekend in Toronto while working on sound effects for *Northland* at the headquarters of the Canadian Broadcasting Corporation. "God, what a weekend this was!" The letter lists eight parties, two films, two theater pieces, a variety show, two dance performances, and a "special sort of exhibition," a striptease that he describes to Eva in minute detail. It is puzzling how exactly all of this might have been accomplished within a period of forty-eight hours, but there is no lack of detail about what he experienced and how one could complete such a routine without sleep.

> You begin to feel so tired that you think you won't survive another minute. Then someone starts the gramophone and someone starts dancing and somehow the din and the muscular effort wake you up again. Then someone gets more liquor and that helps a little, too. Then suddenly you feel hungry and we all go down to Chinatown. . . . Then it's about daylight and that finally wakes you up completely. It's Sunday now and there is always someone to make breakfast with plenty of good coffee and cream

> and the other minor pleasures of Canadian wartime splendour. So then someone says 'Let's go down to niggertown for the breakfast dance.' So we did. And that's where I saw dancing for the first time. It doesn't seem possible. They do anything except go to bed in public.[155]

The scrupulous descriptions of the dancing, whether naked or clothed, of the records purchased, the appearance of the Woody Herman Band and their audience—all of this was not simply a report to his girlfriend but also a study, the expression of an encyclopedic collecting mania, and at the same time elegant, precise prose.

Otherwise than is commonly assumed, a hedonistic lifestyle did not contrast with hard work or for that matter the moral rules that prevailed among the workers at the National Film Board, which were as idiosyncratic as they were typical of the time for young, bohemian-minded, yet professional intellectuals. Marjorie McKay, responsible for the economic affairs of the NFB described these rules, in which Borneman's value system is also easily recognizable, as follows:

> Race prejudice was a bad thing. Interest in music and art was a good thing. Tolerance of different religious beliefs was a good thing. Not believing implicitly in the value of the Board was bad. Having the odd beer or cocktail was a good thing. Treasury was a bad thing. Big business was bad. Labour unions were good. Social security and other social welfare measures were good things. Brilliance was a good thing. "Middle class" was an epithet and "original" was a compliment. Working hard and playing hard were good. Holding up production in any way was bad. To champion the underdog was a good thing. To champion the top dog was bad.[156]

Family Persecution

Differences in opinion notwithstanding, Borneman's enthusiasm, theoretical insights, and practical experience in film all made him a catch for Grierson, who made a concerted effort to bring Borneman's girlfriend, Eva, from London to Ottawa as an NFB employee despite harboring a general suspicion that women distracted their men from work.[157] This finally succeeded in spring of 1943. The reunited pair moved into an apartment on Nepean Street in the city center and married a few weeks later. Eva was as elated as Ernest about the inspiring dynamic at her new place of work and devoted herself to film distribution with as much commitment as her new husband. A trained PR specialist who had gathered a broad set of experiences in film as a journalist and at Columbia Pictures among other positions, Eva pursued her work "with a ferocious professional competence that rather chilled us amateurs," as Graham McInnes recalled.[158]

Throughout this period, one context that defined Ernest Borneman and Eva Geisel's perception of the wartime years should not be forgotten: the German plan to annihilate European Jews, a threat that affected both families. Only a few relatives and acquaintances successfully fled abroad. The majority, as Borneman's father, Curt, wrote in the family history, "vanished by and by, never to be seen again."[159] The family of the mother, Hertha, found itself in particular danger; Hertha herself lived in a "mixed marriage" and did not have to fear deportation and murder but was still subject to repressive measures. Hertha Bornemann died of cancer on 24 October 1943 in a hospital in Lübben. In early 1940 Hertha's sister Käthe and Käthe's husband, Georg Jacobsberg, both of whom Ernest was close to, were deported from Stettin to Majdanek and from there to the Warsaw Ghetto; the other sister, Erna, had gone missing after a final message from occupied Holland in the summer of 1943. In 1942 the parents' business was closed "by order of the local SA leadership."[160] Their son was deeply depressed about the fate of his nearest relatives. On receiving Eva's message in December 1941 that her mother's sister had been deported—who later died at an unknown location in eastern Europe—he noted:

> This is one subject I keep out of my mind by sheer will power. Sometimes, in off-guard moments, when the whole wave sweeps down on me, I feel entirely crushed. You, my people, the war, all the things I ever believed in, my friends in Holland, Denmark, France, my own work interrupted in the full swing of it, Erna in Holland, Georg and Käthe in Poland—it's too heavy; I feel crushed; I escape only by running away from it—and I can never forget or forgive myself for running away.[161]

His constant efforts to bring relatives to England or Canada went nowhere.

Eva was just as depressed. Heartbroken about the persecution of Jews now also taking place in Vichy France, she wrote to her boyfriend that the news was so horrible she could no longer bear it. "My heart and soul revolt at my own incapacity to alleviate such suffering and to hit back at the henchmen."[162] Her British friends couldn't understand her; many even perceived a "ghetto mentality." But the emotions were real, and she could not suppress them. For "I am involved in mankind," she wrote, quoting John Donne, "and feel I may turn to ivory myself if I stay too long in the ivory tower."

Toward the end of 1941 while still in London, Eva had already mentioned lectures on Marx and Engels and friends who were "party members," which may have meant either old or new contacts.[163] By early 1942 at any rate—though now almost thirty years old—she stepped out of the ivory tower to join the Free German Youth (Freie Deutsche Jugend, FDJ) founded by exiled KPD members in 1938 in Prague. With six hundred members and nearly two dozen local chapters after 1939, the organization's strongest national committee was found in Great Britain, whose central London offices comprised two rented houses in Willeden and Hampstead.[164] While the FDJ did establish a political program, cultural activities formed its most important connective tissue. It was here in February 1942 that Eva began to give lectures—first an introduction to film, than an event about Bertolt Brecht—and to write for the FDJ periodical.[165] "You would have loved to watch me keep those rowdies spellbound for some 80 minutes!" she wrote to her boyfriend abroad. She took to several younger members in particular, including Renate Scholem, the nineteen-year-old daughter of former KPD Reichstag representative Werner Scholem. Renate was also the niece of Gershom Scholem, the Jewish intellectual who had lived in England since 1934 and been released from internment on the Isle of Man in 1941. Renee Goddard, as she was called after marrying an emigrant returned from Canada, later made a name for herself as an actress and theater agent in London and Munich. Eva found purpose in the work, writing, "That those youngsters grow up straight and not crooked is a miracle, and in my small way I help to straighten them up."[166] She also described a large FDJ meeting in summer 1942 at which songs and poetry were sung and recited together—"all the old ones" like the "Solidarity Song" ("Solidaritätslied"), "Brothers, to the Sun, to Freedom" ("Brüder, zur Sonne zur Freiheit"), and "Red Flyer" ("Rote Flieger"); "it was all very young and touching." The young men worked in the war industry and came directly from the factories in their work clothes, while the girls, "very unsophisticated," were smiling and in high spirits.[167] Her boyfriend in Canada, who for his part preferred to immerse himself in Spengler's *Decline of the West*, made fun of the social engagement, causing Eva to reply furiously, "And I'm *not* President of a Kid's Club with patriotic songs about the socialist Fatherland. President indeed! Whoever put such a notion into your head."[168]

Borneman's attitude toward politics in these years ranged from euphoria to depression. His period of political activism had ended with his emigration to England, and while he continued to engage in political discussions—not least in the milieu of his shared apartment, the "Hermitage"—he primarily occupied himself with aesthetic questions, with film, jazz, and literature, only picking up Karl Marx again in 1937 and continuing to study it intensively into the following year. He reserved the highest praise for the author and his central work *Capital*, writing that "merely reading the few extracts from *Capital* makes you take part in the biggest intellectual adventure of human history."[169] Although he sometimes called himself a Communist, his Marxism was not committed in any partisan sense.[170] He stated in retrospect, albeit without specifying a chronology, that he had "for many years been an active member of the English Labour Party, the Independent Labour Party and the English Communist Party."[171] It is doubtful whether this involved formal membership. Throughout his life Borneman felt an affiliation for three leftist currents—social democracy, leftist socialism (*Linkssozialismus*), and communism—emphasizing what unified rather than divided them. When he first came to England, it is safe to say that after at least some ties with the KPD in Berlin, he continued to maintain contact with people in the Communist Party, of which he was perhaps a member—Hiller at any rate could later maintain that it had always been Ernest "who tried to bulldoze me into party politics."[172] For a while he was drawn to Trotskyism without engaging practically, however; in 1938 he weighed trying to develop his reputation as a political commentator, possibly at Fenner Brockway's newspaper the *New Leader*. Brockway, with whom Borneman claimed he had long been "associated,"[173] was a Leftist Socialist and the general secretary of the Independent Labour Party who had also published Borneman's friends C. L. R. James and George Padmore in his periodical. Borneman's application for naturalization in England came up during this same period, which Intelligence Officer Turner, a family friend, granted little chance of success so long as Borneman's "revolutionary virus remained the same."[174] And one does in fact find an evaluation of Borneman in the files of the MI5, the British domestic secret service, denying his request for naturalization. Between 1933 and 1938 Borneman, the document states, had been in contact with known Communists and lived with C. L. R. James and should continue to be observed. "We consider Borneman a thoroughly undesirable candidate for British naturalisation. He is known both to the Police and ourselves as a close associate of communists."[175]

Borneman still considered it his duty to change the world, but his hopes gave way to great depression.[176] The years 1938 and 1939 were ones of total failure: the Munich Agreement, Franco's victory in the Spanish Civil War, the German-Soviet pact of nonaggression—a straight line of defeats. "Politics is a too distressing affair nowadays: I can't get away from the despair of constant political defeat—even when I'm not thinking about politics at all the depressing effect of things remains in some back chambers of my mind."[177] Borneman declared in retrospect that the Molotov-Ribbentrop Pact had been the "lowpoint" of his youth: "I wanted to kill myself that day. What losing one's first girlfriend might have meant to someone else at my age was what the loss of Socialism's honor was for me."[178] Then there was the scare that British authorities clearly considered him a member of the Communist Party, denying his release from internment on these grounds. He looked to sidestep the judgment, distancing himself on all counts when he assured Eva that he had "bitterly . . . opposed the C.P. all these years," and vouching to the authorities that he had only been in touch with C. L. R. James because of a shared interest in jazz, and with Jack Chambers because of their common affinity for film, but "never shared their politics."[179] Then there was Borneman's sudden interest in Spengler; it is small wonder that Hiller complained about his friend's ignorance of his own past and Eva was flummoxed by his current political views. Ernest replied that at Huyton he had spoken at length with Arthur Koestler, who was also interned there and whose autobiographical account *Scum of the Earth* (1941) he praised highly, but he tried to calm her: "We found ourselves in agreement on almost all points. He called it an attitude of cheerful pessimism. I said an *attitude*—not a creed, certainly not a philosophy. I have none of that left over. I still hold of the critical parts of my childhood creeds—much of the historical-materialist analysis of history, though none of its hope of fulfillment. Yes, I have broken entirely with the Trotskyists, though not in an aggressive manner."[180] Yet the discrepancy with Eva, who for her part stayed politically active, remained. She believed in the possibility of bettering the world, while he had lost all confidence: "I know that things are bad and I have no hope they'll get better."[181] His mood varied, however. Later, writing in expectation of her move to Canada, he tried to reassure her that his understanding of the need for change in the world had not been clouded. "I don't want you to come hoping for the sky-storming young man of Hampstead and Hermitage and to find an old man with thinning hair and a broth of Schopenhauer vinegar in his veins."[182]

Shortly before Grierson left the National Film Board in October 1945 and set out for Paris to develop the departments for mass media and information at UNESCO, Borneman became the head of international sales at the NFB. This was a large assignment that carried high priority: Grierson wanted to enhance Canada's standing in the international field, and the NFB could build on what was already an excellent reputation. It fell to Borneman to oversee the thirty employees of the NFB's international offices in London, New York, Washington, Chicago, Mexico City, and Sydney and to attend the increasing numbers of international conferences that sprang up following the war's end. The global demand for documentary films also grew dramatically in the postwar period; there was a great need for inspiration and international exchange had again become possible for the first time in years. During the business year 1946–47, forty-one commercial distribution companies and twenty-four foreign government offices purchased NFB films, and numerous countries signed exchange agreements.[183] In one letter to Pete Davis, a filmmaker friend who knew a number of British documentary group members including Legg and McLaren, Borneman gave a mixed report of his work at the NFB: "I made a number of films, doing anything from directing to cutting, but none of the films are very remarkable and on the whole I've been happier during the last year taking care of the Board's international circulation—a distribution job as well as a production job. It meant a lot of travelling and administering and it helped me to learn the things I knew least about."[184] Even if it would prove useful in subsequent posts, Borneman's later depictions of his work at the NFB did not highlight his management experience but his films, in order to assure them a proper place within the historical legacy of the institution. His name and films always appeared next to those of other colleagues, some of whom became famous. There is much to support the fact that during his active time at the NFB Borneman did not consider himself a mature filmmaker able to draw on the full range of his powers under Grierson, but rather as an apprentice who profited from collaborating with experienced colleagues. In contrast to more recent arrivals at the NFB—Norman McLaren or James Beveridge, for example, who were the same age as Borneman and remained successful throughout their entire careers in the film business—after 1945 Borneman fared poorly when it came to earning a living with his own films.

While Borneman was chiefly occupied with administrative tasks at the National Film Board around the time of Grierson's departure, he also found time again to pursue his own projects, especially those relating to jazz. The climate at the NFB had grown chillier; Eva reported that what had been characterized by an "inspiring dynamic and freshness" when she started in 1943 had now given way to competition and mistrust.[185] This two- to three-year period saw the publication of Borneman's well-known article series in *Record Changer*, as well as essays in other, in part well-regarded magazines. Eva had resigned from the NFB in the meantime, working until the end of 1946 for the government in the Canadian Information Service and preparing for the birth of their child afterward. Ernest was also weighing a new field of work with greater freedom.[186] He considered founding a professionally designed, large-scale jazz magazine in place of the amateurish *Record Changer*, asking his friend and jazz critic James Moynahan, who worked for the famous US weekly series *The March of Time*, "What about you and me quitting the film business and starting a magazine together?"[187] He also held out hope of a contract with a US publisher, which would allow him to finish a longer book about "American Negro music" over the next year and for which the National Film Board was ready to give him a leave of absence.[188]

Borneman was also driven by a film project, however. In 1945 he planned the foundation of a "Negro Film Institute" in the United States, a nonprofit organization funded by "various Negro institutions" that would foster the production, distribution, and presentation of films featuring black life and culture.[189] The idea partially coincided with Borneman's research interest, but also went far beyond. His reading of Melville J. Herskovits's famous book *The Myth of the Negro Past* (1941) led him to conclude that the study of black history, in particular the history of their acculturation in the United States, would increasingly rely on film to draw a comparison between the expressions of this culture as found in Africa—dance, gestures or facial expressions, day-to-day behavior, etc.—with those in various regions of the United States.[190] Conceived more broadly, however, the idea was based on a comprehensive analysis of African Americans' representation in film, which Borneman considered fully insufficient in most genres. In dramatic film it was "not intentionally offensive, but invariably patronizing. Uncle Tom mentality at its most pronounced."[191] While musicals featured a sufficient number of blacks quantitatively speaking, qualitatively their roles were reduced to "more flashy aspects of jive and jump music," while more serious forms of music were nowhere in evidence, thus representing a falsification of black folk music. The greatest progress, on the other hand, had come from documentary filmmakers. Films like André Gide's *Travels in the Congo* (*Voyage en Congo*) or Jean Cocteau's *L'Amitié Noire* depicted Africans with respect and understanding. The depiction of blacks in the news, meanwhile, was "either sporadic or sensational," while the area of educational film had nothing at all to offer. There were no film projectors available at African American schools and colleges, despite the fact that visual education in the form of sixteen-millimeter film was a particularly important media for giving young people an impression of black life and culture in Latin America, the Caribbean, and in Africa. Certain aspects of black popular culture such as music, dance, and others could only be compared through film; anthropologists and musicologists from around the world had appealed for relevant research funding. Where commercial film was concerned, a number of black film societies, chiefly in urban centers, had from time to time produced advertising films especially for an African American public, but their undeveloped technique and intolerable mind-set made them a lowpoint for the groups for which they had been made. Figures in the commercial world had nevertheless recognized that the field was badly in need of improvement, as for that matter the others described above.[192]

This project played a significant role in Borneman's filmic oeuvre not because something came of it (which was not the case), but because it provided the foundational ideas for his subsequent engagement with African American music in film and television, some of which did bear fruit in different contexts throughout the 1950s and early 1960s.[193] Writing in 1945–46, Borneman sketched types of films that he later went on to make—the history of a jazz musician that also showed the socio-economic background of the music and its commercialization; the history of a band and the problems it faced; a music film whose story, aside from the images, comes exclusively through the music, that is, without spoken dialogue or commentary. The films themselves typically play out in established musical settings: a bar, music studio, dance hall, or practice space.[194] Borneman also made a case for a new type of musical that would eventually overtake the common Hollywood style of interrupting an otherwise unsophisticated story with song fifteen or twenty times, which over time caused a fair amount of boredom. Borneman saw as an alternative a "plotless musical . . . whose only continuity is the history of the music itself." The "horrible dualism of 'plot' and 'song numbers'" would be discarded in favor of a continuity of music and action, which wouldn't be recorded in the sterile atmosphere of the studio but rather "on location," where the loss of recording fidelity could easily be compensated for, and more fun had, with "the odd sounds of applause, the unpredictable audience remarks and all the banter which usually accompanies any occasion of this kind." "People enjoy this kind of music," Borneman continued, "infinitely more than even the best of concert and opera music." This was all *terra incognita*, "the big open field no-one in the industry has touched as yet," giving the example of René Clair's *Le Million* as a first promising attempt.

The African continent, regarded as the point of origin for present-day African American culture, surfaced repeatedly in Borneman's studies as a point of comparison, a study in differences and similarities used to better understand the transformation of originally African music through its export into the various regions of the Americas. Yet it was also about interaction, about the encounter between Africans and African Americans. This was the point of departure for a film project Borneman developed in 1951 in conjunction with Grierson and Louis Armstrong's management team, albeit one that was never realized—"Satchmo" had participated in earlier film productions, but there was great disappointment in jazz circles when Orson Welles's plan for a collaborative jazz film fell through in the early 1940s.[195] The idea for *Armstrong over Africa* was to bring the star and his band to "the black continent," where they would encounter the music and dance of African tribes in order to see how each played off against the other.[196] One music student from Uganda whom Borneman enlisted as an advisor told him that Africans regarded black Americans as "black white men" and didn't trust them. African Americans could change this, Borneman argued, by demonstrating a direct connection to African music—"Louis could do it by picking up African music and playing it back faultlessly and improved." Not only musically, but also socially speaking the arrival of the US group would impact Africans—Borneman talked about a change in "tribal patterns." He had few illusions about the problematic aspects of the project, however. "Obviously, we can't take a patronising attitude towards the Africans. Louis and his men must learn as much from them as they learned from him." In order to lessen the potential degree of conflict in the encounter, the film should take a lighthearted approach; while many African Americans regarded Africa as a backward continent, Armstrong would see things differently: "To him, Africa is the home of his race. . . . But even Louis does not realise that 'culture' is not something that 'progresses' the way Americans believe that, say, science keeps going on-and-on and up-and-up. That a small African village may have a more complex and subtle life than an American city is something he will have to find out step by step."

UNESCO

Hannes Hiller had predicted that one day his friend Borneman and Eva would wind up in the United States, likely in Hollywood, but this wasn't to be.[197] Instead, Ernest was called to Paris by John Grierson to work in the film section at UNESCO, while Eva initially remained in Ottawa. It had become increasingly clear since the end of 1946 that Borneman would go to France, and on 10 October 1947, with his son not yet three months old, he flew from one city of lights on the Hudson to the other on the Seine to start his new job.[198] He was to become a wheel in the gears of the emerging international bureaucratic apparatus of the United Nations, a political jet set dominated by Western managers. Borneman's universalist sensibility did give him a certain sensitivity toward other parts of the world after all, especially Africa. Yet his anticipation had its limits. The newly minted Canadian spent part of the ten days before his departure in New York in Lake Success, the temporary seat of the UN on Long Island, to acquaint himself with the organization's film policies.[199] He met with NFB employees who had ended up at the *World Today*, such as Legg, Spottiswoode, and Helen van Dongen, Joris Ivens's partner; spent an evening with Mezz Mezzrow and Sidney Bechet; and spoke with a friend from his London days, the publisher Fred Warburg. At meetings with Abel Green, the publisher of *Variety* and Bill Gottlieb of *DownBeat*, Borneman secured journalistic work over the coming months as the Paris correspondent for the two publications. In comparison, he was anything but optimistic regarding his new job. He found the bureaucracy at UNESCO bothersome and counted on leaving early, writing, "Things don't look very tempting any longer and the rumours of JG's early departure from UNESCO seem to be confirmed." His boss did in fact leave in February 1948 to become film commissioner in Great Britain, a move that Borneman noted was "good for him, bad for us."[200] He found New York an exciting contrast, making Canada seem so provincial "that you wonder how you managed to survive the isolation all these years." He wrote Eva that he wanted to live with her in New York, promising to ask Stuart Legg whether in the coming year he might find work at the *World Today*.[201]

Founded in 1945 and based in Paris after 1946, the mission of the United Nations Educational, Scientific and Cultural Organization, or UNESCO, consisted in funding the reconstruction of schools and universities as well as international collaborations in cultural policy, conceived of in the broadest sense. It set out to back mass media initiatives with the goal of improving mutual knowledge of and understanding between nations, providing educational institutions with new impulses, and supporting and disseminating culture and knowledge.[202] The organization's first general secretary, Julian Huxley, recruited Grierson to be the "Director of Mass Communication and Public Information," one of UNESCO's four central departments.[203] The film section, which reported to Grierson, was led by William Farr and had ten employees, including Borneman as the "Director of Information"; Borneman seemed fit for the position, as his position at the head of international distribution for the NFB gave him demonstrable experience in one of UNESCO's key areas: freedom of information beyond borders.[204] As Borneman noted in a piece for a Canadian daily paper, the National Film Board of Canada had done groundbreaking work with its "intelligent internationalism," laying the foundation for UNESCO's own film work.[205] And the ideas, practices, and personnel of the NFB did in fact play a key role in UNESCO's film department; Basil Wright found occasional work there, designing a production plan at Grierson's request for forty-eight films about UNESCO's mission to be produced by member states and distributed internationally. With the help of three assistants, Borneman was tasked with promoting the films' use for educational, scientific, and cultural ends and preparing the logistical groundwork through contact with governmental offices and associations. His future job also included the monumental task of taking stock of every existing documentary film worldwide and identifying any private or public production potential, then making this information available to all member states.[206]

While still in Ottawa, Borneman had developed a two-part concept for UNESCO's film work as a calling card that would set the foundation for his work in Paris.[207] After meeting with Borneman in Canada, William Farr recommended him for the position as a "first-class person" on the basis of his concept, and declaring that "he has the qualifications, experience and enthusiasm necessary for the job."[208] Aside from Grierson, Borneman listed Ross McLean and Melville Herskovits as references, both of whom gave glowing reviews.[209] In two short presentations on distribution methods, Borneman drew from his experience in Canada in presenting films outside of the cinema, paying particular attention to the classification, evaluation, and selection of the films to be distributed.[210] He drew a distinction, however, between requirements during the war, under which all efforts had been directed at a singular aim, from those of the postwar, which had to account for the wide variety of interests present within the global community. In particular, state distribution channels should increase their reliance on commercial structures to reach a mass audience; films whose

Figure 3.5. Ernest (second from left) with UNESCO colleagues in Paris, 1948. Courtesy AdK.

mission coincided with the goals the UN must also meet the commercial needs of the theaters. Borneman described the requirements emerging from this situation in terms of a new type of distribution structure.

Borneman thus already had a concrete program laid out when he began work at UNESCO. A lack of financial resources and political validity (the states of the Eastern Bloc were barely represented) made implementing the plan difficult, however, so that his work essentially consisted of distributing papers and constant appeals to member states and businesses to support reconstruction in countries in need of assistance. As quickly became clear to Borneman himself, the contrast between the high-flying expectations of the possibilities for this new type of organization and the disappointing reality could only lead to frustration. Grierson filled him in shortly after his arrival in Paris: the workplace was ruled by indifference, bureaucracy, too little money, too many bosses, and too few workers. Moreover, in the atmosphere of the incipient Cold War, Grierson—branded as all too friendly to the Soviets—detected "a planned campaign against him and the whole mass communications section from the American side."[211] In contrast to the administration, which was primarily US and conservative, his department was "largely European and Griersonian."[212] Small wonder then, that Borneman described the situation at UNESCO in an early letter to Eva as "pretty disastrous."[213] Not much would change in this regard; a half year later Borneman's Polish colleague (and soon to be girlfriend) Lusia Krakowska let slip to Hannes Hiller on the latter's visit to Paris that "nobody was happy at UNESCO."[214]

Looking back, Borneman recalled his time at UNESCO as particularly frustrating "because we were damned to accomplish absolutely nothing."[215]

Borneman's Paris chapter took a somewhat more positive turn when Farr left at the end of October 1947, and he took over leadership of the film department himself.[216] The work was still unsatisfying enough, however, that by April 1948, seven months into the job and shortly before the stipulated end of his contract, Borneman had decided to return to Canada. Harper's acceptance of his third novel, *Tremolo*, had inspired dreams of a sabbatical in order to write two further books, which he hoped would be turned into films.[217] Borneman wound up extending his contract by a year, however, finally yielding to the temptation of Orson Welles's offer to leave his post in Paris a year and a half later, in the spring of 1949.[218] Borneman's subsequent judgment that his time at UNESCO had been "a complete waste of time" is understandable in terms of the job itself, but his life in Paris must have been another matter, which explains his staying.[219] Everyday life—in particular the cultural life of the European metropole—was a revelation for Borneman. UNESCO's offices at 19 Avenue Kléber in the former Hotel Majestic and Borneman's apartment for the first few months at 20 Rue le Sueur were both located in the beautiful and elegant sixteenth arrondissement, at most ten minutes by foot from each other. He wrote often about the rhythms of everyday French life, which in his view were surprising for being so normal so shortly after the war. People were on the streets, and the stores were full of customers and goods that while expensive were evidently still within reach for many, especially one as handsomely compensated as a UNESCO employee (a salary paid even in dollars not subject to tax).[220] In the end, Borneman earned $6,370 a year—a significant jump in comparison to the previous (taxable) $4,500 salary he had earned at the NFB.[221] He wrote to his father that while life was harder in Paris than in Canada or the United States, he liked it "better in the old world, despite everything." He had longed for a European lifestyle while still in Ottawa, and he now stood by it: "The 'American Way of Life' has always been a pain in the neck for me, and my main relaxation in Paris is not the fine food, but the feeling that I'm once again among civilized human beings. The five senses are not quite atrophied yet, and the sixth sense (how to make more money than your neighbor) has not quite taken hold of everyone, yet."[222]

Borneman saw Margaret and John Grierson and Basil Wright, met with acquaintances like the Skot-Hansens from Denmark or Herbert Steinthal, the current representative of the United Nations Film Section in Paris. He sought out the magical places he had read about in Hemingway's books, drank martinis at Les Deux Magots, a café frequented by Sartre, Pernod at Le Dôme, and Calvados at La Coupole.[223] Shortly after his arrival in Paris he met "Sartre and his girl, Simone de Beauvoir," fresh from an argument on the radio with the Gaullists and Stalinists, "and I'm now right where I started from when I left 9 Heathcote Street. Sartre asked me to write something for his magazine, *Les Temps Moderne*, and I think I'll try and adapt 'Notes on the Realist Novel.'" Overall, Borneman seems to have situated himself quickly within

Figure 3.6. Two dancers from Katherine Dunham's troupe, 1949. In the background from left to right: Eva (wearing a hat), Ernest, Dunham, Othella Strozier. Courtesy AdK.

the intellectual life of the city. He moved in circles surrounding the magazine *Présence Africaine*, whose editors included Jean-Paul Sartre, André Gide, Albert Camus, and Richard Wright, who was living in Paris. He went for walks in the Bois du Boulogne, caught the latest films, and immersed himself in the jazz scene.

After a few weeks in the French capital, Borneman, always one for the "soft voices of women" (Joachim-Ernst Berendt) and finding himself lonely at night, sought out contact with the other sex. "Well now," Borneman joked in one letter to Hiller about his suitcase, which had been fully destroyed while crossing the Atlantic along with all of his clothes, records, and manuscripts, "I just must find a woman to take care of me because this life without underwear must be put to some useful purpose. The sun shines and I will now proceed to the Dôme or some other wholesome place and see what silhouettes look like against the light."[224] One look at Borneman's packed calendar from his time in Paris, which aside from his appointments also contains notes on his experiences, reveals a life packed to the brim with work (often late into the night), jazz concerts, movies, exhibitions, bars, and restaurants—especially around Montmartre and the Latin Quarter—almost a cliché of the highs and lows of life in Paris, in which love and sex played an important role, in art as in life. While his circle of acquaintances included homosexual men and women, Borneman himself, heterosexual throughout his life, openly had multiple affairs with women.[225] Just two weeks after arriving, in October 1947, he wrote to his partner Gullickson, "I don't know what I'm doing here anyway. I guess I just ran away from my newborn son's experiments with the arcadic blues scale. It's cold, dirty, expensive and not good for the morale. . . . Well, I must now put my little midinette to bed."[226] For an extended period of time Borneman was with his assistant Lusia Krakowska, of whom he would later say she had been the only woman aside from Eva with whom he could imagine spending his life.[227] In Paris he was also involved with Jacqueline Lesieu, a UNESCO employee, as well as Jacqueline Walcott, a black dancer from Katherine Dunham's troop, who was performing in Paris.[228]

Back to Berlin

Borneman's work also brought him to other European countries. In July 1948 he inaugurated a special UNESCO program at the Locarno Film Festival with *Hungry Minds*, an NFB film that explored problems in reorganizing the educational system in postwar Europe.[229] One trip between 27 March and 3 April 1948 held particular resonance, taking him back for the first time to his old homeland, a now destroyed Berlin. As a UNESCO employee, Borneman discussed production possibilities in Germany with representatives from German film companies, including DEFA employees Kurt Maetzig and Fritz Arno Wagner and cinematographer G. W. Pabst, visited the French and British film institutes, and took in new German films, among them *Marriage in the Shadows* (*Ehe im Schatten*) and *Murderers among Us* (*Die Mörder sind unter uns*). Coming shortly before the Berlin Blockade, the trip may not have been entirely without personal motives, as Borneman had considered eventually pursuing film in Germany after UNESCO. His impressions—available in the archives of the Deutsche Kinemathek in the form of diary-like entries, as well as a report filed for *Harper's Magazine* in August of that year—are comparable with other visiting emigrants' reports from the early postwar period.[230] The account is largely taken up with a distanced observation of living conditions, in particular of the collective mentality among the population. Sentimentality is in short supply—it had been only four years, after all, since Borneman had made every effort to bolster the fighting morale of Canadian bomber pilots in subjugating Nazi Germany with *Target Berlin*. Borneman registered the outcome—the field of rubble where the former capital of the Reich previously lay—with a careful eye. Encountering the places of his childhood and youth moved him, but not because of the state of destruction in which he now found many; "Better than before," he coolly noted regarding the condition of the

Kaiser Wilhelm Memorial Church. He was much more interested in how people processed the experience of the "Third Reich" and defeat. Similarly to Hannah Arendt on her own trip two years later, Borneman noted a widespread cynicism and amorality, which, as Arendt put it, "is only the most conspicuous symptom of a deep-rooted, stubborn, and at times vicious refusal to face and come to terms with what really happened."[231] On the train east from Forbach, Borneman was struck most by the tireless labor in which people were engaged, clearing rubble, repairs and reconstruction everywhere, smoking chimneys, and bustling factories that operated through the night; "you are entering a workshop which knows no holiday." Soon enough the talk of an "economic miracle" would make questions about the past seem inappropriate. Yet Borneman found himself back in 1933, "back among the faces in the dreamlike horror of *déjà vu.* Nothing had changed; distrust, suspicion, fear were once again stamped in every face with the deep grey dye of hunger and defeat." All moral categories, he wrote to Eva, had completely disappeared.[232] The Germans didn't feel guilty about the concentration camps; they were merely indignant that they had been administered inefficiently. Borneman reported hearing that the gas chambers were a mistake, and work camps would have been more appropriate—that way the weak would have died and the strong would at least have provided useful labor.

The life trajectories of Borneman's closest friends serve as a point of comparison in the report. Of the eleven guests that sat in the apartment on Kaiserdamm for his eighteenth birthday, five had been killed while fighting or in concentration camps, in Madrid, Addis Ababa, Dachau, Sachsenhausen, and Auschwitz. Two others continued to fight, in Palestine and China. Four had stayed in Germany, and Borneman wanted to find out what had become of them. In 1933 all had close ties to the Communist Party; in 1948 one was still a Communist and Socialist Unity Party (Sozialistische Einheitspartei Deutschlands, SED) member, another had converted to Catholicism, a third, a talented Jewish poet, considered political loyalty sophomoric, and the fourth, the son of a Jewish hotel owner, had moved to the Soviet Union and returned to Germany as a soldier in the Red Army. This last friend, disappointed by postrevolutionary Soviet art and convinced that the new art in East Germany was leagues better, said cynically, "I'm a Darwinist. Hitler taught me that. He killed the Jews because they didn't kill him first. This time I'm going to be on top. I'm not going to be kicked around again by anyone." These were the friends of his youth, Borneman wrote soberly, noting a common denominator: a complete lack of interest in moral judgment.

Borneman also took time to visit his father, Curt, who receives a warm description as a thoughtful elderly gentleman, at ease and well educated, "looking exactly like Thomas Mann"—a man torn between the desire to go to Canada with his son and the love he felt for his girlfriend and future wife, who wanted to stay in Berlin. This couple's mentality, Borneman continued, was typical of many Germans—they weren't demoralized but amoral, and they mistrusted all governments and occupational powers. Their attitude was that things would be agreeable to some and awful for others no matter which way history went. As such, it was best to wait and be pre-pared for whatever came. The verdict on the visit was mixed; it was "a weird and won-derful time," Borneman wrote to his father.[233] For his part, Borneman's father was happy to see his son again, writing a carefully considered evaluation: "He has changed a great deal. He is much more forthcoming and is now actually capable of hearing out another opinion, but he remains difficult, as before—or has he become American through and through, while we have remained sentimental, decadent Europeans?"[234]

Borneman had engaged in a systematic way with living circumstances in Germany once before and continued to do so now. His papers at the Deutsche Kinemathek hold numerous newspaper excerpts from the German, British, Canadian, and US press about the situation in postwar Germany between 1945 and 1952 or so. The excerpts concern not only politics, but also economic conditions, in particular prices, cultural events, crimes, and other news stories that might provide insight into the German mentality. Borneman was present for a test screening in Paris of Roberto Rosselini's *Germany Year Zero*, the final film in the director's neo-realist trilogy on the war and early postwar period, and spoke with Rosselini.[235] Around the same time he criticized G. W. Pabst's 1947 *The Trial*, which he considered dangerous for its inappropriate handling of antisemitism. They both had likely been spoiled by the documentary tradition, he wrote to Eva, but he could no longer bear the theatricality of German cinema, regardless of whether he enjoyed the subject matter and the way it was made.[236] Borneman processed the experience of his Berlin trip in *The Maze* (the German version bears the title *Das Labyrinth*), a film project he likely developed before the end of the 1940s. Based on the idea behind his article for *Harper's*, which sets the pre- and postwar within the continuous context of a central character and familial setting, the film is conceived as an alternative draft to the "rubble films" in which Germans depicted the postwar period with "pathos and self-pity."[237] In con-trast to the German productions, but also to Rosselini's work Borneman noted, the project should feature not only Germans but also the Allies, displaced persons, and the "new group of international civil servants" that had emerged within the context of the UN. This would broaden the German focus and place it within an interna-tional context. Warren, the lead character, is a young Englishman who marries the daughter of his professor while in Berlin before the war. Borneman manages to fit all the groups listed above into the project when, after Warren is separated from his wife during the war, he returns to Germany after 1945 to find her and in his search meets with representatives from the occupational powers and with a Haganah group disguised as a black-market ring organizing Jewish emigration to Palestine. When he discovers that his missing wife was killed fighting in the resistance, Warren remains in Germany to play a part in the country's democratization, representing "a new sense of joint responsibility and a new challenge for joint reconstruction."

The project was likely conceived as a springboard for a professional future in Ger-many. After visiting Berlin, Borneman shared with Pete Davis that in all likelihood he would return shortly to begin work on the film; he had already considered moving to Germany to begin by the end of 1947. Borneman continued to see his future in film, a career that might be pursued in England but was best done in Germany and the United States.[238] The cultural life astir amid the rubble of the Reich's former capital had left an impression: "Films, arts, music, literature, theatre are flourishing so violently that Paris seems part of the Backward Territories in comparison."[239] Then there was the fact that production costs in Germany were only a fraction of what one would have to reckon with in the United States. Give him a thousand dollars and he would, as he wrote to Hans Hiller immediately after returning from Berlin, "make the kind of film that we all have always wanted to make." In this way, the present moment in Germany seemed particularly pregnant: "For once, a single person can leave as much of an imprint on a film as a painter or a novelist. Ah, Land of Dreams."[240] His scripts, *The Maze* among them, were based on old NFB, and now UNESCO principles, namely "that you must find a sort of story and the kind of treatment which will be internationally intelligible and internationally interesting without need of dubbing or subtitling—and I think I convinced them." In the following period, Borneman pursued the idea of working specifically in Germany for German film—be it under the auspices of UNESCO or not—but it was difficult. Grierson, Borneman learned, was skeptical because he considered Borneman too rash to make a good producer and too boring to make a director.[241] The true deterrent proved financial, however. This had become clear by summer 1948, leading Borneman to note that none of his German film plans had come to fruition and that his UNESCO job had become pure routine. The result was "complete frustration."[242]

"Dear Ernest, Live Simply": Working with Orson Welles

While in Paris in early February 1949, Borneman met Orson Welles, an already legendary director who had garnered worldwide attention for his radio piece *The War of the Worlds* (1938) and first film *Citizen Kane* (1941). Borneman was the same age as Welles and considered him a genius, a figure inhabiting the upper echelons of the film world with whom it would be a great stroke of luck to work. What began with a disaster soon turned into a lucrative business, especially in the early 1950s, when Welles commissioned Borneman to draft a series of scripts. In 1945, while still working as a documentary filmmaker at NFB, Borneman had noted that Orson Welles was "the only guy in all Hollywood for whom I have some respect," hoping one day to meet him: "We're bound to get together."[243] In 1953, following disillusionment and strife, Borneman could still declare, "Orson is a friend of mine whom I like and admire as a man and an artist."[244]

The two hit it off immediately during their chance encounter in Paris; aside from sharing a leftist political bent, they held any number of interests in common—film and especially jazz. Welles had read some of Borneman's writing on this last subject, as Borneman related to Welles's biographer Peter Noble, and was also familiar with Borneman's third book, *Tremolo*, which had appeared in the previous year.[245]

Figure 3.7. Ernest, Eva, and a young Stephen with the staff at Orson Welles's villa near Rome, 1949. Courtesy AdK.

Meeting again in early April, they discussed in greater detail the basic structure for the project around which their collaboration would revolve—*Ulysses*. It was agreed that Borneman would move with his family to Casa Orlandi, Welles's sumptuous villa in Monte Porzio a few kilometers southeast of Rome, to work on a script for the film. Aside from a very generous salary, Welles would cover all travel and additional domestic expenses, plus room and board.[246] Borneman promptly handed in his resignation at UNESCO, starting work on *Ulysses* on 20 April and finishing 16 August 1949. On 1 May, Borneman also flew from Paris to spend several weeks in Marrakesh, where Welles was at work on *Othello*, to discuss the basic structure of the script and the music for the film with Welles and his team. Borneman then returned to Paris to move out of his apartment before finally flying to Naples on 6 June to pick up Eva and Stephen, two years old by now, who had arrived by ship from New York.[247]

The happiness at Casa Orlandi proved short-lived, however—not only did Borneman's plans to assume part of the directorial and editing work for *Ulysses* in addition to writing the script ultimately fail, many other things also went awry.[248] On 12 June, Welles's secretary Rita Ribolla informed Borneman that "financial difficulties" had arisen, which meant that *Ulysses* could not be produced.[249] Press reports soon began to circulate about a financial bottleneck with *Othello*, which Welles was self-financing.[250] Not only that, but Welles could no longer keep his promise to reimburse the family's expensive crossing from Canada, nor could he pay Borneman's own travel expenses or the agreed-upon salary. Borneman would also have to settle with the servants himself and cover the bills at Welles's home. Debt and lost earnings meant that once the water was shut off at Casa Orlandi, the family had to leave and look for a new home. Borneman could scarcely believe it at the beginning, assuring Welles, "As I said to you when I first met you in Paris, it is more important to me to work with you than to be paid on the dot, and I am more hurt and depressed by the rupture in what I hoped to be a long-term association than by my temporary inability to feed myself and my family."[251] If money were really the issue, then he could seek support from business contacts in Paris, who had said they would finance anything that was directed by Welles and written by Borneman. As the full scope of the catastrophe became clear, however, Borneman asked his father to look about for ways he or Eva might earn money in Germany. Now, after having given up their household in Ottawa and the job in Paris, there was nothing to prevent them from coming back to Germany for the long term.[252] Curt, however, proved unable to conjure jobs out of thin air.

When asked by Borneman what exactly he should do, Welles, ever the playboy, replied, "Dear Ernest, live simply. Affectionate regards, Orson Welles."[253] As a temporary solution, Welles did offer to have Borneman come to Mogador on the Atlantic coast of Morocco, where he was filming *Othello* and would cover transportation and lodging.[254] Instead, Borneman accepted an invitation from David Rawnsley, leaving for Calvi on Corsica in mid-August with his wife and child in tow. The advertised film project promptly evaporated there too, however, and Eva came down with a case of infantile paralysis.[255] Sick, bankrupt, and homeless, in fall of 1949 the family returned to England—Eva and Stephen to Eva's mother in Manchester to recuperate, and Ernest to London to earn money.

Until its collapse, Borneman and Welles's collaboration appears to have functioned at a professional level. Borneman would send over drafts, Welles would critique, Borneman would revise. The few examples of Welles's written instructions give an impression of how the pair worked. Differences of opinion abounded: Should Odysseus's ship sail alone from the beginning (Welles) or split off from a convoy (Borneman)? Should Circe live alone on her island (Welles) or with a number of female servants (Borneman)? Should Pallas Athene be presented dramatically (Borneman) or not (Welles)? Questions of content, aesthetics, but also finances all came into consideration, even if they were not discussed in earnest but rather decided by Welles in his own, imperious fashion: "Pallas Athene is only a subject of conversation. This is a must—must—must—must—must! If you want to write a movie script with a goddess in it, you will have to do it on your own time. I don't want her voice, her shadow or anything to do with her. These Greeks believe in her. That is her entire existence. It is also her entire effectiveness."[256] Borneman evidently was entertaining notions of building model ships or even Troy itself, while Welles left no doubt about his aversion to "model shots." Moreover, Welles's partner was too detail oriented for his taste. Welles found a number of Borneman's suggestions worthwhile, if difficult to realize. The ideas still feel fresh to this day, such as having a single actress play the roles of Penelope, Circe, Nausicaa, and all the other women that Homer describes in similar terms and generally hiring black actors to play the characters, defying conventional modes of representation (Borneman argued that the Greeks had a darker, not lighter skin tone). While nothing came of this latter idea because there weren't enough black actors available to play classical roles, at Borneman's suggestion Welles cast the African American dancer Eartha Kitt in the role of Helen for a theatrical adaptation of *Faust* in Paris, after Kitt had come to France with Katherine Dunham.[257]

Borneman's subsequent, third draft of the "shooting script" adhered strictly to Orson Welles's wishes—gone were the model shots, including those of Troy and the fleet, and Borneman excused himself for any of the misunderstandings for which Welles was in any event so well known. As one of his biographers concludes, Welles was quick to lose patience and expected a familiarity even with minor, unassuming aspects.[258] Borneman dutifully explained that he had worked with great efficiency at Monte Porzio and was certain that the script would be finished well before the dead-line.[259] Shortly thereafter, however, came the disconcerting news of the project's end; the third draft of *Ulysses* "looks wonderful" and Borneman was "heartbroken to see it scrapped—won't you reconsider?"[260] It was to no avail—the project was shelved, although the author continued to work on it while on Corsica, then back in London. In October 1949 he took the measure of what he had done for *Ulysses*: aside from various preliminary work, he had four shooting script drafts, the last of which numbered 183 pages, with 484 scenes.[261]

The issue of Borneman's pay and reimbursement for his expenses stretched out over years. Welles initially paid a monthly fee of one hundred pounds for a period in summer 1951. The two continued working together through the early 1950s, with Borneman's letters—some involving lawyers—often striking an irritable tone and concerning money, or sometimes credit, while Welles's much less frequent signs of life struck a mollifying, congenial tone. The discrepancy arose not from different characters but from the different positions each held in the working relationship. In late 1951 Borneman turned in desperation to John Shepridge, Welles's right-hand man at the time, deeming it reprehensible that Welles would bring his best friends misery while he continued to maintain a lifestyle lacking in all decency at their ex-pense.[262] Not long after, Welles sold the script to Carlo Ponti and Dino de Laurentiis, who then turned around to film *Ulisse* (1954) in Rome in completely altered form, as a large-budget monumental piece starring Kirk Douglas, Silvana Mangano, and Anthony Quinn. They had paid Welles not to make his film. It was only in 1959, when the genius's business affairs were in better order, that one of his belles appeared with a bag stuffed full of bills, putting an end to the matter.

Between 1950 and 1952 Welles and Borneman worked together on the famous radio drama *The Adventures of Harry Lime*, whose protagonist (spoken by Orson Welles) was taken from the *The Third Man* (1949), a film that appeared in German cinemas as *Der dritte Mann* in early 1950. The film was set in Vienna and accompanied by a musical theme played by Anton Karas on the zither that had achieved some renown. The idea of capitalizing on the film with a radio drama was the brainchild of Harry Allan Towers, who also secured the necessary rights, Welles for the lead role, and Karas for the music. By adapting the essential sonic elements of the film for the radio drama, Towers ensured a form of acoustic recognition. Harry Lime's character dies in Carol Reed's film, so the episodes in the radio series were set in the past. Each installment began with the sound of a gunshot followed by an opening speech that delineated a topic much to Borneman's taste—a play of identities: "That was the shot that killed Harry Lime. He died in a sewer beneath Vienna. As those of you know who saw the movie *The Third Man*. Yes. That was the end of Harry Lime. But it was not the beginning. Harry Lime had many lives. And I can recount all of them. How do I know? It's very simple. Because my name is Harry Lime." [263] To popularize Lime, his character was refashioned from villain to adventurer by playing down his asocial tendencies and giving him an ironic, anti-authoritarian streak. In spring 1951 the International Broadcasting Company recorded in London, but also in Paris and Rome—depending on where Welles was at the moment—fifty-two half-hour episodes of *The Adventures of Harry Lime*. They were sold in the United States as *The Third Man: The Lives of Harry Lime*; the BBC acquired sixteen episodes and broadcast them starting in August 1951 as part of their "Light Programme." The series not only enjoyed wide popularity in the English-speaking world, but was translated into numerous languages and sold worldwide.

With *Othello* at a standstill and *Ulysses* a failure, Welles had only accepted the role for the radio piece in order to make money, also agreeing with Towers to write some of the scripts as a side job. Welles didn't write all of these himself, however, but contracted others as well—including Borneman. In June 1951 Borneman delivered the radio script "It's in the Bag," written for Welles as part of the Harry Lime series.[264] On another occasion he affirmed that Welles had asked him to develop a concept into a full radio script—but hadn't received any money for it. Not only that, but his name did not appear anywhere in the credits. He was particularly angered by a report in the US trade press that the series had sold at a premium and his piece "It's in the Bag" "has been singled out as the best of the lot—but with credit going to Orson and no credit given to me."[265]

This version is confirmed in its essence by Towers, who deviates only with regard to the number of pieces Borneman wrote. One day while at home Towers's bell rang. "It's a rather nice guy [Ernest Borneman] . . . and he had in his hand, these six scripts. And he said: 'Mr. Towers, I wrote these scripts for Mr. Orson Welles, and he's never paid me for them!'" When confronted about it, Welles came out swinging: "Don't pay him, Harry, they weren't very good scripts."[266] In the end, none of the broadcast episodes listed Borneman as the author, with Welles claiming to have written them himself. The number of shows Borneman did actually write remains unclear; Towers seems to remember six episodes. While this is entirely possible, there's no concrete evidence, and just as little for the "great many" that Peter Noble mentions with reference to the Harry Lime stories.[267]

Aside from Harry Lime, in 1952 Borneman wrote three radio scripts for Welles for the *Orient Express*: "Orient Express," "The Other Turkish Gentleman," and "A Case of Deviation." He had also written a plot line that unfolded over twenty-five half-hour *Orient Express* episodes. Borneman wasn't paid in this case either, however, and considered selling the stories in London, where a series of half-hour stories around the theme of the Orient Express had just begun.[268] When nothing came of yet another idea advanced by Borneman through his company Screen Playwright Ltd., three and a half years of unequal collaboration with Orson Welles came to an end. Welles valued Borneman's talent as a scriptwriter and repeatedly sent inquiries. Welles also exploited Borneman, however, and soon let him fall by the wayside. For Welles, who in general burned through his collaborators, Borneman became one partner of many who was useful for a time and not much longer. Things must have looked different from Borneman's perspective; he had cooperated with a leading director he admired, taken a first step out of the world of documentary, and worked on a large-scale dramatic film—even if concretely speaking his role in the project lasted only a few weeks before he fell back on smaller formats. He did what Orson had taught him to do, he wrote in retrospect: he wrote scripts for dramatic film and made his first forays into directing.[269] On the negative side of the ledger stood the ongoing dispute over money. Borneman continued to admire Welles as before, but this sentiment was increasingly dampened by the fact that he couldn't bring Welles to fulfill his financial obligations. Borneman's work with Welles accordingly does not play a particularly large role in his autobiography. One could of course adorn oneself with such collaborations, and it does find mention along with other details Borneman thought important, but there is no longer talk of "friendship," as in his letters.

Freelance Work in Television and Radio

His collaboration with Welles at an end, Borneman turned to writing for various television series, including three half-hour episodes for the adventure series *Sailor of Fortune*, produced by the Canadian company Mid Ocean Films and broadcast in England from 1955 to 1958. The show chronicled the escapades of a captain (played by Lorne Greene) involved in somewhat illegal transport operations on the Mediterranean.[270] In the same period he worked on *The Adventures of Aggie*, a show produced by Michael Sadlier for ME films and broadcast in 1956–57 by ITV that chronicled the adventures of a fashion purchaser based in London, Asgaard Agnete ("Aggie") Anderson, and her travels around the world. It is not entirely clear in this case either who wrote the twenty-six episodes. Borneman is only mentioned in "Assignment in Istanbul," while at another point "Peace and Quiet" is attributed to him—it is possible in this case that it concerns one and the same episode, just with different titles.[271] Another show, *Fabian of the Yard* (thirty-six half-hour shows, 1954–56), aired on

BBC as the first police crime series on British television, based on the memories of a Scotland Yard detective and dramatizing famous criminal cases that had occurred in London since the 1920s. The show didn't focus on the violent aspects of the crimes, however, so much as the psychological and emotional conditions of the criminals.[272] Borneman wrote the script for the episode "The Sixth Dagger" (1955), in which locations and works associated with Shakespeare are connected with five knife attacks, all carried out in the same manner by someone who feels called upon to defend Francis Bacon against the plagiarist Shakespeare by assaulting the latter's admirers. Borneman also wrote an episode for the long running series *The Adventures of Robin Hood*, which aired from 1955 to 1960 and depicted the adventures of a band of freedom fighters residing in Sherwood Forest in their efforts to protect England against the machinations of the evil Prince John. In "The Ambush" (1957), Robin Hood and his men plot to thwart Prince John's plans to depose the young, rightful heir to the throne, King Richard.[273] "God knows it was no masterpiece," Borneman reported back to Berlin, "but at least it helped me to take up directing again."[274] He again took the director's chair for the 1958 episode "At the Sign of the Blue Boar."

During the 1950s, Borneman later noted, he wrote, produced, or directed nearly one hundred pieces in total for radio and TV, as well as numerous series.[275] He was given a first chance to realize his ideas for a modern film suited to an international audience with *Bang! You're Dead* and *Face the Music* (both 1954), both feature films in which music and dance play a central role. Looking to the formal style in Borneman's work, one is struck by the general emphasis on musical films or projects that play out within a jazz milieu and communicate principally via nonverbal signals. In this context, music and dance are treated as autonomous forms of artistic expression, alternatives to the customary medium of communication of language. The idea of using music to assist in communication came from jazz, which largely derives its intrigue from the improvised dialogue between instruments. Borneman also looked to overcome linguistic borders by experimenting with films in more than one language and films without speech. The parallels to his literary notions—prompting the fantasy of the reader by omission and hints—are obvious. His films also show post-national potential, allowing for the possibility of a global reception without translation from one national idiom to another. As early as 1944 Borneman had dreamt of a jazz film whose story would be shown visually "while the sound track carries the music instead of commentary or dialogue." As part of his proposal for the concept for the Negro Film Institute, he suggested that "we might experiment with an entirely new departure in film music to which I have given a great deal of time and thought"—a musical film without speech.[276] In *Taps for the Dancer*, a film likely conceived in the late 1940s, the main character communicates by dancing the alphabet, thus re-creating "the world of letters and sentences through dance. The ideal voice in this case is the clack of the tap dancer."[277] *Words Fail Me* (1949) takes place in a country whose citizens have lost the ability to speak and make themselves understood through music, gestures, and color.[278] As noted above, *The Maze (Das Labyrinth* in

German) was intended to be filmed in multiple languages with actors of various nationalities communicating with one another in their native tongues. The meaning of the dialogue is not revealed through overdubbing or subtitles, but rather "with the help of a figurative musical backdrop, from the connection."[279]

Such films took as their model *Carosello Napoletano* (dir. Ettore Giannini), a two-hour filmed adaptation of a theater piece shown in Cannes in 1954 that tells the story of Naples through a family of Neapolitan street singers. This lavishly filmed historical musical does not communicate content verbally but only through music (including well-known melodies from the southern Italian city), dance, and gesture. Borneman was particularly impressed by the film's avoidance of any conventional storyline, instead using methods and techniques from esoteric avant-garde traditions—"in many ways the most remarkable musical film to be made anywhere the world over."[280] The film was "a cinematic freak" in every regard. The most remarkable aspect was that it had been made at all; while it was "a fascinating, ingenious, provocative film," it must have remained practically unintelligible to the vast majority of cinemagoers, "since there is no continuity of plot, all continuity is either optical or acoustical."

A further series of reviews from the mid-1950s offers insight into the development of Borneman's theoretical reflections on film. Among other things, the writing reveals how far Borneman had strayed from Grierson's ideal for documentary film and the collective vision guiding the National Film Board of Canada, and how much more clearly he now adhered to the ideal of auteur film. Something he certainly picked up in part from his interactions with Orson Welles, it was an ideal that, outside a handful of famous individuals, continued to remain an exception in the film business. In a euphoric review of Fellini's *La Strada* (1954), which depicts the relationship between a gruff egomaniac, the actor Zampanò, and his sensitive, slightly mad assistant Gelsomina, Borneman notes that this work "of complete independence of mind, wholly original in concept and execution," could never have been made in Great Britain. A director who proposed such a plot to a producer would be driven out of the British film industry as a dangerous lunatic.[281] In response to criticism that Fellini had overstepped the borders of realism with his poetic tale about the fringes of society, Borneman countered, "I prefer a non-realist film of talent to a realist film that has nothing to recommend itself except truth, and, perhaps, social purpose." Citing the example of Luchino Visconti, a member of the Italian Communist Party, Borneman rejected a socialist realism driven purely by political intentions, but which lacked imagination. "Visconti's heart, no doubt, is in the right place, too, but that does not qualify him to direct films, produce plays, or make pronouncements on aesthetics." Few directors had been able to translate their notion of life onto the screen—Borneman mentioned Charlie Chaplin, Jean Vigo, Carl Dreyer, René Clair's middle work, and the young Orson Welles, who with films such as *L'Atalante*, *La passion de Jeanne d'Arc*, *À Nous la Liberté*, and *Citizen Kane* had revealed a unique signature and opened up new ways of seeing the world, be it through critical, fantastical or utopian, or aesthetically innovative projects.[282] These directors were able to accomplish this only because they largely retained control of their films by combining the roles of scriptwriter, director, and often producer in their own person. Borneman recognized Fellini's merit above all in his effect on the audience: "a wholly unconventional tale told from a wholly unconventional angle which succeeded, by sheer strength of imagination, to persuade us, who had never experienced anything even faintly like it, that it was not merely true but relevant to our own experience."[283]

Borneman experienced a breakthrough in his own productions in the early 1950s; aside from journalistic work for diverse magazines, radio presentations, and television series, he completed five feature films: *Tremolo, Bang! You're Dead, Face the Music, Four O'Clock in the Morning Blues,* and *Betty Slow Drag.* The films also reveal a formal emphasis, with four taking place in the jazz world and three musicals.[284] The exception was *Bang! You're Dead,* written with Guy Elmes (eighty-eight minutes, dir. Lance Comfort, edited by Borneman), a crime film without any reference to jazz that instead explores a subject that was already of interest to Borneman during his time in Canada, and which he would later pursue in studies on sexology—child psychology.[285] The film tells a psychological crime story that begins with the children's game "Bang! You're Dead": A seven-year-old steals a man's watch and shoots him—not symbolically with a toy pistol however, but literally, with a real weapon the child has found. Suspicion lands on the victim's rival, who had argued about a girl with the deceased shortly before the shooting. A friend of the child murderer accidentally discovers the truth, and the perpetrator confesses. As a study in child psychology, the film acquires depth by emphasizing the skewed perception of a child who once heard his single father say that many a person and animal would be better off dead than alive. On a more abstract level, the topic of an innocent child's confrontation with an amoral society is given contemporary relevance and distinguished by its setting in World War II. Classified as noir, the film came out on 9 March 1954 to highly positive reviews.[286] Borneman had already sold the television adaptation of his novel *Tremolo* in early 1950 to the US company CBS (Columbia Broadcasting Company).[287] It premiered in the United States on 4 July 1950 as the new CBS TV series *Sure as Fate,* directed by Yul Brunner and with Paul Lukas playing the lead.[288] *Variety* described an "exceptionally well-scripted adaptation" and "some of the slickest production, acting and dialogue yet seen on video."[289]

In the Boardrooms of British Commercial Television

After contentious debate, on 30 June 1954 Great Britain passed the Television Act, becoming the first European country to abolish the monopoly of state broadcasting and permitting commercial broadcasting, following the US model. It was not only advertising companies making TV commercials that profited in the ensuing gold rush but also commercial regional broadcasters, which were eventually brought under the auspices of Independent Television (ITV) and organized by region. Borneman immediately entered the field, acquiring the reputation of a professional versed in developing commercial television broadcasters. That same year he became director of the film and television department at Alfred Pemberton Ltd., a large PR firm specializing in radio and television that sought to capture a larger audience with its new hire.[290] Borneman worked on the company's commercial television division and wrote TV commercials himself. In summer 1955 he traveled through the United States for six weeks for his new job, studying the US broadcasting system and selling his own manuscripts on the side. He published a summary report about the trip, according to which the comedies and more generally the light entertainment available in the US programs were far superior to the best that the BBC had to offer. The drama, meanwhile, was not always better. He also commented on US commercials, color television, and the possibility of recording TV shows, which he considered absolutely revolutionary.[291]

In 1955 Borneman joined the newly founded Granada TV Network, first in London, then in Manchester. Granada was responsible for the industrial northwest corner of England and sought to establish a media industry there through television.[292] As the head of the script department and personal assistant to programming director Sidney Bernstein, Borneman took on an influential position at the company.[293] He entered the field of commercial television with the ambitious goal of maintaining quality, and thus avoiding the nightmare scenario initially forecast for non-state television in Great Britain. Such pronouncements took the BBC as their standard, which from the beginning had aspired to improve viewer's education and refine the taste of the national public, setting an international benchmark for public television. From Borneman's point of view, however, the quality standards of the BBC were already too low. Like many critics, he was unclear as to whether the ITV audience was anything other than that of the BBC, which served the interests of the elite. An ITV program by contrast was conceivable only for a mass audience, albeit—went the hope—one that would not lower standards or depart entirely from the realm of high culture. Even before his time in commercial television, while still a screenwriter and director, Borneman had argued that "since we don't want to do what everybody else has done in the past, we are bound to annoy them. So be it. The BBC is there to raise the standards of entertainment, not to lower them to the level of the lowest common denominator."[294] Such then was the condition under which Borneman began his work in commercial television: to risk something new that would challenge the taste of the public instead of merely serving it. As reported on in the industry press, he arrived at Granada with a briefcase "bulging with revolutionary ideas for television drama."[295] And Borneman did in fact help to turn Independent Television into an institution that enriched the country with new programming ideas, which in turn spurred the BBC on to reform. "Auntie Bebe" had long looked down on private competition and its audience with disdain but in 1960 found itself at eye level, competing among equals.[296]

One of Borneman's most important projects was the *Granada Workshop*, a series of half-hour televised plays he directed that was lauded as "the most highly acclaimed and daring series of television plays in the history of English television."[297] With the *Granada Workshop*, Borneman played an active role in programming that would give ITV a decisive advantage over the BBC, fully belying the widespread assumption that ITV's forte lay chiefly in the field of light entertainment.[298] The aim was to produce "realistic stories about people in every-day conflicts" and, because television was an intimate medium, in a minimalist style with as little scenery, cast, and crew as possible. "We want plays where the whole action takes place on a person's face."[299] The industry press rightly recognized in Borneman's Granada program "a policy of adventurous, uncompromising plays," including ambitious drama such as *Look Back in Anger* (John Osborne), *Accolade* (Emlyn Williams), multiple works by Arthur Miller including *Death of a Salesman*, pieces by Thornton Wilder, Jean-Paul Sartre, and other contemporary writers.[300] Borneman himself worked on a revision of Ibsen's *Hedda Gabler*, which he also directed.[301] In relation to John Osborne's debut, Denis Forman speaks of a breakthrough in a realistic and topical concept for television, one that took aim against the convention of good taste. The piece treats the radicalization of the younger generation and the socially determined conflict between a young couple—he a member of the working class, she the middle—with the utmost realism. Borneman saw *Look Back in Anger* shortly after its premiere in 1956 and recommended it eagerly to his boss, Bernstein: "This is the most powerful play by an English author that I have seen in the last six years."[302] In its present form the piece was unthinkable for television, Borneman continued, as the language was entirely frank, full of "four-letter words," and depicted scenes that would cause advertisers to shudder. Despite his misgivings, Bernstein decided to give the "angry young man" a national audience. According to Forman, while shooting the piece Borneman got cold feet himself; he had lightly revised the script and was afraid he had cut too little: "Damns and sods I leave in. Lavatory pieces I leave in. I take out six bloodys and four bastards." By Forman's account, Borneman had a nightmare about a censor and that the entire nation, horrified, would flood the *Times* with letters to the editor the next day. The "bloodys" and "bastards" stayed put, however—the station introduced the piece as one before which the children should be sent to bed, while those over forty-five should think carefully about whether they wanted to subject themselves to such a piece. The framing of the show as one for a younger audience hit the mark. The broadcast was a total success because it realistically modeled the everyday speech of young people and contained social critique. *Look Back in Anger*, Forman continued, was Granada's first victory over convention and the cowardice of those tasked with representing commercial interests in the media.

Another goal at Granada was to profile the medium of television as fostering regional identity. Borneman looked to recruit actors from the north of England but also to focus subject matter on the region and show "how conflicts can arise out of Northern life."[303] In Borneman's eyes, this concept gave birth to modern English television. "*Every* English television writer who made a name in the 1960s started with me."[304] Later, when he had to defend himself in West Germany, he even claimed he was "one of the few German-speaking television figures . . . to have a decisive influence on Anglo-Saxon television—the entire program for England's most successful television company, Granada TV Network, was my brainchild."[305] Such an assertion was not especially risky, of course, as there were not all that many German-speaking figures involved with television in Great Britain. More to the point, however, is the fact that Borneman's short stay at Granada, just two years, limited his influence. It was Sidney Newman, Borneman's earlier friend and colleague at the National Film Board of Canada, who would go on to become the great reformer of the British television drama with ITV's Sunday afternoon series *Armchair Theatre*, which systematically introduced the young British avant-garde to the screen beginning in 1958.[306] Later Borneman could not understand why the BBC did not select him, but rather Newman, to be head of drama at the BBC, as all the televised plays that Newman produced in three years at ABC (American Broadcasting Corporation) had been Borneman's ideas.[307] As director of programming at Freies Fernsehen, in 1960 Borneman sought to show a number of these pieces in West Germany and to obtain their directors for guest productions.[308]

Borneman nevertheless found the work atmosphere congenial; Sidney Bernstein was not only "the only Socialist among applicants for a television license," as Borneman emphasized, but Granada was an institution with clear leftist leanings and much more ambitious than the BBC in its willingness to pursue technical experiments.[309] As Denis Forman emphasized, films for a mass audience and artistic pretensions were not seen as being opposed to each other. Bernstein "brought to commercial TV, in the days before the industry apparatchik existed, the aspirations of an impresario of the arts."[310] In short, it was television according to Borneman's taste. And it was in fact Borneman who introduced Granada's highly praised and much loved line of drama.[311] All in all, he adapted twenty-eight theater pieces for Granada and gave the broadcaster new life with the introduction of the series *New Television Plays by New Television Authors* upon leaving in 1957.

By this point Borneman was considered a hot ticket in the television business, "one of the most all-round talented men in commercial television today," as *Kinematograph Weekly* noted.[312] Immediately after he left Granada Television, Wales and West, the new private television station for Wales and west England, recruited him to be the new head of its script department. He was not destined to remain for long, however, reporting to his father by March 1958 that he had given up his position "yet again."[313] When new ideas for projects didn't work out, Borneman again turned to literature. The year 1959 saw the publication of his third novel, *Tomorrow Is Now*, bearing the half-ironic subtitle *The Adventures of Welfare Willy in Search of a Soul*. The character of Willy Proctor stands in for the middle class, in a story that explores generational conflict in a family context. After growing up in London, Willy studies in the United States, where he is involved in the Manhattan Project as a talented young physicist. He returns to England after the war with his American wife, Jean, and their son, Sam, where he slowly despairs of the British social state, which he finds stifling; of his wife, who turns more and more to cognac; and of his Teddy Boy son, who wants nothing other than to be left alone. To Willy's father, Donald Proctor, who was socialized alongside his wife, Maria, during the revolutionary era of the early twentieth century and has devoted his life to changing the world, his son's US brand of liberalism seems both amoral and unethical. Somewhat improbably Borneman has Donald and Maria appear as functionaries of the Communist International at every major hotspot in the global class war during the first half of the twentieth century— at the Kienthal Conference, where they first meet, on the barricades of the Bremen Soviet Republic, at the general strike in Turin, at Bela Kun's side in Hungary, at the Hamburg Uprising, in revolutionary China, at the 1934 Vienna workers' uprising, and in the international brigades in Spain. A brief, if highly schematic "aesthetics of resistance" *avant la lettre* appears in the novel, with the characters regularly reflecting on the morality of their action and—like the author himself—finally disavowing the Soviet Union when it concludes the pact of nonaggression with Nazi Germany in 1939. Donald, who is drawn to Trotskyism after breaking with the Soviet Union and still sees himself as a Communist at the point of narration in the 1950s, badgers his son with the norms of engagement and solidarity. For his part, Willy comes across as an egotistical intellectual, an avowed Tory who only pursues his own benefit even in private, alienating his son and driving his wife to commit suicide in the process. While the elderly generation laments the younger generation's depoliticization and retreat into the private sphere and Willy looks to free himself from the older generation's moral superiority, Willy's son, Sam, takes refuge in the youth rebellion of the late 1950s—"we're a beat generation"—and ends up in jail after wounding a policeman during a brawl. The moment of rebellion and the associated emotions provide a link between the grandparents and their grandson, but deep divides in lifestyle and ultimate aims remain conspicuous.

Even if the generational concept approximates the truth—at least for one part of society—at the beginning of the novel it comes across as overly schematic, an ideal sociological form. As the book progresses, however, competing ideologies cede to psychological conflicts between individuals. To critics the book appeared less a political novel than a profitable "study in decadence."[314] Borneman is clearly concerned with making use of everyday speech in the dialogue, in particular that of deviant youth. The account was praised for its "melancholic brutality," which was superior to that of John Osborne.[315] Looking back, the author deemed *Tomorrow Is Now* his best book. Why? It was his most contemporary novel, moving beyond his specialized interests in jazz and film to address broader social issues. It was also his most political novel, clearly an attempt to come to terms with his own Communist past and present-day position, to set them both in relation to each other and the current rebellion with which he sympathized. Finally, as a declaration of faith in the present, the novel rejected historical determinism and a naïve belief in the future in equal measure. Upon hearing her husband Donald still insist that the future of the past will fall to one side

("The rebels will rise again and blood will be red once more"), Maria—as the only figure who consistently projects warmth, a sense of reality, and a will for unity—counters, "Tomorrow is now, dear."

Back to Germany?

Since his return to Europe, Borneman had been torn between pursuing new, stimulating work in a number of European countries, Canada, and the United States, and returning to Germany. Family was a consideration; Borneman wished to live closer to his father and his father's new partner, Erna Neumann, the widow of a lawyer, who had married Curt in 1948. More important were professional calculations, however—where one might find a stimulating work environment and infrastructure, primarily relating to film, and earn a living. In England the rise of television, coming before it did in Germany, had brought about a decline in cinemas and the film industry, making job opportunities outside television somewhat rare and leaving Borneman relatively out in the cold following his departure from Wales and West. The political situation was also relevant, however; in the first years after the war, Borneman had dismissed out of hand the German self-pity he encountered again and again in his father's letters, explaining to Curt that in Canada nobody would accept his laments for "poor Germany." "We all think . . . that however poor Germany may be now, it is its just punishment for making the whole of Europe poor and killing off a good many of the young men and women of nearly all nations."[316] Borneman's brief visit to Berlin in 1948 had confirmed to him that not much had changed in the essentially maudlin mindset. Then there was his own uncertainty about whether he could live in the Federal Republic worry free, as the Cold War had re-established old front lines. In 1954 Borneman explored the possibility of applying for compensation for losses suffered under National Socialism but lost interest when he heard that applications from Communists were rejected automatically. "I fear it will soon come out that *Schulkampf* wasn't actually a Social Democratic publication, which would not only mean that my application will be rejected, but that I would now also appear again as a Communist in German files. I hardly need tell you what that means in today's political climate."[317] Still, when a longtime family friend returned from West Germany in the late 1950s with a grim report, Borneman, whose own economic prospects were anything but rosy, reacted with nonchalance: "If you can believe her account, it is a Philistine's paradise with anti-Semitism and anti-everything. By comparison, she says, English sloppiness and hyprocisy is a dream. It's never seemed that way to me. I think that one day I will in fact return to Germany."[318]

Borneman had made an effort to develop a foothold in Germany since the early 1950s mostly through jazz and the radio, where he tried to find a home for his work. While he was able to land a number of programs on the radio through Siegfried Schmidt-Joos and Joachim-Ernst Berendt, his progress in film and television was halting, aside from an invitation to the Berlinale. He also worked as an emissary for

German jazz musicians in Great Britain, introducing figures such as Hans Koller and Albert Mangelsdorff. In 1954 alone he produced thirteen jazz programs on both sides of the channel.

In 1959 other parts of the world called. From Ghana came an offer to head the government's film department (which he turned down), traveling instead to India to participate in a British-Indian co-production.[319] The trip was a risk; on 1 September 1959 Borneman had accepted a position as program director at the National Film Theatre and press chief at the British Film Institute (BFI) and was thus responsible, among other things, for the London Film Festival, which began in October.[320] As made clear by his weeks-long absence on a trip for which his colleagues resented him, Borneman still preferred to make films. In the short time he spent at the British Film Institute—the contract had initially stipulated six months and was thus set to end in March 1960—Borneman produced the jazz program for the National Film Theatre's Negro World Festival, among others.[321] *The Girl on the Highway*, which Borneman had originally written for television and was adapted for theater by Peter Cotes, premiered on 15 February 1960. It was a first-rate disaster, unanimously panned by critics and rightly so, as its author declared—"It was terrible."[322] Bad press, the Indian project a failure, unpopular at the British Film Institute, and with no other irons in the fire—Borneman was greatly depressed and considered for the first time retreating from all the noise to an isolated house in Austria.[323] In short it was time to go, and when a truly overwhelming offer came in from Germany, he leapt at the chance.

Freies Fernsehen

Programmatically as well as practically, the growth in Borneman's enthusiasm for live television as a documentation of "real life" can be seen with particular clarity from a large project in the early 1960s that would catapult him atop the German media landscape and, as he later recalled, mark the "most terrible period" of his life.[324] By the late 1950s Borneman's reputation as a media manager had begun to circulate in West Germany. The head of programming at the BBC, Cecil McGivern, had recommended him to film journalist Paul Marcus, a central figure among the German emigrants still in London after the war. Marcus, who was now consulting with the West German government in its search for a capable director of programming for a second German television channel, knew Borneman and held a high opinion of his abilities.[325] On 23 February 1960 two freshly appointed company managers for a new German TV company—Friedrich Gladenbeck, former state secretary at the Ministry of Post, and Heinz Schmidt, until recently the head of press for the Federation of German Industries—interviewed Borneman about his experience in television. Two days later they offered him the post of director of programming and production at the second German television channel that the Adenauer government, against the wishes of the federal states, had in mind to establish.[326] From this important post Borneman would be responsible for driving forward the "rapid and methodical" development of Freies Fernsehen "in keeping with German interests." There was even a "national economic interest" at stake in importing a "British citizen of German descent," as Schmidt wrote to the finance office in Frankfurt, requesting approval of a tax exemption pursuant to § 50 subsection 5 of the income tax law.[327]

Beginning in the early 1950s, figures from mass communications, industry, and newspaper publishing had laid the groundwork for commercial television in West Germany—which they saw as an opportunity to boost product sales—through the Study Group on Broadcasting (Arbeitskreis für Rundfunkfragen) and the Society for the Study of Radio and Television Advertising (Studiengesellschaft für Funk- und Fernsehwerbung).[328] In exchange for receiving a transmission license from the Federal Post Office, they were prepared to give the federal government free rein when it came to content. This accorded entirely with the interests of the government, which in conjunction with the same lobbying associations was also seeking a reorganization of the federal structure of the broadcasting landscape, seen at the time as being run by US fiat, by founding a second television channel as an "organ for state pronouncements" (Kurt Hickethier) that would operate at the national level, to the disadvantage of federal states. The federal government set the wheels in motion when on 30 December 1959 it quietly charged the "Freies Fernsehen GmbH" (or Freies Fernsehen Gesellschaft, FFG for short) with developing a program, the express purpose for which the group had been founded the previous year. Largely unnoticed at first in public, the FFG had one year to prepare a second television program for broadcast. Per the chancellor's wishes, the new institution was to begin broadcasting by 1 January 1961 without fail; he wanted to use the commercial channel to break up the monopoly of what he felt to be an overly critical public radio and to secure direct access to the mass medium of the moment before the upcoming Bundestag elections. Fully overestimating its power, Adenauer thought the outcome of the election to depend on television. This found expression in plans to limit SPD influence on the medium and to counteract the recent media fashion of disputing a journalistic tradition that merely echoed government positions verbatim and turning a more critical eye toward the actions of the powerful instead.[329] It was only in the summer of 1960 with the founding of the holding company Deutschland Fernsehen GmbH that the public first became aware of the project's aims, as well as the fact that the FFG had been at work for months developing the new program. The opposition rallied all its forces against Freies Fernsehen, and shortly before it was to begin broadcast, a constitutional complaint filed by SPD-governed states set up a roadblock. On 17 December 1960 the constitutional court issued a temporary decree suspending the scheduled broadcasting start date of 1 January 1961, with a ruling in favor of the sovereignty of the states and against "Adenauer television" following on 28 February 1961.[330] With the decision, the first attempt to create a dual broadcasting system—one that included both public service and commercial broadcasting institutions—failed, and Freies Fernsehen GmbH dissolved.

The initial conversation in London did not revolve around political matters however, and it is still unclear whether the background of the matter had already spilled out into public. In his memoirs Borneman plays up motives of infiltration, describing conversations with left-wing friends from the Labour Party who advise him to take the post and "push through as much for our cause as you can."[331] In other autobiographical texts Borneman even writes about wanting to return as a sort of "socialist Goebbels and pay those bastards back in their own coin."[332] These later interpretations may be due to the time at which they were given in the late 1970s; at any rate they seem far-fetched. Nevertheless, a political intention may not be entirely off the mark, as the example of Granada had shown that the private sector could provide new room to maneuver for forms of television with leftist politics that understood themselves as aesthetically innovative. The challenge of taking on such an ambitious project made the proposal all the more tempting; by the first broadcast on 1 January 1961, or only eight months after Borneman began work on 1 April 1960, a complete television program had to be devised and implemented, and the majority of broadcasts for the first half year pre-produced. This allowed him the possibility of marking the "style"—as his later competitor Eckert would describe the national character of television in Europe—of the second German television channel, and thus bringing the German television landscape up to speed with the British model.[333] Borneman could never have dreamed of returning to Germany in such a powerful position. It was already a triumph, as his father was soon able to confirm, writing that the newspapers were full of his name and that he had now "become a great man."[334] As soon became clear, however, the returning emigrant had misread several key factors: the political controversy surrounding the company; how serious the FFG leadership actually was about applying British experiences to a German setting not only on paper, but also in practice; the resistance of the political and cultural opposition to commercial television; and finally the connections that FFG leadership personnel held to the politics of the past and their openness to a returning emigrant businessman without German pedigree.

For his part, Borneman was focused on designing a program according to his convictions, from a position of power he had not had before—"German television after an English model."[335] As a returning emigrant with Jewish roots operating in an environment blighted by National Socialism and skeptical toward the West, the goal of creating an innovative, Western television channel that did not at the same time largely disregard the purported cultural mores of its audience created significant problems. Borneman was reproached for looking to push through entirely too much innovation with a staff that was entirely too oriented toward the West, while at the same time isolating himself from the potent media landscape of the federal states and the left liberal scene, which fundamentally rejected the entire premise of "government" or "Adenauer television."

Inventing Forms of Taste: Borneman's Concept

Shortly after beginning work at FFG headquarters in Frankfurt, Borneman submitted a policy paper that took a comparative, transnational approach, identifying areas for improvement in German television, and proposing a draft program that was in many regards ahead of its time.[336] Freies Fernsehen worked as a catalyst for innovation in a number of areas: recording its broadcasts to magnetic tape; producing a stock of programs that it kept in reserve, accelerating the decline of live TV; a stronger orientation toward target groups; awarding external contracts for programming instead of relying exclusively on in-house productions; increased purchase of US series; alternative programming structures and broadcasting formats; politicizing the discourse around television. From the beginning, Borneman broke with the widespread notion in Germany that television should primarily inform and educate its viewers, striving instead for a "synthesis . . . between [a program] of moral, ethical, and intellectual quality on the one hand, and curiosity, a justifiable need for entertainment, and the limited capacity of a TV audience for understanding on the other." While German television was technically superior to other Western countries, the document stated, it also listed a long catalog of shortcomings: neither the start and end times nor the order of the program squared with audience wishes; the pacing was "uniformly slack," and there was all in all "too much talking"; there reigned "instead of self-discipline, self-aggrandizement." Borneman attached great value to the language used on television, which should be closer to the everyday and more realistic than, in his view, it currently was. "The spoken word comes across more stiffly than it needs to. Neither the announcer nor the actor speaks freely. Everything seems affected, unnatural, rhetorical, declamatory."

Borneman considered it a mistake to develop the program based on what had already proved itself on the first channel: "Such a 'Safety First' program is irresponsible to the public. Our program must avoid things that were popular *yesterday*, for popularity is short-lived. We must invent new forms of taste instead of trailing behind." Borneman was ten years ahead of time with respect to his prospective audience, which didn't form one homogenous unit but was highly differentiated, "not an amorphous mass that finds its common denominator at the lowest possible level, but a group of countless minorities and unconscious communities of interest." Accordingly, it was the task of television to gain some clarity about these respective target groups and "at any given time of the day, week, or month, air the type of broadcasts that will reach the largest possible number of minority groups."

Borneman's policy paper also addressed the question of potentially adopting British formats. "Should we adopt the pacing of ITV, which proved itself incomparably more successful than did the BBC during the first three years of competition, or rather the well-tried German pacing of longer broadcasts, longer camera shots, solemn dialogue, and stage direction suited to the theater?" In Great Britain, too, the ITV program had been received with a great deal of skepticism; it was "almost unanimously regarded by the public and all the critics as too breathless, too restless and too 'American.'" Yet not only did it quickly gain more viewers than the BBC, it also triggered reforms at the public broadcaster that mirrored the ITV concept. As it was the founding of ITV had become a success story; the initially pointed skepticism of the public toward experimental pieces had tapered off. This distinguished ITV from the BBC, which had made small changes but remained more traditionally aligned. The public was prepared to accept programs on ITV that it would not have on the BBC.[337]

Four key elements emerge in Borneman's policy paper. First was an aggressive stance toward what was at the time still widespread reservations among cultural critics about television as such, and entertainment in particular, as well as the didactic character of many German programs that came from such misgivings. Second was the conviction that television represented its own form of media, requiring concepts and techniques different from those known to literature, weekly reviews, the radio, and film. Third, there was clear attention given to the needs of individual groups of viewers, much earlier than most of the protagonists of German television, who began to attribute greater importance to the internal diversity of television audiences in the 1970s.[338] Fourth was an intention supported by his time in Britain to adopt patterns in programming for Germany that echoed pioneering commercial shows in the West, even under the expectation of heavy criticism. Such ideas were disputed not only within the German public and world of television, but also among leadership at Freies Fernsehen, where there was considerable doubt about proceeding too blithely with innovation.

The policy paper did not address any directly political questions, and from the beginning Borneman denied working in any political capacity.[339] Such denials took aim in the first place against perennial suspicions within the CDU (Christlich Demokratische Union Deutschlands, or Christian Democratic Union of Germany) of Borneman's instrumentalizing his position, but were also meant to immunize him within Freies Fernsehen, where as a returning emigrant he stood under latent suspicion of having betrayed the fatherland. When speaking to the press, he emphasized the neutrality of the expert. In place of the bipolar view taken by Grierson at the National Film Board, Borneman's statement that "the program director must be neither an artist nor a propagandist" established a third, pragmatic viewpoint that took the interest of viewers as its vanishing point.

The Program

As director of programming, Borneman held deciding influence over its ultimate shape, a key field of which other departments were covetous, as soon revealed itself. He went to work straightaway at a job that knew no normal working hours. Between April 1960 and June 1961 his calendar was full from morning to evening with appointments: committee sessions, meetings with important figures from radio, television, and the entertainment industry. The entries read like a who's who of West German cultural life in the early 1960s. Borneman, for example, met with newspaper publishers who were also involved with Freies Fernsehen, like John Jahr (of *Der Spiegel*); representatives from state-owned radio, such as Dieter Finnern of the SFB (Sender Freies Berlin, or Radio Free Berlin) and Rudolf Mühlfenzl of Bayerischer Rundfunk; actors, like Erik Ode and Heinz Erhardt; scriptwriters, like Herbert Reinecker; directors Michael Pfleghar and Peter Zadek; writers and television authors, such as Heinar Kipphardt and Christian Geissler; journalists, like Klaus Harpprecht, Hans Habe, and—quite often—Peter von Zahn; as well as other important figures, like Jewish theologian and author Kurt Hruby, union functionary Eugen Loderer, historian Fritz Fischer, and music publisher Hans Sikorski. Aside from countless lunches and dinners, his expense report includes "drinks" with Curd Jürgens, Viktor de Kowa, and Georg Thomalla.

The names themselves indicate that Borneman cast a wide net about him, looking for working partners of all walks, and also sought to avoid a conservative profile, instead searching out new fields that piqued his interest in addition to known quantities. Where the faces on camera were concerned, the new was to be given preference over the familiar. Borneman painted a democratic picture for the press: "I never tried to find well-known personalities for our program. I developed my own. Anyone able to speak freely is a potential television star."[340] Finding new people—the same applied for those behind the camera.

Still, the second station could not manage without any stars, even if it meant former Nazi propagandists like de Kowa, but also other professionals like Reinecker and film producer Utz Utermann. More complex cases included pedagogue and scriptwriter August Christian Riekel (pseudonym Harald Bratt), a Social Democrat dismissed from being a high school teacher in 1933 for political reasons, but who then wrote screenplays for National Socialist propaganda films. At the same time, Peter von Zahn, a Washington radio correspondent from 1951 to 1960 and author of the television series *Aus der Neuen Welt* (From the New World) projected the international glamour of a world traveler. Zadek, who left Germany with his parents in 1933 for England, had completed a directing course in the meantime and become friends with Eva's charge Renate Scholem. Habe and Hruby were also emigrants. Then there were the numerous younger individuals from the "forty-five generation," or those who began their careers after 1945, often with democratic impulses—producer Helmut Ringelmann, whom Borneman specifically tried to recruit; directors Theodor Grädler and Jürgen Goslar; writers such as Kipphardt, the son of a victim of National Socialism and Wehrmacht deserter; and the leftist Catholic and later Communist Geissler.

Conceptually speaking, the content of the planned program was international, oriented toward target groups, formally and thematically daring, but politically conformist. It featured an innovative structure, with a number of formats unknown in Germany designed for target groups that for the most part hadn't been specifically addressed before. This included a program between six and seven-thirty a.m. primarily intended for laborers, a high production value afternoon program for children, a consistent framework of opening and closing shows, and a schedule composed predominately of thirty-minute bits. It would be years before many of these aspects became standard features of German television.[341]

British and US series gave the program an international flavor, as did its "champion racehorse" Peter von Zahn, who, although maligned by the CDU and the BDI (Bundesverband der Deutschen Industrie, or Federation of German Industries) as being overly critical, was assigned to produce 104 films in 1961 alone for the series *Weltenbummler* (Globetrotter) and *Diplomatenpass* (A Diplomat's Passport). A glance at the scheduled programming during the first quarter of 1961, the inaugural broadcasting period for the station, shows a diverse array of material that transcended geographical boundaries while also presenting topics with contemporary relevance.[342] In addition to a twelve-part CBS series about the history of flight, the program included three series produced by a Wiesbaden production company—*Kinder in Deutschland, Fremde in Deutschland*, and *Bilder aus Europa* (Children in Germany, Foreigners in Germany, and Images of Europe)—as well as a diverse youth program and a documentary series that included, among other things, the East-West question, China, equality, a women's program, current events, religion, and society.

As indicated by series titles such as *Rote Springflut* (Red Tide) and *Kommunistische Infiltration* (Communist Infiltration), fending off the supposed Communist threat played a key role around 1960 within both government and political education. In such cases, as with the series *An der heißen Front des Kalten Krieges* (On the Hot Front of the Cold War), which was scheduled for broadcast, the domestic secret service itself directed the shows. The author of this last show was Hendrik van Bergh, a public relations man who was well informed on the subject and an advisor to the Federal Office for the Protection of the Constitution.[343] In this case it becomes evident how television aspired to build a national identity by defining an external and internal enemy, and to create a nationally endowed sense of community by mobilizing the nation to repel this enemy. It is also an example of how federal ministries exercised direct influence over content set for broadcast—other series offer similar examples of intervention by the Federal Ministry of Defence and the Foreign Office. Borneman's notion of being able to design a program according to his taste thus had tight restrictions imposed upon it—without question when it came to information and documentary reports.

Borneman did not take active measures against anti-Communist programs, but did try to soften overly rigid concepts of imposing state policy, criticizing, for example, the format planned for the show *Die Jugend fragt* (The Youth Ask). The department head wanted to make sure that the youth discussed affairs "positively and constructively," while Borneman made a case for "totally open questions to men in public life who are fully unprepared"[344] and generally pointed out the inefficiency of political propaganda.[345] Backed by demands from viewers who expected more shows with entertainment from a second television station, Borneman devoted himself all the more to this field, the actual object of his ambition.[346] The traditional distinction between entertainment ("lowbrow") and serious culture ("highbrow") that remained common well into the 1970s in West Germany held no meaning for Borneman. This isn't to say that standards of quality were irrelevant for him. Rather, for Borneman the desire for entertainment was legitimate, and for that very reason it had to be well made. Good entertainment wasn't only to be found in popular series but also, as apparent from his work at Granada, in television plays written by the young avant-garde from countries around the world. And as program director at FFG, Borneman was on the lookout for good West German television play authors, a group that in contrast to Great Britain—where a nucleus had formed over the course of the 1950s— was then just beginning to emerge. It was for this same reason that German television still regularly resorted to filming theater pieces for its programs. The situation did improve through the 1960s, with the increased demand for German television plays from Freies Fernsehen and later the ZDF (Zweites Deutsches Fernsehen) broadening the selection.[347] Seen over the long-term, however, the increased numbers of feature films and series that were programmed meant television plays declined in importance when compared to the 1950s, a turn of events viewed with regret by many a television man, and which seemed to justify the skepticism of cultural critics who considered the television play a mismatch for the medium in the first place.

Borneman's plan of occupying Freies Fernsehen with leftists could scarcely be accomplished. This was due on the one hand to partisan political guidelines for leadership personnel established by the federal government and the BDI, but on the other to political misgivings among the liberal left, who kept a greater distance from the new medium than was the case in Great Britain. In general there reigned an elitist skepticism toward the "consciousness industry" (Hans Magnus Enzensberger), which was in the business of dumbing down the masses corrupted by the economic upturn. Television was its most effective instrument. Some individuals were brought into the fold, but what was on the whole already a considerable degree of mistrust only worsened when Adenauer's unilateral efforts through the FFG—and with them his political ambitions—became apparent. Borneman himself learned where the money for his work came from only in June of that year; he reported on defections among those who didn't want to be "Bonn's mouthpiece" and urged the FFG to release an official statement.[348] In an article entitled "No Tough Questions Please! Employees at the Second Channel Have No Say" for the magazine *Tele*, Manfred Lütgenhorst sketched the image of a conformist television station. Klaus Budzinski and Oliver Hassenkamp, whom Ernest Borneman had tasked with creating cabaret shows for Freies Fernsehen, expressed their doubts "because we cannot reconcile one-sided and potentially censored mass journalism with our consciences."[349] Twenty-one prominent authors would eventually boycott Freies Fernsehen for its commercial character and proximity to the government; in November 1960 the writer's group Gruppe 47 also boycotted the station.[350]

At least in principle, filling leading positions according to the criteria of political loyalty did occur—the entire point of the station, after all, was to secure a reliable mouthpiece for the federal chancellor for the 1961 Bundestag elections and beyond. Fritz Berg, the president of the Federation of German Industries, assured Adenauer in August 1960 that "within the corporation's highest positions" there were "active figures who, selected in close coordination between Mr. von Eckardt and the CDU parliamentary group, represent a positive political line such as no other broadcasting institution in Germany can even remotely exhibit."[351] Berg's assertion that "the Socialist and leftist-intellectual forces setting the tone at these same broadcasters will be removed from our company" did not prove entirely accurate. His words nevertheless make clear how odd a figure Borneman must have cut in Germany—a rare creature elevated from prospective deputy to the head of programming only because the candidate originally intended for the job, the reliable party man and later artistic director of ZDF Karl Holzamer, had decided against the position at the last minute.[352] Suddenly, a returned emigrant with apparently British loyalties sat at the head of the table. Placed at his side as a counterweight, in the position of deputy and chief dramaturge sat Gerhard Eckert, a functionary already known from the television landscape of the Third Reich. The lobbyist's successful 1941 dissertation "Broadcasting as a Means of Leading" had conformed to National Socialist standards, a blot on his record that made it difficult to gain a foothold immediately after 1945. Eckert's fortunes had reversed, however, as the ideal of broadcasting as "the voice of the state" acquired a new popularity with Adenauer's wish for his own television channel, raising Eckert's profile as a purportedly neutral academic advocate.[353] It was Eckert, moreover, who had directed the foundation of commercial television from a key intermediary position as the chairman of the Study Group on Broadcasting and the managing director of the Society for the Study of Radio and Television Advertising. Eckert could have accepted Holzamer as a boss, but not Borneman, all the more so as Borneman initially sought to relegate him to the post of director of program planning, where he would have had no influence.[354] Added to this came conflicting notions about the structure of the program, an issue Eckert brought to management, taking open aim at his boss.[355] It was an argument Borneman was able to win only with difficulty. He demanded that in the future he and Eckert reach agreement on Eckert's suggestions so the impression didn't arise that within the programming department there were "two different program concepts."

Günther Meyer-Goldenstädt, who like Eckert was a former member of the Study Group on Broadcasting and had got his start in television during the Third Reich, also belonged to the group of "old Nazis" who made life difficult for returning emigrants.[356] After 1945 Meyer-Goldenstädt directed live transmissions from the Bundestag and later became senior director at the ZDF. Borneman had originally been designated a production manager and deputy of the program director, but he became head of program production after Holzamer declined, initially leaving the post vacant.[357] This connected "programming" and "production," two areas of responsibility each with a significant workload of their own that when combined with such a short timeframe would have been essentially impossible to master.[358] Borneman thus fought, successfully, to have production separated out. The victory came at the price of Meyer-Goldenstädt assuming leadership for production on 1 October 1960, who then presumed to claim responsibility for areas that to Borneman's mind belonged only to the programming department. The main issue in the intense dispute was Meyer-Goldenstädt's refusal to implement the programming department's guidelines, instead asserting his own power of decision-making.[359] In Borneman's view, production leadership was to be viewed "not as an autonomous, but rather executing department."[360] Company management did not share this view, instead granting the head of production the power to "dictate" to the programming department "when, where, by whom and with which means [shows] were to be produced," in Borneman's words.[361] It was in particular disputes over jurisdiction with Meyer-Goldenstädt and the impossibility of producing the program in the increasingly brief window of time remaining that led Borneman ultimately to resign as program director at the beginning of January 1961.[362]

Borneman's third adversary in the leadership of Freies Fernsehen was Hans-Joachim Hessling, the authorized signatory and cofounder of the Reichspost-Fernseh GmbH in 1939,[363] and a key figure in the founding of NWDR television, as well as its former administrative head. Hessling had been lured away to Freies Fernsehen to direct administration, and Borneman singled him out as the primary reason why his coworker's initial enthusiasm gave way to general frustration. Borneman—and he was not alone—bemoaned the "increasing restriction of our freedom at work," which "has led to such depression among the production and program staff that we no longer take any joy or pride in it."[364] Hessling had drawn Borneman's ire by criticizing the expenses incurred in the wake of the programming department's initial enthusiasm and the productions, series and material rights, synchronizations, and so on it had commissioned. Borneman reproached Hessling for interfering in programming, among other things by deciding whether something was "too expensive," taking offense at the form that productions took or negotiating "with other organizations separately and without our knowledge."[365] It was precisely in regard to the high expectations Gladenbeck and Schmidt had encouraged with promises regarding his "latitude for decisions" that Borneman found the reality so disappointing.[366] The director of programming felt so hamstrung by Hessling and Meyer-Goldenstädt's interference that a half year after beginning work in Frankfurt he wanted the company management to affirm "the recognition that the programming department is the company's most important," as well as "the right to be able to make decisions within my own department without having to defend them at every executive meeting like a defendant at court."[367]

On 15 January 1961, shortly after the federal administrative court imposed a temporary broadcast ban on Freies Fernsehen, Borneman was replaced by Bruno Six, an old collaborator of Eckert's and the CDU state parliament representative for

North-Rhine Westphalia. Six had already obtained a leave of absence from his post as the head of the film, radio, and television department at the Federal Press Office and joined FFG management in November of the previous year. The change in personnel was reported on in the *Frankfurter Rundschau*: "The company denied rumors that hostilities due to the racial affiliation and emigration of the program chief had influenced his dismissal."[368] The denial alone makes clear that such attributions were commonplace, even if those factors may not have led directly to Borneman's replacement. His Jewish background had been common knowledge at least since his introduction at the shareholder's committee meeting on 15 March 1960, when it was briefly and inaccurately announced that his parents "had returned from Theresienstadt."[369] The exact reason for a three-line note preserved in his personal files that states, according to the employee responsible for the wage tax, that Borneman was of the "Jewish religion" remains unclear—the fact of its existence, however, does not.[370] An entire series of indicators hints that at Freies Fernsehen, Jewish heritage was incriminating. Borneman's subsequent ally Erich Rombach himself had made antisemitic remarks around the time of the London meeting with Gladenbeck and Schmidt. According to Rombach, a planned meeting with representatives from Granada TV failed after swastikas were scrawled across the Cologne synagogue and the numerous crimes that followed around New Year's 1959–60, a series of events that had also drawn attention abroad.[371] Of all the British television stations Granada was "furthest to the left" and had "two Jewish directors," including Sidney Bernstein. Writing in the same context, Rombach criticized Granada's show "The Swastika," which aired on 18 January 1960 and "from a German perspective goes far beyond the boundaries of what is tolerable. Those who watched the program were highly incensed afterwards, as it not only denounced issues relating to the Nazis, but was itself anti-German." Rombach's conclusion? For the time being, to shelve the idea of working with Granada. From here it was not far to the conclusion that "from a German perspective," a former Jewish employee from Granada who admitted to British influence should be carefully watched. This mistrust became palpable, Borneman recalled as an older man: "Whenever I walked into the cafeteria, for example, an icy silence would come over several tables. I was followed by their looks until I sat down somewhere, then the whispering would start. So this feeling of being in a totally hostile environment that was behaving conspiratorially was an experience that has stuck with me today."[372]

Resentment is also evident from statements made by the head of entertainment at Freies Fernsehen, who was subordinate to Borneman's programming department. Helmut Schreiber, a once legendary magician with the stage name Kalanag, had performed in private circles for the Nazi elite and come out publicly in support of the party. Borneman would have preferred to install a new recruit like Michael Pfleghar or Dieter Finnern in Schreiber's position.[373] Later Borneman went so far as to petition for Schreiber's dismissal on the grounds that he wasn't fit to meet "the tastes of a modern audience, even that of the average citizen."[374] When Kalanag's first, now highly outdated productions for Freies Fernsehen met with skepticism, he made little secret of his dislike of Borneman. From the beginning Borneman had fought to make Joachim-Ernst Berendt head of the music department; the doors of the station were open to him but Berendt decided to stay at the SWF (Südwestfunk, or Southwest Broadcasting) for reasons of loyalty and because he felt like "more of a listener—and therefore more a radio man than a TV man."[375] Schreiber/Kalanag registered the attempt to recruit Berendt for the job with the comment "My God, for the last time we're making entertainment for the masses, not for individual existentialists or returning emigrants."[376] Nor is this the only example of the degree of traditionalist reservations toward forms of culture perceived as "Western" among the leadership at Freies Fernsehen.

This became painfully clear in a dispute surrounding the question of how "English" the program should be. Borneman—or "the man who thinks English," as Kalanag put it[377]—found himself a target not simply because he wanted to fashion German television after the English model for professional reasons, but also because the prejudice that alleged "traitors to the fatherland" experienced at the time was often projected onto returning emigrants as well—duplicitous figures whose allegiances, when push came to shove, rested abroad. This applied in particular to those who had already attained or were on their way to positions of leadership, such as the SPD's 1961 candidate for chancellor, Willy Brandt. In the run up to that election, during which Freies Fernsehen was supposed to give Adenauer direct access to the hearts and minds of Germans, Adenauer disparaged Brandt by referring to him as "Brandt alias Frahm," in reference to the latter's time in exile.[378] This experience found literary reflection in Borneman's last novel, *The Man Who Loved Women*, when he has his protagonist Will Gregory—a man who has come to Germany in search of work—speak the following words: "The very fact that I spoke German with ease, though not without an accent, served my colleagues as their *Jagdschein*, their hunting license, their official permit to shoot me down. The method of *abschiessen* that they decided on was a whispering campaign that I wasn't a 'real' American but a *Flüchtling*, a refugee who had fled from Germany in some distant age of the past because I'd been Communist or else a coward trying to get away from the risk of war." Gregory had only returned to Germany "because I hadn't been able to make good in my adopted country. The fact that part of this was true—that I had actually come to escape from the downward curve of my fortunes—made it hard for me to strike back. I could not in good conscience stand up and proclaim: 'I'm *not* a Communist,' 'I'm *not* a coward.'"[379] Borneman registered the sensitivity to these points among his colleagues and the public, and sought to rid himself of the image of a returning Jewish emigrant. Once again, he took cover in a television magazine, saying he couldn't "claim for himself the honor of having been a political or racial refugee."[380] Once his time at FFG ended, he continued to try and clear such obstacles from his path in his attempts to gain footing elsewhere. He wrote to the artistic director at NDR that he "had left Germany at seventeen years of age to study in England. I'm neither a returning emigrant nor a refugee, neither a Jew nor otherwise politically bound."[381] It was not the "self-image of a professional innovator working by himself day and night, lost in a sea of incapable 'newspaper editors'" that left him helpless and "hyper-sensitive to 'German' criticism."[382] He saw himself as such of course, but it wasn't the supposed incompetence of others that wounded him so much as the very real German critique of returning Jewish emigrants who supposedly held foreign loyalties that resounded whenever his own position came up for discussion. The term "hypersensitivity" does not accurately describe or assess Borneman's reaction to such forms of hostility. For what was at stake was not an exaggerated perception arising from an inflated sense of self, but a de facto state of mind with which he had to grapple and which he had already noted twelve years prior on his first trip to Germany after the war. Nothing had changed: suspicion and fear—of rock 'n' roll and communism, lipstick and "Americanization"—still marked the faces of many. This characterized the reactions even among those who professed to want to open toward the West, but meant that primarily in terms of political security and economic prosperity—not cultural predilections.[383]

While Borneman thus came across to some as all too unconventional and "Western," others saw him as a reviving force, one to combat bureaucracy and breathe fresh air into the stale world of German television—a "refreshing, casually free-spirited motor," as it appeared in the *Frankfurter Rundschau*.[384] Chiefly responsible for this perception was Borneman's continual appearance as an innovator in the conflicts atop Freies Fernsehen, arguing for moving beyond formats he considered outdated. These conflicts broke out with particular vehemence in four, partially overlapping areas: the value of entertainment, the search for an aesthetic specific to television, the target audience, and with it programming structure, and finally the dispute surrounding the national imprint of the second channel mentioned above.

Entertainment or Information?

Even at its founding, the twin goals set for Freies Fernsehen paired better in theory than praxis. Industry, which was in search of an advertising platform, was interested in achieving the greatest possible resonance among viewers, and this meant entertainment. On the other side there were the federal government's political aims, which could only be accomplished if the share of informative programming were relatively high. Borneman focused chiefly on entertainment, seeking first to lessen the pedantic tone of top-down political messaging that still largely characterized German television, and second to gain the upper hand on the competition within public service broadcasting via entertainment's draw. In contrast to his later self-depiction as a sort of leftist television guerilla, Borneman was hardly able to achieve anything regarding the content of informational and documentary programming given the set political guidelines, and turned his critique instead to formal aspects, which in his view should at least be more entertaining than the competition's. This view set him diametrically opposite the chief editor Konrad Kraemer, to whom the responsibility for this aspect of programming fell. After his stint at the FFG, Kraemer, a "highly dutiful Catholic" and CDU man from Münster, went on to be the editor in chief at the Catholic News Agency (Katholische Nachrichten Agentur). Entirely in keeping with the prevailing view among most journalists during the Adenauer era, he professed a faith in balance and monotony, not opinion and commentary. "I am concerned with objectivity and truth, even at the risk of coming across as boring. For me, sensation isn't something for the screen."[385] It was no surprise that Borneman made little of Kraemer's ideas for programming, which featured titles like "Roundtable Bonn" (Bonner Stammtisch) and "For Our Guest" (Bei uns zu Gast), but also the somewhat more daring "Crossfire" (Im Kreuzfeuer)—all of which seemed "identical and equally boring" to Borneman. The shows were too uncritical, but most importantly they were unfit for television in their formal conception and took too much of a journalistic tack, making them "translations of newspaper articles into television programs."[386] For political programming he recommended that Kraemer's department develop "a program like the English *Panorama*," which "has three or four camera teams filming and presents the week's events in real living color, rather than having four or five newscasters sitting still in a room talking themselves to death." In similar fashion, by the early 1960s Borneman anticipated the trend toward entertainment news that would first break through in West Germany in the 1980s.

As the future program began to take shape in the fall of 1960, a conflict thus arose between Borneman and Kraemer regarding the proper proportions of the two types of programming when a coworker presented a comparison of ARD and Freies Fernsehen. While only 24.3 percent of the ARD's broadcasts were informational or documentary in nature, Freies Fernsehen had plans for 36 percent. The percentage was much too high for Borneman, who thought Kraemer should reduce it to 20 percent or at maximum 25 percent, as with English stations, although this too was on the rise.[387] Borneman's plans shared the same fate as anything else that ran counter to Adenauer's plans—they failed. He did manage to sell the admittedly high proportion of informational programming planned for the first quarter of 1961 as evidence to disprove the regularly aired criticism that Freies Fernsehen offered a "lighter" program than the state-owned competition.[388]

Television Programming and Aesthetics

In principle, Borneman's critique of Kraemer's informational programming rested on an approach he had already developed in his writing and film work during the 1930s and 1940s. Traditional boundaries in text were to be dissolved and various forms of expression woven together intertextually through word, sound, and image, albeit with each medium working out its own specific form first. This in turn provided space for different options, with documentary film, for example, leading either to what Borneman termed "editorials"—partisan explanations about the larger forces at work in the world—or to everyday stories with a "human touch." In the case of television—a medium with sovereign possibilities and borders, most of which had yet to be explored—a cinematic eye was an advantage, in particular if one came from print media or was a writer. On its own it was insufficient, however, as the point was to achieve a visual form that was appropriate to the specific conditions of television and distinguished itself not only from the press, but from the cinema. In his original policy paper on programming for Freies Fernsehen, Borneman named a handful of aesthetic fields whose overhaul seemed urgent. German set design struck him as too restless. Entertainment broadcasts in particular suffered "a type of expressionism run amok—Christmas tree decorations à la Piscator"; the set constructions were too busy and too complicated. Such complexity was conceived of for theater and did not read on the small screen. The result was that the "set design confuses"—"the site of action for the television is the human face. Anything that distracts misses the mark."[389] Here Borneman repeated a widespread assumption among proponents of television, who pointed to its ability to depict internal conflicts—and thus not only its artistic capacity, but also an advantage it held over theater.[390] Over the course of the 1960s, the unique properties pertaining to television came to be defined less formally than in terms of content—as the format that allowed for the quickest realistic, critical, and engaged treatment of contemporary problems. The discussion thus came full circle to where Borneman began with Granada in 1956; in 1958 an adaptation of John Osborne's hit play *Look Back in Anger* for the North and West German Broadcasting Federation (Nord- und Westdeutscher Rundfunkverband, NWRV) set an early example in the trend toward a "new realism" in German television, with critics hailing it as one of the most "impactful television events in recent memory."[391]

Borneman's ideas for program structure also contradicted what was customary on the first channel, not to mention those of the chief editor Kraemer, who came from newspaper. While Kraemer wanted to draw attention and an audience through a constantly changing program—as was currently the case in real-time newspaper reporting—Borneman sought a clearly defined framework: fixed start and end times, fixed time slots for regular broadcasts. "When a patient comes round after a powerful anesthetic and watches our program," Borneman noted, describing his principle in an interview with Rüdiger Steinmetz, "he should immediately know: today is Wednesday."[392] Borneman thus relied not only on quick changes, but also on stability and recognizability, which would have drawn a distinct profile from that of ARD. The "endless succession of twenty-seven-minute films" and subsequent lack of any "real central programming focus" came in for particular criticism.[393] No sooner did Borneman's influence wane than this key element in his ideas about programming was scaled back.

Family or Target Audience Programming?

Nearly every key aspect of Borneman's programming concept was subject to dispute within the upper echelons of Freies Fernsehen, with some members standing directly opposed. This proved problematic not only regarding the prospective program. His deputy Gerhard Eckert clung with an iron grip to his idea of family television, a notion he had defended once before.[394] In his "guidelines" for future television dramatists, he noted that it should be "taken into account that the overwhelming majority of all television plays are seen by families, with different age groups present at the same time." From Hamburg, news magazine *Der Spiegel* considered this "an attempt to talk newcomers into believing that the art of doing right by all is a learnable one." It was a position shared by the managers Schmidt and Six. Borneman protested against a vision of the past and future FFG program that was in line with Eckert's proposal but ran contrary to Borneman and, in hindsight, misrepresented the channel's policy.[395] In this version, it had been fixed "from the outset" that "an explicitly family oriented program should be provided," indeed "every program [should] be suitable for families as a whole." Programming needs not met by this requirement were to be broadcast during the night program. Borneman's response: the head of programming must "never sketch programming so banal that it interests every member of the family at the same time. This 'family program' is . . . the very antithesis of the type of program I have tried to develop for Freies Fernsehen." Such a position was at odds not only with revisionist positions in FFG management after Borneman's departure and the higher power of government policy, but also with a broadly established consensus in West German society: the notion that the family in its classical form—a male provider with a housewife who cares for their children—represented the nucleus that would heal a national community torn apart by the war and its consequences. The federal government had already made some effort to enshrine this harmonious image legally and could have held no interest in then turning around to question it in the media. In general, the electronic "campfire" around which people gathered was assigned a great degree of social cohesive power that extended to any number of imagined communities. The communal act of watching a television program, went the idea, created a connection not only within the nation but also within the family, even if its members might otherwise hold different interests. From this perspective, Borneman's notion of target groups must have seemed destructive. Taking into account Adenauer's belief in the power of television, the danger arose that it might drive forward a trend already visible from some women's part-time inclusion in the workforce: an erosion of the family unit. Seen in this way, Borneman was the enemy within, the "other" threatening the stability of society.

The English material for which Borneman secured the rights to adapt for television plays and his youth program reveal in equal measure the extent to which the program director was prepared, when in doubt, to give preference over the banal to what many in the FFG leadership would deem "shocking." There were few taboos in Borneman's understanding of television programs, which took as its point of departure the everyday life of the viewer and a choice in material and staging that hewed closely to reality. The television play *Das Große Geschäft*, broadcast in 1959 under the title *The Big Client* (dir. Ted Kotcheff) for Sidney Newman's acclaimed *Armchair Theatre* series, nevertheless shows the limits of taste such designs ran up against. Schmidt di Simoni, the head of advertising at FFG, found the satire, which takes place within the advertising industry, as "neither amusing nor intriguing" but "intolerable for German conditions." The level of argumentation becomes clear from di Simoni's objection that "it is simply unacceptable that the client essentially demands the mistress of the contractor he hired as 'compensation.'" [396] Already mildly annoyed, Borneman replied to this and similar criticism of another piece by arguing that it wasn't enough to say that these things were good as works of art but bad for a television audience. "It seems to me that these are works of art because they are honest and deal at the same time with the real problems of normal people." [397]

Borneman also received criticism for the youth program he developed. As the FFG slumped and the finger pointing began, one internal critic, speaking in bad German but all the more pointedly for it, suggested rethinking the entire youth program in light of the first episode of *Für Erwachsene verboten* (No Adults Allowed): "The way it is now one gets the impression as though there was only one kind of youth in Germany, interested only in pop music, dark red lips and blue fingernails. Where are the youth associations assembled in youth councils? Where are the Scouts, the CVJM (YMCA), etc. who accomplish so much that is beneficial?" [398] Other shows were disqualified as "tasteless" or "common," such as the youth music show *Mississippi Illusion*, an early work from a barely 23-year-old Rob Houwer—the Dutch film producer who would find later success with Volker Schlöndorff, Peter Fleischmann, and Paul Verhoeven. What a contrast this was to the actual changes in youth culture such as Borneman had experienced and helped to shape early on in cities like London and Paris. By comparison, stuffy notions of protecting the youth and conservatism, but also a good part of public opinion could come across only as a hopeless form of provincialism. Borneman sought to break taboos not out of principle, but in order to make television that closely mirrored social reality, and thus spoke to viewers instead of putting them off by maintaining a traditional worldview and normative demands. The constitutional court's ruling spared Borneman a final test as to whether this approach would actually make it onto the screen; there is a distinct possibility he would have been disappointed here, as well.

"German" or "English" Television?

Borneman is an interesting case study in the complexity of cultural exchange between Great Britain and Germany, two large countries where television became popular early on, yet which proved more complicated than initially suspected by FFG leadership. As an important actor in the formation of cultural self-images and a medium for the transnational circulation of aesthetic forms and cultural interpretations, television was witness to a clash between constructions of national identity that could not be resolved by the London recruit's double socialization. [399] Borneman returned to Germany in the avowed capacity of a transnational cultural middleman, with the intention of bestowing the blessings of commercial television that had spread so widely on the other side of the British Channel. This had been the reason for his appointment, but it became difficult once the theory of cultural transfer was put into practice.

Transnational media influences have always provided an opportunity to reflect critically on the elements of one's own national culture.[400] While an orientation toward British and US commercial television was one defining feature of its German counterpart, a considerable debate sprang up around the question of national television culture. Industry and government figures involved in developing the new program may well have been open to Americanization in the fields of the economy and politics but otherwise held considerable misgivings, specifically within the cultural field. Eckert, for example, fashioned a "European style" that found its "opposite pole" in US television, not only asserting television's importance to national identity but seeing in it a reflection of national characteristics: "Each country has the programming that it has earned."[401] It wasn't possible, therefore, to leave "a director coming from London"—namely Rudolph Cartier—with the decision of whether a television play should be included in the program.[402] Cartier's origin meant he lacked the special touch for German culture. Oscillating between approval and contempt, Eckert isolated the specific characteristics of German television in the mid-1960s: "Lacking in brilliant sensations, experimentation or avant-garde efforts in its solidity, television constitutes a parallel to Volkswagen, and is thus an unreserved exponent of the conservative aversion to risk in Germany today.[403]

The founders of FFG did aspire to television based on an English model in a concrete sense, but its model characteristics were seen largely in terms of its private commercial basis and formal details, such as a more relaxed appearance for newscasters or moderators, and not the content, which should be "made to conform to German conditions."[404] Especially within conservative circles, German culture was assigned a superiority that must not be surrendered—to the contrary. US culture continued to be seen as superficial and the "increasing Americanization" of television decried, with sex and crime as the gateway for the corruption of German youth in particular.[405] Doubts about the applicability of FFG shows prepared according to a British or US model surfaced repeatedly in evaluations, as with the series *Loretta Young*, of which one critique said it "was not fully in line with our mentality."[406]

An opinion survey conducted by the Allensbach Institute showed a majority of viewers—in particular those among the upper classes—disapproving of "an excess of 'foreign' series" and preferring German shows.[407] Such reservations were widespread not only in public but within the upper echelons of the FFG, who would at times draw on public opinion in their arguments against an overly British or US program. Conflict with a program director who had been brought on board specifically for his experience in developing commercial television programs in Great Britain—and who quickly established that colleagues and the public alike were only partially willing to treat these experiences in earnest—was thus unavoidable. This was made no easier by the fact that Borneman was perceived not as "English" but, correctly, as a returning emigrant. Borneman had settled in Great Britain not just as a "German," but as a former German citizen who wanted to shed his "Germanness" as fully as possible. His Jewish background and political views played a key role in this context; he wasn't a German per se, so to speak, but a true-to-life apostate German with specific opinions and interests that colored his perception of the host country and which—altered by his experiences in Britain, Canada, and France—made their difference felt upon his return. Borneman thus concentrated experiences in his person that transcended borders and were incompatible with the notion of national identity, at any rate as it surfaced in the FFG committee meetings. Nor can one speak strictly of a trade in experiences between Britain and Germany so much as a repeated process of mutual suggestion, a series of intersecting and interwoven stories that can scarcely be explained with reference to the nation. Borneman's effect on FFG leadership thus also shows the extent to which—in this specific situation—television contested national constructions of identity more forcefully than other media.

Borneman took his assignment seriously, contacting numerous British authors, directors, and producers seeking collaboration in one form or another. These included documentary filmmakers Tony Isaacs and Denis Mitchell as well as producer Jack Good, who was intended to produce his trademark "beat" programming à la *Oh Boy* or *Wham* for FFG.[408] Borneman knew many of them personally and did succeed in winning over a number of British and US television figures, like choreographer Bernhard Hall and Austrian screenplay writer and director Rudolf Cartier, who as a Jew had emigrated first to the United States then to Great Britain, and whose work at the BBC earned him the reputation of being a rejuvenating force in television drama. Directors Mark Lawton, Peter Graham, and Herbert Wise (also born in Austria) also joined, as did Allan Buckhantz (of Lithuanian descent) as a director, producer, and head of director training.[409] He also built support among British broadcasters. He recommended others, like former colleagues Paul Rotha and Stuart Legg, for contract work.[410] Erich Rombach, a 34-year-old economist who had previously played an important role in conveying British experience to Germany through his role at the London office of the Federation of German Industries, also joined the programming department and became one of the few figures Borneman trusted within the FFG apparatus.[411]

Borneman later recalled that he had recruited a majority of the members on his production staff among former emigrants.[412] Most were leftist, leaving the Freies Fersehen—which had been set up with the opposite intention—"occupied by Socialists." Whether it was truly "the most progressive television team that has ever existed in the history of Western mass media," as he goes on to claim, is doubtful. Leftists certainly found work at Freies Fernsehen, but the placement of loyal CDU people in leading positions alone, when paired with the network's strong ties to previous propagandists for the National Socialists and the hostility toward Borneman, all make such talk seem like wishful thinking.[413] This could be chalked up to a subsequent interpretation of what Borneman perceived to be a catastrophic failure or may also have served as a form of political justification written from the specific perspective of the

1970s—empirically, however, it is untenable. Even at the time there were few signs of Socialist infiltration. SPD media-orientated politician Fritz Sänger, at any rate, said in October of 1960 that Freies Fernsehen was "cut entirely from the same cloth," that is, of BDI and CDU figures: "There isn't one of us, except maybe the porter."[414]

As early as summer of 1960 Borneman ran into criticism within his own department, when Eckert raised widespread, culturally critical reservations related to foreign material coming from the West. Borneman's appointment to head of programming had itself been logical to the extent that the work of young British authors had livened German television since 1958 with its pointed, realistic, and critical tone—John Osborne especially, but also John Mortimer, Harold Pinter (Borneman staged his piece *A Night Out* for Freies Fernsehen), Tom Stoppard, and others.[415] This was not to everyone's liking, however, as would become clear not only from the press response. Eckert was struck by an "almost overbearing emphasis on sexual motives," which "can likely only be explained in terms of certain Anglo-Saxon attitudes."[416] Eckert considered *At Home*—a play that had recently premiered in London and to which Borneman took a strong liking—"practically unstageable" "because the problems, words, and entire premise of the conflict are indeed true and could also be true for Germany, but would cause such protest that we can never afford to broadcast the piece."[417] A short while later Eckert criticized the purchase of numerous English or US shows. Nor did he forget to single out as the reason for his misgivings that "we, and in particular you have come in for harsh public criticism for pieces that are much too Anglo-Saxon.[418]

Borneman made an effort to allay these fears by constantly professing to seek a middle path between custom and novelty, "to create a compromise between the tested and successful program structure of ITV in England and the tradition of German television."[419] A conflict flared around the structure of the timing; Borneman wanted to up the tempo and adopt the quicker pacing of ITV's programming format, which featured numerous half-hour shows. He had made up his mind "to put together an entertaining television program with no pauses, in the best Anglo-Saxon tradition." This concept, as radio historian Rüdiger Steinmetz has noted, stood in "the greatest possible contrast to the state-run television programs at the time" and was "essentially an anticipation of what . . . privately owned commercial channels offer today."[420] As Borneman anticipated however, there was to be no lack of contemporary criticism. Specifically with regard to the structure of the programming and fully in keeping with Eckert, the German professional public remained skeptical.

As public criticism of the channel mounted and the constitutional court's ruling then brought a halt to the entire enterprise, especially after New Year's 1961 Borneman's adversaries sought to give the impression that he was culpable not only for the alleged surplus of English-US material but for other missteps as well. Managers Schmidt and Six lamented that in the first quarter "there is a predominance of foreign material and directors" and announced that this would be compensated in the second quarter by a "predominance of German manuscripts"—something Borneman doubted, as he considered most of the German television plays already purchased to be unworkable.[421] His own deputy and the chief dramaturge Eckert, concerned with distancing himself from the "scapegoat" like many of his colleagues, issued a radical critique of the program in which he postulated that "*German* television plays were needed." Borneman protested that "this sounds as though the program leadership had sworn off a search for German television plays. The opposite is true. We were *forced* to buy foreign television plays because the script department wasn't able to provide any German television plays."[422]

Years later Eckert, an early champion of commercial television, still looked back on New Year's 1960–61 with incomprehension. The situation was "grotesque"; "a second station, while lacking here and there due to the rush, was ready for broadcast."[423] If, however, one takes a closer look at early 1961, the period set to begin broadcasting, things were still a far cry from the stated goal of a channel ready to air with sufficient pre-produced material for the first half of the year. While nobody apparently had a thorough overview of the material, the station had far less than the 1,030 prepared hours of programming that Borneman claimed, and even the 440 hours that FFG administrative leadership registered with Bonn were not entirely ready for broadcast.[424] At the beginning of 1961 Borneman was ready to throw in the towel for the very reason that the program still wasn't nearing completion two weeks after the planned start of broadcast, and he considered it impossible "to broadcast with this staff, on 1 April or at any other point."[425] A sober assessment leads rather to the conclusion that the new television program would "not have survived the first four weeks."[426] The constitutional court's decision spared the FFG the disgrace of appearing in public with an unfinished and scanty program. Given the set conditions— an overly narrow time frame dictated by political calculations; positions filled based on political, rather than professional criteria; in general the lack of professionals at every level; internal competition and disorganization—anything else would have been a miracle. The quality of the shows was also subject to external and internal inspection and came in for thorough criticism;[427] in the eyes of the station's advisory board—a group dominated by conservative, traditionalist thinking and marked by outdated preferences—the program failed on account of its Western character. There was "much too much of an Anglo-American atmosphere," ran the critique, while on the other hand it was lacking in "good farce, good comedic tales or situations, light entertainment."[428] Internal critique similarly chipped away at the foundations of the program as they had been laid out by Borneman. His trademark rapid pacing with its thirty-minute segments met with disapproval, as did the predominance of British-US influence ("foreign elements") and individual shows and series for which he was responsible.[429] A number of projects from the educational/documentary department received similar verdicts, but ultimately Borneman was selected to bear responsibility for the defeat. The *Frankfurter Rundschau* learned the same from well-informed circles; difficulties that the "'programming advisory board' of 'Deutschland Fernsehen GmbH' had with accepting current productions" had Borneman's departure as a result.[430] This was not entirely the case. Rather, by the New Year Borneman had grown so fed up with the bureaucratic squabbling and inefficiency in production that the appointment of the federal government's proxy Six to "program director," to whom Borneman was subordinate as "program leader," went right along with Borneman's plans. He requested either to be put in charge of production or to rewrite his contract as an independent contractor for program consultancy and production, with a guaranteed salary equivalent to his current 5,000 Deutschmarks a month.[431] Neither happened. FFG leadership naturally tried to save face, professing esteem for the man they had given the boot—Six avowed that he was "very interested in retaining Borneman as an internationally recognized television professional"—but once the results of the program review had been leaked and a showing specifically devised for the press elicited similar reactions, the impression that Borneman had been deposed due to a bad program changed his perception in public.[432] Borneman himself viewed all this as a confirmation of his earlier prognosis, namely that regardless of its actual qualities, the program he had designed would face "sharper critique" than would commercial television in Western countries.[433]

All in all, Borneman's experience with German television was depressing, a result that owed not least to his status as a returning emigrant. Had he spoke with an English or American accent, he later recounted, he would "possibly" have been accepted as typically English or typically US American. "But because I spoke like a German, anything I did that deviated from the straight and narrow was chalked up to affectation or theatricality. Nobody could or was willing to grasp that something such as a native German with an English mentality could exist."[434] It was, however, the "foul concoction of slander, attempts at sabotage and the simple-minded affronts of reactionaries connected with the era of National Socialism" that proved most vexing. There was nothing to the reputation that Germans held for efficient working methods, as the disorganization and disputes over areas of responsibility within the leadership of Freies Fernsehen illustrated. In Germany, work was evidently far "less disciplined than in the seemingly looser order of the Anglo-Saxon world," he protested.[435] It was absolutely "impossible for anyone who had grown up in England and possessed a certain degree of sensitivity and tact . . . to live and work in this country." England, he continued, was a country of genuine civilization precisely because of how widespread characteristics such as lethargy, inefficiency, and conservatism were; like Egypt, Rome, and Greece, "a dying empire is a magnificent place for self-observation."[436] And to then compare this to Germany!

External opinion of Borneman's style of leadership was split. Many considered him "dictatorial," while others thought the opposite—that he was not capable of asserting himself. As leadership qualities, however, both were unwelcome in a system experiencing a shift in hierarchy. Borneman himself located this within the German-British cultural divide. He was an employee, not a fighter, he told Hessling: "Up until my return to Germany I did not even know that grown people can fight. I'm helpless against this thing because I don't have any weapons against it."[437] "God knows

I don't have a dictatorial temperament," he protested to a second opponent, Meyer-Goldenstädt, "and when faced with the dilemma of a principled decision that could harm an employee and a quiet tolerance I always choose the second alternative, even if the illusion of a lack of will to decide may come from that."[438] Borneman knew quite well what he wanted and was on no account helpless, but worked determinedly with the people he considered amenable to designing the program according to his wishes. At the same time, he was such an outsider that he stood no chance of actually mixing with the intrigue playing out among the "German," politically uniform majority. Borneman's inability to assert himself, as was reported here and there once the entire affair came to an end, was blamed less on the implied weakness in leadership than on the power relationships at the leadership level.[439] It was entirely possible that given the unfavorable circumstances and a time frame that was much too narrow, Borneman had seen from an early point that the plan of realizing his high ambitions was doomed to fail. By late summer 1960, Borneman had already intimated to his father "that it would be best for him if the whole episode were to fall through."[440]

Even after his work at FFG took a downward turn, Borneman did not sense the political nature of the entire business, but instead asserted the opposite. There had never been an attempt made to exert political or artistic influence; the business had failed due to lack of time, money, and professional staff alone.[441] This took no stock of all the hostility that had to do with his English taste, Jewish background, position as a returning emigrant, or progressive ideas about a new and improved television, which may themselves not have been of a partisan political nature, but absolutely carried political implications. Borneman also clung fast to his belief that Adenauer had offered him, a leftist, "the unrestricted and uncensored opportunity to build up a television organization that may have been the most progressive of its time."[442] This may have owed to a need to defend a project of major importance in media politics within the history of the Federal Republic, in which he had once played a prominent role. Yet the model has been refuted by research, as has the supposition that following the end of the FFG, in addition to the "triumph of the conservatives," a "gradual eradication of all leftists within the institutions of public law" had also taken place at ZDF. Quite the contrary—at least for a few years around 1968, the ethos of engaged journalism especially brought more leftist journalists into the fold of broadcasting corporations than ever before. It is entirely possible that the public opinion effected by this shift placed Borneman under particular pressure to justify himself while writing his autobiography. With its "first television judgment," the federal constitutional court had guaranteed the independence of federal television from the state as well as economic interests, thus encouraging the investigation of contemporary issues and engaged journalism. The claim that the ban on Freies Fernsehen also hampered the modernization of West German television, as Borneman believed—in analogy to what had happened in Britain—must be evaluated with a discerning eye. On the one hand, widespread criticism of the shows produced at the FFG, including from Borneman himself, gives cause for doubt. On the other hand, any number of shows created during the decisive year of the FFG's buildup would later achieve success on other channels, and a reserve of television professionals was assembled that to that point had scarcely existed and which began to remedy the staff bottleneck in the field. Last but not least, there was the rapid assimilation of many of Borneman's ideas and initiatives by state-run broadcasting institutions and their implementation in various formats.[443] Nevertheless, looking back as an ex-manager on the reality of his experience in commercial television, Borneman was not always convinced by what he regarded as the institutional enshrinement of his earlier ideas. In an interview with Steinmetz shortly before his death, he "cursed" the dominance of the series in commercial television.[444]

Borneman's position at Freies Fernsehen ended on 30 June 1961. At his wishes, his contract was initially shortened by a year, and the company did not intend to extend it beyond 31 March 1961, despite press releases to the opposite effect.[445] For this reason Borneman was not eligible for the same high settlement pay that other leading managers were. Instead his former deputy Gerhard Eckert, who had sought to change Borneman's key positions since Six's arrival, assumed his post.[446] Borneman stayed on for another three months in a freelance consulting role while FFG was dismantled.[447]

Borneman's frustration did not run deep enough however for him to give up on television altogether. In 1962 a bizarre epilogue unfolded when he applied for a director-generalship at ZDF that did lasting damage to his already unsteady footing in German television.[448] That February the press was tickled to learn of the strategies he had allegedly employed when applying for the position. Letters dated from the

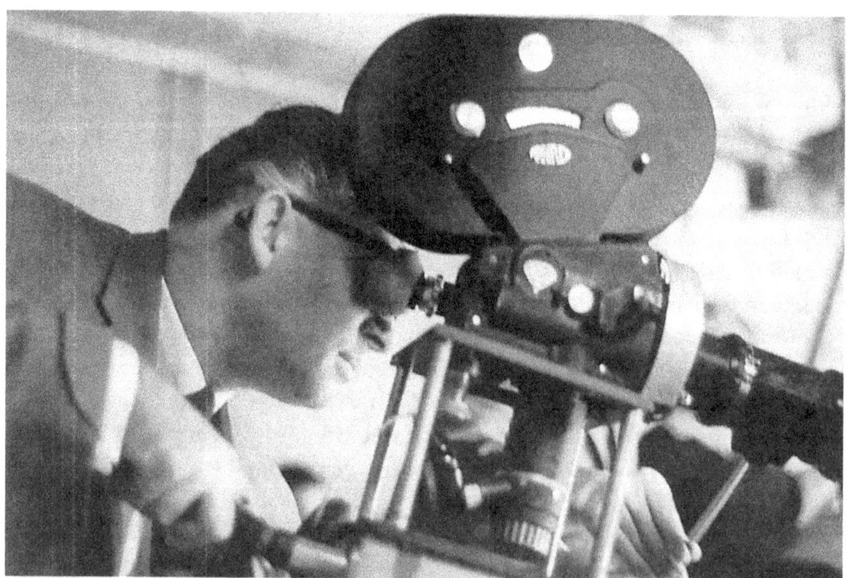

Figure 3.8. Filming in Italy, 1961. Courtesy AdK.

nineteenth of the month had been sent out to members of the television advisory council at ZDF, the group responsible for making personnel decisions, in which Borneman's qualifications were supported by individually tailored arguments in each case. The letter to the union representative emphasized Borneman's standing as a trade unionist, while Hans-Dietrich Genscher, the federal managing director of the FDP (Freie Demokratische Partie), received a letter stating that Borneman was an "active party member." The SPD's Jockel Fuchs learned that Borneman had "been active on the Republican side of the Spanish Civil War," Fuchs's fellow party member Willi Eichler read that former Leftist Socialist Peter Blachstein could tell Eichler more about Borneman's political views, and the head of the committee, who was from Hannover, was told Borneman's father had been "a Hannoverian of old," etc. This smacked so clearly of opportunism—the members of the council read the letters aloud to each other during their first session on 20 February 1962—the Kölnische Rundschau conjectured that already at Freies Fernsehen the candidate had been a "shoo-in" for the position "not only because of his professional aptitude, but also certainly due to his 'loyalty.'"[449] In its next issue, *Der Spiegel* characteristically poked fun at "Earnest (also Ernest) Borneman."[450]

Publicly exposed in this way, Borneman suspected a plot between his girlfriend, with whom he had separated a day before the application, and newspaper publisher Fritz Niehus.[451] Seeking revenge, his girlfriend had taken his typewriter, then typed out and sent the letters, while Niehus had long sought to secure the position for his preferred candidate, the ultimately victorious Karl Holzamer, and to root out any real competition. As a reward, Niehus promised the lady a ZDF post. A lawyer was supposed to help silence Borneman, who for his part still tried to iron out the wrinkles, congratulating Holzamer, for example, on his eventual appointment to ZDF director and looking to set the record straight on what was said about him, "as though I were a political opportunist, or at least a political organized being."[452] To no avail.

It is difficult to say what actually happened. Resorting to such an uneven strategy would presuppose a considerable degree of stupidity, a quality one would be hard-pressed to apply to Borneman. On the other hand, the conspiracy Borneman describes sounds no less improbable. It is possible that Niehus, a confidant of Borneman's archenemy Gerhard Eckert, did harbor intentions of driving Borneman away, but the story with Borneman's girlfriend seems much too bizarre, all the more so as their liaison continued afterward. Whatever did occur, the episode shows the force of the pressure bearing down on Borneman, the limited control he had over the situation, and his uncertainty about how to solve the problem.

With the publication of his novel *The Compromisers* in 1962, Borneman returned to the path of zero compromise, committing himself entirely to freelance work that would give him greater artistic and political independence. He kept his head above water in other ways in the meantime, however, quickly finding a new job that led him back to the advertising industry and ensured a good income, at least for several years.

From 1961 to 1964 he was the head of the Television, Radio and Film Department at the Frankfurt branch of the ad agency Foote, Cone and Belding, where he made advertising films. After a period of unemployment, in 1966–67 he had a short stay in the same capacity at the Ted Bates ad agency in Frankfurt. Borneman was paid very well for his work—at first he drove a Mercedes 190 SL roadster and later a Jaguar— but he grew bored and kept on the lookout, as always, for something new. Neither job was particularly challenging, although they did give him the freedom to pursue creative interests on the side.

With his attempted re-entry into television failed, Borneman turned to the mass market, trying his hand as a popular nonfiction writer. Eva also developed her reputation as a translator. The couple bought a house in Frankfurt in early 1962 and moved in together that spring; Eva gave up her position at Oxford University Press and followed her husband to Frankfurt, even though his situation had deteriorated in the meantime. She wasn't afraid but did experience a case of "emigritis." Short-term alternatives in Cologne and the United States were turned down to allow the family to set down new roots. Stephen, fifteen years old by now, attended the boarding school at Schloss Salem until completing his Abitur in 1966, and he went on to study economics in Ottawa and law in London. He worked later as a lawyer, manager, and management consultant.

The foundation for this new direction was a literary agency that Borneman began with Eva in 1966 in Frankfurt. Ebohaus was dedicated especially to literary exchange between German- and English-speaking countries. They couldn't do the work of the agency themselves, however. Eva also tried to land English-language exposés on West German television channels under her maiden name of Geisel (at the prompting of her spouse, who considered his own name less judicious given recent events),[453] an effort that succeeded only in part, and not only because it was largely German material that was filmed in Frankfurt—the increasing distance to London also meant connections to the world of film and television in the UK had grown weaker. When Eckart Stein, the future leader of the renowned ZDF series *Das kleine Fernsehspiel* received a letter from Eva proposing—aside from two pieces by her husband—work from the "younger avant-garde" in Great Britain, Stein replied that the editorial staff found her suggestions "unsuitable": "We aren't of the opinion that the suggested pieces belong to the ranks of the younger avant-garde in England. We are absolutely interested in this younger avant-garde, and would also like to obtain as many original language television plays as possible."[454] Interest in British television plays had in fact expanded in the meantime; the second half of the 1960s saw new authors gain recognition, such as Clive Exton, who had five pieces shown on German television in 1966. Leo Lehman, the most frequently performed British author, had had nineteen pieces shown since 1964.[455] This was a generation that had come up after Eva and Ernest's time in London, however, and whom they didn't know. Nearly ten years had passed since Borneman had played an active role in British television, and he had lost contact in Germany with the state of television on the island. An argument with

LeRoi Jones had given a similar impression in the field of jazz, when Jones showed Borneman's positions to be outdated. Journalists similarly dismissed Borneman's "revolutionary ideas of yesterday."[456] While this was unfair, it was indicative of his problem in the second half of the 1960s. He was over fifty years old, and thus anything but young and avant-garde, which he did not really reflect. Without a doubt he sensed the crisis and was bowled over by it. Shortly before his fiftieth birthday he remarked that for him it was "the most depressing [birthday] of my life—lord knows there's no reason to celebrate. When you turn so old and still haven't gone anywhere—quite the opposite, when you're so clearly on a downward trajectory, you don't feel much like celebrating a birthday."[457] Two years later, he lamented that he "still had not had any real success in life." "If I had ever been successful in something I enjoyed, then I definitely would have begun to relax a little by now."[458] There could be no thought of this, however, since "nothing had worked out." Borneman did make a change, gradually withdrawing from his old topics of jazz and film/television and immersing himself in a new field that was set to become enormously popular and offer new, fertile terrain for rebellious views.

Notes

1. Borneman to his father, 8 January 1951.
2. As mentioned in a letter from his mother, who was skeptical about it due to his young age, 13 November 1934. See Borneman, *Die Ur-Szene*, 156, 289.
3. Rudolf Hans Hiller to Borneman, 27 August 1941.
4. For this quote and the following, see Borneman, "Sound Rhythm and the Film"; Borneman to parents, 13 April 1934; Jim Harris to Borneman, 20 December [no year given].
5. This and the following from Borneman to Davis Rawnsley, 3 January 1948; Borneman, *Die Ur-Szene*, 156; Borneman, "Autobiographisches zur Geschichte des Films und Fernsehens," 41. See Borneman, "Sound Rhythm and the Film."
6. Editorial in *Harper's Magazine*, February 1947.
7. Borneman, "Autobiographisches zur Geschichte des Films und Fernsehens," 41.
8. Ernest Borneman, *Novels, Films, TV Shows, Musicals, Radio Shows, Broadcasts*, n.d.
9. Borneman, *Die Ur-Szene*, 157–58; Borneman to Karl Holzamer, 18 February 1962; Borneman to unknown, 19 February 1962.
10. J. Weston Parle to Borneman, 18 June 1936.
11. Borneman, *Die Ur-Szene*, 157–58; Borneman, *Novels, Films, TV Shows, Musicals*, ca. 1957.
12. As in a letter dated January 1981 reprinted in the appendix of Borneman, *The Face on the Cutting-Room Floor*, 270.
13. Borneman, *The Face on the Cutting-Room Floor*, 38.
14. Ernest Borneman, *Socialist Films for a Capitalist Government: The Wartime Experiment in Canada*, n.d. [presumably from the early 1970s].
15. See Borneman's diary as well as a typed summary in in LAC, RG2408-0-5-E, vol. 1. See Brunnhuber, "After the Prison Ships."
16. Meeting of the National Film Board, 14 December 1943, LAC, RG53-2, T-12771. On the overall internment system, see Seyfert, "'His Majesty's Most Loyal Internees'"; and Koch, *Deemed Suspect*—on Borneman in particular, see 187–88.
17. Borneman to Herskovits, 17 July 1941, NUL, 35/6/4/5.
18. Alexander Paterson, Prison Commission, Home Office, 26 September 1939.
19. Koch, *Deemed Suspect*, 186–90.

20. Meeting of the National Film Board, 14 July 1942, LAC, RG53-2, T-12771.
21. Borneman references seven individuals when discussing fellow internees: *Die Ur-Szene*, 295. See the reflections of a fellow detainee in Brandt, "Internment and After." See also McKay, *History of the National Film Board of Canada*, 37.
22. National Film Board Minutes, 6 November 1945, LAC, RG53-2, T-12772.
23. Alexander Paterson to Geisel, 2 August 1941.
24. Fritz Grundland to Borneman, n.d.
25. Report of the Controller and Secretary, 31 August 1942, LAC, RG53-2, T-12771.
26. Ernest to Eva, 11 July 1941 and 17 July 1941.
27. Borneman, *Die Ur-Szene*, 158; interview with Eckart Frahm, 28 January 1984. On this context, see Gittings, *Canadian National Cinema*.
28. Ernest to Eva, 18 November 1941.
29. Ernest to Eva, Easter Sunday [1942].
30. Ernest to Eva, 17 July 1941 and 21 July 1941.
31. For an overview of Grierson's milieu at the time, see Rotha, *Documentary Film*. On the problematic "totalitarian" traits of Grierson's understanding of propaganda and his goal of establishing a new world order, see Nelson, *The Colonized Eye*.
32. Evans, *John Grierson and the National Film Board*, 247. Borneman went so far as to claim, "We were all Socialists and Communists" (in *Socialist Films for a Capitalist Government: The Wartime Experiment in Canada*, n.d. [presumably from the early 1970s]). The following quote from ibid. For secondary scholarship, see Khouri, *Filming Politics*, 87–95; Druick, *Projecting Canada*; McKay, *History of the National Film Board of Canada*, 37.
33. These figures are drawn from Ellis, *John Grierson*, 155; Evans, *John Grierson and the National Film Board*, 169.
34. Ellis, *John Grierson*, 158.
35. Ernest to Eva, 1 November 1942.
36. Khouri, *Filming Politics*, 119–36.
37. Ibid., 126. On the Russian films, see also Evans, *John Grierson and the National Film Board*, 200–05.
38. See Khouri, *Filming Politics*, 132–33; Evans, *John Grierson and the National Film Board*, 127.
39. Rielle Thomson to Grierson, 21 January 1944 and 20 May 1944, NFB, Production Files.
40. Walter Wilson of the Famous Players Capitol Theatre, 22 March 1944. Newspaper reports in the *St. John Times-Globe* on 1 February 1944 and the *Montreal Daily Star* on 16 February 1944 emphasized that the film was to be shown to the thirty-eight thousand workers in the defense industry, and would strengthen combat spirit and generate pride in Canada's part in the fight against Hitler's Germany.
41. Khouri, *Filming Politics*, 149–52.
42. Ernest to Eva, 20 December 1942 and 1 January 1943.
43. Ernest to Eva, 31 January 1943.
44. Khouri, *Filming Politics*, 169. For more details about the film, see Evans, *John Grierson and the National Film Board*, 135–36.
45. Ernest Borneman, "John Grierson or the Creative Treatment of Reality," n.d. See also Ellis, *John Grierson*, 149.
46. Ernest to Eva, 3 February 1942; Ernest to Gullickson, 14 December 1945; Ernest Borneman: *Novels, Films, TV Shows*, ca. 1957.
47. Production credits, ca. 1950. Most of Borneman's films—but not all, such as the important *Zero Hour*—are listed in the standard reference work on the National Film Board of Canada, *The NFB Film Guide*.
48. On the social classification of the population as reinforced through the NFB films, see Druick, *Projecting Canada*, 45–72.
49. "A Black-Out-Ing."
50. Ernest to Eva, 10 January 1942.
51. On this film, see Evans, *John Grierson and the National Film Board*, 191–93.
52. Stuart Legg, Talk on "Cutting," 17 January 1946, LAC, R738-5-6-E, vol. 7.

53. McInnes, *One Man's Documentary*, 116f.

54. Ernest to Eva, 12 February, 1 April, and 5 May 1942.

55. Ernest to Eva, 15 May 1942.

56. Ernest Borneman, *Socialist Films for a Capitalist Government: The Wartime Experiment in Canada*, n.d. [early 1970s].

57. Ernest to Eva, 27 August 1944.

58. Ernest to Eva, 23 August 1941.

59. McKay, *History of the National Film Board of Canada*, 49.

60. See Gene Waltz's introduction in McInnes, *One Man's Documentary*, x.

61. Ernest to Eva, 20 December 1942.

62. Ernest to Eva, 20 May 1942.

63. Ernest to Eva, 1 November 1942.

64. Handwritten note, n.d.

65. Ernest to Eva, 1 July 1942.

66. Meeting of the National Film Board, 13 January 1942 [actually 1943], LAC, RG53-2, T-12772.

67. Spottiswoode, as quoted in Ellis, *John Grierson*, 152.

68. For this quote and the following: Ernest to Eva, 22 July 1942.

69. Meeting of the National Film Board, 12 October 1943, LAC, RG53-2, T-12771.

70. Ernest to Eva, 16 July 1942.

71. Ernest to Eva, 27 July 1942 and 12 November 1942.

72. Ernest to Eva, 20 November 1942.

73. Ellis, *John Grierson*, 152; Beveridge, *John Grierson, Film Master*, 126. See also the introduction by Hardy in *John Grierson: A Documentary Biography*, 41f.

74. Ernest to Eva, 1 November 1942.

75. Winston, *Claiming the Real*, 12.

76. Khouri, *Filming Politics*, 190–91. On this discussion see Ellis, *John Grierson*, 156–57.

77. Grierson, "The Documentary Idea: 1942," 179. The critique of Grierson's protégés according to D. Jones, *Movies and Memoranda*, 40.

78. Grierson, "The Documentary Idea: 1942," 188.

79. Ernest to Eva, 20 May 1942.

80. Undated excerpt from *Die Weltwoche* in AdK, EBA.

81. *Weltwoche*, n.d.

82. Ernest to Eva, 4 October 1941.

83. Newspaper excerpt and leaflet collection about Borneman's radio and television activities since 1940 in AdK.

84. Ernest to Eva, 21 July 1941.

85. Ernest to Eva, 16 August 1941.

86. Grierson to John Devine, 2 July 1941, NFB, Production Files War Saving Film.

87. Ernest to Eva, 17 July 1941; Ernest Borneman: *Novels, Films, TV Shows*. A statement of costs confirms that Borneman wrote the script (Spottiswood, Estimate for War Savings Trailer *5 for 4*, 12 September 1941, NFB, Production Files War Saving Film).

88. Borneman, *Die Ur-Szene*, 366.

89. Ernest to Eva, 4 October 1941.

90. Ernest to Eva, 14 December 1941.

91. Ernest Borneman, *Notes on the Realist Novel*, n.d.

92. Borneman, "Macht und Sprache," 28–29.

93. Borneman, *Die Ur-Szene*, 354.

94. Ernest to Eva, 6 December 1941.

95. Ernest to Eva, 7 December 1942.

96. Hardy, *John Grierson*, 138–39.

97. Ernest to Eva, 7 December 1942.

98. Ernest to Eva, 31 January 1943.

99. Ernest to Eva, 2 March 1943.

100. NFB Minutes, 13 March 1945, LAC, RG53-2, T-12771.

101. NFB Meeting, 9 May 1944, LAC, RG53-2, T-12772.

102. Borneman to Grierson, McLean, and Legg, 7 February 1944, NFB, Production Files for *Zero Hour*; Borneman, "D-Day."

103. Ernest Borneman, *Socialist Films for a Capitalist Government: The Wartime Experiment in Canada*, n.d. [early 1970s].

104. Infomaterial in NFB, Production Files for *Zero Hour*. Further see McKay, *History of the National Film Board of Canada*, 46; James, *Film as a National Art*, 83.

105. Thus Borneman in an interview in *The Face on the Cutting-Room Floor*, 265.

106. NFB Meeting, 9 May 1944, LAC, RG53-2, T-12772. Press cited in Reviews and References, ca. 1947.

107. Ellis, *John Grierson*, 154. Stuart Legg phrased this even more forcefully, stating that one practically no longer filmed by oneself anymore (Beveridge, *John Grierson, Film Master*, 184).

108. Ernest Borneman, *Socialist Films for a Capitalist Government: The Wartime Experiment in Canada*, n.d. [early 1970s].

109. This and the following according to Khouri, *Filming Politics*, 173–92; Ellis, *John Grierson*, 37–38, 156–57, and 172–73.

110. See Aitken, *Film and Reform*, 89.

111. Quoted in Hardy, *Grierson on Documentary*, 11. See Winston, "John Grierson Versus Ethnography," 49.

112. Grierson, "The Documentary Idea: 1942," 179.

113. Ellis, *John Grierson*, 172. For greater detail on Grierson's aesthetic in the 1920s, see Aitken, *Film and Reform*.

114. This and the following in Grierson, "The Documentary Idea: 1942," 179.

115. Khouri, *Filming Politics*, 192.

116. Borneman, *Die Ur-Szene*, 344.

117. This is the (to my mind) somewhat lopsided interpretation in Brunnhuber, *The Faces of Janus*, 47–70.

118. Beveridge, *John Grierson, Film Master*, 69. See Winston, *Claiming the Real*, 59–60.

119. Borneman, *Die Ur-Szene*, 344–45.

120. Quoted, e.g., in D. Jones, *Movies and Memoranda*, 42. The actual line comes from the pro-Nazi play *Schlageter* by Hanns Johst.

121. Lethen, *Cool Conduct*.

122. Ernest Borneman, "The Documentary Film in Canada," 20 October 1945, University of Sterling, John Grierson Archive.

123. Ernest Borneman, *Socialist Films for a Capitalist Government: The Wartime Experiment in Canada*, n.d. [early 1970s]. This draft, from Borneman's estate, bears his address in Scharten and is paginated from 122 to 161, thus clearly conceived of as part of a longer text. It is based on an original draft of nearly the same length, a thirty-eight-page piece entitled "The Documentary Film in Canada" dating from 20 October 1945, which has been cited differently in research (copies are available in NFB and LAC, where it is wrongly attributed to John Grierson in Sidney Newman's estate; an incomplete version is located in John Grierson's estate at the Univeristy of Stirling archives). In comparison with the earlier version, the later reveals a series of cuts that also hold political implications, while additions notably reveal Borneman's role. A heavily edited version reduced to technical aspects appears in Feldman, *The Canadian Film Reader* (Toronto: P. Martin Associates, 1977) under the title "Documentary Films: World War II."

124. Quoted in Jones, *Movies and Memoranda*, 33.

125. Ernest to Eva, 31 January 1943.

126. Grierson, "The Documentary Idea: 1942," 179.

127. Ernest to Eva, 31 January 1943.

128. Ernest to Eva, "End of March" 1936.

129. Quotes from an interview in Borneman, *The Face on the Cutting-Room Floor*, 264.

130. This and the following according to Ernest Borneman, *Socialist Films for a Capitalist Government: The Wartime Experiment in Canada*, n.d. [early 1970s].

131. Legg has a similar description in Beveridge, *John Grierson, Film Master*, 185.

132. Borneman refers to this in his first novel from 1937, *The Face on the Cutting-Room Floor*, 205, quoting Edmund Wilson.

133. Quoted in Ellis, *John Grierson*, 154.

134. Ernest Borneman, *Socialist Films for a Capitalist Government: The Wartime Experiment in Canada*, n.d. [early 1970s].

135. Ernest to Eva, 1 November 1942.

136. Beveridge, *John Grierson, Film Master*, 185. See also Evans, *John Grierson and the National Film Board*, 112–13.

137. Ernest Borneman, *Socialist Films for a Capitalist Government: The Wartime Experiment in Canada*, n.d. [early 1970s].

138. Ernest Borneman, "The Documentary Film in Canada," 20 October 1945, University of Sterling, John Grierson Archive. Borneman's own film *Mosquito Squadron* (1944) and McInness's *Coal Face Canada* are given as further examples.

139. Borneman to Spottiswoode, 12 July 1944, NFB, Production Files.

140. See the extensive correspondence with Applebaum in Borneman's estate in AdK.

141. Quoted in Evans, *John Grierson and the National Film Board*, 120–21.

142. Ernest to Eva, 31 January 1943.

143. Ernest to Eva, 11 November 1942.

144. McInnes, *One Man's Documentary*, 117.

145. Ernest to Eva, 16 August 1941.

146. Ernest to Eva, 10 January 1942; Norman McLaren to Borneman, 3 August 1949; James Beveridge to Borneman, 11 July 1951.

147. Richard, *Norman McLaren, Manipulator of Movement*; Dobson, *The Film Work of Norman McLaren*. For biographies, see the entries on James Beveridge and Norman McLaren in *The Canadian Film Encyclopedia*, http://legacy.tiff.net/CANADIANFILMENCYCLOPEDIA/, accessed 1 June 2013.

148. Borneman, "Remembered Faces," 26.

149. For this quote and the following: Ernest to Eva, 18 February 1942.

150. National Film Board Minutes, 6 November 1945, LAC, RG53-2, T-12772. See James Beveridge, *John Grierson, Film Master*, 126.

151. Ernest to Eva, 10 August 1941.

152. McKay, *History of the National Film Board of Canada*, 38.

153. Ernest to Eva, 7 January [1942].

154. Ernest an Eva, 16 July 1942.

155. Ernest to Eva, 27 February 1942.

156. McKay, *History of the National Film Board of Canada*, 49.

157. On Grierson's attitude toward women and work, see Ernest to Eva, Easter Sunday [n.d].

158. Eva to Curt Borneman, 3 March 1948. Quote in McInnes, *One Man's Documentary*, 117. On her work at an English film magazine, see Ernest to Eva, 19 July 1937; as the "girl for everything" for the head of Denham Labs, the film laboratory for Alexander Korda's Denham Film Studios see Borneman, *Die Ur-Szene*, 157.

159. [Curt Borneman], *Familiengeschichte der Bornemanns*, n.d. [ca. 1969].

160. Curt to Ernest, 12 January 1946.

161. Ernest to Eva, Easter Sunday [1942].

162. Eva to Ernest, 11 September 1942.

163. Eva to Ernest, 21 November 1941.

164. Bernhard, "Die Geschichte der FDJ in Großbritannien 1939–1946."

165. Eva to Ernest, 16 February, 21 May, and 3 July 1942.

166. Eva to Ernest, 29 July 1942.

167. Eva to Ernest, 3 July 1942.

168. Eva to Ernest, 8 September 1942.

169. Ernest to Eva, n.d.

170. For example, in Ernest to Eva, 9 June [mid-1930s].

171. Borneman, *Die Ur-Szene*, 397.

172. Rudolf Hans Hiller to Borneman, 1 November 1947. Borneman stressed that similarly to his Berlin friends, he "had been close to the Communist Party, but had never been a member" (Borneman, "Back to Berlin," 64).

173. Ernest to Eva, n.d. [1938]; "Korrupte SPÖ, Gott-Vater Kreisky & sexfeindliche Eminenzen."

174. Ernest to Eva, n.d.

175. Copy of excerpts from report re: Ernst Bornemann, associate of James, 9 May 1939, NA, KV2/1824.

176. Ernest to Eva, 20 September 1942.

177. Ernest to Eva, n.d. [1938–39].

178. Borneman to Jürgen Bettcher, 24 April 1974.

179. Ernest to Eva, 14 December 1940 and 14 June 1941.

180. Ernest to Eva, 14 December 1941.

181. Ernest to Eva, 5 May 1942.

182. Ernest to Eva, 20 September 1942.

183. The Annual Report of the National Film Board, 1946-47, LAC, RG53-2, T-12772.

184. Borneman to Davis, 20 September 1945.

185. Eva to Curt, 3 March 1948.

186. Eva to Curt, 4 December 1946.

187. Borneman to Jim Moynahan, 30 January 1945.

188. Ernest to Curt, 25 July 1946.

189. Borneman to Dale Curran, New York, 10 September 1945; "The Negroe Film Institute," n.d.

190. Excerpts from Melville J. Herskovits, *The Myth of the Negro Past* (New York: n.p., 1941).

191. This and the following according to untitled and undated handwritten notes. There also exists a precise listing of films of various genre produced by different societies: Ernest Borneman/JF, Negro Film Production and Distribution, 13 September 1946. A detailed treatment addresses questions of distribution and production and lists potential subjects: Finance and Story Aspects, n.d. (also available in the Beinecke Library, Richard Wright Papers, 89/1087a).

192. Untitled, undated handwritten notes.

193. Ellen Wright to Borneman, 10 October 1946, YUBL, Richard Wright Papers, 94/1225.

194. This and the following: Ernest Borneman (National Film Board), "A Draft Prospectus on American Negro Film Production: Finance and Story Aspects," n.d.; "Box Office Research, Treatment and Financial Breakdown for a Proposed New Type of Musical Film to Be Issued as a Monthly One-Reel Screen Magazine," n.d.

195. Charles Fox in *Jazz Journal*, August 1953, 15.

196. Borneman to Grierson, 30 April 1951.

197. Hiller to Borneman, 28 July 1946.

198. Borneman to his father, 8 November 1946; Borneman to Grierson, 26 May 1947; *Variety*, 8 October 1947.

199. William Farr to Grierson, 2 July 1947, UNESCO Archives, PER/REC 1/79.

200. Borneman, no addressee (presumably Rudolf Hans Hiller), 27 January 1948.

201. Ernest to Eva, 4 and 11 October 1947.

202. UNESCO, Report 1947; UNESCO, Report 1948.

203. Evans, *John Grierson and the National Film Board*, 266–68; Ellis, *John Grierson*, 229–39.

204. UNESCO Personnel Action Form, 20 July 1947, UNESCO Archives, PER/REC. 1/79; Ernest to Eva Borneman, 16 October 1947; to his father, 19 October 1947.

205. Borneman, "Canada, Unesco and the Movies."

206. *The Evening Citizen*, 13 October 1947.

207. On film section assignments in general, see Borneman, "Films for International Understanding."

208. Farr to Grierson, 2 July 1947, UNESCO Archives, PER/REC 1/79.

209. UNESCO, Application for Employment [Ernest Borneman], 18 June 1947, UNESCO Archives, PER/REC 1/79; Ross McLean to S. Samuel Selsky, Director of Personnel, UNESCO, 14 November 1947, ibid.
210. Ernest Borneman, "A Brief on Distribution Methods with special reference to the classification, evaluation and selection of films to be distributed," n.d. [1947], UNESCO Archives, PER/REC 1/79; Ernest Borneman, "A Second Brief on Distribution Methods with special reference to the classification, evaluation and selection of films to be distributed," n.d. [1947], ibid.
211. Ernest to Eva, 12 October 1947.
212. Ernest to Eva, 22 October 1947.
213. Ernest to Eva, 16 October 1947.
214. Rudolf Hans Hiller to Ernest, 4 April 1948.
215. Interview with Eckart Frahm, 28 January 1984.
216. Ernest to Eva, 22 October 1947.
217. Eva to Curt, 3 March 1948.
218. Request on Personnel Action, 28 April 1948, UNESCO Archives, PER/REC 1/79; Curt to Ernest, 5 July 1948.
219. *The Listener*, 26 March 1987.
220. Ellis, *John Grierson*, 237.
221. [Approval of salary raise], 9 December 1948, UNESCO Archives, PER/REC 1/79; UNESCO, Application for Employment [Ernest Borneman], 18 June 1947, ibid.
222. Borneman to his father, 16 November and 13 December 1947.
223. For this quote and the following, see Borneman to Eva, 12 and 22 October 1947.
224. Borneman, no addressee (presumably Rudolf Hans Hiller), 18 January 1948.
225. Borneman's calendar, 1947–48.
226. Borneman to Dr. Glockenspiel (Gordon Gullickson), 29 October 1947.
227. Borneman, *Die Ur-Szene*, 252–53.
228. Ibid., 367.
229. Leporello, n.d.; undated excerpt from *Die Weltwoche* [late 1940s]; *The Evening Citizen*, 10 September 1948; details in the "Locarno Festival" file of the UNESCO Archives.
230. Borneman, "Back to Berlin." The following quotes from the two sources mentioned.
231. Arendt, "The Aftermath of Nazi Rule," 24–25.
232. Ernest to Eva, 5 March 1948.
233. Letter from 5 April 1948.
234. Curt to Eva, 24 May 1948.
235. Borneman's calendar 1947–48; Ernest to Eva, 29 May and 4 June 1948, ibid. The finished film premiered 1 December 1948.
236. 29 May 1948, ibid.
237. "The Maze": An Original Screen Story by Ernest Borneman.
238. Ernest to his father, 13 December 1947.
239. Borneman to Pete Davis, 12 April 1948.
240. Ernest, no addressee (presumably Hiller), 4 December 1948.
241. Ernest to Eva, 29 May 1948.
242. Ernest to his father, 24 July 1948.
243. Borneman to Gordon Gullickson, 14 December 1945.
244. Borneman to Moody & Epstein, 18 May 1953.
245. Noble, *The Fabulous Orson Welles*, 195.
246. Borneman to Welles, 30 May 1951. See also Peter Noble's account in *News of the World*, 6 May 1956.
247. Diary entry, May 1949; Borneman, *Die Ur-Szene*, 262; Noble, *The Fabulous Orson Welles*, 196–200.
248. Borneman to Welles, 20 April 1949.
249. Borneman to Welles, 30 May 1951. See Brady, *Citizen Welles*, 431.
250. *New York Times*, 25 July 1949.
251. Borneman to Welles, 17 June 1949.

252. Ernest to his father, 24 July 1949.

253. Quoted in Noble's report in *News of the World*, 6 May 1956.

254. Welles to Borneman, 14 July 1949.

255. Borneman to G. Williamson, 15 August 1952, StDK, Borneman Collection.

256. [Welles] to Borneman, 28 May 1949.

257. Borneman, *Die Ur-Szene*, 368; interview in Borneman, *The Face on the Cutting-Room Floor*, 257; Noble, *The Fabulous Orson Welles*, 221–22; Brady, *Citizen Welles*, 453–54; Thomson, *Rosebud: The Story of Orson Welles*, 309–10.

258. Brady, *Citizen Welles*, 438.

259. Handwritten draft of a letter, n.d.

260. Borneman to Welles, 13 June 1949.

261. Borneman to T. M. Carter, Canadian Embassy, Rome, 12 October 1949.

262. Borneman to Shepridge, 8 December 1951.

263. Quoted in Drazin, *In Search of the Third Man*, 138.

264. Borneman to Pritchard, Englefield & Co., 24 June 1953.

265. Borneman to E. Gordon Lawrence, 20 November 1951.

266. Quoted in Tavares, "Orson Welles, Harry Allan Towers, and the Many Lives of Harry Lime," 175. Brady similarly states that Borneman wrote "many of them" in *Citizen Welles*, 460.

267. Noble, *The Fabulous Orson Welles*, 229.

268. List of short biographies, n.d.; Borneman to Welles, 2 September 1952; Borneman to Shepridge, 27 September 1952; Welles to Borneman, 29 September 1952.

269. Interview in Borneman, *The Face on the Cutting-Room Floor*, 258.

270. http://ctva.biz/UK/SailorOfFortune.htm.

271. Ernest Borneman: *Novels, Films*, etc., n.d.; http://ctva.biz/UK/Aggie.htm, accessed 15 July 2013. Borneman's estate includes the stories for "Trial in Camera," "A Portrait of Death," and "Ordeal by Fear."

272. Trinity Productions Ltd., *Fabian of Scotland Yard*. A recording of "The Sixth Dagger" is available in LAC.

273. Borneman's estate contains numerous additional scripts for other shows including pieces written by others, as well as two Borneman wrote with Patrick Morely, "An Apple for the Friar" and "A King's Ransom."

274. Ernest to his parents, 20 November 1957.

275. Interview in Borneman, *The Face on the Cutting-Room Floor*, 258.

276. Borneman to Jim Moynahan, 25 November 1944; Ernest Borneman (National Film Board), "A Draft Prospectus on American Negro Film Production: Finance and Story Aspects," n.d.

277. "Taps for the Dancer," A Screen Story by Ernest Borneman, in StDK, Paul Kohner Collection. German translation and commentary in Borneman, "Geheimtipps für den Tänzer," 408.

278. Ernest Borneman, *Words Fail Me*, televison play [1949].

279. Ernest Borneman, *Das Labyrinth*, n.d.

280. Ernest Borneman, *Carosello Napoletano*, undated manuscript.

281. Ernest Borneman, discussion of Fellini's *La Strada*, undated manuscript [1954].

282. At another point, aside from Clair and Vigo he names contemporaries Elia Kazan and William Wyler as his "favorite directors" (untitled, undated). Also in Eva Geisel, "Betty Slow Drag," n.d.

283. Ernest Borneman, "Verismo, Socialist Realism and the Italian Films," undated manuscript [1954].

284. Borneman himself talks about this period in terms of "twenty-eight television programs in thirty-two months": "twelve as an author, seven as a director, nine as producer" (Borneman, *Die Ur-Szene*, 158).

285. Borneman to Welles, 30 May 1951. In 1961 *Bang! You're Dead* was broadcast in the United States, albeit as a thirty-minute epidsode for the NBC series *Alfred Hitchcock Presents* (http://www.imdb.com/title/tt0508131/, accessed 16 August 2013).

286. Borneman to this father, 20 March 1954; [Overview of reception in the press], n.d.

287. Borneman to P. V. E. Terni, 19 October 1950.

288. Columbia Broadcasting System, press release, 7 March 1950.

289. *Variety*, 12 July 1950.

290. Advertisement with Borneman in *World's Press News* from 5 November 1954.

291. Borneman, "Eight Points on American TV"; *World's Press News*, 29 July 1955.

292. Sendall, *Independent Television in Britain*, 193–200.

293. Borneman, *Die Ur-Szene*, 159.

294. Borneman to Charles Morell, 17 March 1954.

295. *TV Times*, 19 July 1957; *The Times*, 14 June 1958; *Guardian*, 2 July 1958.

296. Sendall, *Independent Television in Britain*, 339.

297. Marcus Wittacker to the directors of Süddeutsche Rundfunk, 25 September 1958.

298. Sendall, *Independent Television in Britain*, 345–46.

299. *TV Times*, 19 July 1957.

300. *Commercial Television News*, 24 May 1957; Forman, *Persona Granada*, 98.

301. *TV Times*, 31 May 1957.

302. This and the following in Forman, *Persona Granada*, 78–81.

303. *TV Times*, 19 July 1957.

304. This and the following in Borneman to Wolf Hanke, 17 December 1973; Borneman, *Die Ur-Szene*, 159.

305. Borneman to Walter Hilpert, 19 June 1961.

306. From the early correspondence: Newman to Borneman, 15 January 1942.

307. Borneman to Sean Graham, 21 September 1962.

308. Borneman to McGregor Scott, 26 May 1960; MacGregor Scott to Borneman, 22 April 1960; Borneman to Sidney Newman, 7 June 1960, all in BAK, B 263/144.

309. Borneman, *Die Ur-Szene*, 159.

310. *The Independent*, 7 February 1993.

311. *Kinematograph Weekly*, 26 December 1957.

312. Ibid.

313. Ernest to his father, 15 March 1958.

314. John Davenport, *Observer*, 12 July 1959. Cf. Peter Green in *Daily Telegraph and Morning Post*, 26 June 1959.

315. *Observer*, 12 July 1959.

316. Ernest to Curt, 25 July 1946.

317. Borneman to his father, 23 November 1954.

318. Ernest to his parents, 15 May 1958.

319. Borneman to Marcel Leduc, 24 April 1959; Ernest to his father, 8 November 1959.

320. Ernest to his father and Erna, 27 September 1959; Borneman to Sigmund Seifert, 1 October 1959.

321. *The British Film and Television Yearbook*, n.d.; Borneman to the Secretary Council for African-British Relations, London, 28 September 1964; Ernest to his father and Erna, 27 September 1959.

322. See *Daily Mirror*, 17 February 1960.

323. Borneman's letters from 19 February and 1 March 1960.

324. Borneman, *Die Ur-Szene*, 160–67.

325. See his report from the 1954 Berlin Film Festival, quoted in "Betty Slow Drag": Press Reports, n.d.

326. Gladenbeck to Borneman, 3 March 1960.

327. Schmidt to the Frankfurt am Main tax office, 3 June 1960, BAK, B 263/96.

328. On the history of Freies Fernsehen, see Steinmetz, *Freies Fernsehen*. Also see the overview in Hickethier, *Geschichte des deutschen Fernsehens*, 114–18. See also Bausch, *Rundfunkpolitik nach 1945*, 385–462.

329. Hodenberg, *Konsens und Krise*.

330. Details in Bausch, *Rundfunkpolitik nach 1945*, 433–38.

331. Borneman, *Die Ur-Szene*, 161.

332. As stated in an interview, reprinted in Borneman, *The Face on the Cutting-Room Floor*, 266. Similarly in an interview with Eckart Frahm, 28 January 1984.

333. Eckert, *Das Fernsehen in den Ländern Westeuropas*, 28–32.

334. Father to Ernest, 18 October 1960.

335. *Frankfurter Rundschau*, 12 October 1974.

336. Ernest Borneman, "Das Kontrastprogramm: Konkrete Vorschläge zur Form und zum Inhalt eines zweiten deutschen Fernsehprogramms," n.d. In parts identical to his piece in *Spots*, no. 7, from 10 August 1960, 5–6, and *Tele*, 15 October 1960, 5.

337. Sendall, *Independent Television in Britain*, 335.

338. See Hickethier, *Geschichte des deutschen Fernsehens*, 314–340.

339. *Tele* from 15 October 1960, p. 5.

340. *Tele* from 17 September 1960.

341. On the children's program, see, e.g., Kübler, "Vorführstunde," 358–59.

342. Kraemer, "Betrifft: Überblick über die ungefähren Kosten der Programm-Produktionen der Aktualitätengruppe im 1. Quartal 1961," 13 September 1960; "Übersicht über die dokumentarischen und aktuellen Programme der FF GmbH, 1. Quartal."

343. *Der Spiegel*, 8 December 1965.

344. Borneman to Kraemer, 9 December 1960, BAK, B 263/42.

345. Borneman to Schmidt and Kraemer, 24 November 1960, BAK, B 263/42.

346. Find the results from the Infratest opinion poll commissioned by the FFG and conducted in September 1960 in Eckert and Niehus, *Zehn Jahre Fernsehen in Deutschland*, 193–207.

347. Hickethier, *Das Fernsehspiel der Bundesrepublik*, 221–225; the following conclusion on 35.

348. Borneman to Schmidt, 2 September 1960, BAK, B 263/42.

349. *Tele*, n.d.

350. Steinmetz, *Freies Fernsehen*, 369–70; Hickethier, *Das Fernsehspiel der Republik*, 222.

351. Quoted in Steinmetz, *Freies Fernsehen*, 202.

352. Ibid., 296–97.

353. On Eckert's biography See Steinmetz, *Freies Fernsehen*, 109–15 (with quotes from Eckert's dissertation on p. 112). See Hickethier, *Geschichte des deutschen Fernsehens*, 117–18.

354. Eckert, memorandum from 28 June 1960, BAK, B 263/42.

355. Borneman to Gladenbeck and Schmidt, 5 September 1960, BAK, B 263/42. See Eckert's memorandums from 19 and 22 August 1960, BAK, B 628/108.

356. Quoted in Steinmetz, *Freies Fernsehen*, 338.

357. Schmidt to the Frankfurt am Main tax office, 3 June 1960, BAK, B 263/96.

358. Gladenbeck to Borneman, 3 March 1960.

359. Borneman to Meyer-Goldenstädt, 7 October 1960.

360. Borneman to Meyer-Goldenstädt, 26 October 1960.

361. Borneman to Six, 14 January 1961, BAK, B 263/109.

362. Ibid.

363. The Reichspost-Fernseh GmbH was created by the Nazis to bring about the technical introduction of television.

364. Borneman to Hessling, 3 September 1960. See Steinmetz, *Freies Fernsehen*, 336–37.

365. Borneman to Schmidt, 22 October 1960 (see also 24 November 1960).

366. Quote from Borneman, *Die Ur-Szene*, 161.

367. Borneman to Gladenbeck and Schmidt, 5 September 1960, BAK, B 263/42.

368. *Frankfurter Rundschau*, 18 February 1961.

369. Quoted in Steinmetz, *Freies Fernsehen*, 297.

370. Meyer, memorandum from 25 October 1960, BAK, B 263/96.

371. KER (Rombach) to Schmidt, 17 February 1960, BAK, B 263/143.

372. In an interview with Werner Pieper in *taz*, 12 April 1990.

373. Borneman to Schmidt, 27 July 1960, BAK, B 263/42.

374. Borneman to Gladenbeck and Schmidt, 18 November 1960, BAK, B 263/42.

375. Borneman to Berendt, 23 September 1960; Berendt, "Ernest Borneman und die weiblichen Stimmen," 117.

376. Schreiber-Kalanag to Schmidt, 19 November 1960, BAK, B 263/42.

377. Ibid.

378. Brandt's mother's maiden name was Frahm.

379. Borneman, *The Man Who Loved Women: A Landscape with Nudes*, 57.

380. *Tele*, 15 October 1960, p. 5.

381. Borneman to Walter Hilpert, 19 June 1961.

382. Steinmetz, *Freies Fernsehen*, 371.

383. Borneman, "Back to Berlin," 59.

384. *Frankfurter Rundschau*, 20 September 1960.

385. *Der Spiegel*, no. 33 (1960): 24.

386. Borneman to Schmidt, 17 January 1961.

387. Borneman to Kraemer, 7 December 1960, BAK, B 263/42. The development in England: from 19 percent in 1956 to 26 percent in 1959 and 36 percent in 1962 (Sendall, *Independent Television in Britain*, 343).

388. FF Program Leadership (Borneman), "Freies Fernsehen: Programmkonzeption des 1. Quartals vom 1. Januar 1961 bis 31. März 1961," 20 October 1960.

389. Ernest Borneman, "Das Kontrastprogramm. Konkrete Vorschläge zur Form und zum Inhalt eines zweiten deutschen Fernsehprogramms," n.d.

390. Hickethier, *Das Fernsehspiel der Bundesrepublik*, 42; the following on 54–58.

391. Quoted in ibid., 126.

392. Quoted in Steinmetz, *Freies Fernsehen*, 342.

393. Loeser to Gladenbeck and Schmidt, 13 February 1961, BAK, B 263/111.

394. *Der Spiegel* no. 33 (1960): 23.

395. At issue was the text "Programm-Abteilung," n.d., BAK, B 263/114.

396. Schmidt di Simoni to Eckert, 13 October 1960, BAK, B 263/42.

397. Borneman to Gladenbeck et al., 17 October 1960, BAK, B 263/42.

398. This and the following in A. N. Schneider to Six, 6 February 1961, BAK, B 263/112.

399. Bignell and Fickers, "Introduction: Comparative European Perspectives on Television History," 7.

400. Morley and Robins, *Spaces of Identity*.

401. Eckert, *Freies Fernsehen*, 30–31.

402. Eckert, memo from 22 August 1960, BAK, B 263/108.

403. Eckert, *Freies Fernsehen*, 37.

404. Lindegk, "Warum erst nach zehn Jahren?," 86.

405. Eckert, *Freies Fernsehen*, 34.

406. A. N. Schneider, note from 27 January 1961, BAK, B 263/112.

407. Quoted in Schildt, *Moderne Zeiten*, 297.

408. Borneman to Edward H. Sommerfield, 9 June 1960, BAK, B 263/144.

409. Borneman to Schmidt, 27 July 1960, BAK, B 263/42.

410. Borneman to Kraemer, 28 November 1960, BAK, B 263/42.

411. *Stage and Television Today*, 27 October 1960; Steinmetz, *Freies Fernsehen*, 341.

412. Borneman, *Die Ur-Szene*, 162–63.

413. Steinmetz, *Freies Fernsehen*, 287.

414. Quoted in ibid., 302.

415. Hickethier, *Das Fernsehspiel der Bundesrepublik*, 125–26, 248–255. On Pinter's piece, see Borneman to Gladenbeck and Schmidt, 13 October 1960, BAK, B 263/42.

416. Eckert to Borneman, 4 July 1960.

417. Borneman, memo, 5 August 1960, BAK, B 263/42.

418. Eckert to Borneman, 2 August 1960.

419. Ernest Borneman, "Freies Fernsehen: Programmvorschläge für 1. Quartal vom 1. Januar 1961 bis 31. März 1961."

420. Steinmetz, *Freies Fernsehen*, 330.

421. Borneman to Schmidt and Six, 3 May 1961.

422. Borneman to Schmidt and Six, 23 March 1961.

423. Lindegk, "Warum erst nach zehn Jahren?," 93.

424. Borneman, *Die Ur-Szene*, 163. At another point he even spoke of fifteen hundred hours (Borneman, German TV).

425. Borneman to Six, 14 January 1961, BAK, B 263/109.

426. According to Steinmetz, *Freies Fernsehen*, 372.

427. See also ibid., 376–83. The press arrived at a somewhat more balanced conclusion; see, e.g., *Die Welt, Der Tagesspiegel*, and *Das Handelsblatt* from 26 January 1961.

428. Conference with the committee from the program advisory board, 17 February 1961, in BAK B 263/111.

429. Quoted in Steinmetz, *Freies Fernsehen*, 379.

430. *Frankfurter Rundschau*, 18 February 1961.

431. Borneman to Six, 14 January 1961, BAK, B 263/109. Essentially the same to Schmidt on 27 December 1960, ibid.

432. *dpa*, 18 Feburary 1961. See *Der Spiegel*, 15 March 1961.

433. Borneman, "Wie frei war das 'Freie Fernsehen'?"

434. This and the following in Borneman, *Die Ur-Szene*, 162.

435. Borneman to Gladenbeck and Schmidt, 5 September 1960, BAK, B 263/42.

436. Borneman to Sean Graham, 21 September 1962.

437. Borneman to Hessling, 3 September 1960.

438. Borneman to Meyer-Goldenstädt, 26 October 1960.

439. "Bornemann hadn't been able to assert himself in the 'chaotic circumstances,'" well-informed circles reported to the *Frankfurter Rundchau* (18 February 1961).

440. Borneman's father to Eva, 3 September 1960.

441. Borneman, "Wie frei war das 'Freie Fernsehen'?"

442. Borneman, *Die Ur-Szene*, 164.

443. Such was Heinrich G. Merkel's contemporary assessment in Steinmetz, *Freies Fernsehen*, 370–71.

444. Steinmetz, *Freies Fernsehen*, 371.

445. *fff-press*, 10 April 1961.

446. Eckert, memo, 11 July 1961, BAK, B 263/108. On the revision, see Eckert to Six, 30 January 1961, BAK, B 263/113.

447. Borneman to Arno Seeger, 30 June 1961.

448. For the context, see Bausch, *Rundfunkpolitik nach 1945*, 487–97.

449. *Kölnische Rundschau*, 22 February 1962. See also *Aktueller Fernsehdienst*, 23 February 1962; *Spots*, 28 February 1962.

450. *Der Spiegel*, 28 February 1962.

451. Borneman to Paul Haag, 18 March 1962.

452. Borneman to Karl Holzamer, 18 February 1962.

453. Ernest to Eva, 15 March 1962.

454. Geisel to Hajo Schedlich, ZDF, 5 July 1967; Eckart Stein, ZDF, to Geisel, 10 August 1967.

455. Hickethier, *Das Fernsehspiel der Bundesrepublik*, 250–51.

456. Such was the opinion of Hessischer Rundfunk editor in chief Wolf Hanke in *Medium*, n.d.

457. Ernest to Curt, 25 March 1965.

458. Ernest to his father, 26 March 1967.

Chapter 4

TOUCHING
SEX AND SOCIETY

When Ernest Borneman began to note down children's everyday phrases and sexual rhymes in Frankfurt in the early 1960s, he entered a field that was to play a key role in social change.

Freedom from Fear: The Sexual Revolution

It wasn't the sale of anti-pregnancy pills beginning in 1961 alone that triggered the "sexual revolution" of the late 1960s; more broadly, it was the confluence and reciprocal impact of technical innovation, shifting values, and sexual discourse in the media and advertising.[1] The most important outcome, however, was that by the early 1970s, many more people could have sex with relatively less anxiety than before. The fact that people could now practice their sexuality outside the setting of heterosexual marriage was a win for democratization of the first degree. Yet liberalization did not only make sexual life simpler. Rather, new boundaries and conventions emerged that again complicated the newly won freedoms, leading over the course of the 1970s to new norms and rules for what could and could not be said and done. Under the auspices of a conservative "turn,"[2] a backlash against sex education gained footing at least by the beginning of Kohl's government in 1982, which led in the context of HIV/AIDS in the mid-1980s to a renewed effort at regulating sexual orientation by means of prohibition and punishment.

As the state loosened its interventions in sexual life during the 1970s amid these shifting perceptions, leaving the decision about how to conduct this aspect of one's life to the citizens themselves, sexology, psychology, and the media took on the role of advising authorities to be consulted in case of doubt and as aids in individuals' self-monitoring. From the late 1960s onward, Ernest Borneman rose to become a sought-after expert in this field, addressing issues of sexuality in the form of dictionaries, treatises on the history of sexuality, advice columns, and talk-show appearances.

The course of the sexual revolution was propelled by actors from different generations, as a brief look at some of its most important protagonists reveals. Journalist

Oswalt Kolle (b. 1928) provided one source of education beginning in the late 1950s, addressing the masses of West German society in deliberately sober language about the emotional meaning and techniques of a sexuality based on equal rights through magazine series, books, and films. Entrepreneur Beate Uhse (b. 1919) opened her shop with practical products for "marriage hygiene" in the late 1940s, promoting "contraception in the republic with authority and circumspection" (Gunter Schmidt). Her breakthrough, however, came with the commercialization of sexuality and the erosion of the pornography ban. In 1970 social scientist Günter Amendt (b. 1939) published *Sexfront*, a tract on sex education written from a leftist perspective whose blunt language and graphic representations unleashed a flood of petitions to ban it. Like Amendt after him, Borneman (b. 1915) began with language, albeit one that kept a certain reserve, as with his *Lexikon der Liebe* (Dictionary of Love) in 1968 (in contrast to the student leader Amendt, who used taboo terms like "Schwanz" [cock] and "Möse" [pussy] in his book for adolescents). At the same time, Borneman engaged in a profound, unprejudiced exploration of the sexual language of children and adults within popular culture, lending his subject legitimacy in the process. Within wide segments of the population, this allowed for speech about sexuality that fell outside the professional terminology of medicine or psychology, even if the gates of "high culture" remained closed as before. Speech ultimately occupied a less important role than did immediate sensory experience in the acquisition of sexual knowledge for Borneman, in particular observing sexual intercourse between one's parents.[3] Still, a years-long engagement with the language of sex allowed him to draw far-reaching conclusions on changes in sexuality within West German society.

Following in succession of Hans Giese, in the late 1960s a young, empirically based school of academic research took root in universities in the figures of Volkmar Sigusch, Eberhard Schorsch, Gunter Schmidt, Martin Dannecker, and others. In 1972 this was recognized institutionally and by discipline under the term "sexology" (*Sexualwissenschaft*) in Hamburg and Frankfurt.[4] In contrast to the sexual research now pursued at universities by professors, Ernest Borneman, like Kolle and Amendt, found himself dependent on uncertain sources of income—chiefly the media, which played a central role in the "sex wave" of the 1960s and the ensuing upheaval in the field of sexuality. He saw his own work as one part research and one part education, and gained a wider audience principally through his position in the mass media. Until his death Borneman was considered a renowned sex researcher with opinions that while grounded in academic research were also provocative, and thus a source of scrutiny.

Sex Dictionaries

Borneman began publishing on sexuality with *Lexikon der Liebe* (Dictionary of Love), a two-volume work that "rose above the erotica of the Kolle era like a glacial erratic," as his editor at the time phrased it. Published in 1968 by the Paul List Verlag in

Munich, the book anticipated both Amendt's *Sexfront* and Helmut Kentler's *Sexual-erziehung* (Sexual Education) and came out before the younger sex researchers around Volkmar Sigusch had found a voice in broader circles.[5] In his first book written in the German language, Borneman lamented the state of sexual science in its land of origin but also the population's aversion to psychoanalysis: "The German doesn't like to investigate his motives."[6] The book was intended to address a need and fill a gap: the need, especially among young people, for clear-headed factual information on issues of sexuality that was "written without condescension." The book should bring about something "that has not existed before . . . a dictionary that satisfies the requirements of science and is nonetheless written in understandable language."[7] Borneman explained the great meaning attached to love in the present moment of the 1960s with twin reference to the crisis that had gripped religion, politics, and the family as well as the unprecedented upswing in education and leisure. He defended contemporary suspicions regarding monogamy but challenged a consumerist attitude toward love that failed to assign a prominent place to a reciprocal give and take. The dictionary entries show an interest in both breaking with reigning taboos and educating the reader. Beside the term "onanism," for example, which describes self-satisfaction as a matter of course, there is also an entry for "preventing onanism," which reviews the numerous methods used in earlier times to stop masturbation. Writing with reference to the normative demand of loyalty and the widespread practice of infidelity in a long article on the term "marriage," Borneman raises the "contradiction between what marriage should nominally be and what it actually is." On the notion of "sexual transition," a rare occurrence in his day, one reads, "Because the basic nature of the human being is bisexual, these kinds of interventions come as less of a surprise to the doctor than the layperson, who can only rarely free himself from the illusion that masculinity and femininity are unambiguous and absolute phenomena."

The press reacted positively to the book; the *Süddeutsche Zeitung* issued somewhat tentative praise as a "tremendous, downright obsessive feat," while the political left waxed enthusiastic.[8] *Pardon*, a satirical magazine located firmly at the center of the outbreak in 1968 that had a young and educated readership and a permanent interest in breaking taboo, found *Lexikon der Liebe* not only informative, but unavoidably tendentious: "All the information is directed against an outdated moral code. That's also necessary."[9] And for Henryk M. Broder, a spokesman on sexuality who was present on every channel of the counter- and mainstream culture, Borneman came as a revelation. On West German Broadcasting (Westdeutscher Rundfunk, WDR), Broder welcomed the returning emigrant's work as a breath of fresh air for German sexual culture and praised "the unpretentious style, clarity of the formulations and the social engagement that provides an agreeable counterexample to the well-preserved German tradition of academic impartiality, that is, non-engagement." He expected great things from the new figure on the scene of popular West German sex literature: "Borneman's book will hopefully help liberate sexuality from the small-town atmosphere of double morality and repressed dirty-joke tellers." The "movement toward humanization and emancipation of sexuality [receives] a fresh impulse from Ernest Borneman."[10]

Two more dictionaries followed: in 1971 Rowohlt published *Sex im Volksmund* (Sex in the Vernacular), a compendium, as the subtitle advertised, of "obscene German vocabulary"; in 1972 a comprehensive collection of children's rhymes with commentary was published as a three-volume set by Switzerland's Walter Verlag. Borneman began work on the dictionaries in the early 1960s during his time at Freies Fernsehen, a point at which, now permanently returned to Germany for the first time in twenty-seven years, he had taken up a study of language on the side. His autobiography describes how after work he would make his way through the bars and restaurants of the neighborhood surrounding Frankfurt's train station by night with a notebook in his pocket, jotting down everyday speech. "So what began to accumulate in my notepads was one part vocabulary from the Nazi era, while another part was new formulations from the postwar period and years of occupation. Finally there was the language of prostitutes and pimps, which I took for typical West German neologisms at the beginning. It took at least a year until I learned that one was different from the other."[11]

This work would provide the basis for *Sex im Volksmund*, an encyclopedia with a stated fifty thousand entries (containing, as many have confirmed, 256 synonyms for "breasts" and more than one thousand for "penis"). Borneman saw "in the vocabulary, syntax and grammar of the forbidden a process of linguistic innovation," which might bring down the "dictatorship of ruling class speech" then holding court in West Germany. As it was, everyday German speech attempted "to deny its regional and class-based structure." Yet in "popular speech," "one finds even today innovative turns of phrase that illuminate the life of the senses." Even writers who valued such language, like the "young savages" (*Junge Wilden*)—Borneman named Rolf Dieter Brinkmann, Peter O. Chotjewitz, and Hubert Fichte—ended up using the "dandyism of a fashionably alienated prose." Extra-parliamentary opposition would never win over the sympathies of the masses, because it uncritically repeated "the worst mannerisms of middle-class academic speech." Borneman thus stuck to documenting popular language without his works becoming "popular" in their own right.

Borneman's first books on sexuality demonstrated once again his encyclopedic working methods, with the explanations he assembled for his entries entering into the greatest possible detail. His estate contains long lists of terms on every subject imaginable—phenomenological, descriptive, and analytic concepts that address a diverse range of aspects within each subject and are arranged hierarchically. It also contains an extensive collection of slang terminology from innumerable fields: body parts, emotions, social relations, clothing, amusement, etc. One folder from his estate that contains letters addressed not to him but the Hamburg sex magazine *St. Pauli Nachrichten* shows Borneman to have relied on not only his own notes and interviews for material, but also a friendly environment. The letters, counting well over one hundred in number, were written in response to a question the magazine posed in May 1970, about alternatives for the verb "to fuck." They include answers not only from professionals in the prostitution business, but from entirely average citizens who report back on their families' and circles of friends' use of speech.[12] After the book's appearance, the publisher received numerous letters (mostly positive) as well as a large number of suggestions for new terms yet to be included—Borneman had called for them in his foreword—so that over time a thick folder with "addenda" came together.

The public response to the monumental work was mixed but fundamentally appreciative. Liberal media like *Der Spiegel* wrote about the amount of work involved and its "imposing abundance," and the *Times Literary Supplement* noted "herculean field research"; more conservative minds spied an "aberration in taste" running through the work or criticized its veneration of "street and gutter jargon."[13] Karl Krolow lay down this "crucial book" from a "crucial author" exhausted: "One can learn about conversational German of a certain type until he runs out of breath or fantasies, until his eyes grow dim. Attention has its limits."[14] Robert Neumann similarly considered Borneman to be "insatiable" and saw him as wandering about a "labyrinth without end," but celebrated a "in many respects fascinating work" and a "treasure."[15] Finally, the Darmstadt literary jury accorded the book a princely accolade, selecting *Sex im Volksmund* as its book of the month for August 1971.[16] The book's reception also saw the rise of the moniker "Pornomann," a word association that would be tacked on time and again despite rhyming with the author's last name only with difficulty.[17]

If Borneman had limited himself in *Sex im Volksmund* to presenting his collection and refrained from drawing further conclusions, over the course of the 1970s and 1980s he would use that same material to reach seminal conclusions regarding sexual development. It was no longer the creative potential of "popular language" that

Figure 4.1. Borneman in bib and brace: an encyclopedist at his card index. *Spiegel*, 1971.

formed the focus now, but rather its development as an indicator for changes in sexuality—and those for the worse. Borneman detected a "trend toward objectification and alienation running through the erotic vocabulary of everyday speech when the language of love turns into that of depersonalized sexuality."[18] This did not only have to do with the commodification of sexual services; Borneman saw an early objectification of love turned commodity in children's education, where nonconformism was punished by withholding love. This expressed itself in sexual phrases that emphasized the inanimate character of love objects or sexual organs. Long lists cited example after example: girls were referred to as "slices," "screws," or "pieces"; penises as "hammers," "rods," or "bolts"; vulvas as "drill holes," "sockets," or "mines," etc. Even more pronounced was a tendency to refer to sex organs with images of weaponry—in this case, too, Borneman found dozens of examples. "The language of love," ran his pessimistic appraisal in 1977, "is not only changing in our contemporary bourgeois world from a language of tenderness into one of fear and aggression—it is also revealing in the course of its metamorphosis that lovers are losing their grip on love, which no longer appears as a relationship between I and you but as one between drives, and that the feelings the lover himself has produced now confront him as foreign forces that rule over him."[19] Borneman was convinced that as with the economic, social, and political consequences, the human being in bourgeois society was increasingly incapable of seeing through "the sexual consequences of his being and his actions." "Thus the creative process of popular language," the author concluded, "is in the end again negated by the alienation of bourgeois society."

In *Lexikon der Liebe* Borneman describes how he first came upon the field of sexual science. He has a precise date at the ready: 10 October 1940, when as the head of the library at his war prisoner camp in Canada he "happened upon a creased copy of the *Journal of Criminal Psychopathology*" in which the Marxist psychoanalyst Géza Róheim—to whom Borneman dedicated his dictionary—"had tried to analyze the dreams of an African prostitute."[20] No mention is made yet of the other related activities in the field that would appear later in his autobiography from 1977, such as a position at Wilhelm Reich's sex-counseling clinics in Berlin in the early 1930s or studies during his early years of emigration with other world-renowned teachers including Bronislaw Malinowski in London, Vere Gordon Childe in Edinburgh, and Helena Wright in London in the 1950s. One wonders why he did not call attention to these qualifications in his early publications, to legitimate his work; there is much to speak for the fact that he affixed such biographical laurels only once he was better acquainted with the works of these key thinkers. Using Wilhelm Reich as an example, in a detailed autobiographical account from 1969 written for the magazine *Underground*, Borneman explored the sexual debate within the Weimar KPD, and thus Reich's theses, without mentioning any collaboration.[21] There is only a discussion of "lessons" at the Socialist student federation at which Wilhelm Reich is said to have been present, among others. Nor is there any mention of Reich in an article for the *Times Literary Supplement* from 1971 on recent literature combining Marx and Freud.[22] That same year he wrote to his childhood friend Herbert Steinthal in Copenhagen, explaining that he was "at work on an attempt to resolve the dialectics of Marx and Freud to one another, and have read and worked through everything in print by Wilhelm Reich. But much has disappeared."[23] He asked Steinthal for recommendations about antiquarian bookshops that might have the writings Reich published while in exile in Copenhagen and Oslo, and he sought to be introduced to a Danish or Norwegian psychoanalyst who had worked alongside Reich. No reference to a close acquaintance with Reich in their common youth appears in this letter, either. It is only in his autobiography from 1977, then again in a 1981 essay that Borneman describes an alleged connection with Wilhelm Reich in greater detail, claiming to have joined the German Federal Association for Proletarian Sexual Politics (Reichsverband für proletarische Sexualpolitik) in 1931, after Reich enlisted him as a sexual counselor; to have worked alongside Malinowski in London in anticipation of Reich's move to England; and to have been in touch with Reich via letter until 1942. Recent research on Wilhelm Reich has established that a sex-counseling clinic never existed at "Charlottenburg's Schlossstrasse," the address Borneman gave in a 1986 interview as the site of his purported collaboration.[24] It seems doubtful that this owed merely to the "clouded memory" of a 71-year-old man, as does his claim in the 1981 essay that Reich withheld Borneman's coauthorship on an article.[25] Working at a counseling clinic as a teenager, as Borneman purports to have done, "would [itself] have been a novelty and likely unique for a long time," Reich scholar Andreas Peglau cautiously concludes.[26] In the face of multiple autobiographical claims, one is left unsure as to whether such a thing ever happened. Borneman himself hinted at the fictive nature of his account, explaining potential contradictions to Reich biographies by way of gaps in his memory and conceding that in such a case "I'm also not able to say who is or isn't right here." His version came at the risk of publishing "screen memories" as he wrote, thus immunizing himself against potential objections.[27]

What is clear at any rate, is that by the end of the 1960s, with an article in the youth magazine *Underground* that combined leftist schooling with revolutionary sexual politics, Borneman was at pains to compensate for the generational disadvantage at which he found himself in the cultural revolution of 1968 by establishing an intellectual and, as far as was possible, close personal proximity to the forerunners of the present movement. It was from this effort that one characteristic aspect of his publications in the late 1960s sprang: the perpetual recourse Borneman made to his autobiography when accounting for his current activities. While such autobiographical references had already made an appearance in his texts on jazz, they did not serve the purpose of legitimating his own actions to the extent they did in his writings on sex.

By spring 1967 the die had been cast for the time that was left to Borneman, by now fifty-two years old. He resigned from the Ted Bates advertising agency, where he had begun work in December 1966, remarking that "like everything I do, it is likely the wrong decision—but I can't lead three operations at the same time—the ad agency, the literary agency and my own minor scribbling. So I will give it another shot with writing, now that I've established so many contacts through the literary agency . . . that I can sell all of what I'll write over the course of the coming year."[28] Borneman had concluded once before at an early point that he could work better "alone than as a salaried employee"; this would now continue to prove itself.[29] After his departure from advertising, Borneman was like a man possessed; the following years were filled with a profusion of writing projects, including the already mentioned *Lexikon der Liebe, Sex im Volksmund,* as well as *Psychoanalyse des Geldes* (The Psychoanalysis of Money). With self-employment, the question of where to live resurfaced yet again. Eva, who like Ernest could work from anywhere as a translator and literary agent, suggested buying a house in the countryside to accommodate their enormous library of around ten thousand volumes, and where both could work undisturbed.[30] In 1969 the couple made a find in Upper Austrian in Scharten, a town of two thousand souls a half-hour drive west of Linz and two and a half hours east of Munich: an old farmhouse with room for multiple workspaces and guests, in which they would live up until the end. After almost ten years in Frankfurt, the move to such a rural area did not come as easily as expected to Borneman, all the more so as concentrating on his written work also meant saying goodbye to previous passions. At the end of 1970 he reported to his father, "I have a long but peaceful workday here without the telephone or disruptions. Actually, for my entire life I've wished to live one day in the way I'm doing now . . . but on the other hand I often feel so sad that I've left the levers of power as early as I have, and am no longer making any films or leading any television stations. After London, New York, Paris and Rome, Scharten really does feel lonely."[31] Added to this came a disillusionment with which anyone who has lived in a foreign country is familiar, as any romantic notions that may have been associated with the land of Freud and Schnitzler soon gave way to a more sober assessment:

> If one grew up in England, then spent ten years suffering under the pernicious spell of German boors, Austria, with the urbanity it has managed to salvage for the bourgeois era from the holy land of Kakania,[32] seems at first like salvation. The soft, ingratiating voice of the television interviewer, the cheekiness with which he questions statesmen and politicians with an incisiveness that is unheard of in Germany, his ability to fluidly portray complex things in simple terms, his will to use dialect and popular idiom—all this at first gives Austrian Radio [Österreicher Rundfunk, ORF] great appeal . . . after three months one sadly begins to discover that a part of this elegance has come at the price of rejecting the power to decide and a loss in the will to decide, at a shift of all values from matters of content to formal affairs and flight from social reality and social responsibility. As in England, another dying land, it is still some consolation to experience the good manners of a vanished era, but it lulls even its guests into a certain intellectual indolence, to a merry, semi-conscious state that lasts from this year's harvest until one is fit to cry.[33]

Childhood Sexuality

Borneman addressed a wide variety of questions pertaining to sexuality, but his true specialization—one with which he engaged continually from the early 1960s onward—was the sexuality of children, a field in which discursive changes between the late 1960s and the mid-1990s are particularly evident. If *Studien zur Befreiung des Kindes* (Studies on the Liberation of the Child)—the title of a three-volume work by Borneman from the 1970s—spoke to a central project of the 1968 movement, by the 1990s children were no longer even halfway perceived as self-determining sexual beings, but rather seen primarily as victims of masculine violence in need of protection. Borneman's concepts and his increasingly defensive position in light of the shifting public discourse offer an opportune means to reconnoiter this field of tension. As Borneman established on his outings to playgrounds and schools, the "bad uncle" was also a familiar metaphor in the 1960s for the ubiquitous threats confronting children, who prior to their education were seen as innocent, pre-social beings. Subsequent perception would range from an interpretation of the child as a pure, but easily swayed being to its opposite—that of an independent or aggressive creature, not least when it came to sexual proclivities. Drawing in no small part on psychoanalysis, the emphasis within the '68 movement soon shifted to the latter interpretation. Following Freud, to someone like educational theorist Johannes Bilstein, the child now seemed "from the very beginning [to be] a compulsive, sexually active being which develops the complex psychological apparatus of an adult step by step via its interaction with the environment" and undergoes different phases of sexual orientation.[34]

The three volumes of *Studien zur Befreiung des Kindes* (Studies on the Liberation of the Child) appeared in 1972, 1974, and 1976, respectively, initially through Walter Verlag in Switzerland, then through Ullstein. All three feature an introduction and succinct commentary and present new material on the sexual language of children. Volume 1 is arranged according to forms of verse—counting rhymes, simple rhymes, tongue twisters, etc.; volume 2 is arranged by subject and deals with the "Environment of the Child"; volume 3 deals with the "World of Adults" as reflected in "forbidden" rhymes. Explicit references to research in popular song on the one hand and to psychoanalysis on the other reveal the work as a transitional point between Borneman's earlier study of ethnomusicology and his more recent work in sexology.[35] For the first time, one finds more extensive reflections and opinions regarding Freud's drive theory and its neo-Marxist reading within the student movement. Even at first glance, prefaces by well-known academics—folklorist Lutz Röhrich, musicologist Wolfgang Suppan, and psychologist Igor Caruso—lend the volumes a scholarly dignity. The work enjoyed largely positive feedback, even if isolated voices registered methodological concerns.[36] In a review of the first volume for *Der Spiegel*, Peter Rühmkorf, who had himself published a similar, if somewhat methodologically distinct collection in 1967 under the title *Über das Volksvermögen* (On the National

Wealth), smugly pointed out the parallels: "At first," it seemed to Rühmkorf, "to be an original discovery that certain phases within childhood sexual development also find reflection within this collective medium." But then Borneman, "without our discussing it . . . had developed exactly the same theory from his research lab in Wolfsburg—a fact that far surpasses the notion of an anonymous and authorless popular literature, and brings the truly democratic concept of dialectically sublated authorship within reach."[37] Borneman brushed aside the accusation with the observation that in the end it is about popular culture, for which no copyright law exists.[38] His collection—exhaustive as always—of nearly five thousand verses is still used in ethnology; a comparable work has not been undertaken to this day. Freiburg folklorist and head of the German folk song archive Lutz Röhrich meanwhile found words of praise for the author: "It remains Borneman's indisputable service to have raised this type of elementary poetry from the unseen and made it visible in the first place." In the work a "long neglected genre [was] presented in a hitherto unachieved fullness and completeness."[39] Röhrich himself had made "erotic folklore" the subject of his academic work and invited Borneman to visit as a guest in his courses as early as 1971.[40]

More strongly influenced by field research than by "thinking at the desk" from his socialization in England,[41] Borneman collected "forbidden" children's rhymes on his ethnological outings, or songs and verses with sexual content that children exchanged among themselves but concealed from adults. Within these forms Borneman made out the structural elements of an "alternative order," a "children's underground." It was only in these ongoing "creative activities" that the child ceased "to satisfy or challenge adults" and was only a child.[42] Yet the point was not merely to document this secret world. The idea, which Borneman attributed to Géza Róheim, was to test whether Freud's model for the stages of development in infantile sexuality was borne out in the use of everyday sexual rhymes.[43] To this end, the rhymes common among predetermined age groups were correlated with Freud's stages. Borneman's conclusions reaffirmed the continued validity of Freud's theory about child libido, as one reviewer noted, in order "to support children in their right to sexual-sensory experience."[44] For Borneman, the essence of Freud's model endured—the sequence of an initially "polymorphous," or multiform, phase characterized by a nonspecific sexual sensation over the entire body followed by oral, anal, and phallic or oedipal phases, a latent period after the sixth year, and finally the dominance of the genitals in puberty.[45] Drawing on Herbert Marcuse and Norman O. Brown, Borneman nevertheless took a critical view of the model's teleological construction, seeing the true liberation of human sexuality as consisting in a return to the pan-eroticism of the primary stage. From this follows the postulate that it is not children's sexual knowledge that is a misunderstanding of adult knowledge, but the opposite; it is rather the present sexual life of adults that is a "corrupted form of early childhood sexuality." Following Marcuse, Borneman argued that "'normal' does not mean subordinating partial drives to the dictates of the genital stage, but rather the pan-sexuality of the newborn, which is free of all subordination. 'Perverse' does not mean regressing to a pre-genital phase of childhood, but rather the tyranny of the genital stage over the partial drives."[46] Then there was the fact that Freud considered his model universal for being biologically grounded. For his part, Borneman considered the matter at hand to be a "specifically Western, specifically bourgeois syndrome that appears in no other culture." "It registers nothing more than the self-imposed forms of repression of a social system that gains its social dynamic from the suppression of childhood sexuality."[47] The "most dangerous legacy" of Freud's theory of "civilization and its discontents"—that is, that culture emerges from the sublimation of sexual desire—was the notion that happiness and desire must be sacrificed in order to establish culture. All in all Borneman, as Igor Caruso phrased it, wanted to turn Freud on his head in order to "no longer acknowledge the systematic suppression of childhood sexuality as a *conditio sine qua non* for the emergence of culture."[48]

Set against this backdrop, the widespread opinion that the sexual language of children had been picked off from listening to adults became untenable. Rather, the language reflected a series of discrete steps in an evolving sexuality that followed Freud's model. Borneman did find, however, that rhymes in the anal and latent phases set in and stopped with a delay of one to two years, while his observations regarding the phallic period deviated "completely" from Freud's analysis.[49] There were other results that were incompatible with Freud's assumptions, too: it was less "penis envy" that Borneman observed in girls than it was "vulva envy"—later to become "breast envy"[50]—that he observed in boys. The author registered more dynamic activity from girls in general, leading him to consider a female-dominated future as a real possibility (if the bourgeois system were even to survive the next quarter century). Boys and girls alike, the children in Borneman's studies come across as fearless beings. He regarded them as extremely self-conscious actors in expressing their sexuality, not only between each other but also in relationship to adults, and was unable to understand how one could reduce the sexuality of children to abuse by adults.

Adults—this was to be Borneman's "most important discovery" in the course of the project—suffered from a "post-pubertal amnesia," usually not or only vaguely recalling their sexual behavior during childhood or denying it in full.[51] Those who assumed the existence of children's sexuality and engaged with it in scholarly fashion were thus commonly denounced "not just as swine, but mostly as liars or slanderers,"[52] something Borneman had himself often encountered in the course of his field research. Since his arrival in Germany in March 1960, he reported, he had visited the playgrounds, swimming halls, and schools of the large cities in which he was working to ask children about sexual rhymes. In doing so he was often subject to suspicious questioning from housemasters, parents, or police. He grounded the work, a form of "self-therapy" as a returning emigrant, in his aversion to "the affectation, artificiality and unsettled nature of a language that tried to deny its roots in work and popular dialect."[53] In his search for a popular language, he "quickly came across certain types of children's songs that differed fundamentally from the hoary songs of the organized youth movement. . . . These obstinate, often seemingly nonsensical rhymes with which children communicate in a language scarcely accessible to adults soon revealed themselves to be a virtually inexhaustible source of unconscious, preconscious and semi-conscious material on sex."

Within the context of the educational models then emerging from the student movement, Borneman's approach could not have been more timely. This scene was characterized not only by sectarian experiments in communal living or day-care centers, but by a profound revaluation of children in a wide range of fields. The term "children's culture" (*Kinderkultur*), used for the first time in 1973 in the magazine *Kursbuch*, points to the independent space that had opened up for society's youngest members, where new ideas regarding education, pedagogical initiatives, consumption patterns, and children's independent play all mingled. The goal was to develop children into free individuals, or rather to allow them to develop themselves into free individuals. Beginning in the 1960s, increasing numbers of West Germans came to consider the twin educational goals of independence and free will as goals worth striving for. Formal authority no longer sufficed, and the previous, matter-of-fact use of violence toward children became both anathema and prosecutable; empathetic communication and rational discussion were used as educational methods in its stead. Broader social change provided other settings: a sharp drop in the birth rate due to the pill, rising female employment, higher divorce rates, and a general differentiation in lifestyle also shifted the place value of children. From the early 1970s, on children came to satisfy emotional needs more greatly than before, with their importance in the family growing accordingly. In "partnership families," children were not only paid careful attention, they also became projective surfaces for the era's high hopes regarding social change. Contemporary ideals no longer involved childhood idylls removed from society or restrictive education, but confronting reality—including its less idyllic aspects—and education in self-guidance, something that found expression in children's books, theater, and TV shows.

At the same time, the question of whether projecting hopes onto children would not overburden them was also raised regularly. On reading Rühmkorf's *Über das Volksvermögen*, it occurred to critic Reinhard Baumgart that demythologizing (in this case the time-honored stereotype of the asexual child) frequently proceeded hand in hand with the production of new myths: "These magnificent children! I hear him crying out (certainly with more complicated wording), this by no means sweet, but still magnificently rascally popular tongue, rebelling line by line against any type of authority."[54] For Borneman too, the culture of children held a provocative element that called bourgeois capitalist society into question. Borneman would continue to maintain the concept of a child as a sexual being with its own wishes and options for action up until the end of his life. He did oppose romanticizing children and their subversive texts, in which he saw a reincarnation of the "noble savage" from the Enlightenment. "The sexual content of these verses is not the expression of developed sexual desires but a desperate form of compensation, the blooming scar of the prohibitions with which childhood is hemmed in and obliterated by bourgeois society."[55] In such a context the libidinous behavior of the child "was no occasion for admiration or esteem, praise or acceptance."[56]

Borneman's initial thoughts on sex education boiled down to a fairly simplistic system: first, it was not words but acts, that is, the parent's behavior, that showed children the proper way to approach sexuality; second, a model sex education was strictly speaking impossible under capitalist conditions—it was only under free social relations that education could lead to a truly free sexuality; third, a "liberation of the child" was therefore only conceivable once the prevailing order had been dispensed with.[57] He did not revise his position until the concept was criticized from a pedagogical perspective as disdaining "the educationally effective possibilities within the context of the present order" and "concrete, politically feasible action plans" were demanded. The critique also called attention to the fundamental conflict between the notion that education could in principle enable independent judgment and at the same time improve individual lives.[58] Borneman would not stand for the accusation that he had "no constructive notion of education" and immersed himself the field. While he did keep the view that sex education was unnecessary if the parents led an open sex life, he now engaged earnestly with the question of how the vast majority of people for whom this was not the case might be helped. "In such cases," he concluded in one text from 1988, "careful sex education in schools . . . could help a great deal."[59]

In 1981 Borneman published another book on the topic, *Reifungsphasen der Kindheit* (*Childhood Phases of Maturity*), conceived of as the first part of a three-volume series on the subject of "sexual developmental psychology."[60] Over eleven chapters, the book details the stages of sexual development in children up to age eight, supporting the assumption of a sexual life in children and in order to help teachers "answer questions from concerned parents about whether their child of such and such an age is mature enough for certain sexual information."[61] The work's conception as a textbook for training sex educators was innovative; there was not yet a chair in the field of sex education at any university in the German-speaking world. The book nevertheless saw itself as "preparatory work" for the founding of such a position—and it was obvious who might be first in line.[62] The thought was not at all misplaced; sex education drew increasing attention in West Germany in the 1970s, eventually becoming an ideological battlefield, with the Catholic Church in particular—in association with the CSU (the Christlich-Soziale Union, or Christian Social Union) and the conservative wing of the CDU—challenging the schools' contention that sex education should not be left to the parents, but rather carried out within a public context. The need for corresponding teacher training courses was obvious in this context, allowing one to conjecture reasonably that a new academic field that went beyond the purely biological aspects of sex would soon emerge. When the Kohl government took office the year after the book's publication, however, it announced a general rollback of initiatives in sexual policy, and the idea remained stuck in its initial stages until being taken up again in part with the advent of HIV/AIDS.

Borneman's research on childhood sexuality—which appeared in English first in 1990 as a journal article, then in 1994 in book form as *Childhood Phases of Maturity*—was a source of great interest in the United States, where a lack of social acceptance meant there were few works on the subject.[63] At the same time, Borneman's US colleagues criticized the fact that the author had not published his empirical data, preventing closer inspection.[64] What was more, Borneman's heavy reliance on a psychoanalytic approach made assessing the details difficult for those who did not work within the paradigm.

The topic also found literary reflection in Borneman's writing, where an early interest in psychological issues is evident in *A Face on the Cutting-Room Floor. Tremolo*,[65] from 1948, is a crime novel revolving around a series of peculiar events in the everyday routine of the Sommerville family: a present arrives that nobody has ordered, a clarinet disappears, a food delivery never appears. The events trigger mutual suspicion and end up provoking fear and terror. The psychological study seems at first to be populated exclusively with polite, well-adjusted family members from a prosperous New England suburb, a normality that soon proves fragile, however. The answer to the riddle comes from an oedipal complex, but with a pointed twist: it is not the son who kills the father and marries the mother, but rather the mother living at home with her son (the novel's protagonist, Mike Sommerville) who has staged everything so that Mike's wife and son come across as psychopaths, in order to eliminate them and live alone with her son again. As it turns out, she has already assisted with the death of the father. To Mike, the mother represents the certainty of what she herself sees as the "American way of life"—"in its wider meaning of voluntary submission to the norms of the nation and to the conventions that served to perpetuate the rule of the families who had coined and developed the norms."[66] Only when Mike exposes the mother as the guardian of this tradition and recognizes her destructiveness can he free himself and begin to model an independent life path for his son, who trusts completely in his father.

The year 1968 saw the publication of Borneman's last novel, *The Man Who Loved Women: A Landscape with Nudes*. In the novel, the author surveys the field of sexuality in experimental fashion, depicting fantasies and practices that deviate widely from the norm. The book chronicles the sexual exploits of US set designer Willard Gregory, who takes a job in 1954 at a theater in the provincial German town of Landsburg, later moving to Berlin's "Goethe Theater." While in Germany, Will discovers lesbian sex and intercourse with two women as a passion—one that he increasingly gives into after his wife Ruth begins an affair with the fashion designer Magda, whom he also takes as a partner. The story is packed with detailed depictions of sexual practices of every conceivable arrangement, sometimes of a sadomasochistic nature, and an image emerges of the trials and mishaps of an artist in search for his identity as a sexual being. From gay and lesbian meet-ups in the provinces to private orgies in the villas of West Berlin, Gregory increasingly loses himself to his obsessions, only to determine in the end that his love and sexual desire are reserved for Ruth and Magda

Figure 4.2. The German edition of Borneman's final novel (published by
C. Bertelsmann in 1971). The cover was designed by Raymond Bertrand, whose
erotic drawings appeared in numerous works of underground literature. The book
is dedicated to the surrealist artist Hans Bellmer, a German emigrant whose
own work shows a preoccupation with female anatomy.

alone. Both die in an automobile accident on their way to meet him, however—with
his wife pregnant. In the background of this family tale that was not meant to be,
the image Borneman gives of West Germany in the 1950s is of a society that is just
as prude as it is promiscuous—at least among the upper crust—with a tendency to

deviate from the norm. In large part, the preferences assigned to Will coincide with Borneman's self-description of his own—a desire for female sexual partners, a "soft spot for games in bed as a trio," and an aversion to sadomasochistic practices and sex between men. German society is depicted as holding double standards not only for sex but also for foreigners, who are brought into the country for their talents, then viewed as a threat and eliminated through contemptible plots.

Publishing the Private: Borneman's Sex Life

It is not uncommon for sexologists to be asked about, grouped by, and classified according to their private lives and sexual preferences. While such needs are often driven by voyeuristic motives, there also exists an understandable epistemic interest: any kind of sex research, as Volkmar Sigusch has emphasized, is "subjective," that is, the researcher cannot fully separate him- or herself from the object of study.[67] Even if those consulted justifiably decline to address this aspect of their private lives, it continues to play a certain role in their public perception. Borneman was extraordinarily open about his sexual experiences and proclivities, not only with friends but also in his writings and interviews.

During most periods in his life after his release in Canada, Borneman had amorous relations outside of his central relationship with Eva, a connection that never entertained any doubt. At points during the war years he gave up hope of ever seeing his beloved again, advising her, "Darling, don't become an old virgin before it is too late." She herself did not desire any other relationship, but expressed understanding for his: "Physical unfaithfulness on your side would, I know, not change your feelings towards me for a second. When you have the feeling that you can no longer hold out and need more intimate human contact, you know that I understand. I cannot deny that the *knowledge* of it would hurt me somewhat . . . and I know that similar things went through your mind when you were in prison and knew I was free." She herself felt more like a prisoner of her love for him, one that excluded other romantic relationships. Later, Borneman would interpret her statements as an invitation to an open marriage.[68] While he suspected Eva of affairs during his internment, his Paris years, and then again around 1960, it is difficult to judge the extent to which these were projections.[69]

Borneman, at any rate, made much greater use of the alleged openness of their relationship than did Eva, initially living with another woman in Ottawa until he succeeded in bringing Eva to Canada,[70] and later holding relationships with multiple women in Paris. In Frankfurt, as notes in his calendar show, he began seeing a woman in 1960 who at times also brought her friend, a relationship that would extend for at least three years. It was here he gathered experience with ménage-a-trois, something that had fascinated him since a liaison with two sisters in London before the war and which he worked into his 1968 novel *The Man Who Loved Women*.[71] The dedication in the English-language edition reads, "For you both"; a later letter revealed that he meant the two friends mentioned above.[72] As is clear by this point, Borneman's relationships were of an exclusively heterosexual nature, although this does not mean they were reducible to "coitus germanicus simplex," as Sigusch disparagingly entitled the preference. Rather they aimed at tenderness in a broad sense, as Borneman repeatedly described it in his polymorphic ideal.

Borneman continued to see other women during his years in Scharten, in cities where his business would bring him from time to time. He met Sigrid Standow before Eva's death. "I've slept with two or three hundred women in my life," he stated in one interview, before going on to explain what remained important to him throughout: "These weren't 'one night stands'—there were few relationships that lasted less than a year."[73] Even if the number may (as usual) be exaggerated, this had little to do with advertising sexual prowess. Borneman considered extramarital affairs practically necessary and, what was more, an important source of human experience. It was clear to him that the relationships were problematic, morally speaking. When asked about his own experiences at the end of a long interview about sexual development, he replied, "My relationship to my own sexuality is bad, to the extent that I haven't succeeded in being as honest with my wife as I would like. Because she is hurt when I hide something from her and becomes angry, and rightly so, when I sleep with someone else. So after all this talking, I can't answer the simplest question of all for you."[74] The death of Eva, the love of his life, on 19 December 1987 shook Borneman to his core; nor was it something his new girlfriend Standow could console him over.

Figure 4.3. Eva and Ernest in Scharten, 1986. Courtesy AdK.

"The Marx of the Women's Movement": *Das Patriarchat* and Contemporary Feminism

In 1975 *Das Patriarchat* (The Patriarchy), Ernest Borneman's 671-page "magnum opus" (his own description) was published by S. Fischer Verlag. The book opens with a bombshell, the dedication: "*Das Patriarchat* is dedicated to women. It is intended to serve the women's movement in the same way that *Capital* served the workers movement: as an analysis of the past, a key to the future and a weapon in the daily struggle." This sounded the fundamental tenor of the book, not only in the self-sure historical analogy, but also the ambition of providing the raison d'être for a significant present-day political movement. In doing so, *Das Patriarchat* placed itself among the books that had achieved similar goals for US feminism and appeared in German translation during the second half of the 1960s: Betty Friedan's *The Feminine Mystique* (1966) and even more importantly Kate Millet's *Sexual Politics* (1969), which attacked patriarchy as a relationship of domination. Borneman's work cited Millet as well as the US women's liberation movement. Alongside Alice Schwarzer's bestseller *The Little Difference and Its Huge Consequences* (*Der kleine Unterschied und seine großen Folgen*)—a book published at the same time by the same publisher, albeit to much greater acclaim—Borneman's was one of the first in the German-speaking world to provide greater legitimacy for the aims of the incipient women's movement. As did feminism, although with greater ties to the Marxist tradition, the book combined a critique of capitalism with one of patriarchy; as with feminism, Borneman viewed the women's movement as revolutionary, with the task of raising consciousness about power structures. Within this pluralistic field he did not, however, participate in an increasingly strong trend that assumed the need to effect a fundamental separation from men and the institutions they ran, such as political parties and unions.[75] If one follows the distinction between "social" and "cultural feminism" and takes Borneman's self-description as a "feminist" seriously, his approach holds the most in common with social feminism, which begins with the fundamental equality of the sexes to then reproach prevailing power structures that construct inequality through ascription, as in education. It does not seek to establish difference between the sexes, but equality. Cultural feminism on the other hand begins with the difference between the sexes, either on biological, cultural, or physical grounds. As historian Kristina Schulz summarizes, "If cultural feminism argued for a society that recognized the 'other,' social feminism sought to overcome the 'other.' If representatives of cultural feminism sought to abolish sexual *hierarchies*, social feminists supported overcoming sexual *differences*."[76]

The book drew from a wide stock of primary and secondary literature, including literary and philosophical sources, excavation reports from archaeology, and "bourgeois" research. When it came to the detailed findings however, and especially his interpretation of them, Borneman relied on a small cast: Friedrich Engels and Engels's inspiration, Lewis Henry Morgan, but above all the Marxist archaeologist Vere

Gordon Childe—whose student Borneman considered himself to be—the Marxist student of ancient Greece George Thomson, and the Soviet ancient historian M. O. Koswen. The work only cites its often extensive quotations and gives no references for the overwhelming quantity of specific information it contains, making an assessment by academic standards well nigh impossible. A bibliography of one hundred pages, rendered difficult to understand and therefore practically useless by its miniscule font size and arrangement into extremely specific subject fields, provides a brief summary of one part of the primary and secondary literature.

The books situates itself in the field of "historical sexual anthropology," which its author views as an up-and-coming "young discipline" that exists in a certain tension with the "few professorships in sexology," which "today are held by doctors, sociologists and psychoanalysts."[77] Concentrating on the heartland of the matriarchy in the Mediterranean region, Borneman initially looks to the transition from prehistoric matrilineal societies (those organized around the mother) to patriarchal, male-dominated societies that occurred during the New Stone Age (Neolithic), a period Borneman dates between roughly 4000 and 1800 BCE in Europe. Detailed studies of the patriarchy in both Greece and the Roman Empire follow, including several hundred pages devoted to the "sexual superstructure" after a description of the "social basis," thus contradicting the widespread notion within feminism that sexual oppression served as the primary basis of domination in patriarchy. This historical excursion ends not with a contemporary analysis but with a look to the future. In 1979 a paperback version appeared with an afterword in which Borneman addressed the controversy that had erupted around the book in the meantime. After appearing in multiple editions, its final printing came in 1991, at forty-six to forty-seven thousand copies. The work was conferred countercultural status when it was pirated,[78] although the publisher was less thrilled by the illegitimate child and contracted a private detective.

The author concedes in the foreword that a significant part of the book should be regarded as a "thought model" and "working hypothesis" due to the nature of his sources, which are as incapable of disclosing human thought and feeling as they are the constitution of society. Borneman takes a materialist approach to account for the superior position of women vis-à-vis men in prehistory, speaking in terms of a gradually emerging division of labor between the sexes. The woman's appointed task of gathering foodstuffs was more important for sustenance than the more or less sporadic hunting in which the men engaged, making her the pivotal sex until the Neolithic. Borneman rejected the term "matriarchy," as it was not a society dominated by women but a nonhierarchical order that had prevailed, speaking instead of a "matrilineal" or "matristic" society, in which one's descent was traced back exclusively through the mother. Borneman casts the period referred to as "primitive communism" in Marxism in a romantic, idealizing light, as a "world of modesty: timeless, constant, unperturbed, undemanding, and unassuming, but also considerate and dignified; a world without exceptionalism, but also without individualism; without individuality but also without blatant nonconformism; an existence free of property, but also greed or theft."[79] On this "isle of the blessed," sexuality was not directed only toward coitus, but also found gratification "in body contact, holding hands, embracing and being embraced, contact with breasts and breastfeeding."[80] Nor was it restricted to long-term relationships between couples, but was promiscuous and included members from one's own clan as well as relatives once removed. The incest taboo only arose after a growth in consciousness that distinguished the individual from the community had emerged and with it, Borneman argued, the enforced faithfulness of the woman via the emergence of property and related law of inheritance.

Borneman further explains the matriarchy's replacement by the patriarchy in terms of a revolution in the relations of production: male domination begins with agriculture and livestock breeding—that is, a settled life—as the forces of production for which men are responsible hold rank over the female activities of collecting foodstuffs and hoe-farming. Theft, a phenomenon unknown in the matriarchal clans, emerged with the advent of private possession of livestock. Borneman goes on to extrapolate the characteristics of patriarchy as such from this finding: "Patriarchy is thus not only a system of hereditary rule, a way of describing relationships, regulating sexuality and a law of inheritance, but also an ideology of theft, a justification of exploitation dressed up as morality, a glorification of armed robbery and appropriation of property. Whoever wants to understand the patriarchy must never forget its origins in robbery."[81] The shift in the relations of production triggered by male domination also accounts for the rise of the monogamous family, which succeeded the larger, mother-oriented clans.

The woman's transfer from the father to the husband via the system of bride purchasing, and thus her status as a commodity, had repercussions for sexuality. Once the wife became the property of her husband, freedom was seen as wasteful, infidelity as theft, and jealousy appeared for the first time in the history of Greek tribal society. "Jealousy is not actually sexual excitement, but only the sexual form of an entitlement to private property and the fear of its loss. This was a turning point in the history of sexuality."[82] In a nutshell: the "Neolithic revolution" (Childe) amounted in sexual terms to a "counterrevolution, a conspiratorial male revolt, a sort of original coup."[83] The matristic order is described in ideal terms; the patriarchy appears as the origin of all things evil. Events in Greece and Rome were of global significance "because they shaped the later actions and thought of the European plunderers who have plagued humanity since the fifteenth century of our era by conquering, colonizing and exploiting almost the whole of the non-European world."[84]

In contrast to a broad consensus among feminists that sexual oppression formed patriarchy's basis of power, Borneman held that sexual repression was socially determined. Emancipation from patriarchy was a process that must be accomplished by women and men working together, he argued, and would lead to the liberation of both sexes. This set him at odds with "radical feminist" women authors who took the hostility between the sexes as their starting point, such as Kate Millett or his antagonist Marielouise Jurreit. In her 1975 autobiography *Shedding*, Verena Stefan, a former Socialist and feminist activist, describes a similar process of female self-discovery that consists in a sexual rejection of men and an exclusive focus on one's own, female sexuality, leaving behind both Freud's assumption of a gender-neutral libido and the utopia of a free sexuality for both sexes.[85] One sketch of the battle between the sexes came from the United States in Valerie Solana's SCUM (Society for Cutting Up Men) Manifesto, which appeared in 1969 through März Verlag, a publisher with ties to the underground. Alice Schwarzer further popularized this process by grounding it in the "myth of the vaginal orgasm," a theory of Anne Koedt's that describes the clitoris as the primary sex organ capable of causing orgasm. The penis—regardless of whether it belonged to a conservative patriarch or a leftist student—was rejected as the physical manifestation of men's domination over women. Marielouise Jurreit (who would also use the last name Janssen-Jurreit from time to time) backed up the turn against the male sex with the theory that the empirically observed "greater willingness of the man to engage in aggressive acts has one of its foundations in male biology."[86] In a not entirely inaccurate, if somewhat overstated view, Borneman characterized Schwarzer and Jurreit's position as "sheer biologisms, and the derivation of a total feminist concept from biology."[87] Leftist men were singled out in particular as enemies, as in Svende Merien's 1980 autobiographical novel *Der Tod des Märchenprinzen* (The Death of the Fairy-Tale Prince), in which Arne, the boyfriend the female protagonist has picked up in her search for an "unmanly man," is exposed as a "misogynist." The widespread acceptance of the book's perception and the need it served is shown by its numbers, with over 160,000 copies sold by 1983.[88] Among feminist groups, studying one's body and rejecting "prick fucking" (*Schwanzfick*) became an essential part of a practice regarded as political, a boycott of sexual intercourse as a strategy for combating the patriarchy. Through physical and mental exploration, encounter groups provided a broad spectrum of possibilities for constituting the feminist self, but in addition to solidarity also generated the subjective feeling of a "permanent state of war."[89] In this context too, the private was political. Amid the heady atmosphere of a process of self-discovery justified on biological grounds, the reappearance of culturally conservative ideals harking back to a time of traditional gender dualism but dressed up as a new alternative could hardly be avoided. If, as Ulrike Heider observed sardonically, there was any talk of men "in the blossoming ghetto of women's centers and women's communes," it was filled with "warnings from mothers and grandmothers about the wicked scoundrels who could destroy a girl's life in the blink of an eye."[90]

Borneman considered cultural feminism's encounter groups to be reactionary navel-gazing, rejected the gender dualism of the new women's movement as apolitical, and argued, drawing dangerously close to the language of an old boys' club, that feminism had led to "sexual disorders": "If emancipation amounts to the ruin of heterogeneous sexual life, then its good name falls into disrepute."[91] Although he criticized the "stale, petty bourgeois air in the battle of the sexes," his analysis was also based on a clearly polarized, essentialist notion of two sexes, in which the woman held the positive role and the man the negative.

> In her ability to give birth, woman is the original producer. In her capacity to nurture, she is the mother of civilization. By contrast, man's millennia-long occupation as a hunter and fisherman has made him an exploiter of nature and predator *par excellence,* and it will take thousands of years more until he has attained the degree of civilization that woman has during the same time as the guardian of warmth, the architect of the home, protector of offspring and producer of sustenance.[92]

In contrast to an increasingly predominant trend within the women's movement that advanced the polarization of the sexes on the basis of biological characteristics and considered reconciliation impossible (at least for the foreseeable future), Borneman did not take anthropological constants as his point of departure, ultimately viewing gender identities and roles as historically mutable categories and aspiring instead to a future perspective that would do away with sexual identity as such—again, entirely in keeping with many a classical feminist text. To this extent Borneman was a prominent representative of sexual difference, even if it was women who ultimately (and currently) represented the better side of humanity for him, and who—just like the working class in overcoming capitalism—should lead the effort to overcome patriarchy. With such thinking Borneman helped to clear the way for the developing cult of femininity and "new motherhood." As more and more conversations about the sexes became subject to polarized notions, what was at heart a universal humanist stance and insistence on both sexes' common struggle for a different society made Borneman's arguments appear less and less timely.

To stay with Borneman's historical parallel: whereas Marx and Engels avoided more precise statements about the future of communism, in the final chapter of *Das Patriarchat* Borneman sketched the basic contours of a future non-patriarchal social order—and thus naturally opened himself up to attack. As for Friedrich Engels or Alexandra Kollontai, social and sexual liberation proceeded hand in hand for Borneman. In this regard his thought was largely in line with the sexual revolution of the 1960s, with works drawing from Wilhelm Reich and Herbert Marcuse linking the two processes in similar fashion. Yet this also put him at odds with lines of development that had emerged in the meantime, as represented by the political successors to the student movement and the new social movements. Communist groups counted entirely on class struggle and condemned the sexual revolution as a "secondary contradiction," while the social question did not play a particularly important role for the majority of the new women's movement, and cooperation between sexes was ruled out.

Because gender difference was not biological for Borneman but socially conditioned, he also saw the classless society of the future as a "sexless" society, in the sense that "in a society of free individuals, we will also decide whether we want to live as a man or a woman."[93] In this connection he cites contemporary statements from Susan Sontag and Frank Böckelmann. His thesis that economic or cultural equality must be accompanied by the sexes' biological convergence (as was already symbolically anticipated by the long hair and unisex clothing of contemporary youth) made him particularly vulnerable to criticism. An advocate of technology in his Marxism, the image that Borneman sketched of the future, and what has in part become reality today—artificial insemination, surrogate mothers, gender reassignment—must have met with all the more resistance for coming at the beginnings and continued ascendancy of a discourse of authenticity that was based precisely on biological factors. As Borneman stated unequivocally, "Women's liberation can come about only through the liberation of sexuality. No matter which rights women's liberation wins for itself, no matter how far it succeeds in deconstructing the prejudices against it, no matter how far the cause of equal pay advances, three biological disadvantages remain in place for the time being: menstruation, pregnancy and the vulnerability of the breasts. Until we have eliminated all three, there can be no equality among sexes."[94] He spoke of an "abolition of menstruation" and "alternatives to carrying the child in the womb."[95] While these pointed passages were singled out for criticism within the book's reception in West Germany, the ideas they represented were anything but new in feminist thought.[96] Simone de Beauvoir sketched a similar utopia in *The Second Sex*, in which full equality between the sexes would lead to new forms of sexuality, while Shulamith Firestone, a leading feminist intellectual in the United States, wrote about the elimination of sexual difference and "overcoming sexual dualism" as the goal of a liberated society in her defining 1970 work *The Dialectic of Sex: The Case for Feminist Revolution* (published in Germany in 1975). For Firestone, the future should not only be classless but also sexless, or better yet androgynous.[97] In public debate Marielouise Jurreit was alone in criticizing Firestone's calls to abolish pregnancy as a "full denial of the female body," writing that "a naïve belief in science and revolutionary attitudes enter an oddly illusory relationship in Firestone's thought."[98] When presented by Borneman, such utopian sketches became all the more threatening, not only because they came from a man who resembled a patriarch, but also because the progressive euphoria that prevailed around 1968 had in the meantime given way to skepticism toward technology and an emphasis on authenticity. This was a shift to which Borneman's cult of the mother had partially contributed, as the newfound sexual dualism among feminists not only rediscovered the allegedly biological nature of women but—in contrast to feminist pioneers like de Beauvoir and Millett—now sang its praises, celebrating menstruation, for example, as an aspect of identity.[99] Then came the fact that since 1971, the campaign against the ban on abortion—with its slogan of "My Stomach Belongs to Me!"—had resulted in a new consciousness directed against others' control of the female body that made ideas of "deconstructing femininity" seem reactionary.

If the "sexual revolution" had eroded the binding nature of traditional norms such as heterosexuality, marriage, or monogamy within the population, this was especially true of younger social groups, especially students and those within leftist circles, where it was connected with more radical demands made of the self. If one looks to its effects on social practice, the aspiration to broader sexual emancipation within the alternative milieu of the 1970s and 1980s by no means led only to greater pleasure, but also to greater insecurity, unsatisfying relationships, and new norms. When the first volume of *Sexualität konkret* appeared in 1979, its editors detected "the broken sexual relations around us . . . and our helplessness before them."[100] *Der Spiegel*'s decision to select this quote in announcing the volume shows just how current the perception was.[101] The intense pressure to love newly, differently, more freely, and more individualistically made such statements common fare[102] and was discussed openly by members of this milieu under the aegis of authenticity, without a solution to the conflict being immediately proposed. The politicization of sexuality lent the topic a gravity with implications that reached far beyond private preference to enter collective conversation and evaluation. Because individual behavior was no longer a private matter, sexual views and preferences became an essential and publicly discussed part of one's self-description within alternative scenes, and subject to criticism. In Sven Reichardt's judgment, for these actors "and their sexuality, such demands ultimately represented a fatal burden."[103] The women's movement held particular sway within this context and constructed "new regimes of sexuality" to which individuals would at times defer or make their own sexual practices conform.[104] After 1977, a lively debate about which goals would result in an equitable form of sexuality coursed through numerous leftist publications, including Frankfurt's *Pflasterstrand* and especially the magazine *Konkret*, which released the series *Sexualität konkret* at irregular intervals between 1979 and 1986.

For Borneman, the central issue of the women's movement did not involve arriving at a specific definition of "woman" as such; rather it should look to "the notion of motherhood," which "has formed the economic and ethical core of all matristic cultures in the past."[105] In the future, the concept of "motherhood" should be transformed from a fixation on individual children to the needs of the community. By abandoning the idea of woman "as a reproductive machine," Borneman fantasized, "all her attention, nurturing and caring could be devoted to the general environment. Motherhood will transcend biology to manifest as a social force."[106] Even if it proceeded from the assumption of properties specific to each sex, the concept stood diametrically opposed to the "new motherhood" that would soon emerge from one corner of the women's movement and which arrived in the form of biological determinism. In contrast to earlier feminist thought, which regarded the excessive importance attached to motherhood in determining biology as debilitating, women's ability to bear children was now interpreted as a sign of their superiority to men, an opportunity for self-realization or even true fulfillment. Taking root in the mid-1970s, this new cult of femininity proceeded from a central "assumption of the natural 'difference' of the woman, of the 'woman as a natural being,'" according to "social feminist" Alice Schwarzer.[107]

As it was, Borneman's "magnum opus" presented an impressive, even overwhelming overview of all the primary and secondary sources describing the shift from matriarchal to patriarchal orders, their respective characteristics and concrete form. The work was marked by the present moment: Marxist, but without an unconditional belief in progress; inspired by the rise of the women's movement, but without sharing in the polarization of the sexes or recognizing that the opposition between a "bourgeois" and "proletarian women's movement" had grown obsolete; taking an interest in sexuality as a key element in relations between the sexes, where other Marxists saw only a secondary contradiction. Borneman delivered a full-throated criticism of "bourgeois research" and its share in legitimating the patriarchy, as well as the contemporary bourgeoisie as such, but also noted shortcomings within his own camp: an "extremely coarse tone" toward women and the discourse on sexuality in general within the new left, traditional sexual stereotypes in Marx and Engels, and patriarchal wage and employment policies in the unions.[108] He rejected calls for "equal rights" that continued to orient themselves exclusively by the maxims of the patriarchy—emancipation could only be reached by its "destruction."[109]

The Origin of the "Magnum Opus"

How did Borneman come to appoint himself a leading luminary of the women's movement? The story behind the book's genesis offers a number of clues. The author traced his interest in sexual relations in the ancient world back to a debate with Malinowski at Malinowski's home in London in the summer of 1935, when the professor had objected to the theories of Friedrich Engels. The conversation had piqued Borneman's interest, whose eventual research sought to establish "who was right in this case."[110] Assuming that Borneman did actually debate social anthropology with Malinowski, the conversation did really occur, and the subsequent phases also match Borneman's account[111]—assembling materials from 1935 on, a study of the archaeological reports until 1948, beginning analysis after 1950—his engagement must have been only of a limited intensity, for references to any activity are scarce. Evidence for a first English-language version drafted between 1934 and 1947 and a second between 1950 and 1958 that allegedly circulated "among friends and colleagues" has not yet appeared, either in manuscript form or in Borneman's correspondence.[112] Collections of quotations from books and newspaper excerpts—mostly in German, with isolated fragments in English—do appear after 1954. There is also a more intensive period of engagement with Greek mythology during his collaboration with Orson Welles in 1949, although there were no further projects that dealt with the subject. As such, much in the record indicates that Borneman began to take interest by the late 1940s and to collect material in the 1950s, but did not begin to work on the project in earnest until the second half of the 1960s. Nor would he have had the time to work on the project intensively beforehand; there were other priorities. In 1965, for example, he was still reporting to his father that he was at work on a "history of U.S. negro music."[113] A concrete project about prehistoric forms of life surfaces for the first time in 1966–67; in conjunction with Scherz Verlag, Borneman planned a thirteen-part book and television series called *Die Sitten der Menschheit* (Human Customs). In an exposé written by the head of publishing at Scherz Heinz Klüter, who wanted to hand over the entire project to Borneman, the series looked to "take stock of the various human traditions, customs and cultural forms of expression from prehistory to the present" and to illuminate the "relative nature of human behavior." Taking its cue from methods in ethnology and cultural anthropology, the series would focus on birth, marriage, and death and play out in "prehistory and among primitive peoples," both within the course of world history and in the present day. In the end, "individual observations" were to be compressed into an "outline of 'cultural' history," with "culture understood in the sense of U.S. anthropology as a people's way of life and the social inheritance the individual adopts from his group."[114] The broad tack taken by the exposé not only coincides with Borneman's focus on relations between the sexes; the long line of historical development and emphasis on the "social inheritance" still functioning in the present day are also recognizable in *Das Patriarchat*. Other projects, too, point to an increasing engagement with prehistoric sexual relations; the *Lexikon der Liebe* from 1968 contains a number of references. It can be assumed then that Borneman began work on the project in the second half of the 1960s, albeit initially with limited energy.

The early 1970s show a more intensive focus on prehistoric forms of life; in a letter to Heinz Kamnitzer from summer 1971, Borneman asks for help finding literature on a "history of matriarchy in antiquity" in the antiquarian bookstores of the GDR (German Democratic Republic).[115] By 1972 he had completed more extensive manuscripts about Greek and Roman history that were intended for publication as books—presumably under the auspices of the project with Scherz Verlag—but never came out after plans for the series were canceled for financial reasons.[116] Another book on a different subject had to be completed, he wrote his father in September 1972, "then finally my magnum opus about matriarchy in antiquity."[117] Everything points to the fact that by composing a foreword, moving several chapters forward, and adding a conclusion, Borneman reframed a manuscript he had authored for another purpose about the (patriarchal) customs of the Greeks and Romans, then set it within the context of the incipient women's movement—a cause with which he no doubt strongly sympathized and considered a decisive force in changing society. In this light, one conclusion at which a handful of the book's reviewers arrived based on its disparate structure proved correct: Borneman had taken two highly detailed manuscripts about the love life of classical antiquity that originated in a different context and "somewhat forcibly enlisted them in the service of the feminist cause."[118] This would also explain the book's limiting itself to antiquity, something that is otherwise not necessarily understandable given the long history of patriarchy that followed. When it came time to hand in the work as a dissertation, Borneman again restricted it to his highly praised, empirically based central chapter about Greece and Rome. Years later, this chapter has still been deemed "exceptional" from a feminist perspective.[119]

Borneman's Psychology and the Scientization of the Social

Before that however, Borneman had to defend the work against any suspicion he had merely jumped onto the bandwagon of the feminist movement by professing a lifelong engagement with the subject, based on studies with experts in the field and a tremendous amount of work. Given the origins of *Das Patriarchat* it is more than improbable, as the author claims, that an entire five thousand manuscript pages had been finished by 1973.[120] There is no question that Borneman worked intensively throughout the early 1970s on the manuscript, which was the "most important book that I've written to date," as he wrote to his father a half year before its publication.[121] The teaching position he accepted for the summer semester of 1974 at the University of Salzburg doubtless came as a help. His first lecture course on "social cultural psychology" focused on his study of children's verses, the psychoanalysis of money, and the patriarchy.[122] The course's de facto concentration on the ancient history of patriarchy meant that by 1975, Borneman had hundreds of pages of lecture material prepared on the subject. The give and take of research and teaching brought Borneman a new sense of hope: "My university work has rejuvenated me and helped me through my initial depression about Scharten's loneliness. I'm starting the third semester of my teaching position and although it's a tough routine to drive two hours in the car, speak for four, then drive back for two hours without time to eat or rest, I don't want to miss any of it."[123] After *Das Patriarchat* was published in the fall of 1975, Borneman set his sights on a life goal now within reach through the position at Salzburg: obtaining a doctorate. That spring he had written to his father that his "great wish" to write a dissertation would have to be postponed for financial reasons—he couldn't pursue unpaid work at the moment.[124] When he first received a teaching position at Salzburg, he considered handing in one volume of his work about children's verses to "some favorably minded professor as a doctorate."[125] Then Bremen University entered his field of view, and he fell upon the pragmatic solution of using the more substantial *Das Patriarchat* as a basis once it was finished.

Bremen presented itself as an option because the institution, founded only in 1971, also awarded doctorates for distinguished accomplishment to those who hadn't completed their Abitur.[126] Bremen was considered a leftist university that embodied reform movements in education such as research-based learning, an orientation to praxis, and social responsibility; gave Marxist researchers a chance; and took a more lax approach to academic convention than was traditionally the case with German universities. Subsequent partisan accusations that Borneman had only received his doctorate from Bremen out of "leftist solidarity" were thus unfounded, as the reformist university accepted criteria other than formal education.[127] It was not, as may have appeared from a conservative point of view, an exceptional case of manipulation and nepotism, but rather a structural principle. Without any clear history of contact with the university, in early 1974 Borneman wrote directly to Thomas von der Vring, the founding rector and former SDS (Sozialistischer Deutscher Studentenbund, or

Socialist German Student League) intellectual, describing his work at *Schulkampf* and ensuing exile and asking whether he might "belatedly" obtain his doctorate from Bremen.[128] The psychologist and previous SDS colleague Thomas Leithäuser represented Borneman's doctorate in faculty area eight of the university, suggested reviewers, and otherwise arranged for the undertaking to proceed in an orderly fashion.[129] The dissertation reviewers, like the candidate, did not fully follow academic convention either. They included sociologist Gunnar Heinsohn, who had received his own doctorate shortly before, in 1974, but only became a professor of social pedagogy at the University of Bremen in 1984; and returned Jewish emigrant Ulrich Sonnemann of the Frankfurt School, who first made a name for himself as a freelance author after returning to Germany and worked as a guest professor in Bremen from 1971 to 1974, before becoming a professor of social philosophy at the University of Kassel. Frankfurt sexology professor Volkmar Sigusch, who initially proposed Borneman and stated his willingness to serve as a reviewer, later withdrew; nothing is known about the reasons.[130]

As far as is known, it is during his doctoral defense that Borneman first mentions Malinowski, Childe, and Wright as academic mentors and his work with Wilhelm Reich as a sex counselor. Borneman had good cause to refer to Hornbostel and Herskovits in his musicological work; Róheim was first named in 1972 in the first volume of his *Studien zur Befreiung des Kindes*. Now, however, the task at hand was to furnish proof of academic achievement at the intersection of anthropology, prehistory, and psychology, which accounts for the references Borneman included in the curriculum vitae that he handed in to Bremen. As he explained:

> I had to leave Germany only a few months before my Abitur and my English was not yet good enough to take English qualification exams (matriculation). As such I was unable to pursue a university course in any normal sense of the word "study" (collect certificates), and therefore to receive my doctorate or qualify as a lecturer despite thirteen semesters at English and U.S. universities. On the other hand, I have learned things thanks to personal friendships with Malinowski, Childe, Herskovits and Róheim that I could scarcely have expected from "post-graduate studies," in the U.S. sense of the term.[131]

Borneman's resume was trimmed in other ways, too, to cut an academic figure: the period of his ethnological study of Eskimos under Grierson was lengthened to three years, his time at UNESCO was attributed to developing a section of "academic film," and his film and television work of the 1950s purported an emphasis "in the branches of ethnological, sociological and psychoanalytic" film.

In the 1980s, at a time when his academic pedigree was repeatedly called into question, Borneman explained that "the trunk with all our documents had gone missing" in the move from Frankfurt to Scharten. "With it were my birth certificate and all my university papers from England, Canada and the U.S. I received my birth certificate following a four year wait after applying to the German authorities, the university papers are nowhere to be found."[132]

The candidate wanted only a 370-page excerpt from the middle of his book to be considered for his dissertation, the section that empirically reconstructed relations in Greece and the Roman Empire. "I wanted," he explained, "to leave the pamphleteering of the fore- and afterword, the heuristic constructions of the pre-historical section, speculations about the future and my polemical remarks on the bourgeois women's movement outside academic discussion, as they had been written at the wish of the publisher and were not a part of my original work."[133] In his "theses" for his dissertation defense, which took place on 4 May 1976 as part of a public colloquium, Borneman responded positively to his reviewers, who raised a number of the same issues that had surfaced in public debate surrounding the book—in particular the formulations in his final chapter. Otherwise, his theses concentrated on the connection between productive forces and relations between the sexes, which the candidate wanted to discuss in concrete settings.

Before Borneman received his academic credentials, Igor Alexander Caruso had invited him to teach at the Psychological Institute at the University of Salzburg for the summer semester of 1974. Caruso himself was appointed professor of clinical psychology and social psychology at the University of Salzburg in 1972 after a somewhat problematic and winding academic path—he had recently been shown to have participated in the Nazi euthanasia program at a children's clinic in Vienna. Over the course of the 1960s he turned from a form of existentialism inspired by Christianity toward Herbert Marcuse, teaching psychoanalysis "as a socially critical and politically engaged science."[134] Aside from sharing political sympathies, there were biographical parallels: Caruso held a doctorate but in the subject of pedagogy; he hadn't qualified as a university lecturer, nor could he furnish any evidence of training in psychoanalysis. Borneman, too, looked back on an unorthodox career and had published his first books on sexual anthropology without a dissertation—and received the lectureship. Caruso was taken with his new hire and reviewed a number of his books positively.[135]

Borneman's first books on the subject of sex already referenced Géza Róheim, the leftist Freudian and founder of ethno-psychoanalysis, whose work Borneman had read in the 1940s and whose "student" he claimed to be.[136] Only later, however, does a reference to training analysis appear, which he claims to have completed with Róheim over three years somewhere between 1942 and 1947 or possibly in the early 1950s—statements vary.[137] The claims aren't supported by other sources (and are also difficult to verify, as Róheim's personal documents haven't been preserved). How likely is it, as Borneman asserts, that he flew from Ottawa to New York every weekend for years to undergo the process? One wonders all the more as there is no mention of Róheim in what is otherwise a quite well preserved letter correspondence from the war and early postwar years. In this case too, it is more likely that Borneman may have known the analyst, but the relationship was not nearly as close as he maintains.

Be that as it may, at the Salzburg Psychological Institute Borneman's unconventional academic profile, the institute's reputation for a proximity to contemporary issues, and a teaching staff with a reputation for charisma drew a following among leftist students who were enthusiastic about the field of psychology. Early students recall Borneman's appearances in Salzburg with euphoria. Josef Christian Aigner, co-editor of the second commemorative volume for Borneman and today a professor of psychosocial work and psychoanalytic pedagogy at the University of Innsbruck, is of the opinion that even for German students, in the early 1970s the school ranked among "the most interesting for a psychology major," as the classes "offered in the field of psychoanalysis and sexology" became "a meeting point for critically engaged intelligentsia," while Borneman's "intrepid, lively intellect as a teacher and researcher" had been "enormously important for a number of us and for the climate at the university."[138] As contemporary author and psychologist Ingram Hartinger recalls, it was not always classical psychological issues that were discussed; lectures that were given titles like "Libido Theory" as "a disguise" were then witness to discussions about every conceivable topic in the broad field between sexuality and social critique. "Students came by the droves to the epochal 'Patriarchy' lecture, because he was always fascinating and captivating."[139] Psychologist Gerhild Trübswasser encapsulates what was evidently a widespread opinion when she writes, "For me and presumably for an entire generation of students he was . . . an extremely important teacher."[140] Aigner concedes that many of Borneman's theories "seem overdone and unreasonable, and not only to me," but these had "always been the most thought-provoking elements in his teaching . . . as he always tried to spur on public debate about sexuality with such provocative, daring statements."[141] A number of Borneman's former students went on to become noted therapists or, like Aigner, were among "the very few in our country who teach and research sexuality in earnest."[142] Borneman's contract was not extended following Caruso's death in 1981, after he accused other professors in an obituary of driving their "charismatic colleague" to his demise.[143] In a newspaper article, the well-known physician Hans Czermak quoted Caruso as saying, "The only thing that will remain of the Psychological Institute at the University of Salzburg is the fact that Borneman once taught there." For Czermak, "that is why the institute was so persistent in trying to rid itself of Borneman."[144] One of his students spoke in less personal terms in this connection about an "elimination of psychoanalysis" and a "purge"; Borneman himself considered it symptomatic, summarizing the dismissive attitude toward psychoanalysis in its native land as follows: "The only professorship that has ever existed for psychoanalysis is . . . empty and certain not to be held again by a psychoanalyst."[145] In 1977 Borneman was bestowed the title of professor by the Social Democratic Austrian Ministry of Science and received, by his own account, an exceptional offer from Salzburg of a professorship in psychology. This did not come to pass after the finance minister objected to Borneman's age—he would soon qualify for retirement. Still, science minister Hertha Firnberg awarded Borneman an "honorary salary" of 5,000 schillings monthly.[146] Between 1979 and 1985 he also taught at other universities in Klagenfurt, Bremen, Marburg, and Innsbruck, though his dream of a full professorship went unrealized.[147]

As a psychologist and sexologist, Ernest Borneman was directly involved in the "scientization of the social" (Lutz Raphael), a process that from the 1960s onward saw a dramatic rise in the number of experts specializing in every realm of social life and was characterized by an increased demand among West Germans for guidance in their individual lives. The radical changes society had undergone since the 1950s—the rise of mass consumerism, generational upheaval, challenges to traditional gender roles, greater sexual freedom, and later fears of environmental pollution and the arms race—provoked uncertainties that one sought to address through interpretation and advice. In this context, psychoanalysis, which experienced a renaissance beginning in the late 1960s, had a number of terms and theories at the ready to set social development in relation to individuals' psychological and physical constitution, discussing, for example, the connection between "sexuality and class struggle" (Reimut Reiche). The rise of the Frankfurt School, which took a psychoanalytic approach to combating authoritarian tendencies by a "turn to the subject" (Theodor W. Adorno); psychoanalysts Alexander and Margarethe Mitscherlich's account of Germans' insufficient reckoning with the National Socialist past in terms of a narcissistic "inability to mourn"; a glorification of sexual liberalism in the name of "sexual revolution" in line with Wilhelm Reich; early experiments in communes with individuals' "inner revolution" as a precondition for the "outer revolution"—each of these serve as an example of the "historical formation of the 'counseled self'" in the late 1960s.[148] Against academic psychology and prevailing psychiatric methods, the viewpoint caught on that it was not the patient who was sick, but the society that declared him to be so.[149] Counseling not only took the form of psychotherapy but was offered by a wide variety of institutions and actors, including communes, churches, private services, and the media. From marriage to drug counseling, these channels provided assistance with handling what was perceived to be the increasingly overwhelming nature of everyday life and supported citizens in the lengthy "process of self-transformation," as Fritjof Capra, one of the most important spokesmen of the esoteric "New Age" movement, described individuals' self-optimization.[150] Psychology became a fashionable course of study in the 1970s, especially among leftist students, while the rise of magazines like *Psychologie heute* (1974) and *Warum! Zeitschrift für Psychologie und Lebenstechnik* (1975) spoke to a broader demand within society for guidance in handling psychological problems. A sufficient number of experts, needs, institutions, and media channels thus all converged, ensuring psychology's place in society as a technique for coping in a seemingly ever more complex world.

In 1969 Borneman singled out one part of the media landscape for praise, Darmstadt's März Verlag. That year the publisher had reissued works with a grounding in psychology by leftist educational theorists from the Weimar Republic, including Siegfried Bernfeld, Edwin Hoernle, and Otto Rühle, financed in part by pornography from the Olympia Press Verlag, as he also noted approvingly.[151] In a long review of Marxist and Freudian literature written in 1971 for the *Times Literary Supplement*, Borneman discussed the renaissance of Wilhelm Reich, Herbert Marcuse, Erich Fromm, and a handful of new arrivals on the German book market.[152]

While Borneman was a ferocious critic of the trend, he also played his part in the decade's "psychoboom."[153] He wrote for numerous popular scientific and leftist periodicals such as *Psychologie heute* and *Warum!*, but throughout the 1970s and 1980s he worked primarily as a columnist, sex guide, and talk show guest on nationally broadcast programs. As the book title *Psychoboom* (1976) makes clear, Borneman took part at the time in what was already a growing critique of therapy culture that took aim at an alleged "discouragement by experts" (Ivan Illich). Borneman's critique did not limit itself to the self-proclaimed "soul tinkerers" and body therapists promising people psychological stability, but took a more basic approach. The explosive growth of a "new professional class of urban shamans" built of physicians, quacks, "group therapy charlatans," natural healers, and religious sects, Borneman argued, "proved the existence of a need for solace and assistance within an entire generation of mentally unsound industrial dwellers."[154] When psychological ailments appear to such an extent, however, they are no longer the exception, but the rule. "Their symptoms can no longer be diagnosed as signs of deviation from social norms within an individual's psychology, but must be judged as the actual norm of society." Borneman recognized the compulsion to manage oneself that arose in the name of freedom, but he did not view the popular "psychoboom" as an attempt by citizens to gain a firmer grip on this freedom—rather, it was a form of repression with psychic consequences. With education seeking to "convey to the citizen the illusion that he is the master of his own fate, there emerges an entirely new field of tension between reality and the psyche. The recognition that the world isn't the way we have been taught it is at school or our family home is repressed only with difficulty, and in such a way that we find ourselves confronted with entirely new, neurosis-like symptoms. These 'neuroses' are no longer treatable because they do not find their origin in an individual psyche." Nor for that matter could they be addressed using the known methods of psychotherapy. The layperson believed "he could help others in 'self-awareness groups,' through 'sensitivity training' or in 'encounter groups' with 'transactional games' or touching rituals, breathing exercises or meditation." Professional psychiatrists, psychoanalysts, or neurologists must recognize that "their profession is outdated, and that the one form of assistance they can offer to those suffering psychologically in Western industrial society is changing society." Only by participating in this process could people "regain the pride and security that bourgeois society has deprived them of."

The world hadn't changed as expected however, and in the 1970s the leftist scene increasingly distanced itself from the idea of revolution to focus instead on "the subject," or the individual and his concrete social environment. Within the alternative scene a different life was tested out in the here and now. For the most part political goals were not wholly abandoned, but were either set among the "therapeutic self-liberation utopias" already proposed by the early communes or turned into a "psychotherapeutic do-it-yourself subculture," as the historian Maik Tändler terms it, "in which acting out psychological problems was interpreted as expressing resistance and critical consciousness."[155] Coming amid an effort to gain a reflective experience of the self that was still loaded with political aspirations, Borneman's radical solution seemed too remote for many. As one reader dryly noted in response to his statement that these types of neuroses were incurable, "I confess, that is not enough for me. If I have a disease, then I want to deal with it."[156]

While Borneman continued steadfastly to assert the rhetoric of liberation as inherited from Reich, supported theoretically by Herbert Marcuse and others, and practically implemented in "1968," in the 1970s there emerged a new hero within the firmament of leftist theory who, still unnoticed by many of his contemporaries, conceived of the alleged emancipation of the individual as a new form of domination. According to Michel Foucault's theory of "governmentality," psychology and sexual practices should be seen as "technologies of the self."[157] They were mobilized in the name of self-determination, but de facto represented a modernized form of domination, an "individualizing and totalizing form of power" that claimed all the more legitimacy for not being imposed from above, but defined by individuals themselves. In the 1970s the mechanism of integration via personal responsibility, now common in our neoliberal present, was still difficult to see through because the "technologies of the self" were understood as technologies for liberating the individual from state guidelines and the power of tradition. Only in hindsight did the situation become somewhat clearer: "a constitutive element of the political emerges from a political countermovement," as sociologist Sabine Maasen writes regarding the function of therapy and counseling.[158] "At the end of the sixties," Maasen continues, "the message was still: you're sick because society is sick, so you must change society; by the early seventies the message had reversed itself: society is sick, so you must change yourself."[159]

Public Debate Surrounding *Das Patriarchat*

On the one hand, *Das Patriarchat* arrived at an opportune moment, as Borneman's Marxist approach could hope for a certain receptivity within the West German public that would have been unthinkable before, as again shortly after. Then there was the fact that Borneman did not advocate an economically derived Marxism but assumed a dialectical relationship between the structure and superstructure, feeding expectations that the book would be welcomed by Western Marxists. On the other hand came the increasing distance that the new women's movement held to its historical materialist foundations, making Borneman's Marxism seem orthodox, and thus dated by comparison. Moreover, the sexual dichotomy within feminism had developed to such an extent—and was given additional forward momentum by the idealization of the female—that Borneman's grand gesture to the movement he set out to serve was regarded as a sort of presumption. Whether the women's movement needed a *Capital* of its own was anything but certain; it was impossible, however, that its author be a man.

Borneman's book was discussed in every major publication in the Federal Republic, Austria, and Switzerland, as well as in numerous smaller newspapers and magazines. Lengthy, uncritical reports in popular magazines that regularly discussed sex such as *Stern*, *Petra*, and *Spontan* stood opposite the condescending discussions carried out by the "high culture" of the "quality press," which generally held distractions such as sexuality at arm's length and regarded blatant partisanship as unscientific—at least when it was Marxist and committed to the women's movement.[160] The *Neue Zürcher Zeitung* thus spoke of "grandiloquence," the *Deutsche Zeitung* of a "radically reactionary book," and predictably, the *Bayernkurier* called it "unrestrained."[161] In a double review of Schwarzer and Borneman's books for the *Süddeutsche Zeitung*, Richard Kaufmann imperiously dismissed both the "'frustrated lesbian,'" who had spotted "a couple of very grave problems of the infantile neurotic woman," and the admittedly "tireless industry" of Borneman, who had combined "a sort of dream about the prehistory of mankind" with a "collection of dirty jokes from the ancient world," making for a "superfluous" book.[162] In *Die Welt*, Arnold Gehlen dispensed altogether with argumentation, upbraiding the text with statements like "That galls" or "Nothing occurs to me in this case."[163] Ivo Frenzel faulted Borneman for the "all-consuming thoroughness that informs us of sexual techniques from classical antiquity, anal eroticism and pederasty, prostitution and infidelity" as well as "the impression . . . the author is actually ashamed of and must excuse himself for coming into the world as a male being."[164]

A few reviews in less conspicuous places discussed the book exclusively in positive terms.[165] Without reserving their critique, an entire host of voices was well disposed to the project, however. For Hans Krieger of *Die Zeit*, there was "a tremendous amount to learn" from the book, though he considered Borneman's ambitions of being "a Marx of the women's movement" exaggerated.[166] Wolf Lepenies's review in the *Frankfurter Allgemeine Zeitung* proceeded respectfully with Borneman's "polemical work," observing a contradiction between the "hypothetical character" of the treatment and the seeming authority of the material's presentation, and generally criticizing a certain "show to impress."[167] Arno Plack welcomed the "ethical postulate" of the matriarchy in his review for *Der Spiegel*, even if it were under dispute as a model of development, and also found the book corrected idealized notions about Greek and Roman society. At the same time, he held Borneman's turn to socialism as a solution to be overly simple.[168] On SFB, Udo Reiter praised the large amount of unfamiliar and little-known material, as well as its organization into theses that "are truly original and worthy of consideration," but saw this "ruined . . . by an ill-tempered form of dogmatism that blends Marxist doctrine with feminist fanaticism to create a strange, inconsistent message."[169]

The left showed a critical interest. Günter Herburger reviewed "Borneman's historical digging" positively in *Konkret*, calling for the work's continuation into the present. Walter Hollitscher considered the "case against male domination" to be the "most significant contribution" to the UN's "Year of the Woman." While critical of some details, Gunnar Heinsohn praised *Das Patriarchat* in *Päd.extra* as an "out-and-out exceptional book" addressing the current question of sexual emancipation.[170] In the magazine *Psyche*, ethnologist and author Hans-Jürgen Heinrichs saw Borneman as showing the way for a new debate in the humanities.[171] And social psychologist Klaus Ottomeyer gave an in-depth, comprehensive review of Borneman's book from a Marxist perspective in *Das Argument*, valuing it as an important contribution to the debate on the left and the possibilities of interpersonal emancipation, but criticizing, among other things, the "naïve belief in technical progress" and humans' unlimited ability to adapt.[172]

Reader response to Borneman's book contained the usual cultural reservations; one reader from Upper Bavaria considered discussion of women's oppression to be "an invention of excessively spoiled . . . women egotists while Borneman, a good natured fool, seems to believe every word in his naïveté."[173] Hans Paeschke, the editor of *Merkur*, couched his anti-feminist stance in more delicate language, judging the book as an index of the irrational spheres among which the discussion of sexuality meandered, a failed attempt to make the women's movement more palatable: it is "a truly remarkable case, insofar as a male disposition, using every conceivable gesture of adolescent boyishness, looks to set down a complete statement of the present madness of emancipation literature in letters of fire and brimstone. The disgrace comes in equal measure. In short, the book would be treated most productively as a symptom."[174]

The considerable number of skeptical responses may not have been entirely free from a desire to brush aside a perceived upstart who was focused on a socially unacceptable subject, lacked any academic credentials, and—what is more—appeared in the publisher's advertising in proper anti-academic fashion, in "work clothes made of drillich fabric and a bib" as "they are known from various laborers," Reiter commented in the SFB. Caroline Neubaur meanwhile confronted such dismissive stances on West German Radio (Westdeutscher Rundfunk), wondering "why this man succeeded in causing such a stir in the academic camp" and finding the reason in a common "aversion" among academic reviewers to the "dilettante."[175] Neubaur could not "shake the fatal feeling that in this case—to women's detriment—a scapegoat was yet again being sent to the slaughter as an example."

There was certainly some truth to this, but reaction to *Das Patriarchat* cannot be treated at this level alone. Summarizing the most important arguments against the book beyond any combative or denigrating opinion pieces, four central points of criticism emerge. First, Borneman was faulted for the speculative character of his account. And it is true that Borneman's sources allowed no conclusions to be drawn about people's prehistoric or early intellectual and emotional life, so that the argument in the *Das Patriarchat* should have been considerably more measured than was the case. In this connection, Borneman was also accused of declaring the overall form of his argumentation to be a "working hypothesis," but then presenting an image of firmly established facts in an unequivocal interpretation of the material, a "final theory" (Krieger) that he represented with "missionary zeal" (Reiter). Third, the book contained a concealed biologism. While Borneman repeatedly emphasized economic and social conditions, his arguments took a biologistic turn in his comparisons with the animal and vegetal world and in his concluding chapter, which assumed the elimination of women's purported biological disadvantages to be a decisive precondition for bringing about equality between the sexes. Finally, the work was associated with an overly dichotomous image of the matriarchy and patriarchy, as well as a "unilinear line of development" (Ottomeyer). In reality, matriarchal and patriarchal societies had existed simultaneously at various times and could not be associated unilaterally with positive or negative characteristics. Borneman's thesis of women's natural superiority represented a "new mythos" (Lohmann). Such objections were valid arguments that could not be dismissed out of hand and were largely advanced by authors who were fundamentally well disposed toward Borneman.

Instead of silently accepting what he felt to be unfair treatment in the critique of his book, Borneman often went on the offensive, a strategy that only strengthened the impact of the critique. He wrote letters to the editor, convinced editorial boards to give him space to reply, defended himself against accusations in a long piece for the magazine of the Humanist Union, and issued another thorough account of his views in his 1977 autobiography, as well as in the afterword to the paperback edition of *Das Patriarchat* in 1979.[176] While Borneman defended his arguments, he also tried to neutralize the faults found with the book, explaining that the most heavily criticized parts merely constituted "a summary of the most important thoughts" that he had "heard discussed and noted down" in discussions between feminist and Socialist women's groups, and therefore he was "actually only responsible as a reporter, not the author."[177] This was no doubt true at a factual level—such positions were clearly in evidence in feminist literature—but he could by no means extract himself from the affair so easily; as the author, he was responsible for his account. Clearly worn down by the criticism, he silently withdrew individual positions, including his theory of the need to dispense with the "three biological disadvantages" of the women, which no longer appears in the paperback edition from 1979.[178] That same year, he relativized the nature of the very book he had submitted as his dissertation, designating it "popular science and academic journalism."[179]

Interest abroad was much more limited than hoped for. The book appeared in French translation in 1979, but that is where it remained. An English translation, which would have seemed obvious due to the feminist debate's origins in the United States, failed for doubts regarding both content and form. A well-known New York literary agent, Joan Daves (in a former life Liselotte Davidson, a Jewish emigrant from Berlin), criticized the effusive wealth of detail—"exhaustive (and exhausting)"—and felt an overall line of argumentation was lacking; at the very least the Jewish-Christian tradition would have to be included. Borneman's combination of psychoanalysis and social radicalism, Daves continued, was classic Wilhelm Reich and thus lacked in originality. Daves recognized the book's topicality but wondered at the fact "that a house like S. Fischer would bring out a book like this in its present form (are their editors asleep?)" and advised against it.[180]

Reception in the Women's Movement

The categorical rejection of *Das Patriarchat* that came from within the women's movement wounded Borneman more deeply than any routine cultural conservative critique. More so than in other countries, the women's movement in West Germany had coalesced outside of existing institutions and looked to establish equal rights through self-awareness, self-organization, and fighting the "patriarchy." Taking a number of cues from many initiatives of the earlier bourgeois women's movement, the contemporary struggle was "staged" within the student movement to great public effect.[181] It was in this same context that the movement's "autonomous" self-conception emerged, likewise its distance from men and the state. The political turmoil of the early 1970s gave way to form a feminist counterculture—the substrate of the "cultural feminism" under discussion by that point.[182] If the movement's social structure was relatively homogenous—most of the activists were under thirty years old and received higher education—even a passing glance at the different arguments and forms of action present within the "women's movement" makes its extreme diversity readily apparent, such that the term can only sensibly be referred to in the plural. Female union laborers and leftist feminists linked the struggle for equal rights between the sexes to social aspirations—and it was to them that Borneman appealed in particular.

It is not, therefore, possible to discuss a controversy with the women's movement as such, as there were no collective positions articulated by "the" movement. Opinion on Borneman's book varied, with many an activist considering him an ally. While the book's appraisal by a nonprofessional female readership is naturally difficult to gauge, letters to the editor and other public utterances reveal a response that was not only negative. One female reader of the *Frankfurter Rundschau* welcomed Borneman's "intellectual 'field kit,'" while later Viennese journalist Barbara Freitag described an impactful experience reading the book on the Côte d'Azur; for her the book was a "milestone."[183] Roland M. Schernikau, too—not a woman, but one of the "new men" on the left—counted *Das Patriarchat* among the "couple of texts that made me think differently than before."[184] The longer that public discussion of the book within the new women's movement carried on, the more negative the tone grew, leading in the end, it is safe to assume, to widespread resistance. This resistance was not only connected with the factual record, but also, significantly, with the ways in which Borneman responded to criticism. At the same time, the book addressed a highly charged field, as it had grown increasingly clear by the time of its appearance that the bright hopes for a liberated sexuality would not be so easily fulfilled for everyone, leaving some frustrated and strengthening a negative stereotypes of "the man" or "feminism." Opinion remained divided in the immediate wake of the book's appearance; its exposure of patriarchy as a form of male domination and the utopian counterexample of a nonauthoritarian, female-driven order were generally well received. At one meeting Antje Kunstmann, then student editor of *Materialien zur Frauenemanzipation* (Materials for Women's Emancipation), was taken not only with the wealth of information in *Das Patriarchat*, but also by the provocative interpretation. Borneman "does away . . . thoroughly with women's naturally imposed inferiority. The thesis of human sexual behavior developing away from genital primacy and toward a sort of 'polymorphous tenderness' spread across the whole body is certain to find resonance with feminists and others who are dissatisfied with the customary forms of sexuality." Kunstmann criticized Borneman's idea of liberation from sexuality per se but had little doubt about *Das Patriarchat* as a tool in the women's struggle and wished it a wide readership.[185]

The work spoke in a similar capacity to 28-year-old journalist and author Ursula Krechel. In a largely respectful discussion of the book for the *Frankfurter Rundschau* shortly before her own book was set for publication, Krechel criticized Borneman's notion of changing motherhood from a biological to a social trait. Whereas men had "only ever" encountered motherhood as "something given," for women it had principally been a normative duty that "restricted their existence . . . in the name of motherhood."[186] A double review of Krechel and Borneman's books on Radio Bremen in spring 1976 gave cause to believe that Borneman's account of sexuality was received with greater skepticism, both within the women's movement itself and the public sympathetic to it, and that the academic angle he represented with such aplomb had now given way to a subjective approach. Krechel's book was not, as author Vera Gaserow and coauthor Rüdiger Krohn maintained, a "euphoric polemic," but rather "a fastidious and candid view of the conversation within individual women's groups. By contrast, *Das Patriarchat* impressed with its "wealth of knowledge" but disappointed as a "men's magazine dressed up as history" and in its call to liberate women from "*their* sexuality." "One can only hope that the women's movement does not take its cues from Borneman's ideas," wrote Gaserow and Krohn—a wish that would not go in vain.[187]

Erika Wisselinck, the editor of the evangelical news service *Korrespondenz der Frau*, a seemingly humble periodical that reported on feminist action and thought before *Emma* or *Courage* had been founded, summarized the cool response within the women's movement to *Das Patriarchat*:

> They noted his theories regarding a peaceful matristic—by which he means a woman-centered—primitive culture with some satisfaction . . . yet on the other hand Borneman considers women to be at a "biological disadvantage." He wants to do away with their female functions and organs by means of biochemical technologies, so that motherhood no longer exhibits biologically, but as a "social force." Setting aside entirely the abstruse nature of such a line of thought, women reject it as a profoundly

patriarchal point of view: once again it is women who are to change, to make themselves conform to male notions (this time Borneman's). With it, Borneman has disqualified himself as one of patriarchy's detractors.[188]

One controversy that proved longstanding—and first established Borneman's negative reputation in the women's movement—came shortly after the book's release, with Marielouise Jurreit's review in *Vorwärts*. For Borneman, it was crucial for the text to appear specifically in the mouthpiece of German social democracy, to whose left wing he felt bound in solidarity and which he constantly had in mind when he referred to the "Socialist" or "proletariat" women's movement. The context of Jurreit's review undermined Borneman's self-assigned role as a spokesman of the Marxist left for the women's movement. A journalist and activist within the movement herself born in 1941, Jurreit was particularly well qualified for the review as the soon-to-be author of *Sexism: The Male Monopoly on History and Thought*, a book published in 1976 by Carl Hanser Verlag that would become a standard work within the milieu. Like other reviewers, she faulted *Das Patriarchat*—with its patchy references and inadequate bibliography—for its lack of rigor, insistence on a theory of evolution that contradicted the research, vulgar use of Marxism, and speculative approach. Jurreit praised the empirical chapter, as others had, but concluded her review with the verdict: "From an academic perspective however, the book is a nuisance. This means further that it cannot do justice to its political claim of serving the women's movement."[189]

Six weeks later this review, which was comparable to others in any other regard, was met by a rejoinder from Borneman that exceeded in scope alone the source of his ire. Dispensing with any conciliatory gesture, as he had in his response to Gehlen's critique for example, he issued a parochial rebuke to the young woman, not only bringing the full weight of his biography and years of study to bear against Jurreit, but also weaponizing a strict adherence to Socialist principle. It simply wasn't acceptable that Jurreit, "in *Vorwärts* of all places," accused him of vulgar Marxism, "thereby using me as a pretext to attack the mothers and fathers of the party." A grim memory of another party's techniques for excluding its enemies may well have lain at the root of Borneman's self-centered statement; his adversary wanted to use him "as target practice in order to gun down the party's founders." The sixty-year-old Borneman questioned Jurreit's qualifications and saw in her "perverse reactions" a "strategic error in the struggle for women's liberation." For her part, the accused responded dryly in the same issue of *Vorwärts*, asking, "Does Borneman not actually see how 'I-centered' the type of self-promotion that constantly invokes the ghost of Karl Marx is, and how much damage he thereby does to himself?"

The dispute with Marielouise Jurreit culminated in the fall of 1976 with the publication of Jurreit's book, which exceeded even Borneman's in scope and resulted in establishing difference feminism. Importing the term "sexism" from the United States, the book defined it in analogy to racism as approving of women's inferior place in society, and thus of their "exploitation, mutilation, destruction, domination and persecution" on the basis of their sex.[190] In thirty-six extended explorations of the most varied social and academic fields, Jurreit describes, for example, the systematic exclusion of women in male-dominated historiography, reconstructs the patriarchal attitudes that Socialist forefathers Marx and Engels took toward their wives, criticizes biologism and psychoanalysis as techniques for denigrating and "disempowering" women, and advocates against working from within institutions, contrary to what Rudi Dutschke had advised the student movement.[191] Jurreit's work engages intensively with the "Marxist lines of thought" that had played such an important role in US and European feminism, as with de Beauvoir and Firestone for example,[192] and whose persistent influence in West Germany Jurreit believed should be limited. There was no harmonic primitive society ruled by a peaceable matriarchy. "In all societies," Jurreit summarized, "we find the sexes standing opposed to each other, as with two political parties."[193] Because the male party had always held power, ran the conclusion, "only in settings where women possess their own structures of solidarity . . . does one observe them demarcating room for maneuver within the economic and sexual spheres." When applied to the current situation, this meant female self-consciousness could not develop in parties and associations created entirely in men's image; it was only extra-parliamentary struggle, in the shape of autonomous struggle and a "permanent institution of human society,"[194] that could exert political pressure in the defense and consolidation of female identity. Jurreit likewise considered the utopian vision of a harmonious future between men and women that many feminists shared to be mistaken. Such "extreme wishes for abolition" were bound to lead astray in the first place because male aggression was in part biologically determined.[195] Sexual characteristics, potential technological developments notwithstanding, were an "irrevocable biological trademark of humanity." "A human being who does not consider oneself or others in terms of male and female is unthinkable,"[196] Jurreit argues, in a thesis that seems outdated from today's perspective but at the time served to draw the line to men as sharply as possible.

Silence would likely have been the better option in this case as well, not least because the previous year's dispute had undoubtedly left Borneman in an awkward position. He did not hold back however, but lambasted Jurreit's book in the style and often the language of a grand campaign, availing himself of various media channels. The two squared off early in 1977 in *Konkret*, without spending much time discussing the content of the book, Borneman reproached Jurreit for abandoning her collaboration with Socialist parties and unions and instead setting her hopes on feminism as an independent force, without offering any strategy for combating the patriarchy. Drawing encouragement perhaps from the moment it was experiencing on the international stage, Borneman instead recommended the popular front (*Volksfront*), this time even including the Socialist camp as an ally: "Changing a militant patriarchy can only be managed with militant means. It is the unions who possess such means, the Socialist and Communist parties, people's republics and Socialist states. No matter how bad the situation may also be for women in Socialist states it is only there, and only with the assistance of Socialist and Communist parties, that we can overcome and strike down the bourgeois patriarchy."[197] Jurreit's rejection of an alliance with these forces despite her "high intelligence," Borneman wrote, once again in the role of the leftist patriarch, must have its reasons beyond that of "rational logic." Pique, defeatism, bitterness—such is the tone that characterizes the concluding passage of Borneman's critique. Borneman went further in other texts, reaching at times for questionable historical analogies: "the sexually segregated women's centers and forums" were only the "inverse image of a pre-Hitlerian old boys' club"; authors such as a Susan Sontag, Alice Schwarzer, or Marielouise Jurreit had only changed the "sexual prefixes" when compared to authors from the turn of the century, etc.[198]

Jurreit's reply described a "defamation campaign" against her book, a "personal and premeditated retaliatory effort" and "calumny."[199] Other female authors responded to Borneman's critique in similar terms, calling the media outlets that had placed their pages and microphones at his disposal to task. "There is a madman running about the editorial offices of the West German media," went Barbara Schleich's image in *Vorgänge*.[200] Writing for the leftist feminist periodical *Courage* in the language of the times and her milieu, one writer criticized the fact that Borneman had "transformed his grief into hitting below the belt," going on to note that "the women's movement can do without such West German comrades with confidence."[201] Journalist Friederike Münch saw a "monopoly on debate" and a "defamation" not only of the author herself, but the entire women's movement, coining the slogan "A recommendation to everyone: read Jurreit, not Borneman!"[202]

Borneman could not let the matter be, truly taking aim below the belt this time by attesting that the author was actually suffering from a "private psychological problem," her sexuality.[203] Jurreit replied soon after in the *Deutsche Zeitung*, criticizing an essay Borneman had written for the same periodical and repeating her objection to the "liquidation of female biology" that Borneman proposed as "in and of itself positively discriminatory against women." In her summary of the Borneman-Jurreit dispute for Hessen state radio, Erika Wisselinck censured the media outlets that considered Ernest Borneman to be an expert on the women's movement, as well as the fact that "his sorties against Ms. Jurreit's book are reprinted with a unique show of unanimity by press outlets of every affiliation."[204] This reflected the imaginary boundaries drawn between, on the one hand, a media landscape that was correctly perceived as dominated by men and that imagined one of its own to be a pioneer of the women's movement and, on the other hand, the movement itself, which fell victim to this patriarchal alliance. Certainly, Borneman's widespread media presence was problematic for the reception of Jurreit's book; however, there was of course no way that he could fully control opinion in a media landscape as differentiated as that of West Germany—as his clash with Jurreit over his own book had shown all too clearly.

Jurreit's work received high praise from numerous reviewers and was translated into Swedish and English—at the time of its final printing in 1987 as a paperback for Fischer Verlag, it had reached an impressive count of twenty-seven to twenty-nine thousand copies, even if this was significantly less than what Borneman's bestseller sold. The book further revealed a potential value for strategic political arguments, with the Social Democrat intellectual Peter Glotz designating it a "great success" and a "point of departure for women's continued self-organization in our society."[205] Glotz's position differed from Borneman's in the fact that the former directed his calls for greater openness not to the women's movement, but to politics. The fact alone that the state secretary for the Ministry of Education would utter such a statement while rising to the post of scientific senator for West Berlin indicates that there was plenty of leeway for such a position. If Glotz was not much less patriarchal in his thinking, he spoke from the outside however, while Borneman saw himself as part of the movement and stood under stricter observation for this reason alone.

As the female readership's reaction in *Vorwärts* had already shown, the altercation confirmed for many what Borneman had been accused of multiple times before: holding a patriarchal attitude toward the women's movement, in this case toward Jurreit.[206] There was no doubt that the behavior of the accused fed this perception, a particularly delicate affair in West Germany given the origins of leftist feminism in debates within the SDS that had focused in no small part on the machismo of the movement's leaders. Borneman's disappointment at the lack of support, even hostility, that greeted him from this camp was certainly genuine, and one can easily imagine the first months following publication of his book, as he admitted, counting "among the most painful of [his] life."[207] Borneman surely wanted to be on the side of progress and to support the women's movement, which seemed to him the most important contemporary force for social change. Such motives were naïve, however, to the extent that he was not sufficiently informed about the inner composition of the movement, its various currents or intellectual constitution, and moreover exempted both himself and his positions from the movement's critical reflections about the structural phenomenon of patriarchy. Borneman learned from the dispute, publicly declaring that he had "recognized mistakes" and been forced to examine himself "in light of feminists' emotionally aggressive criticism." This provided the backdrop for his autobiographical book *Die Ur-Szene* (The Primal Scene), which was published in 1977.[208] In a way, the book represented a swing of the pendulum when compared to *Das Patriarchat*—radically subjective instead of scientific, yet all the more egocentric for it.

A Wishful Autobiography: Borneman's *Die Ur-Szene*

Die Ur-Szene ended up as self-congratulatory as it did because the attacks against Borneman's "magnum opus" had placed him under pressure to justify himself, prompting him to set his past as a widely traveled Socialist and hardworking autodidact on the scales and describe it in detail. In doing so, Borneman sought to undergird the strength of his positions by drawing the closest possible personal connections to academic figures and other authorities.

Borneman had begun work on an autobiography while still in Ottawa in 1942—*A Cage for the Strange Birds*—at the tender age of twenty-seven. It was to no avail, however; as he lamented, "It's dull and dead."[209] He picked the project back up at a high point in his life, when he had found a viable approach with the potential to lift it beyond the boundaries of an *ego histoire*. At Borneman's encouragement from Austria, his father researched the family history, then wrote down and sent it to his son in 1975. Childhood and youth experiences played a prominent role in the father-son letter exchange from these years. Late in 1970 Borneman announced to his father his plan to write an autobiography "not as in my own story (which would be too vain) but rather as a mirror to the times."[210] He declared the book a "self-analysis," modeling its structure on the Freudian concept of the "primal scene" (*Urszene*). He describes a defining experience from early childhood at the beginning of each of his eleven chapters, then proceeds to describe either the preference arising from it or the path he took to overcome it later in life. The sight of his parents engaged in sexual intercourse, for example, becomes the originating experience of the protagonist's fulfillment in his own sexual life; witnessing two couples making love leads to a lifelong fascination with lesbian sex, while he regarded homosexual acts among men with a "certain disgust." At its heart the book spoke not only to the development of individual personality, but also to its connection to societal development. It was not, as Freud thought, the psyche that determined the structure of society, but rather, according to Borneman, society that determined the structure of the psyche. Thus closeness to the mother and rejection of the father is described as an Oedipus complex, as it is in Freud, but is applied at the political level. Borneman despises his father's "political haplessness" as a member of the left liberal party of the Weimar Republic, and thus a democrat disposed to compromise,[211] while the son's shift to the KPD "was an unconscious attempt to transfer the function of my own mother to that of an ideal mother, i.e., to break through a fixation with the mother before it could adopt oedipal forms."[212] As one might expect from the book's approach, such politicized psychologizing appears frequently and laden with Freudian language in descriptions of Borneman's personal trajectory, although it largely operates only as a prelude to more tangible autobiographical chapters, which provides the book's actual fascination. As the self-analysis of a psychologist, the autobiography's form was novel for the mid-1970s; it suggested candor and authenticity and hewed closely to contemporary conversation in its combination of Freud and Marx. Despite a generally positive reception, the book had limited resonance. The bright idea of using one's own biography "to interpret society's fate within the political coordinate systems of our time is dashed to pieces against the amount of material from a highly eventful, highly active life that tempts one to spin yarns," Hans Krieger wrote in *Die Zeit*, going on to note that this "in many regards brilliant man" had been forced to come to his own defense by listing agreeable character traits.[213] In *Konkret*, media commentator Friedrich Knilli situated the book "between novelistic self-depiction and self-critical essay."[214] For writer Paul Kruntorad, Borneman's autobiography contained "numerous puzzles" that remained "unsolved." His "show of accomplishments" combined to give the image of a "completely atypical intellectual: one free from all self-doubt, in no way ponderous, and self-sure and self-opinionated to the point of overconfidence."[215]

Borneman's flights of fancy took inspiration from Peter Weiss's "wishful autobiography" *The Aesthetics of Resistance*,[216] which is written in the voice of the author and tells an engrossing story of young, independently minded Communists and Social Democrats in their resistance against the Nazis, contact with Communist luminaries like Willi Münzenberg, Richard Stahlmann, and Herbert Wehner, and their participation in world historical events alongside such figures, be it in Berlin, Paris, Madrid, Moscow, or Stockholm. Weiss's book also wrested Max Hodann from oblivion, a leftist doctor and sexual pedagogue from Berlin, whom Borneman also described in *Die Ur-Szene* in 1977 as the "friend of our home doctor" and a link to Wilhelm Reich.[217] Borneman makes reference to this parallel himself in an essay about Wilhelm Reich from 1981, writing that "not long ago I discovered that he [Hodann] played an important role in the lives of other young people born in the same year as myself; Peter Weiss for example, who made him a central character in his novel *The Aesthetics of Resistance*."[218] The line between "life" and fiction blurs here in symptomatic fashion and remains just as unclear in Borneman's own autobiographical depictions. The first volume of Weiss's work appeared in 1975 to instant acclaim and could easily have served as inspiration for Borneman's own "wishful autobiography." As in Weiss's book, *Die Ur-Szene* combines documentarian with fictional elements, albeit while purporting to be purely documentarian. Weiss was more daring in this regard, describing his book as a "self-biography that follows my own development in numerous regards but at the same time attempts the following experiment—what would I have become, how would I have developed if I hadn't come from a petty-bourgeois but a proletariat setting?"[219] Borneman reversed the thought experiment; the one whose biography did actually proceed from the Berlin milieu of intellectuals and working youth that another author of the same age imagined for himself (Weiss was born in 1916, one year after Borneman) fashioned an academic environment after his own wishes. Truth, as Borneman had long recognized, was a relative term. He took for granted the possibility that problems of verification might arise.

It was not all "cover stories," however, as Borneman would call his autobiographical inventions elsewhere. It would not escape anyone who took the trouble to read *Die Ur-Szene* that the author held no high school degree, had never enrolled as a student, and had only pursued research on his own, without institutional backing. He stated it openly. He did, however, set up a number of new smokescreens, making the actual record difficult to discern. What did Borneman have to lose? By 1977 he had achieved what there was to achieve—his dissertation and the title of professor (it was more than unlikely that he would receive a full professorship at the age of sixty-two) attesting to his qualifications and standing. On the other hand, there was his reputation to defend—one that would certainly not suffer from the fact that he had achieved everything as an autodidact. Still, a couple of references couldn't hurt in order to compensate for the lack of formal training.

Hereafter Borneman no longer spoke of the "bourgeois women's movement" but "feminists"; he did not distance himself from the latter, but did note the hostile line between them and the women's groups of the "old left," a line that was itself only of limited solidity, however. He made his position more concrete: he had "always completely accepted and supported the critiques of feminists against men and patriarchal institutions," but considered sensitivity training and other techniques for self-discovery to be unsuitable in the political struggle, where it was not isolation from, but alliances with political parties and unions that was necessary, or better still, their "feminization" through mass participation.[220] In retrospect, he realized, he had been accused of "typical patriarchal arrogance . . . to imagine that as a man, one could help women. That was patronizing condescension, a disguised form of disdain."[221] He still failed to see, however, that the cause of this perception did not lie exclusively in a polarized image of the sexes held by the feminist side, but also in his own decisive contribution to it. This did not mean Borneman's read of the women's movement was entirely misguided; he was not at all mistaken in his observation that the old dichotomy between "feeling" and "reason" was given new life in the hostility to a rationality considered "masculine" (and which was assigned a prominent place in Jurreit's book),[222] a notion that to his mind represented a relapse into the "whole patriarchal nonsense of woman as nature and man as civilization."[223]

Judging by the at times vehement reaction to his appearances at panel discussions and conferences, not much changed in Borneman's perception as a leftist patriarch who was cozying up to the women's movement for reasons of self-promotion. A half year after *Das Patriarchat* came out, he wrote to his father that "my book was discussed peacefully and objectively" at an international "feminist conference," "so maybe there's still hope."[224] The master was mistaken, however; Borneman was and remained persona non grata within the women's movement. "Borneman was ugh. Nobody read him," one former activist recalls.[225] Despite his profound disappointment, the outcast stuck by the idea of feminism, not relinquishing hopes of one day achieving recognition within the women's movement, though they would go unrealized. "He was always pressing for this recognition," one of his former female students recalls. "There was something unbearable about it."[226]

Nonetheless, even if his book was surrounded by an "air of forced intellectualism," as former *taz* journalist Ute Scheub wrote recently, male authors with a feminist orientation were a rarity in West Germany.[227] It is obvious that Borneman could not pass muster with the strict views of radical feminists who were just as ideologically minded as he. True, he confronted a real problem in good faith, but the persistence of patriarchal attitudes within his thinking could scarcely be overlooked, and it was precisely this to which the feminist camp reacted with such sensitivity. Then there was the fact that by international comparison, debate concerning the sexes within West Germany was conducted "with particular venom" as Dagmar Herzog writes.[228] To be sure, Borneman never partook in the partway maudlin, partway aggressive rebuke of the women's movement that became fashionable among leftist periodicals such as *taz* or *Ästhetik und Kommunikation* during the second half of the 1970s. During these years, Herzog finds, "mocking feminists in the rudest way possible" formed a part "of everyday West German life."[229]

Ultimately, it is open to debate whether feminist critique proved itself to hold the golden standard. Looking past its uncontested accomplishments and its contested details, Borneman's book can in any event be credited with having provoked discussion. He was the first within the German-speaking world to tap into the US debate around the patriarchy—and the matriarchy along with it as a positive, if somewhat less developed counter model—as well as to justify the terms' use as a battle cry in designating a power relationship and introduce it to the wider public. Borneman's book has often been looked back upon as a breakthrough in the discussion surrounding the conflict between the sexes. In the *FAZ*, one reads that since *Das Patriarchat*, historical discrimination against women has been "a fact taken for granted within women's research that can hardly be foregone in today's academic discussion."[230] Despite her own ambivalence toward the term "patriarchy," the founder of gender history Karin Hausen considers the "bold gesture of declaring war against the overpowering 'patriarchy'" to be "an act of liberation" for the incipient women's movement. In Germany the "obvious nature of the discussion about *the* patriarchy" likely had Borneman's book "to thank in some respects."[231] Marielouise Jurreit's challenge to the notion of the matriarchy from within feminism did not mean the debate ended here. To the contrary, it has since continued across the political spectrum; since Jurreit, opponents of the theory have included legal historian Uwe Wesel and psychologist Jutta Menschik writing from a Marxist feminist perspective, while Klaus E. Müller has outlined concerns from an ethnological perspective.[232] It was not with academic but identitarian aims that the theory of the matriarchy first took root in "cultural feminism" beginning around 1978, where it was advanced as a projection of wishes and fantasies surrounding the "counter mythology" of a "female principle" and accompanied by the belief in a definition of woman as an intrinsically natural being as well as a growing interest in mysticism, esotericism, and occultism.[233] "Cultural feminism" thus linked an all-encompassing "matriarchal research" to the "necessity of an entirely concrete utopia that can heal the planet and provide a truly human way of thinking and being for everybody."[234] For decades now Heide Göttner-Abendroth, the self-appointed "pioneer" of a "new form of matriarchal research," has pursued the historical existence of a matriarchy from a feminist and spiritual perspective under the premise that its research is "better accomplished [by feminists] than in the hands of men."[235] Against such a backdrop, her deep-seated critique of Borneman, which doesn't ground itself in the paradigm of research but rather in the feminist movement's claims for autonomy, becomes clear. "We are only too happy to take this self-described Marx of the women's movement into consideration, but would in any case prefer to raise our own voices, formulate our own worldview, develop theory from our own self-understanding. Within the patriarchy, there is a history of men speaking for women."

Borneman's reputation also suffered among West German sexologists who hadn't been involved in the discussion surrounding *Das Patriarchat*. Volkmar Sigusch shook his head at Borneman's idea of doing away with "all that is basal female," while Reimut Reiche even spied a concealed "hatred toward women" in the book's glorification of them that found expression in the "fervent call to castrate women completely in the name of revolution."[236] The fantasy of the woman "as a utopian bringer of salvation" was widespread—in Herbert Marcuse as a philosophical idea and in Borneman, he argued with excessive force, as a "totalitarian psycho-surgical vision."

"Sex Uncle" in the Media

While Borneman's books may have brought him renown on the pages of the culture section, it was his journalistic work that initially introduced him to a wider public, and then—to a much greater extent—his role as a sex counselor and commentator on radio and television. Borneman wrote for leftist publications such as *Konkret* and new mass-market magazines that addressed the growing field of popular psychology, but he also appeared in the pages of *Der Spiegel* in the early 1970s and youth magazines like *Bravo*, as well as men's periodicals like *Playboy* and *Lui*. As his publications from the 1940s and 1950s showed, Borneman had always been eager to hold a prominent position within the media. This was not only because such positions generally paid well—doubtless a relevant concern for a freelancer like Borneman—but more so because he was constantly looking to move beyond the small circles of the initiate, be it in the world of jazz connoisseurs or the leftist enclave of the 1970s. While he fought for what he considered right within more specific contexts, he was also intent on reaching a broader public, independently of financial considerations. For its part, the media took an interest in Borneman not only because he had something to say, but also because what he had to say was often provocative and polarizing—and drove sales in the process. His ability to do so in the scandal-ridden field of sex had been clear since ascending to the firmament of West German publishing on the back of three sensational works on sexuality between 1968 and 1972. After *Der Spiegel* contracted him to review books by Friedrich Hacker and Esther Vilar, German *Playboy* gave him a three-part series about the sex life of the future, followed by a four-part series entitled "Das Tabu" (taboo).[237] The work did not involve his lifeblood; Borneman did not value the magazine, as he wrote to his father, but it paid well, unlike leftist periodicals. He was "proud of the fact," he continued, "to appear as the sex uncle amid the thicket of German street magazines."[238] The *Playboy* series drew an instinctive counter-reaction from the women's movement and, independent of its content, was subsequently weaponized within the war of opinions. "He takes care to prove his 'emphatic subordination' to the aims of the women's movement by gracing *Playboy* with his views," Jurreit noted caustically in *Konkret*.[239] In his reply,

Borneman made no attempt to pacify the leftist readership but rather escalated the affair, writing that "I am thankful for the chance to write for *Playboy* (and would also be thankful if I could write for the Springer press empire), because that way I get out of a restricted circle of comrades and for once reach my political opponents with my writing."[240] The sexist magazine was ripe for attack of course, but the concept was not entirely new either, especially in West Germany, where after the fallout from its GDR subsidies, it was of all publications *Konkret*, the flagship periodical of the left, that could only be saved by and make its name based on a mixture of sex and politics, as dictated by its founder, Klaus Rainer Röhl. *Playboy* was not left, but it published discerning entertainment in addition to its images of naked bodies; that same year, Klaus Budzinski, Gerhard Zwerenz, Kate Millett, Hans Habe, Stefan Heym, and Ann Thönnissen appeared in its pages.

The *Neue Revue*

Another major channel of influence came in Borneman's involvement with *Neue Revue*, a periodical in the yellow press that began in 1966 with the merger of *Revue* and *Neue Illustrierte*, and which profited from the surge in public debate around sex by publishing a combination of images of scantily clad women and erotic stories. Indeed, it was the *Neue Revue* that had first unleashed the "sex wave," with a sex column starting in 1966 by Borneman's predecessor, Oswalt Kolle. To this extent, as Kurt Koszyk writes, the *Neue Revue* was at the "avant-garde of sexual education," though it was soon overtaken by other periodicals that let all the clothing drop.[241] Published by the Heinrich Bauer Verlag, the magazine continued to convey "the slightest air of gravity" in comparison to competitors such as *Praline*, *Quick*, or *Wochenend*, presenting not only sex but a wide spectrum of everyday topics, including politics.[242] The "direct connection to the everyday life of its readers" took the form of actively bringing the advice craze to a mass audience, featuring working reports from psychologists and marriage counselors, numerous series offering guidance (on the subjects of partnership and health, among others), and advice columns (e.g., "guide for the whole family," "how to save money"). The magazine took a strategic approach to the field, acting as though a growing need for advice were already perceptible. As sociologist and psychologist Peter Kaupp astutely noted by 1971, "Given that in the future social change throughout all sectors is more likely to increase rather than decrease, this 'stabilizing function' may be permitted to take on a significance at least as great as that of entertainment and diversion in the future editorial offerings of the *Neue Revue*."[243]

Marriage and partnership played a distinctively larger role in the *Neue Revue* than any other comparable publication, forming a good quarter of the material selected for publication.[244] More than the readership of other journals, the *Neue Revue*'s audience (in particular those under forty) considered "sex education and problems" as well as "marriage problems" to be particularly important.[245] The magazine treated sex "as an index for the modernization of partnerships, a way to break with old taboos and to develop an uninhibited, free and open relationship with one's partner."[246] Borneman wasn't the magazine's only advice columnist in the field of sexuality; the column "Ask Dr. Heimberg" was already in print when he began, and he would later be joined by Erika Berger's "The Erotic Interview," making for a total of three sex columns by the end of the 1980s. With a circulation that reached two million at points during the 1970s, the *Neue Revue* offered serious competition to *Stern* (published by Gruner + Jahr), which though less by comparison wasn't stingy itself with the amount of skin that it showed.[247] Circulation sank continuously through the 1980s to 800,000 by 1993, although still with a total reach of 3.77 million readers.[248] An effort was made to strengthen the impression of seriousness, but in vain; as the numbers dwindled, reader age rose above that of *Stern*. Borneman's involvement brought him the accusation of pawning his credentials as a sexologist in order to give the entire affair an academic veneer. While *Der Spiegel* considered the *Neue Revue* "never easy to classify," Volkmar Sigusch, the sharpest critic of Borneman's involvement, dismissed it without further ado as a "sex and crime rag."[249] Between 1982 and 1984 the magazine published a series entitled "Love from A to Z" written "exclusively" for the *Neue Revue*, as it was advertised, by Borneman. The series was conceived of as a dictionary for those whose reading habits didn't involve books: "If you clip it out, you will have a detailed and complete compilation."[250]

Most importantly however, from 1983 onward Borneman wrote a weekly column for *Neue Revue* under the title "Sprechstunde über Sexualprobleme" (Office Hours for Sexual Problems). Appearing in the magazine's imprint as an "academic advisor," he was paid 2,500 Deutschmarks per week, a considerable monthly salary that provided a welcome source of financial stability for a freelancer.[251] "New! Professor Borneman answers your most intimate questions," the series announcement read, making special reference to the author's familial status. The "bon vivant, who likes his food and wine," had been married to his wife for fifty years. "That is more than is usual for a sexologist—most of his colleagues may be entirely capable of offering advice when it comes to others' marriage or sexual problems, but often lead troubled love lives of their own."[252] Exactly how "normal" Borneman's love life really was or was not mattered little in reality. What did matter was not upsetting norms that continued to exist, a feat that could be accomplished all the more definitively by mobilizing known prejudices against the field of sexology. The content for Borneman's column was provided by reader letters, a small number of which—around three to five per issue—he personally addressed in the magazine. The vast majority were answered directly by letter, an effective mode of establishing a connection with readers, for which the magazine paid an additional 30 Deutschmarks per letter. With some one hundred letters addressed to Borneman arriving daily and the stated goal of answering each letter, the columnist couldn't manage the workload himself, so additional assistants were brought on—around twenty by Borneman's reckoning.[253] His motives for working with the magazine were not only financial but also grounded in the idea of a research project, a study of contemporary sexual problems as reflected in readers' letters commissioned by the board of the German Society for Social-Scientific Sexuality Research (Deutsche Gesellschaft für Sozialwissenschaftliche Sexualforschung).[254] Readers' letters, Borneman argued, constituted a diverse source of material on the population's state of affairs such as had never existed. He had previously petitioned magazines with advice columns to share their readers' letters with him, "because I had the impression that most of these letters . . . must be forgeries, as their authors seemed to be so thick and misinformed that I thought children . . . could not be as thick and as misinformed as the writers."[255] All the magazines refused; only the chief editor of the *Neue Revue* gave him access to the archive of "Dr. Heimberg" and offered him, what was more, a column of his own to generate further material. Beyond the written sources, opinion polls taken of the letters' authors would deepen understanding. In response to his critics, Borneman justified the project by pointing to doctors' and psychotherapists' limited ability to establish a general image of sexual problems, as they could "draw only limited conclusions about the sexual behavior of the general population" based on the small, socially selective number of their patients.[256] People who wrote letters turned to advice columnists in magazines precisely because they did not want to visit the doctor or a therapist, but preferred seeking advice at a safe distance. "What do sexual therapists know—especially those who take a psychotherapeutic approach and depend on their patients expressing their troubles in words—about people who aren't able to verbally express themselves, who in the best cases make spelling mistakes in their postcards or punctuate their lines incorrectly, and would descend into panic if their mail-order uncle or aunt were to suddenly show up at their door?" As it was, this was an entirely apposite observation that Sabine Maasen has analyzed, writing in terms of normalization, as an expansion in disadvantaged classes' ability to conduct their own lives: a search for advice in the field of sex "provides every individual who considers him- or herself uneducated or awkward with a way to talk about their person."[257] Borneman first discussed the interim findings of his research project in 1984 on Southwest Broadcasting (Südwestrundfunk, SWR), again in 1985 for *Die Zeit*, and finally in 1987 before an audience of sex educators. He foresaw great things for the project, vowing, "When our book comes out in 1987 . . . no one will believe what it is we've heard. Compared to it, the Kinsey Report is child's play."[258] He initially set publication for 1987, then for 1989, and was still discussing it in 1991—in the end it was never completed.[259] This was not due to a lack of primary sources, as is clear from the collection of reader correspondence in Borneman's estate, which is preserved in numerous archival boxes and organized by keyword. According to Franz Altrichter, a close collaborator of Borneman's for years who was also involved in the project, other assistants came from a circle of young gay men in Dusseldorf centered around Rolf Gindorf who were active counselors to the gay scene. The large number of replies in Borneman's estate testify to the tremendous amount of work accomplished by the team: hundreds of written replies, often drafted by assistants, but always bearing Borneman's signature.[260] There was no public financing for answering the letters, which meant the project was funded by the fee the publisher paid for answering the letters.

A steady source of income plus project financing was nothing to be scoffed at, but Borneman found it difficult. He was still of the basic opinion that within the context of the existing social order, change for the better was impossible, and he had always avoided taking up his own therapy practice. Because diagnosis at a distance was impossible, the most a columnist could offer in effect was information, but not advice or therapy. He considered comparable columns that assumed the opposite to be true irresponsible. Nevertheless, he managed to adopt a pragmatic position, which he characterized as follows: "Columns can accomplish three things: 1. Communicate information, as most sexual problems arise from pure ignorance. 2. Console those who believe themselves to be entirely alone in their misery. Those who think they are the only ones to suffer on the planet. . . . 3. I can convince people who are afraid of the doctor to seek medical treatment." It may not "be much, but it is better than nothing."[261]

Beginning in 1986, Borneman also took over a column at the *Arbeiter Zeitung*—the gazette of the SPÖ (Sozialdemokratische Partei Österreichs, or Social Democratic Party of Austria) and the second largest Austrian daily newspaper after *Presse* in the 1980s—grounding his decision in leftist arguments. First, he was interested in "countering the daft bourgeois notion that marital or other sexual difficulties only have private causes. In actual fact it is bourgeois dog-eat-dog society, with its class-specific educational certificates, disastrous form of competitive thinking that holds humanity in contempt, and its labeling of the economically weak as 'failures' that is directly to blame for a large part of sexual misery today." Second, he wanted to reanimate the "long tradition of liberal and emancipatory views on sexuality" within the working class that had been forgotten "by many SPÖ members." "The present column thus has the task of continually recalling the differences between our sexual morality and that of bourgeois or ecclesiastic culture."[262]

Evaluating the enormous amount of source material assembled within this context is a task that must be left to other works. At present I only provide a rough outline of what differentiated Borneman's advice from that of others, taking as an immediate point of comparison "Dear Marta," a popular Swiss column penned between 1980 and 1995 for the tabloid *Blick* by journalist Marta Emmenegger and recently the subject of thorough analysis.[263] Borneman's point of departure in his advice, his standpoint on sexual morality, did not differ from his contemporary Emmenegger: "The ethics of sexual intercourse is based solely and exclusively on nobody doing what the other does not want, and no third party receiving injury."[264] Such a statement did not, of course, clarify the details of what was actually "advised" or, in Borneman's words, taught or encouraged. A contemporary analysis of Borneman's columns from 1987 found that the *Neue Revue* focused on sexual excitement; letters were often selected for publication that "described sexual practices in painstaking detail . . . without a problem thereby becoming visible or advice seeming necessary." As for Borneman's answers, the conclusion was reached that they focused on overcoming informational deficits or "allaying insecurities about taboo questions. This is modeled after a relatively liberal image of sexuality that is accepting of many forms."[265] An initial sample of the material shows four pronounced differences to "Dear Marta."[266] First, as for "the sex advisor to the nation" on the other edge of Lake Constance, a heterosexual relationship between two people represented the normative ideal for Borneman. Such a relationship should furthermore be characterized by love and in particular by altruism, that is, aim at a partnership. In contrast with Emmenegger however, Borneman did not advocate for monogamy but encouraged those who breached the precept, instead counseling understanding and a mutual effort to resolve problems with one's partner. Second, Borneman did not exclude social causes from his advice as did "Martha"; to the contrary, a society based on competition stood opposed to sexual relationships based on partnership, meaning those in search of a satisfying sexual life had structural obstacles with which to contend. To a certain extent, this already undercut the exclusive self-responsibility assigned to the individual within radical liberal ideology and by Emmenegger herself. Third, while "Marta" overlooked differences between the sexes when it came to readers' self-assigned roles and their own self-images, for Borneman these were a constitutive element in offering "fitting" advice. Men and women alike should be informed about the socially determined nature of their self-perception in order to understand the context, attune their own individual behavior, and overcome this state of affairs. Fourth, it strikes one that Borneman by no means always saw a positive way out of the problem through education and encouragement. Not infrequently he would censure the behavior of the letters' authors—for example, if they showed no interest in their partner, treated them badly, or spied on them—and would counsel separation or divorce. As Günter Amendt with *Sexfront*, Borneman thus made the case that there were alternatives to perpetual coupledom, even to marriage itself. Rotraud Perner later recalled of her radio work with Borneman that the latter's "standard pronouncement"—"You have the wrong partner! Separate!"—had "in the meantime become the stuff of legend."[267]

A more detailed look at specific cases quickly reveals that for the most part, replies usually took up the affairs of those concerned with empathy and in detail. To give one example from many, a man who has just turned sixty cannot reach orgasm. Borneman: "All I can tell you is that psychological processes are more important than physical processes, all the more so the older one is. Even with a diminished ability to get an erection, an experienced women and an empathetic man can give each other satisfactory orgasms."[268] A man's partner loves to wear tall heels during sex, and has begun to stand on his stomach ("It hurt of course when she danced or hopped about"), and has recently taken up asking him to lick her soles. Borneman's response: "Anything that both partners want in love is 'normal.' You shouldn't be jumping up and down on your partner's chest or stomach however, especially not if you're wearing high-cut heels."[269] All in all, one finds comprehensible opinions and advice that boils down to motivating the person in search of help. No, masturbation isn't harmful; try to overcome the inculcated attitude that sex is dirty; if your boyfriend is constantly criticizing your breasts, go find another. He would often advise seeking out a conversation with a local sex counselor or professional literature. There were isolated cases, however, in which Borneman—who appeared in the column wearing a white lab coat resembling a doctor's—overstepped the boundaries of information and encouragement he himself had set. Such exceptions partially explain themselves in terms of the unequivocal nature of his fundamental positions. Like Freud, for example, Borneman believed that the most important prerequisite for a satisfying sexual life in adulthood was found in childhood. The fundamental condition was warmth and attention from one's parents, who undertook the sexual education of the child through their own sexual practices. If this were not the case, as could be assumed for a considerable number of citizens, what options remained to begin with? In response to one man who complained that his wife had refused him, Borneman wrote, "If the parents have a disturbed relationship with their own sexuality, feeling sexual intercourse to somehow be sinful or dirty or disgusting, it will be very difficult for the children of such parents ever to develop a healthy sexuality in their own lives."[270]

He regarded masturbation with skepticism—not for the moralistic reasons with which poisonous pedagogy (*schwarze Pädagogik*) concealed its disciplinary intentions, but rather, in reference to Freud, because he considered it a form of sexuality that was entirely too self-referential. It was unproblematic during transitional times between sexual partners, but one shouldn't grow too used to it, because it concealed the danger of leading one away from the less simple matter of sex between partners. He didn't see that for increasing numbers of people, self-satisfaction was a sexual practice that was not only pursued when one was single, but could also happen in tandem with partnership and in no way detracted from it. He rejected forms of sexuality that rested on violence or subjugation. He defended the legitimacy of homosexuality as "one of the many erotic relationships between two people deserving of equal rights" and defended homosexuals against attacks coming within the context of the political response to HIV/AIDS.[271] From time to time his skepticism does show through, likely set off by his own explicitly heterosexual tendencies, but he was not homophobic, as he was occasionally accused of being. In 1977 he conceded that "I have often, and with good reason, been accused of saying something wrong, unsatisfactory or distorted about homosexuality," going on to clarify: "The 'toleration' of homosexuality and other manifestations of human sexuality that one finds so often in progressive, 'sex positive' educational literature simply isn't acceptable. They must be recognized as autonomous, absolutely equal and equivalent forms of sexuality, and accepted as a part of the enormously broad diversity of human sexual tendencies."[272]

Another fundamental position that made itself felt in his answers was the conviction that there were right and wrong choices in partner, with far-reaching consequences for both sides. In certain cases, as described above, Borneman might thus advise a reader that he or she had chosen the wrong partner in the first place and that separation or divorce was unavoidable. He clearly overstepped his own maxims, as well as his authority in these instances. On the other hand, such advice—unlike before the sexual revolution and the women's movement, where the relationship was to be preserved at all costs—was also easy to find. A comparative study of advice columns on partnership problems in "entertaining weekly newspapers" finds that "in 1962 it was exclusively tactical intelligence, understanding and patience that was counseled for everyday marital difficulties. In 1992 separating from one's partner (after taking certain measures to save the relationship in some cases) was commonly suggested as a solution."[273] To give an example: a man whose wife is pregnant writes in assuming that there won't be penetrative sex for a long while and seeking advice because his partner finds it repellent to satisfy her husband with her hand or mouth. Borneman's reply: "I find it truly difficult to advise you because if your wife, despite all her 'liberalism,' is disgusted by using her hand or mouth, you should never have married in the first place. I don't mean to say that intercourse with hand or mouth must be accepted, but if one partner considers it normal, then he must find a partner who also considers it normal. Two people with such fundamental differences in their sexual preferences simply must not marry each other, otherwise one's entire marital life becomes an absolute hell of sexual needs at odds with each other."[274]

In 1990 Borneman was awarded the Magnus Hirschfeld Medal for service in the field of sexology from the German Society for Social-Scientific Sexuality Research. The award was given with explicit reference made to his public role; the decision read, "He often selects the public sphere as his preferred location to practice and transmit his science, at the very site where the people who need it can be found, and in a language they can understand."[275] Coming on his seventy-fifth birthday, the award was a welcome recognition of his work over the past quarter century. The only blemish was that the acknowledgment came from friends—other sexologists greeted Borneman's public role and his positions with much greater skepticism.

Crossing Swords with Volkmar Sigusch

Borneman's columns in the *Neue Revue* were subject not only to praise but also to criticism, eventually raising a mini-furor among West German sexologists, which, unlike the debate surrounding *Das Patriarchat*, barely reached the newspapers but is still of interest for revealing profound disagreements about sexual development and its interpretation. In a 1987 article entitled "Der Ratschläger" (The Advisor), Volkmar Sigusch, a professor of sexual sciences at Frankfurt am Main University who had completed his dissertation in Hamburg, issued a sharp critique of Borneman's *Neue Revue* columns in *Pro Familia*, the magazine of the German Society for Family Planning, Sexual Education and Sexual Counseling (Deutsche Gesellschaft für Familienplanung, Sexualpädagogik und Sexualberatung).[276] Sigusch attacked Borneman first for publishing with the *Neue Revue*, a "trashy tabloid" published by the "reactionary" Bauer Verlag, which traded on sex and people's sexual difficulties for hard currency. This argument echoed heightened traditionalist reservations toward the popular press that had re-emerged in leftist critique since the 1960s, as expressed in countless critical accounts of their manipulative effect. Now in 1987, the all-too-familiar topos of moral panic in the field of "filth and trash" still hadn't been laid to rest, as demonstrated by the focal point of the volume in which Sigusch's article appeared: a critical appraisal of sexual content in the media—rock music, pop stars, action films—that cited Borneman's work as exemplary for gossip magazines.[277] Using a number of the advice columns Borneman wrote between 1983 and 1984 as discussed above, Sigusch came to a "devastating assessment," as the editorial board of *Pro Familia* termed it. In Sigusch's words, "Anyone looking for an object lesson in the worst conceivable sex advice, and who would like to see in plain print just how cynical anti-educational sexology can be, would be well-advised to read Borneman's murderous phrases. Nearly everything that he presents with such flourish is false from the perspective of sexual science, and is irresponsible as advice."[278] Sigusch criticized the very premise of an advice column, which, unlike a therapist, was based on nothing aside from a letter—but also, and in particular, Borneman's advice itself. "Without really knowing anything about his victims, he deems them unfair, unjust and cowardly, their behavior wrong or unforgivable, their fears totally unfounded or imaginary. He dares to accuse them of having made the wrong choice in partner, tries to convince them of the hopelessness of their situation and even—on a repeated basis—counsels separation and divorce, all by way of long-distance treatment."

An emotional involvement cannot be overlooked in assessing Sigusch's polemic. It was what had induced him to make a precise study of his colleague's autobiography and columns in order to pick them apart piece by piece, and which then guided his pen while writing the article. After lightly mocking Borneman's numerous self-stylizations in a style as amusing as it was accurate (skilled in every field, endless workdays, decisive interventions in politics and society—Borneman and his wife did not find it funny in the slightest), Sigusch then described his disillusionment. Even after *Das Patriarchat*, whose theories he "spared" only with "a heavy heart," he was uncertain whether Borneman "was not showing up our academic and cultural pursuits in some subversive manner by parodying it, writing satires that he then skillfully paraded about as science." Any remaining "inhibitions" evaporated when Borneman attacked him in 1986 however, and he had lost all "illusions" since the columns for the *Neue Revue*. The target of the attacks, shocked and bewildered by a broadside he considered "defamation," could only think of personal reasons: Sigusch must be "nearly mad with jealousy—firstly of my private life, secondly my public 'success' and thirdly of the loyalty of my friends," and pressing for greater public recognition:

> What brings Sigusch to the brink of despair is his own ineffectiveness. Somebody who imagines himself to be incomparably more clever than all his colleagues yet is known only to a microscopic number of his satellites, and never manages to exact any influence whatsoever on his country's medical, social or political landscape. This explains his embarrassing,

self-revelatory rage toward any colleague with a greater public impact. On the one hand he whips himself up into a frenzy railing against the "yellow press" and the "media," while on the other clearly longing for nothing less desperately than to receive mention and praise in the media more often.[279]

Borneman and Sigusch had previously been friends, as Borneman repeatedly testified. "I've sent many patients to him over the years. It was disappointing to me that he never took the time to treat even one—it's also why I broke off the relationship. This made him angry, which is why he is now attacking me."[280] At another point Borneman mentioned that when his colleague had "showed up penniless from the GDR, [he had] supported, sponsored and praised him for years," while Sigusch, twenty-five years Borneman's junior, viewed the relationship in an opposite, though no less patriarchal light. Granted, he hadn't served as advisor to Borneman's thesis, but he hadn't "set up any roadblocks on the unusual path" Borneman took to achieving his doctorate.[281] Two positions emerged here that would never be reconciled to one another.

As always in his long rejoinders, Borneman went on counterattack, accusing Sigusch of a general aggression toward former friends and doubting his accomplishments. "A man of unquestionable intelligence, one with a unique chance to follow in the distinguished footsteps of Hans Giese and to restore the reputation of German sexology to what it was before the National Socialist period, now spends his days writing tidy little anthologies written in aphoristic, coquettish academese and peppered with foreign terms."[282] Where the subject matter itself was concerned, Borneman denied all responsibility for the editorial line of the *Neue Revue* and spoke of "minor derailments by my coworkers," for which he "naturally" took responsibility but allowed that "small errors might be forgiven" in light of the large number of reader letters. A crowd of readers protested Sigusch's attacks, including a group of Borneman's friends that he rallied himself, as revealed in his letter correspondence from early February 1987. One distinctly independent voice, sex educator Karla Etschenberg, called attention to the deplorable fact that "two of sexology's most recognizable figures . . . had been made to look ridiculous," "the one by means of what has been written about him, the second by the way that he writes about the first." "As thrilling as I find it to observe stag fights at the zoo or in the wild, I find such demonstrations equally inappropriate for a respectable magazine in an area (sexuality) that has enough difficulty depicting itself with any respectability in public." Karl-Heinz Twele, the responsible department head at the *Neue Revue*, revealed that Helmut Kentler, a well-known sex educator previously within Borneman's orbit who was now allied with Sigusch, was among the sexologists writing for the paper and that he had also offered Sigusch work.[283]

The conflict ran deeper than such a sudden outburst would lead one to suspect. At its heart lay an entire complex of reasons that had come increasingly to the fore beginning in the late 1970s and involved competition between two professional associations and people, but more importantly differences in opinion. In 1971 a new association of sex researchers interested in the social sciences had formed outside of the well-established German Society for Sexual Research (Deutsche Gesellschaft für Sexualforschung, DGfS). The leading light of the new society was Rolf Gindorf, a former interpreter and businessman who took up his studies late but had since become a sexologist, even earning his doctorate.[284] After internal squabbling, the association disbanded, giving rise among the same circle to the German Society for Social-Scientific Sexuality Research (Deutsche Gesellschaft für sozialwissenschaftliche Sexualforschung, DGSS) in 1982, a group that, in Sigusch's words, "with the name alone meant to signal that it would take up competition with the thirty-year-old DGfS." While a de facto rivalry existed, the DGSS was never able to challenge the DGfS seriously with the latter's institutional grounding in the universities. The DGSS also became Borneman's organizing platform; he served as its president from 1982 to 1986 and as honorary chairman afterward. A number of active members withdrew following the internal split, including Helmut Kentler. Into the early 1980s, the relationship between the DGfS and Gindorf's circle seems to have been relatively unproblematic; in 1980 they issued a joint call to parliament and the government to strike paragraph 175 from the statute books, which made sexual relations between people of the male sex punishable.[285] Shortly after the new association's founding, it also undertook to carry on its relationship with the DGfS "as free of conflict and in friendly a manner as possible."[286] It soon became clear that this was easier said than done—when Eberhard Schorsch didn't reply to a letter from Gindorf, the latter commented, "I suppose they view us as a form of uncomfortable competition on which fine people don't waste their time."[287] And again: "It is increasingly clear to me that those in the DGfS leadership are concerned with a highly specific type of sexual research and politics whose agenda is defined in such personal terms that the locker room air itself seems to decide. 'How one keeps outsiders outside' [Wie man Außenseiter draußen hält] was the name of one essay by Lautmann. That is likely what we will remain forever." Borneman joined the chorus, adding a personal edge: "I believe Schorsch to be a forthright person who is overburdened by the DGfS. In my view the problems lie exclusively with Sigusch—I have my doubts about his honesty."[288] In the previous year, as the dissonance between the two groups grew, Gindorf described the trait that he and Borneman held in common: "We are both outsiders and as such are constantly threatened by stigmatization; whatever we say, write or do (or permit) is met not only with criticism . . . but highly emotive reactions, from joy to hatred . . . thus those of us who do not exude the requisite smell of accomplishment instill a more or less well defined fear of contact in the well bred, the Sigusches or Schorsches."[289] Despite the confrontations between the two associations, Sigusch acknowledged the guiding force of the DGSS in his *Geschichte der Sexualwissenschaft* (History of Sexology). Gindorf's "life accomplishments," in particular his persistent "struggle for the recognition of homosexual partnerships" and his belated doctoral defense "command respect."[290]

Sexualität konkret

In such a context, Sigusch's attacks in "Der Ratschläger" could not have come entirely "for no apparent reason," as Borneman claimed shortly after the article's publication.[291] Discord was already evident by the late 1970s with the appearance of two competing magazine projects on the public stage, one to spectacular acclaim, the other less so. At the time, however, everyone was still speaking with one another. In a review of Sigusch's *Die Sexuelle Frage* (The Sexual Question)—a book published by Konkret Literatur Verlag in 1982 that summarized a number of articles from the first three issues of *Sexualität konkret*—Borneman reported proposing to Sigusch, Schmidt, and Schorsch that they edit three issues of the magazine *Psychologie heute* devoted especially to the subject of sexuality.[292] They waved the suggestion aside; in Hamburg and Frankfurt there likely already prevailed a certain skepticism toward Borneman as a black sheep, not to mention his ideas, which were only somewhat contemporary and may or may not serve their own designs. The incident also indicates that Borneman's plan to build a "unified and centralized consciousness for the rapidly growing and expanding universe of sexual research" by means of a joint periodical was not only doomed from the start, but even propelled the schism.[293] The fact that this plan was to be accomplished under his editorial lead in cooperation with his home journal reinforced the perception that Borneman was attempting to "conquer the West German sexology scene," as Sigusch continues to characterize Borneman's public appearances between 1968 and 1977 to this day.[294] While Borneman was a prominent figure by that time—known throughout the press, on radio, and on television—he evidently did not want to limit his role to that of a media star or of a figure subverting the scientific paradigm, but to be taken seriously in the sexual sciences. It was not only his dissertation and title of professor that left little doubt about such aspirations, but also his initiative to collect material from within the "universe of sexual research." Since *Das Patriarchat*, Borneman had actually risen to the level of an "impactful liberation sexologist," as the *FAZ* later put it.[295] Yet his research was not transparent enough for him to be recognized as an authority among sexual scientists. Intellectually he did not bring much new to the table; at over sixty years old he was cut off by habit from the scene of young sexologists, who were also influenced by the Frankfurt School, but even more by post-structuralism, pop culture, and other postmodern cultural currents. Then there were the normative attitudes he held toward "proper" sexual behavior, positions that often derived from his own practices but were either not necessarily comprehensible or besides the point for others. The definitive gestures with which he drove home the mandatory nature of his positions also disturbed many. In practice, Borneman's strong suit—the fact that he had no fear but spoke up for what he considered right, without consideration of losses—could also be a deterrent. This was daring for an otherwise unaffiliated freelancer; on the one hand, it brought a breath of fresh air when it came to traditional clichés on the subject of sexuality, but on the other, it was regarded as irritating when it called group consensus into question. Confrontations were in any case unavoidable, and Borneman pursued them as might a military commander, as the disputes with Jurreit and Sigusch show. In an article written for her husband's seventieth birthday, Eva Borneman subtly called attention to the pronounced narcissism on display in these cases, noting that the "most interesting, but likely most painful tensions [arise] from the discrepancy between the image one carries of oneself and that others hold of him."[296] She had often tried "to make Ernest Borneman aware of his overly uncompromising style of writing and presentation and to modify it. Nonetheless I am conscious of the fact that it is precisely his style of exaggeration and hyperbole that can be, and is much more provoking and fruitful than my overly finicky precision. . . . I've often accused Borneman of dealing all too casually with his own insights and discoveries. But it would be narrow-minded, dense and petty if I weren't to consider this the expression of a fascinating and versatile emotional life."

The special issues of *Psychologie heute* did not come to fruition as conceived by Borneman, although a special edition of the magazine edited by Borneman was published in 1979 by the Beltz Verlag as a compact, 250-page volume under the title *Sexualität: Beiträge zur Sexualforschung* (Sexuality: Articles on Sexual Research). It was this special edition that Borneman claimed Sigusch and his people had "imitated," just as they had the idea for releasing it as the special edition of a magazine, albeit under the name *Sexualität konkret*. This last series, a total of seven issues devoted to sexuality and edited by Hermann L. Gremliza and Volkmar Sigusch, was published by *Konkret* between 1979 and 1986 and achieved tremendous success because it permitted the "immense and flickering sea of lights of sexuality," which, following Foucault, first arose through bourgeois efforts to control it, to appear in all its brilliant splendor.[297] The issues were printed in multiple editions; the first run of 140,000 copies sold out at the kiosks. One hundred pages long and laid out as a magazine, the publication featured well-known authors such as Günter Amendt, Günter Herburger, Peggy Parnass, and even blues singer Eric Burdon, with two photo snippets of pubic hair and a bottom on the cover.[298] The crowd of young sexologists and recognizable names from the leftist cultural scene paired with a wealth of imagery and illustrations by F. K. Waechter, Robert Gernhardt, Ernst Volland, and Robert Crumb to create a highly attractive setting in which to discuss contemporary issues around sexuality. Police seizures and investigations only increased the appeal. Borneman's paperback (the cover—symptomatic without wanting to be so—featured a stone penis that had broken off) also assembled prominent experts including Helmut Kentler, Rüdiger Lautmann, Bernd Nitzschke, and Peter Gorsen, but it lacked the sex appeal of the competition; it wasn't made for a mass audience and appeared in one printing only. It was obvious that the elderly gentleman from an Austrian province held a different idea of such a volume. While he had a respectable professional publication in mind devoted to "normal" sexual life,[299] Sigusch and Gremliza addressed themselves to a broader public through a combination of specialist articles (e.g., Sigusch, Schmidt, Schorsch) and popular pieces from the political and cultural scenes that were meant to include all the sexual manifestations of the present. Borneman grumbled about the fact that many important German sexual researchers were not represented in *Sexualität konkret* (he himself wasn't asked, nor did the list of recommended literature contain a single one of his titles); the series was a "leftist variation of hypocritical bourgeois indignation."[300] The first three issues "at first paraded the most seductive details in word and image before us . . . only to damn them later as the evil spawn of corrupting capitalism." "What I find indecent," his criticism came to a head, "is selling soft porn as socialism." In an interview with an alternative newspaper he spoke in more concrete terms, discussing an argument with Sigusch and Dannecker about the first issue of *Sexualität konkret*. The editor at the *Marburger Zeitung* had read the issue "in fairly great detail" and, the interviewer declaimed, "been somewhat shocked, as the political tendencies in the analysis reminded me a bit of Spengler's *Decline of the West*. Where is a critical, leftist perspective to be found? Is this not a culturally conservative form of fatalism?" Borneman replied enthusiastically:

> I find it thrilling what you say. On my way back to Austria from Marburg last Tuesday, I spent a half-day in Frankfurt with Volkmar Sigusch and Martin Dannecker. . . . I said practically the same thing using the same words. Both were not only stupefied, they were truly horrified. They said they couldn't imagine what kind of perverse mind could have read such a thing into the issue, which after all was by far the most optimistic, most progressive, likely most Marxist-based volume ever to be written anywhere in the history of West Germany. Since then we've practically stopped speaking with one another. Because we were both quite closely aligned, and both think practically the same thing, and for one of us then to edit such a publication . . . I mean he found my book of the same title Sexualität . . . just as bad as I found his. And despite this there have hardly ever been two people in German sexual research to stand so closely aligned, ideologically speaking.[301]

While that would change, it helps to explain one part of the force with which the two came into conflict.

Sexualität konkret did not only generate waves of enthusiasm, a fact that emerged farther afield than the questioned posed by the alternative Marburg newspaper. One reviewer broke her stylus while reviewing the 1983 issue number 4 for *taz*, "not from enthusiasm but disgust," leaving another to finish the assignment.[302] Journalist and educator Dieter Schnack spotted a great deal of cynicism and talked about a "pornography for intellectuals" in light of the series' numerous introductions to porno shops, red light bars, and porno films (his brief summary alone caused the layout designer "to refrain from further reading"): "The entire crafty affair, all the emancipatory hullabaloo seems to me to be not much more than the briefcase of Professor Garbage looking to save face."[303]

When asked by the interviewer from the *Marburger Zeitung* to explain the growing interest in "deviant" forms of sexuality, Borneman responded in part by criticizing an article by Hans Eppendorfer (a pseudonym of Hans-Peter Reichel) in the first issue of *Sexualität konkret*. Eppendorfer, a social outcast turned Hamburg author and lead editor of the gay magazine *him applaus*, had made a name for himself through his reports on the homosexual sadomasochist scene over three long interviews from 1970, 1973, and 1976 with Hubert Fichte, who took an ethnological interest. For Frankfurt criminologist Herbert Jäger, an important agent for reforming the sexual penal code and a steady skeptic of "aggressive norm enforcement," it remained an open question whether the "forms of play involving sexual cruelty described have an amplifying effect or rather a therapeutic, liberating effect."[304] Such nuance was less relevant in the broader public, where it was more the sensationalist aspects of Eppendorfer's reports that were valued. For the "nearly two-meter-tall studded neighborhood lord" (*Berliner Zeitung*), homosexuality was associated, as *Der Spiegel* fancied, "with the notion of blood, assault and leather."[305] Many a reader was fascinated with Eppendorfer's motto "Make others your victims before you become one yourself." The interest shown by arts sections and theaters indicated that the zeitgeist had struck out in a new direction, as did the fact that the interviews were collected and published in 1977 by Suhrkamp Verlag, one of the era's most reliable bellwethers.[306]

In relations between men and women, too, there were signs that the high hopes associated with liberalization had now given way to disappointment and disquiet and that everything pointed toward conflict in the realm of sexuality—and this long before HIV/AIDS became prevalent.[307] In the "contempt for the sexual" that had spread throughout leftist radicalism in the first half of the 1970s, be it of an anarchist or Maoist persuasion, "sex," as Massimo Perinelli observed, "had been driven off the horizon of liberation."[308] In his analysis of soft- and hard-core pornography between the early 1970s and early 1980s, Pascal Eitler speaks of a "steep increase in the brutalization of sexuality."[309] Following detailed fieldwork on the Reeperbahn in Hamburg, in 1978 *Stern* concluded that "sex had never been as harsh as now." In 1978 and 1980 violent "leftist pornographic fantasies" were periodically described or sadomasochistic scenes depicted in the alternative magazine *Pflasterstrand* as well as *taz*, which sparked a wave of indignation in the alternative scene coming amid other sexist incidents and called forth a "revolutionary council" among feminists that assigned itself the task of constantly "monitoring the behavior of left-wing men."[310] In this setting, the discourse also began to change in unmistakable ways. No de-escalation of the conflict between the sexes lay in sight—to the contrary. "A desire for the obscene finally received intellectual consecration," Ulrike Heider wrote, "once discriminating magazines like *Ästhetik und Kommunikation*, Klaus Wagenbach's *Freibeuter* and Konkursbuch Verlag, founded in 1978 under the banner of a critique of reason, began to adorn themselves with it."[311] While the subculture in the high-rise offices of *Der Spiegel* applauded the arrival of a "new Genet", others were less enthusiastic.[312] For Borneman, this "desire for the obscene" also—and especially—found expression in *Sexualität konkret* under the editorial lead of young sexologists who in his view should have another mission. Eppendorfer's text, which gave a detailed report from New York of the most brutal sexual practices, should "under no circumstances" have appeared in *Sexualität konkret*, as it allowed its author's fascination with the "contemporary forms of what are truly the most severe degradations of human sexuality" occurring in the United States to "show through." Eppendorfer "even believes that a certain cathartic cleansing can occur through them, that we must identify ourselves with this scene." Faced with a choice between socialism or barbarism, Borneman wrote, looking out on Sodom and Gomorrah, humanity had evidently chosen the latter.[313] A number of years later, when what had initially been fascination turned fashionable, he reaffirmed his position once again. It seemed to him "that this new sadomasochistic wave, which filters out the negative elements from the sexual experiences of our genus and then offers them up as the essence of sexuality does not do justice to human sexuality, but rather looks provocatively to make regressive desires pass as norms. What proffers itself as progressive is a rationalized justification of regression."[314]

Taken as a whole, the confrontation between Borneman and Sigusch delineates the contours of a fundamental rivalry that had already appeared by the late 1970s. Borneman's wish, as Sigusch aptly remarked, to become the "Nestor of sexual research in the German-speaking world" doubtless contributed to the dispute.[315] The academic sexual sciences in Hamburg and Frankfurt pursued empirical studies in order to take stock of factual sexual behavior and to set it against the normative observations that had to that point largely dominated the conversation. As Martin Dannecker phrased it, sexuality should be treated "neither mystically nor moralistically," but rather "functionally and in a useful manner."[316] Borneman himself also worked empirically, in his studies on the sexual language of children as well as his historical reconstructions of sexuality in Greece and Rome. If he wasn't mystical, he was, however, moralistic, albeit not in the sense of a bloated and restrictive sexual morality. Borneman's value judgments on sexual behavior were well matched to 1968, which advocated for a form of sexuality free of fear and based on reciprocity between the sexes, and likewise sexuality's important role in overall societal change. These judgments were less welcome once the emphasis on sexual revolution tapered off, hostile attitudes toward women and men alike spread, and pain's reputation as a precondition for lustful sensations was rehabilitated, a shift that became palpable toward the end of the 1970s. It became clear that Borneman did not want to go in this direction when he ended up begging off a foreword he had originally promised to write for the first volume of Claudia Gehrke's book series *Mein heimliches Auge* (My Secret Eye), published in 1982. The series brings together many better- or lesser-known figures from the left and has them present their favorite erotic photographs. The series ran under the motto "Everyone his own pornographer."[317] Gehrke quotes Borneman's letter of cancellation: "I can't write the foreword. This is for two reasons, both of which came as completely unexpected and unanticipated: either in word or image, a majority of these articles show such little esteem for one's own sex or others, and such an inclination to subordinating or humiliating one's own sex or others, that I see a complete failure of the sexual revolution in them."[318] Gehrke justified herself with reference to the images and the argument that there was an "aggressive, warlike side to eroticism that also has to do with subjugation, humiliation and destruction," one that had only been further repressed after the sexual revolution or masked by "alternative softness" and had now suddenly burst to the surface. Ulrich Greiner, one of the authors (non-leftist) railed against the "drivel of the unity of the body and soul," which boiled down to one thing only: "we should keep lust in check with the bit of reason."[319] Enough. Now it was lust's turn to romp about unrestrained.

Borneman had already voiced his skepticism toward the rampant discourse around sexuality both within the media and relationships, which had less and less to do with his conception of a "sexual revolution." In an interview given during the summer of 1979, he argued that "sexuality is talked about and depicted much too much in the bourgeois institutions, not too little," depriving it of all content in the process.[320] In light of the ubiquitous conversation about sexuality, Borneman even distanced himself from Wilhelm Reich, declaring the latter's assumption that the liberation of society would occur through the liberation of sexuality to be outdated. "I don't believe a word of it any longer. I think there may be one final hope, namely the liberation of sexuality through the liberation of society." That did not come about automatically, however.

Each subsequent dispute similarly revolved around how current trends within the field of sexuality were to be judged. On the one hand, Borneman considered developments in the recently established academic field of sexual science misguided. He criticized the "laziness of contemporary German sexologists," their "refusal to conduct research," the "degradation of German sexology and [its] constant decline as well as . . . in its reputation abroad."[321] This was both unjust and inaccurate; West German sexologists had in fact produced an entire series of empirical studies that considerably expanded understanding about sexual development in society. Among these, Gunter Schmidt's long-term study on changes in student sexuality from 1966 and 1981 represented a crowning achievement, a study later replicated in 1996. In the late 1960s and early 1970s the emphasis lay, for example, with Schmidt and Sigusch's study on worker sexuality from 1968–69, Günter Amendt's examination of adolescent sexuality in the drug subculture (1970), Martin Dannecker and Reimut Reiche's 1974 study on homosexuality, etc. Then there were the numerous interventions by the DGfS—its part in reforming the sexual penal code between 1969 and 1973, in psychosurgery, childhood sexual abuse, decriminalizing homosexuality, and other issues pertaining to the law or sexual politics.[322] Borneman evidently expected more from Sigusch—in particular large empirical studies comparable to those of Alfred Kinsey about the sexual practices of US citizens from the 1940s and 1950s, or William Masters and Virginia Johnson's work on the psychological and physiological mechanisms of sexual behavior in the 1950s and 1960s—and considered the Frankfurt professor's essay collections akin to the culture section in the newspaper. Entirely in keeping with German tradition in the humanities, Sigusch did not want to restrict himself to definitions and measurements, however, but considered sexual research a "subjective science" and sought to grasp its complex phenomena via interpretation.[323] As an enthusiastic review of one of his books noted in *FAZ*, he took up a "decidedly anti-positivist position" that took love to be just as difficult to comprehend fully as our psychological drives, ascribing a secretive quality to them instead that would only profit by its prohibition—all in all, praise was reserved for a "life of the drives that elides social control and assumes a subversive quality."[324] Anti-enlightenment mysticism, was Borneman's rejoinder.

Sigusch's approach also brought him into conflict with a close colleague from Hamburg, Günter Amendt, who criticized Sigusch for adopting the speech of "drives" without first defining them—"especially he," who after all had studied under Adorno, should have recognized that the "need for definitions was pre-critical."[325] His chief critic, however, was Gunter Schmidt, who considered the assumption that energies accumulate internally, then demand to be discharged— what was for him and Eberhard Schorsch both a "vulgar theory of drives"—to be a historically specific ideology that could never be scientifically proved.[326] Instead, Schmidt proceeded from more neutral motives that were not physically determined but guided rather by a variety of intrinsic and extrinsic impulses. He considered Freud's theory of drives to be an opinion conditioned by history and since outdated by the liberalization of sexuality. Presently, control did not occur in the form of repression but rather, as he saw it with reference to Foucault, through satisfying the search for desire.[327]

For his part, Sigusch wanted to bring an end to this turn from the drives, a process that had already gained broad social acceptance. "Motivational psychology," he declared in an attack on Schmidt at the fourteenth DGfS convention in Hamburg, means "the sexual has lost its explosive power, has nothing more to do with tension, pressure, breakthrough, explosion." Rather, it was "without juice or power, image or sound, because [it has been] de-substantiated and rationalized." The Frankfurt professor came out against relinquishing the drives in order to save what he considered the subversive impulse of human action. "What is adhered to, then, is all that is unruly and not yet fully tamed; what is transverse has not yet been set straight; that humans with their urges and abilities have not truly and fully been assimilated by the lowest common denominator."[328] For Sigusch, Eros represented a great secret that could not be fathomed by rational means, in which resided a rebellious force. Freud be praised, this secret could not be disclosed no matter how much sexologists counted or measured. He opposed the "tyranny and nightmare of the factual" to the "anarchy of lust," whereas for Schmidt theoretical positions explaining sexuality were subject to historical change. He could not see how, as Sigusch thought, "combativeness would betray" anyone who "denied his impulses," because the capacity for rage was part of the human condition, with or without drives.[329] According to Schmidt, the intensity of resistance that accompanied the denial of one's drives resulted not from a scholastic dispute about the proper school of thought, but was instead about "mourning," about "the loss of the subversive innocence of sexuality, its unredeemed promise of freedom."[330]

Schmidt's bitter commentary on his friend's crusade gives an impression of the role that Sigusch fashioned for himself: "I confess to murder: of the sexual drive . . . not only have I thought and surmised wrongly, I have failed politically and morally. The camps have now been cleanly divided, the wheat separated from the chaff. The fall from grace has been named for what it is, the criminals branded, and unto Volkmar Sigusch be the power and the glory to do so."[331]

The discontent had long been palpable by the time Sigusch and Borneman came to open blows in 1986–87. The conflict was not limited to the publication of *Sexualität konkret* or the feuding associations; in a laudatory discussion of Helmut Kentler's *Taschenlexikon Sexualität* (Paperback Dictionary of Sexuality) for issue 4 of *Sexualität konkret*, Sigusch deemed Borneman's *Lexikon der Liebe* "quite unpleasant" and opined that he could "do without all the indexed slips of paper" "with a clear conscience."[332] The next year, in a review of Sigusch's collected volume *Vom Trieb und von der Liebe* (On the Drives and Love) for *Psychologie heute*, Borneman criticized the author's supposed ignorance of academic research on sex and a tendency to "freewheeling inventions": "the stylistic reaching and the opportunistic prose Sigusch offers us once again in his little volume is no substitute for research."[333] Two years later he opened up a general line of attack in a collected volume edited by Ulrike Heider that undertook a critical revision of the "myth of new sensuality" and was conceived of as an "answer to the erotic irrationalism of contemporary cultural output, with its anti-enlightenment approach to thinkers like de Sade, Nietzsche and Bataille," and which also featured contributions from Giesela Elsner, Lothar Baier and Joachim Bruhn.[334] In his piece Borneman accused Sigusch, with reference to *Sexualität konkret* and the 1984 *Vom Trieb und von der Liebe*, of having associated himself "in the most cringeworthy fashion" with the new romanticism.[335] At issue was the latter's contention that the life of the drives was "anarchic and irrational, instinctual, indecent and unclean," that the "the vast majority of the editors at international scientific journals would reject the coarse song of love and praise of the drives that I look to sing here, some indignant, some bemused."[336] "Rightly so," came Borneman's reply, which recognized within Sigusch's writing a reactionary force that had to be set within a broader context. Sigusch's "mockery of science and the rational mind, this apology for the irrational, advances in lockstep with the new counter reformation, the new renunciation of the classical enlightenment, the decline of the great French tradition of clear thought, with the nostalgic wave of Nietzsche-Wagner-Hitler, with the infiltration of the 'poetic' into what is verifiable and what falsifiable in 'new' French philosophy." Borneman by no means labeled Sigusch a "follower" of such a "wave," as the latter accused him of in his article for *Pro Familia*. As Sigusch had nonetheless conceded in his own book, "whoever wants to sing the praises of the drive must pay terribly close attention not to fall into bad company, for it is surrounded by all the ideologies of blood and soil, just as it is beguiled by the disciples of the new irrationalism."[337] Borneman did not say that Sigusch had become an ideologue of blood and soil, but considered such statements—when made within the context of the current, postmodernist rehabilitation of anti-rationalism, as well as trends within contemporary West German culture that found new words of praise for Ernst Jünger, Leni Riefenstahl, and Arno Breker—to be dangerous, as they seemed to point to a "romantic and irrational worldview."[338] In a positive review of Heider's book for *FAZ*, Hans-Martin Lohmann noted with approval the authors' view "that the ultimately wistful, religiously inspired program of the critique of rationalism is indebted to a regressive, resigned gesture that takes cover behind the position of an enlightenment grown self-reflexive, and which casually appeals to ideological reserves whose dubious fascistic footing shines through at multiple points."[339]

Borneman exaggerated fully when he wrote, referring to Sigusch's remarks on "lower love," that the "mockery" described above went "hand in hand with a new justification for torment, torture and cruelty to humans." Sigusch had in truth given an ambivalent image of love, first sketching out the utopia of harmonious coexistence in his "high song of love," "easy, cheerful and childlike, like an evening breeze on the Aegean," then following it with the other, "perhaps more familiar" side in his "lower song of love, which was "an orgy of the lowest forms of cruelty. It is full of refined humiliations, frantic disempowerment, bitter disappointment, malicious revenge and spiteful aggression. It is greedy, clammy, all devouring, boundless, breathless, touchy, hypocritical and insatiable. It is home to feelings of danger, not of well-being: hatred, fear, rage, guilt, weakness, defeat, envy and jealous obsession. . . . This love is egocentric and asocial, a close relation of madness and obsessive desire."[340] Sigusch not only named love's ambivalent qualities—for him it was the less ideal aspects that clearly outweighed: "one stanza from the high [song], a thousand from the low's daily chorus and lifelong reprise." More recently, as he writes in his book from 2005 *Neosexualitäten* (Neosexualities), "sexual democracy" is still a "horror," while he reserves his highest praise for "perverse lust." It is what keeps sexual relationships alive: "Fantasies must be 'dirty' because purity, cleanliness, conscientiousness and rationality are poisons that drive out any kind of eroticism."[341] Lust emerges in the dark zones of what is illegitimate, of the forbidden—where the Catholic Church and its followers have always located them, in other words, with the only difference being that they are now interpreted positively.

By the mid-1980s the atmosphere had grown poisonous, a fact that was not lost on Borneman. He wrote to his new girlfriend Sigrid Standow, a doctor interested in pursuing a further degree within the field of sexual science, that while he would like to recommend her to Schorsch and Sigusch, he could not facilitate a connection "because I stupidly angered both of them with not particularly enthusiastic reviews of their latest books."[342] The fight continued in a *Der Spiegel* article from early summer 1986 that reported on the feud among German sexologists, stating that thirty professionals, along with the three hundred or so cronies in their field had gotten in a scrape "over the others' scientific qualifications, and the one who had gotten his frizzy mop the most tousled was Volkmar Sigusch."[343] In this case, the context of the article is illuminating: coming shortly after the "Operation AIDS" issue of *Sexualität konkret* had taken *Der Spiegel* to task for its sensationalist and homophobic reporting on HIV/AIDS, the article was written solely at Sigusch's expense and filled with arguments from the opposing camp: aggression toward colleagues, behavior worthy of a stag fight, and scanty research.[344] On the "day of vengeance" (Gremliza), *Der Spiegel* cited Borneman's criticism of the "lower song of love" (the magazine let the other side, the "higher song," fall completely to the wayside) from his article in Heider's collected volume, which had appeared that spring; Borneman was quoted as saying that Sigusch "did not [describe] objective reality, but a subjective experience of misery."[345]

By fall 1986 Ernest Borneman's wrath had still not abated, and he now accused Sigusch of having "urged" "those ill with AIDS [to] infect their sexual partners with an easy conscience, because it was unworthy of being human to give up the life of the drives."[346] This was a fairly audacious interpretation of what Sigusch had written, which only contained the idea that organizing one's sexual life rationally and thereby controlling it "skipped out on reality."[347] Borneman certainly felt challenged by Sigusch's categorization of sexual researchers into "rational sexologists" (also "the affirmatives") and "subjective sexologists" ("the critics"), with the former taking their cues "directly" from the results of natural science and the latter operating "in a halting, playful or speculative" manner. The affirmatives set stock in "instruction and control," while the critics adhered to "what is subjective in sex" and "mourned" "the calculated exclusion of individual drive-love." To the "rational sexologist" Borneman, Sigusch's declaring himself to be a "subjective sexologist" likely came across as far too adventurous in the context of HIV/AIDS. As a doctor, Sigusch's time would be better spent pursuing AIDS research and searching for a cure. What was more, the former DGfS chairman had also recently come under fire from the women's movement; at the 1985 DGfS annual conference in Hannover, Alice Schwarzer labeled him a "pseudo-progressive author" and accused him, based on his texts, of pursuing sexual science without consideration for the female sex.[348] By 1986 Sigusch stood under a great deal of pressure; seeking the easier way out of a situation that had become too much for him, he took Schwarzer's side and launched a counterattack against Borneman. From the DGSS side, Gindorf saw a tit-for-tat response in Sigusch's attacks. It was the hour of "revenge"; "whoever knows Sigusch knows that he cannot stand any other positions or personalities on 'his' territory."[349]

Volkmar Sigusch republished his "Der Ratschläger" article in 1990 in slightly expanded form and continued to maintain the piece's basic conclusions in successive publications on the history of sexology.[350] Borneman—indisputably a controversial figure in the field—was nevertheless included in a biographical dictionary of sexual researchers compiled by Sigusch and Günter Grau, in a work that acquired temporal dimensions worthy of Borneman himself ("we've searched and collected for three decades, and studied and made notes for one"). The volume featured the biographies of 199 deceased researchers from the nineteenth and twentieth centuries from within Germany and abroad, including some two dozen figures active after 1945 but who were no longer living, among them Hans Bürger-Prinz, Hans Giese, Helmut Kentler, and Eberhard Schorsch. While Sigusch was certainly far from conceding Borneman his desired role of "Nestor," he still considered him a prominent sexual researcher despite everything. Familiar points of criticism prevail in Borneman's entry, and the praise comes tipped with poison: "Admirably, he succeeded in pursuing an academic career without having completed secondary schooling or a demonstrable university course."[351] Nevertheless, Borneman had clearly been a stimulating teacher and played a leading role in professional organizations. The fact that his works "were practically no longer cited . . . for a number of years" now, the entry continues, is generally the fate due to empirical research and time-bound opinions.

Drive and Punishment

A number of years ago Gunter Schmidt described the context in which his second study on student sexuality from 1981 emerged; his account may help explain Borneman's pessimism and dogged fight. Entirely in keeping with Dagmar Herzog's findings, Schmidt wrote that since the end of the 1970s, "the blues had [descended] over the landscape of love": "Sex and relationships changed, but high hopes went unfulfilled, and contentment—political and private—a dream deferred. The swan song of the 'sexual revolution' was delivered with the greatest pathos in . . . *Sexualität konkret*. 'Eroticism is just loneliness' went the saying, with Bob Dylan mumbling somewhere in the background. And with a great sadness an important process began: sexuality's demystification from its overload."[352] Volkmar Sigusch was surprised by Schmidt's view, which was little wonder given Sigusch's earlier defense of *Sexualität konkret* against Borneman's criticism on account of its being particularly optimistic and progressive, finding in its diverse depictions of "new sensuality" a sign of the subversive power of the drives.[353] For his part, Borneman's criticism did not spring from reasons of ego but from the attitudes and practices it depicted, which had nothing to do with his concept of a liberated sexuality. Gunter Schmidt's explanation carried further; he argued that the popularity of an ethos of negotiation in sexuality—as opposed to normative opinions of what counts as "good" and "right," that is, what it is that unites the involved parties—was not the result of a belief in the "ability to rationalize sexuality," but rather pointed to the "stirring belief in its *irrationality*."[354]

> Venerable images and concepts within our culture—sexuality as a drive and form of wildness, as the final refuge of our human nature, as an unrestrained, taboo-shattering and transformative force, an eternal drama and an involvement with life and death—we reverently appreciate all of this in

the cinema, as recently with *The Titanic*, while having long known that all that was yesterday and has since gone under like the ship. Thus we are on the verge of dissolving the myth of damnation and salvation by way of sexuality, one to which the student movement also subscribed. "Drive" is no longer a metaphor for sex, but rather a search for stimulation, amusement, thrills; the goal is not satisfaction in the sense of peace or a lack of needs, but rather diverting oneself with excitations and collecting sensations.

Just as enthusiasm waned for the libidinous and anarchic qualities to which Sigusch gave voice in the early 1980s and continued to represent, the entire basis for psychoanalysis was similarly called into question.[355] Borneman had surely watched on with some satisfaction as Catholicism and patriarchy's standards for sexuality were shaken to the core—he himself had made every effort to do as much. It was not his doing, however, that sexuality also be "thoroughly cleared" of its association with psychoanalysis, and thereby demystified and made less dramatic. He offered resistance but also made concessions when the principle of enlightenment seemed to suffer for it. When Sigusch's thought drifted off into the irrational, he took Schmidt's side.

Yet the fascination with unleashing impulses that is so evident in *Sexualität konkret* and other venues could not be put off so quickly. It was the flip side of the new federal government's reactionary sexual regime, which arrived in the form of restrictions imposed in response to the process of individualization. In 1985 Jürgen Habermas made the case for a "new obscurity" in his work "Die Neue Unübersichtlichkeit," arguing for an "everyday communicative practice and method of discursive decision-making that can put the participants themselves in the position of developing concrete possibilities for a better and less precarious life shaped according to *individual* needs and insights, and according to *individual* initiatives."[356] At the same time, Habermas saw the emancipatory potential of "self-realization" as undercut by a politics that, aided by traditional culture, sought to preserve "the ruling powers of conventional morality, patriotism, bourgeois religion and popular culture." By the same token, "conventional morality" should again prevail within the realm of sexuality. With its plans for an "intellectual and moral turning point" in politics and culture, the CDU/FDP government under Helmut Kohl sought to bring about a rollback in liberalization, which under the catchphrase "1968" was considered responsible for a general decline in morality and tradition, but especially regarding sexuality. Under the leadership of Heiner Geißler, the new ministry for youth and families did away with the seven-part video and workbook series *Betrifft: Sexualität* (Topic: Sexuality), a project from 1976 produced for extracurricular youth work that no longer matched the moral precepts of the government.[357] It was not government policy alone, however, that led Ulrike Heider to discuss the 1980s as a high-water mark in the "contempt [both] for reason" as well as "measured consideration or conversation in connection with sexuality, including the policies once so highly valued as enlightened." Like other defenders of the sexual revolution in Germany, including Borneman, Heider made Michel Foucault out to be the intellectual provocateur for this shift, with the recently rediscovered leftist Nietzschean Georges Bataille in the role of prompter, "the elder statesman of all enthusiasts of the mortal passions, the abysses of human lust, victimhood, death and sacrificial death."[358] According to Foucault, all social relations were permeated by power relations; this included the field of sexuality. "No desire without power or the exercise of power," Heider writes. "It is from here that Foucault proceeds, with only a passing grin for the "humanist fantasy of a sexuality that is perfectly developed for all." Seen in this way, Foucault's perspective was not only political, but amounted to a counterreformation when it came to sexuality.[359]

Among the left, too, there arose a perception that the tender form of sex in which the hippies engaged had put an end to lust. "The social project of a 'soft prick,'" Reinhard Mohr crudely joked, "not only ran up against biological, but also cultural limits."[360] Resurrecting the idea of sex as an incomprehensible, demonic primal force, sexual desire, indeed, the nostalgia for a "more intense life" (Cora Stephan), could be satisfied only in connection with subordination, violence, and pain. In 1983 feminist Barbara Sichtermann took aim at "pancake sexuality," going on to explain that "a sexual relationship without 'militancy,' without pain-desire is something artificial, an absurdity."[361] The fascination with Carlos Saura's 1983 film of the opera *Carmen* and the ensuing wave of confessions among women on the left to fantasies of passion, eroticism, lust and even rape also provided a resonant chamber for "any amount of excessive kitsch," as Silvia Bovenschen wrote in 1988.[362] While the link between desire and violence remained a controversial topic in the women's movement throughout the 1980s as well, in 1988 the magazine *Emma* started its "PorNo" campaign, which was directed against "propagating and enacting the humiliation of or contempt for women" and demanded an anti-pornography law.[363] Critics of the campaign feared a rollback entirely in keeping with the government's intentions. Günter Amendt, for example, rejected such a law despite his criticisms of sexuality's commercialization, as the regulation of "sexual relations by means of laws and state executive bodies" would create a climate of moral panic and reanimate the spirit of law and order, instead of emancipating the individual.[364] To be sure, the *Emma* campaign also addressed a problematic contemporary phenomenon: the rampant romanticization of pornography, prostitution, and sadomasochism within leftist circles. Confronted by such a situation, it is small wonder Borneman showed skepticism toward a lack of restraint in talking about sexuality that came under the pretext of "breaking with taboos" at any cost; for him, free sexuality was directly tied to the notion of equality, which also meant freedom from compulsion, violence, and exploitation. In his mind, sexuality and society were directly connected; those who acted in a spirit of partnership and altruism during sex did the same in the nonsexual realms, and vice versa. He thus saw his vision of a liberated sexuality fundamentally threatened from three angles: the anti-educational incursions of the Kohl government, the fashion of a philosophy that was skeptical of rationality, and sexual overkill of every variety, even the most brutal, as driven by its commercialization. The threat increased when, starting around 1983, the rise of HIV/AIDS placed a potent weapon in the hands of society's standard bearers—against promiscuity in general and homosexuality in particular.[365] Apocalyptic visions of societal collapse were conjured up in order to bring West Germans grown overly permissive back into line with controlled forms of sexual intercourse and fixed, heterosexual relationships. Violations were threatened with jail time, as happened to a number of individuals with HIV in Bavaria. The defensive lines weakened as increasing numbers of early protagonists from the revolt of 1968 backed away from the idea of "sexual revolution," including many a figure from the alternative scene, from Reinhard Mohr to Matthias Horx, and one of the movement's leading intellectual forces, Reimut Reiche, who—now reformed—retroactively dismissed the idea of a "guilt-free sexuality, an act of the drives without guilt" as an illusion.[366]

The year 1990 saw the end of Borneman's popular columns in the *Neue Revue* and the *Arbeiter-Zeitung*; his stint at the *Neue Kronenzeitung* also came to a close. Instead, from the middle of the year on he wrote for *Salto*, a newly christened leftist magazine with high aspirations, which, as he wrote to a friend, "was made by apostate Communists and shares my own baseline attitude—fundamentally Marxist, but hostile to the Communist party."[367] This reduction in work—after the *Salto* column finished in early 1993, he would not take on any comparable projects with other publications—was accompanied by a growing general frustration that had gripped him since Eva's death, privately at first, then politically since the "change" in the GDR. A new inability to assert his will at the *Neue Revue* further served as an indicator that his importance as a public figure had diminished. The end of Borneman's eight years at the magazine in December 1990 was brought about by a conflict that arose when the editor responsible for his column was out sick. Borneman insisted that his texts be printed without changes, a stipulation that was first agreed upon in 1982 and had been implemented for years. Nevertheless, throughout 1990 the number of editorial interventions had increased, meant to adapt his pieces to the moment. Borneman not only resisted paraphrasing the original text, but took particular issue with any moderation of his sparse style. "The columns sound more and more like Erika Berger. Yet I think, feel and write totally differently. If my style doesn't remain intact, my content goes with it."[368] Most importantly, Borneman complained, the magazine had decided to "only publish 'positive' letters to the editor with 'positive' answers in my column."[369] To his surprise, editor in chief Klaus Wolfram did not defer but fired the indignant author without further ado. Borneman received 20,000 Deutschmarks as a consolation prize, but as he wrote to his old editor Jean-Jacques Kroeber, he was personally affected, "aggrieved and hurt."[370] He had asked Wolfram whether three columns in one periodical "wasn't a little much. But I wouldn't have supposed that he would cancel my columns instead of Berger's. I was dumb, in other words." There was truth to this. Borneman had underestimated Erika Berger, who sported exclusively journalistic credentials and was also the spouse of the magazine's former editor in chief. In the late 1980s Berger experienced an astronomic rise to become "the sex expert of the nation" (Oswalt Kolle) with the television advice show

Eine Chance für die Liebe (A Chance at Love, broadcast beginning in 1987 on RTL plus) and presented a much more attractive alternative for the magazine than the contrarian septuagenarian.[371]

A Permanent Guest on Talk Shows

Throughout the 1970s and 1980s, Borneman was likely television's most frequently consulted expert on sexuality. His ability to provoke reached its greatest potential on the format, with his presence enlivening the German airwaves from 1973 onward and proliferating in the late 1970s on live talk shows. Television series like *3 nach 9* (3 after 9, airing on the third channel of Northern German Broadcasting) and *Je später der Abend* (The Later the Evening, on West German Broadcasting 3/ARD) brought the contemporary ideal of a "culture for all" to the world of the screen, a notion that aimed at bringing as many people into the fold as possible in debates about how to arrange society. Talk shows undergirded the communicative aspect of television as a receptive medium and served as an important mediator in the heated debates coursing throughout society.[372] In the 1980s, conversations explicitly about sex became a new topic for the talk shows. They also helped individuals to orient themselves by meeting a growing need for information and direction, as well as advising on and presenting models for self-identification or differentiation. As media researcher Heinz Bonfadelli has shown, talk shows fulfilled an increasing public need for "personalization, emotionalization and staging," and provided experts who were able to speak knowledgeably about a topic but also to evaluate "the experiences and knowledge of the layperson," whose "authentically" perceived experiences now found a forum and served viewers as a "parasocial comparison."[373] By presenting disagreements between experts at odds with one another and the opinions and practices of people "like you and me," the "therapy of saying it all" served to demonstrate different ways of living life that could help viewers situate themselves.[374] Borneman filled an ideal slot as an expert in these discussion rounds, not only as a professional with long-standing experience in television, but also because he never avoided a conflict that came his way. His role was that of the leftist agitator, a defender of the sexual revolution, women's issues, and socialism—although his concrete opinions on the matter under discussion were rarely predictable. It was built into the logic of the format, which was set on emotionalization, that this combination would enrage other talk show guests and viewers alike, all of whom let their opinions be known. At the same time, the mixture mobilized the ideas' numerous supporters, creating a polarization par excellence. One can speak about "staged fights" only to a limited extent, as the positions represented real differences within public opinion.

Borneman was a provocateur only when it came to content; formally speaking he did not break character. In fact, his positions gained acceptance because he did justice to his role as expert, explaining why his supporters were correct in sincere fashion. The transcript from one talk show about teenage sex and abuse contains a comment from an audience member that articulates a common perception: the "calm certainty" of his appearance "leads one to suspect that you know what you are talking about, and are on steady footing with reference to the facts you give."[375] It was not only Borneman's well-considered scientific arguments but his steadfast quality. The same audience member was "impressed by how openly and candidly you have represented your perspective, even though all the other discussion participants were against it, and public (or published) opinion without a doubt." The combative streak in the nonconformist made his halo shine all the brighter.

Borneman took part in numerous discussions on a host of West German channels throughout the 1970s and 1980s. Shortly after the premiere of the series *3 nach 9*, he was invited alongside Inge Feltrinelli, Conrad Ahlers, the "Hamburg call girl 'Nicole,'" and her colleague "Bärbel" to participate in a 11 December 1975 round-table on the topic "The Year of the Woman: Is the End of Patriarchy in Sight?"[376] In 1982 he made an appearance on Sender Freies Berlin alongside Rosa von Praunheim, Carmen Thomas, and Elisabeth Motschmann, a pastor's wife, on *Arena*, the pro-gram of the ARD cultural magazine broadcast. A conversation on the subject "The New Nudes—A New Discovery?" followed a striptease by an Italian performance art-ist[377] and took a turn for the startling when sixty-year-old Helga Götze, well-known in West Berlin as a tireless sex propagandist, insinuated herself into the conversa-tion from the audience, getting a rise out of Motschmann ("Shameless"), who then found herself under attack from von Praunheim and "Götze fan" Borneman, until the "freewheeling discussion" (*Der Spiegel*) fully slipped from the moderator's con-trol.[378] On 26 May 1991 Borneman joined Harald Schmidt for a discussion on the show *Schmidteinander*; the host introduced him as a "distinguished guest" and "one of Europe's most renowned sexologists."[379] Borneman struck a dignified, informal appearance for these occasions, sporting silver-gray, combed-back hair and casual clothing. Speaking with a sonorous voice in print-ready phrases, he would pause visibly to consider the questions he was asked, making his case seriously but reacting with a quick wit and allowing himself the occasional jest. Borneman also discussed his private situation openly. The conversation on *Schmidteinander* revolved around common sex problems in marriage. When asked about his relationship with a woman who was forty-two years his junior, Borneman replied that normally such a large age gap would mean things did not go well. Nor did they live together. He went on to say, however, that it wasn't only older men who could be with younger women, but also older women who could be with younger men—even if the latter arrangement found less social acceptance. Once one's needs were recognized, the person should follow them. "If anything is harmful, it is conforming to the prevailing norms. That is always harmful."

One revealing source for the public response that Borneman's appearances elic-ited are recordings of viewer calls to the Austrian Broadcasting Company (Öster-reichischer Rundfunk, ORF) directly following the programs' broadcast. The calls show with crystal clarity just how polarizing he was, with those who had been left behind by the cultural shift giving vent to their anger, pining for days gone by and lamenting the decline in morality. It should be kept in mind that only the most agitated among the audience would have reached for their phones; for those who were less decided, the shows provided an opportunity to learn more and form their own opinions about an area with which they were only partially familiar and to scrutinize their own thoughts and actions.

Beginning in 1976 the ORF series *Club 2*—often moderated by the same host as *3 nach 9*, actress Marianne Koch—took up specifically controversial topics, making it a subject of daily conversation—all the more so as there was no set end time to the program, so that conversations would carry on. A 1979 broadcast during which Nina Hagen illustrated how women pleasure themselves caused a particular stir. Borneman, now an Austrian citizen, played a key role in this setting—mostly as a guest, but at times as a moderator.

One episode of *Club 2* moderated by Koch that was regarded as particularly scandalous had the provocative title "Lolita 1981: Childhood Sexuality and Commercial Exploitation." Borneman appeared alongside a schoolgirl, her father, a child psychologist, a teacher, a mother, and a teaching apprentice. ORF received 257 calls immediately following the show's broadcast—a large number that would only rise in the days to follow—that contained almost exclusively negative messages: "Borneman is a perverted old fool. His time is long gone." "A perverted swine." "Borneman himself is disturbed; he shouldn't talk about others." "Borneman can't force a population to his opinion. The types of behavior he talks about don't exist; he's making it up." "Nothing but pigs. They all belong in the gas chamber. A bunch of disturbed people." "Bringing Mr. Borneman into Austrian high schools is typical of the left. It contributes to the depravity of the youth." "Borneman is an imposition for the audience; does he always have to be on?!" Positive voices were in the minority: "Borneman is completely right—children masturbate."[380] Such comments laid bare the strongly opposed views that prevailed within society not only regarding important issues in cultural change—questions of sexuality in particular, and above all the sexuality of children—but also regarding Borneman's person, a figure with whom some identified and who for others appeared to be evil incarnate. He was also made a projective surface for xenophobic, anti-intellectual, and especially antisemitic positions.

The call transcript for a *Club 2* episode "The Porno Industry: Freedom vs. Human Dignity?" that Borneman moderated, for example—whose guests included two porno actresses, a representative from the Catholic Academic Association (Katholischer Akademikerverband), a feminist student, and René Durand, the head of the Hamburg red-light establishment "Salambo"—featured comments like the following: "Mr. Borneman is a dubious, repulsive, lip-smacking old lecher." "All the guests are perverts." "Borneman is a swine. The ultimate scum in this club." "Why isn't it mentioned that these people are Jews?" "Borneman should have stayed put in the camps."

The strongest reactions, however, were elicited by "Sex in the Alpine Republic," a *Club 2* episode from 12 February 1985 that addressed the findings in Borneman's book on sexuality in Austria, *Rot-weiß-rotes Himmelbett* (Red White Red Four-Poster Bed). In the role of adversary the show had Martin Humer, the notorious "porno hunter" and sworn enemy of sex education and abortion, who had attacked the book's author for years. In his book Borneman certified the Austrians as being sexually inhibited, a conclusion that had already triggered a wave of anger leading up to the broadcast that had an involuntary humor to it; as part of a public opinion survey by the *Kurier*, Karl Moik, an elder statesman of television from the program *Musikantenstadl* (Musician's Barn), replied, "Well, I don't know how it is for others, but in Kärnten, or more specifically at home, things run totally normally as far as that is concerned."[381] During the show, which sought to ratchet up conflict by making the most of the hostility between the "porno hunter versus sex researcher," Humer turned into his own worst enemy when his absurd positions took center stage. Borneman mostly stayed quiet throughout, in part because his opponent did not let him get a word in edgewise. The reactions of the public demonstrated that the good old days were gone forever; numerous newspaper reports mocked Humer as a moral standard bearer.[382] Telephone responses—214 the day of the broadcast, 345 the next—were mixed. Many criticized Humer, and it was repeatedly asked, "Why doesn't Mr. Borneman speak more?" The familiar antisemitic and anti-foreigner comments were also in evidence, however: "Is Borneman a Jew?" "Borneman should send a couple of properly circumcised men our way." "It is outrageous what that foreigner Borneman makes us out to be." "That foreigner Borneman shouldn't blacken our country or us Austrians." "Borneman should go back to where he belongs." At the same time, numerous callers came to his defense: "Borneman should be allowed to speak more; he is far and away more sensible." "Borneman is putting up with far too much; why doesn't Ms. Koch step in?" "Koch and Borneman are the most intelligent conversation participants." "Excellent, finally Mr. Borneman is putting up a fight." Once again, numerous viewers complained about the sex researcher's frequent appearances on screen: "Why is the terrible, filthy Borneman always on?"[383]

Summarizing reactions to this and other *Club 2* episodes, a pattern emerges of a minority supporting Borneman's position and defending him as a pioneer in sex education, while a majority responded with aggressive criticism, often open antisemitism, and hostility to foreigners. Borneman was constantly consulted in the role of an academic, which brought forth anti-intellectual attacks. His age increasingly became a factor; while opponents disparaged him as an "old lecher," others saw in him an authority given his experience, a sort of "grand old man" of sex research, which heightened identification among viewers favorably disposed to sexual liberalization. His own interest in securing himself privileged status is on display in *Die wilden Alten* (The Old Savages), an Austrian television project conceived of in 1986 that set Borneman alongside cultural luminaries Alfred Hrdlicka, Christine Nöstlinger, and Robert Jungk. The show intended to portray them as models of obstinacy and lifelong engagement, "those rare examples of intellectual youthfulness who do not keep silent for propriety's sake, who doggedly oppose the zeitgeist and forbid themselves to lose pace."[384]

Borneman also went on the radio in the classical role of counselor, starting in 1985 on Radio Luxemburg's *Prima intim*, where he answered three to five calls per show. The call-in format of the show came from the United States, where presenting live counseling sessions on personal problems to a broad public had achieved tremendous popularity. It was no different on the European continent; the "Sex Hotline" became an institution on the ORF's third radio program, *Ö3*. The program went live in early 1988, broadcasting on a two-week schedule between midnight and 2:00 a.m. and featuring a rotating cast including Borneman, journalist and psychologist Gerti Senger, sex therapist Rotraud Perner, and Gerhard Schmutzer of Vienna AIDS relief.[385] Combing a casual moderation style with a well-matched musical soundtrack and counseling, the show became a "hit," especially because the late-night conversations succeeded in creating an intimate atmosphere that facilitated speaking about sexuality.[386]

To be sure, the population in Austria was not necessarily well disposed to Borneman. "Nearly without competition" as a sex expert, a founder of the Austrian Society for Sexual Research (Österreichische Gesellschaft für Sexualforschung, ÖGS), and for a long time the sole sexual scientist holding a professorship, Borneman provided an ideal image of the enemy to anyone for whom the changes in tradition since the 1960s had gone too far.[387] With the ÖGS, over which he presided as its founding chairman from 1979 to 1985, Borneman had awoken Austrian sexology "from its sleeping beauty with a kiss," as his former student Josef Aigner put it, creating a gathering point in the process for all those who wanted to take up a national tradition that had since faded, and wasn't looked upon favorably in many circles.[388] His growing media presence went one step further in making him an ideal target of reactionary efforts. He was hounded in particular by Martin Humer, mentioned above, who for the liberal Austrian public was the incarnation of a backward-looking Catholic rural population that stood opposed to all progress. Born in 1925, Humer was a photographer by trade who gained recognition in the early 1970s as a politically right-wing guardian of public morality. He railed against the screening of pornographic films (or those he considered to be so), and in 1981 he inspired a campaign against a candid educational theater piece staged by Rote Grütze, a children and youth theater from Berlin, that was entitled *Was heißt hier Liebe?* (What Does Love Mean Here?) and was set to tour various Austrian cities. Humer spoke of "the moral decay of the people" and called for a performance ban in the name of a silent majority,[389] with partial success: the performance in Linz was banned due to protests staged by parents and teachers; in Innsbruck it was canceled after a bomb threat. Throughout the 1980s Humer reported Borneman to the authorities on multiple occasions; all were dismissed, but it was not merely a matter of the public sphere, Borneman's lawyer, and the courts.[390] Humer put pressure on bookstores that sold

Borneman's books, nor did he stop when he reached Borneman's own backyard but proceeded, now by virtuous means, to send the aging sexual researcher scrambling, with mailers sent out to the residents of Scharten denouncing Borneman. Exhausted, Borneman turned to his lawyer for help, asking "if we can somehow get rid of the terrible Humer."[391] Humer could not be shaken off, however, and outlived his nemesis by years.

Pedophilia and Child Abuse

Borneman did not change his opinions regarding the sexuality of children once they came under pressure from the conservative turn in the 1970s and early '80s. At the same time, a debate had emerged among pedagogues in the magazine *Betrifft:Erziehung* (Topic: Education) around the question "Does it hurt children when sexuality is not only spoken about between educator and student?"[392] Among actors from "1968" there prevailed a general opinion that the legitimate sexuality of children was persecuted, while an all-in-all violent society, including all of its "poisonous pedagogy," took out its anger on those in its keep. As early as 1963 Theodor W. Adorno had attacked the hypocritical defense of childhood innocence, noting that "unauthorized tenderness toward minors is still punished more severely than when parents or masters beat them half to death."[393] Borneman himself saw the increasing vehemence of the conservative pushback toward the end of the 1970s as a cultural struggle between a reactionary and a progressive camp and threw himself headlong into the debate, pulling no punches in a 1978 handbook published by Wilhelm Fink Verlag about the emergence of "children's culture." In his article on the topic of "sexuality," Borneman drew on ethnological studies by Bronislaw Malinowski, Margaret Mead, and Peter Buch that investigated the sexual life of children in the Pacific region, describing sexual intercourse between children and the practical instruction of sexually mature boys by older women in a matter-of-fact manner, contrasting it to the cold attitude taken by West German society, in which a Berlin youth group's failure to separate sexes by tent on a camping trip to Scandinavia had been cause for scandal.[394] "As opposed to us, where children are regarded as sexless and any effort made by an adult to prepare a child for sexual responsibility is seen as a form of betrayal of one's pedagogical duty, the Balinese viewed their educative mission precisely as practicing one's sexual roles." Borneman criticized the Old World for having

> somewhere, totally arbitrarily and varying country by country . . . [drawn] an age boundary between what is allowed and what is forbidden. . . . At the same time, it is implied that the older person must use violence to reach his goal. *Pedophilia* is confused with *pedosadism*, and the *gerontophilia* of an immense number of children and youth looking for older partners is ignored, as though the desire to couple flows only from the older to the younger, and never from the younger to the older.[395]

For Borneman, the "in and of itself harmless and developmentally supportive act" between children and grown-ups caused fear and had a negative impact on the child only because of the permanent warnings, because of prohibition and punishment. In this and other texts he drew repeatedly on Reinhart Lempp, a well-respected child and youth psychiatrist from the University of Tübingen who maintained—much in line with Alfred Kinsey—that bringing sexual actions before a court put much greater stress on children than the act itself and advocated for declaring sexual contact between children and adults that occurred without physical or psychological violence exempt from punishment. "It is only by investigating whether something shameful or punishable has occurred that the thought forces itself upon him [the child]," Borneman wrote, "that what would otherwise scarcely have bothered him might be shameful or punishable." Sexologists from Hamburg and Frankfurt had protested a brochure released by Baden Württemberg's Ministry of the Interior for the same reason; "sexual behavior is equated with 'bad' behavior" throughout the entire text, thereby instilling in the child a "lifelong fear of love." Borneman questioned the incest prohibition on similar grounds, suggesting, contrary to popular belief, there was no scientific basis; it was instead the "arbitrary power of the lawmakers" that ruled the day.[396] A bundle of papers from Borneman's estate containing numerous quotations and copies of handwritten letters has those involved explaining that intercourse between children and adults—in this case, relations within families—could be a beautiful and satisfying experience, but one accompanied by fears of being found out and persecuted.[397] The extent to which Borneman's material contained opposing views and the relative proportions of each must be left for another study—his theories at any rate evidently drew from an empirical basis, about whose representative quality, nonetheless, no further conclusions can be drawn presently.

When a debate about child abuse broke out in 1980, triggered by a campaign to legalize sex between adults and children started by groups of pedophiles, positions like these came under attack.[398] It became common practice to distance oneself publicly from Sigmund Freud's theories, while books by Florence Rush and Alice Miller raised interest. This early debate chiefly concerned the abuse of young girls, a topic for which the women's movement felt well qualified. In 1982 in the magazine *Brigitte*, eighty-one women reported what had happened to them, an event that had a snowball effect as more and more spoke out about their own experiences.[399] The following year the first local self-help group for women who had been abused as children was founded in West Berlin under the name "Wildwasser" (White water). In the years to come such groups would form in numerous cities throughout West Germany, eventually taking institutional form as counseling centers. Such groups also viewed it as their mission to expose the culprits, feeding a wave of paranoia in the early 1990s regarding abuse that grew with an ever-expanding perpetrator profile. "As opposed to the former 'child abuser' [*Kinderschänder*], conceived of as an abnormality," Ulrike Heider writes, "the 'culprit' [*Täter*] is now seen as an entirely normal man. This was in keeping with feminist logic and the discourse surrounding rape."

Beyond the positive effects that came from public attention to victims' suffering, this development also brought questionable symptoms in tow, such as wrongful accusations and the resuscitation of a "sound popular sentiment" that was able to accomodate traditional sexual enmities. Last but not least, the weaponry of prohibition and punishment in sexual political policy again became socially acceptable. In the early 1980s "the pedosexuals" pressure group was allowed more space to maneuver within the alternative scene, while opinion remained divided among sexologists.[400] For his part, Helmut Kentler recognized "a possibility for therapy" in intimate relationships between adults and children, and Eberhard Schorsch, like many of his colleagues, held the relevant paragraphs 174–176 in the sexual legal code to be "not rationally justified," while Günter Amendt raised the concern that given the real differential in power, pedophilia meant adults' freedom to act against the weaker.[401] Amendt voiced his opinion on the question once again shortly before his death and at the height of the recently rekindled debate, simultaneously distancing himself from the "discourse of child abuse" (Gunter Schmidt), taking account of the "tragic" situation of pedophiles, and criticizing a trend driven by media hype of abetting discipline and distance in regaining their position as pedagogical principles.[402]

Borneman likewise distanced himself from the "abuse" of children by adults; for him the very notion of a free sexuality was directed expressly against violent forms and their idealization. He continued to insist however, on the right of children to develop their own sexuality together with those of the same age or with adults, considering the will of the child to be decisive. He noted the publication between 1982 and 1984 of an entire succession of bestsellers whose subject of child sexual assault brought significant public resonance and high sales. In his view, the books' recipe for success consisted in singling out, of all the variety of possible relationships between children and adults, those between young girls and grown men that rested on violence. The result was a one-sided and false image: "Behind the hypocritical façade of concern for the well-being of the defiled child there lies concealed a new, dangerously reactionary form of hostility to the body in all of these books. For under the pretext of protecting the child from rape, writings of this kind deny the child's own autonomous sexual wishes and their fulfillment. With it nearly one hundred years of sexual reform, sex education and struggle to liberate the child from sexual restrictions are undone."[403] In the face of public pressure, Borneman found himself obliged to reassert—as he had done so often before—that his own preferences were for adult women. "My interest has always and only been in strong, independent women, not weak, helpless, unprotected young girls."

If Borneman's name was rarely mentioned in any denunciatory capacity in the still relatively quiet media debates of the early 1980s—aggressive calls following the *Club 2* broadcast from 1981 notwithstanding—he appeared in the resurgent debate of the early 1990s, if not as a pedophile, then as a sort of prompter for a pedophile lobby that appropriated his arguments as its own. In the late 1980s the number of book titles dealing with sexual abuse increased sharply, with public interest driven by a number of cases in which male educators were accused of sexually abusing children with whom they had been entrusted. In response a truly hysterical witch hunt for pedophilic abusers broke out in kindergartens, schools, and extracurricular institutions, but also within one's immediate family and circle of friends, leading to a series of false accusations. The general suspicion against men in itself came as no great surprise, for, as *Emma* proudly announced at the height of the campaign, "feminists have said it loudly for fifteen years now: fathers and stepfathers rape their daughters, brothers their sisters, and uncles their nieces."[404] It was a generalization that opened the floodgates to sweeping suspicions. There is no question that making an issue of sexual abuse in cases where it actually occurred was both right and necessary—not simply for the victims, but for society as a whole. As Sophinette Becker argued, however, there also had to be an effort to find a position "between demonizing and minimizing."[405] The general denunciation of male relatives or men in toto as sexual predators was directed not only at the male sex but also against sexuality as such, or in any event sexuality between men and women, which was subject to the blanket suspicion of an abusive relationship. In an atmosphere as charged with denunciation and persecution as that of the early 1990s, a rational debate about the sexuality of children that included more than abusive relationships wasn't possible. While Martin Dannecker found a "comparatively rational attitude" toward the topic in 1987, by 1997 he found that "in the present day" sexual contact between adults and children was "declared 'sexual abuse' regardless of the type of contact, its intensity or duration, and the sex of those involved."[406]

In Austria, where Borneman's standing among expert circles was practically uncontested, he came under attack from Rotraud Perner, a sex therapist who had worked with him at the "Sex Hotline" for the Austrian Broadcasting Company. Around 1980 Borneman and Perner shared a close and—according to their letters—friendly working relationship at the Austrian Society for Sexual Research (ÖGS), even enjoying a brief sexual encounter, as was later exhaustively reported on in the publicly staged "war of the sex popes" (*Basta*). The relationship cooled over the course of the 1980s; Perner convinced the lead editor of the *Arbeiter Zeitung* to discontinue Borneman's column, arguing, according to Borneman, that it was "obsolete and played out" in both content and form.[407] He described the subsequent course of events as follows:

> At one point Rotraud and I were fairly in love with each other. The relationship went off track somewhere along the line, and I ended it. This was happening in the very same period that she gave up on her education as a lawyer and her efforts to become an SPÖ politician, and struck out on a third career as a sex consultant. At the time—these were her own words—she wanted to learn "everything about sex" from me. Then when she had learned enough, she naturally wanted to destroy all evidence of her apprenticeship, which she did by saying and writing the exact opposite of whatever it was I had just said and written. I put up with it for more

than a decade. And now, when I react to the slightest thing for the first time, she plays the part of a poor woman being attacked by an evil macho. The opposite is true.[408]

For her part, Perner viewed her relationship with Borneman as an "utterly marginal affair" in her own account of the details.[409] In a dispute that was carried out in the press, Borneman claimed that the book in which Perner attacked him was "full of Nazi speech, envy and malice," and accused her of occupational bias—the overly narrow perspective of those who dealt primarily with sexually abused children.[410] Perner retorted that she had "done nothing more than quote his own sentences," accusing him in turn of nothing less than indulging in a "form of behavior" that "is contemptuous of humanity."[411] Wrong, Borneman countered, "she acts as though I were responsible for all the horrible actions. She does not just reproduce the original quotation, she also interprets them." He took her to court for defamation but failed, predictably, on all counts. The tabloids reveled in the fight, all the more so as Borneman's girlfriend also got involved, attacking both her partner's adversary and her spouse in private letters.[412]

More interesting than the mudslinging in which the press gloried, however, was the content of the dispute itself, which initially revolved around Borneman's position on child sexuality before moving on to other topics. In 1989 Borneman published a revised edition of his handbook article on "sexuality" from 1978—which had already caused "a tremendous stir among 'emancipated' women" when it was first delivered in Austria as a lecture[413]—where he took up with developments since its first publication and incorporated results from a long-term study on sexual relationships between children and adults.

> Neither psychological disturbances nor sexual disadvantages of any type were determined as a consequence of such relationships if they came from the child's initiative, and if the older partner hadn't subjected the child to violence or psychological pressure. For this reason, I find as little credibility in the horror stories that are so popular today about the grave and unavoidable eventual consequences of a sexual relationship between a child and an adult as I do in the similar myth of damaging one's spinal cord by masturbation.[414]

Borneman made it clear here that he was talking about relationships not marked by pressure or violence. Nevertheless, he conceded that the structural power difference between an adult and a child could not be ignored, aligning himself with Günter Amendt. Both argued, Borneman wrote, "that no matter how much effort an adult went to not to sexually exploit a child, he or she possessed such an additional degree of experience and power that they could scarcely help but to steer the situation toward his or her favor."[415] Instead of taking this point fully into account, however, he minimized it in part with reference to Eberhard Schorsch, who had found that pedophiles "were more docile than aggressive" and wanted only to "caress and be caressed, discover and be discovered." In this way, the structural power relationship was again negated. Borneman stuck by the thesis that instilling fear was just as damaging as an act of sexual violence itself: "When the mother warns her daughter about a man, or even about her own father, as a potential rapist, she causes at least as much damage in the soul of the child as in the case of actual rape, though the damage resulting from violent incest or rape during childhood must in no way be doubted or denied—on the contrary."[416]

Beginning in early 1991, Borneman's position on this issue put him "under heavy fire from the Austrian women's movement," as he wrote to Rolf Gindorf. He felt persecuted: "The campaign is taking similar dimensions to that of the horrible right extremist Martin Humer: abusive phone calls day and night, threats (castration, rape, etc.) and more than thirty articles of the utmost harshness in women's magazines. It has never bothered me to be attacked from the right. But to be attacked by my own people has given me real (at times physical) difficulties."[417] Rotraud Perner's previously mentioned discussion from that same year of Borneman's theories formed the focus of attention. She argued from the point of view of a feminist sex counselor, whose work had taught her to take the perspective of victims seriously and to mistrust men's ignorant statements on the subject of abuse. Such men referred chiefly to "'the' expert" Borneman. Perner quoted from Borneman's 1989 essay as well as *Die Ur-Szene*, criticizing not only his theories on child sexuality, but especially their authoritative and uncritical air. "I fear an 'incapacitation by experts' when men, no matter how renowned they may be, formulate theories contradicting women that are then used by men," Perner wrote, and especially feared "'messiahs' in the realm of sex education."[418] In truth it was about power, she continued; Borneman generally did not want to allow the perspective of victims because it might call his own opinion as an expert into question.

Perner's text did not so much rely on reasoned argument with Borneman's theories as it did self-exposure—an effective strategy within the heated debate surrounding abuse—and an attack against his status as an authority. For his part, Borneman did not understand that while there was an essential disagreement about content, there was also an issue with the attitude, regarded as typically male, of an "expert." Rather, he faulted the tactical machinations of an ambitious woman prepared to resort to rotten tricks. "Ms. Perner certainly isn't stupid. She knows very well that I'm neither a child abuser nor one who approves of the sexual abuse of children. She specifically selected the subject because it is a sensitive issue for women—and rightly so—and she can be certain of her ability to rally all women against me by falsely pinning such views to me."[419] Criticism of Borneman would linger in the ensuing years, in particular Rotraud Perner's accusation that he was providing academic cover for pedophilic groups.[420] The matter was made no easier by the fact that the attacks no longer came only from the feminist camp, but also from the left. Yet no matter how forcefully he came out against them, the fight against Perner—thirty years his junior—left him exhausted, for the simple reason that he wasn't able to cope. In spring of 1993 he confessed to an acquaintance that he felt "helpless before the wave of slander, accusations and insults and am no longer enjoying my life."[421] He found one interview with Perner for *Stimme der Frau*, the mouthpiece of the leftist League of Democratic Women (Bund Demokratischer Frauen Österreichs), particularly bad. This "calumny" sought to "brand him an enemy of women" and "probably accomplished this successfully as propaganda throughout the entire Austrian women's movement."[422] Soon the debate was no longer restricted to Austria, but reached the German public. In 1992 his statements in favor of an interest and advocacy group for fathers having to pay child support came under criticism. "Sex professor excuses child abductors," blared the tabloids inaccurately.[423] The German Association for the Protection of Children (Kinderschutzbund) was outraged and easily found a sex therapist willing to damn the "contemptuous statements" from the "sex pope." Once again, Borneman was forced to defend himself in the *Süddeutsche Zeitung* and other media outlets: "I consider the sexual abuse of children to be a crime and have never called for greater leniency or exemption from punishment in cases of such crimes."[424] Yet the wave of criticism did not subside. In the fall of 1993 he saw himself accused in *Emma* of providing scientific cover for a pedophile lobby that used his name to justify its unmistakable intentions. Putting him among the ranks of pedagogue Reinhart Wolff, an important actor in the 1968 student movement, sexologist Helmut Kentler, and Rüdiger Lautmann as well as—and especially—the author Katharina Rutschky, *Emma* deemed him part of a "pro child sex alliance."[425] Rutschky's 1992 book *Erregte Aufklärung* (Aroused Education) took up with the persecution and forced confessions around the subject of child abuse that had recently gained a second wind, concluding that at its source lay a new hostility to sexuality, one that caused "disgust, lack of enthusiasm, depression."[426]

> The Puritanism of modern societies no longer shows itself in interventions by the police, censorship authorities or state attorneys when a naked breast appears on the big screen, but in the compulsion to continually occupy free spaces opened up by reason with a panicky fear, and to succumb to wild visions of catastrophe. What were once society's most legally deprived groups, those most sharply affected by immobility and moral repression, such as women and children, now suddenly appear, in a complete misjudgment of the course emancipation has run, as the victims of a liberal social order in which they can be ruthlessly exploited, disregarded and even abused.

Borneman shared in others' enthusiasm for the book, from *FAZ* to the psychoanalyst Paul Parin, writing that "it is the best thing that was been written on the subject to date." At the same time, public response underscored his own sense of paranoia. "Now Rutschky can't publish any more ever again on any subject whatsoever, as every single female journalist has threatened to strike if their newspaper or magazine publishes something by her. Incredible. Back to the Nazi era."[427] In the debate surrounding child abuse, Borneman's central role was as the object of attack; those writing in defense of sex education referred to his texts only rarely. This may have been due to the texts' overconfident, theory-driven style. It was above all "methodical factual work" that was in demand for arguments countering the "abuse of abuse," and Borneman had not done any actual research in the area that might have justified its use for a long time.[428] It was also likely that his pariah status within the women's movement and increasingly marginal position did not necessarily make him an ideal ally in bringing society to perform an about-face.

Finis!

"We now live," Dagmar Herzog recently commented "on the other side of the sexual revolution, in a melancholic post-history plagued by inner turmoil and boredom."[429] The decline of the project Borneman had devoted all his energy to in the early 1990s coincided with a broader political and personal crisis. He was about to turn eighty, Eva's death at the end of 1987 had come as a lasting private shock, and he stood under professional pressure as never before—from colleagues in Germany (nobody, he noted bitterly, came to his defense in Austria); from the right by traditionalist enemies of sexuality, led by the indefatigable Martin Humer; and from the left by feminism and from the strong feminist anti-pedophile contingent within the SPÖ, KPÖ (Kommunistische Partei Österreichs, or Communist Party of Austria), and the Greens. Then there was the collapse of socialism in Eastern Europe, which he had still considered more progressive than Western capitalism despite everything and on which he had continued to set his hopes. Despite a critical stance, he admitted in a 1990 interview with Werner Pieper for *taz* that "one piece of my heart nonetheless is still attached to it [socialism]; it is impossible if one spent his early youth in the Communist Party to shake off the characteristics of that time in one's own character and development."[430] He had registered his failure in the political realm years before the turning point of 1989/1991, as early as 1983, describing a phenomenon that also took a physical toll. Reflecting on withdrawing from the Communist Party in the mid-1930s, he wrote:

> Somehow, we are all failures. The morality that was the defining force in our lives proved itself unattainable in the hands of others. But when faith collapses in the face of irrefutable knowledge, it is not only the head that rules, but also the body. The verve is gone. One grows tired earlier. The joie de vivre is gone. You often wonder why as a nonbeliever you still plod your way through the everyday routine. The reward at the end of the day is replaced by sheer work habit.[431]

Even by comparison to all previous disillusionment, what came now was a setback down the line. "We live in an age of political and sexual counter reform," he stated in 1991.[432]

Borneman had long been a controversial figure within his professional milieu. Important West German sexologists "doubted many of his stated views," with only a small faction remaining loyal, despite their many critiques.[433] Even with his obvious longing for recognition as an academic, Borneman maintained an anti-academic air that became especially evident from his frank speech and an unqualified penchant for all things popular. This position earned him the early support of the counterculture, which showed a fundamental skepticism toward the academic world and appreciated his rebelliousness. For the Stuttgart literary scholar Thomas Rothschild, Borneman was first and foremost a "controversial contemporary" who was shut out by his colleagues "because as a resolute force for enlightenment, he does not refrain from bringing the discussion to the people whom it concerns. And is not too refined to publish it in the tabloids."[434] In the opinion of ethnologist and cultural historian Hans Peter Duerr, this "witty and educated man" should not have been named "in connection with the university prigs."[435] And in 1990 Rolf Schwendter, a tireless organizing force in the counterculture within Austria and Germany since the 1960s, gave the encomium for Borneman's seventy-fifth birthday. "Austria has never been good to its nonconformists," it began, then traced a long biographical trajectory leading up to Borneman's role as chairman of the author's association in Graz. "The holes haven't been plastered over, and the aporia still show nakedly," but it was clear to Schwendter that those who "have branded [Borneman] at best as a forgettable mail-order uncle in order to close their eyes out of self-interest to the type of fragmentation that they and their kind have themselves produced" did just as little justice to the now humbled giant as those who could not stand the combination of the "prehistory of Marx's 'prehistory'" and the question of "utopias of intimate human socialization in the future." Small wonder then that in the future the "standing of Ernest Borneman among streamlined neckties who have made a savior of the global market and a religion of Karl Popper may be somewhat limited."[436] While Borneman certainly enjoyed the praise of the nonconformist, affirming as it did his own self-image as a nonconformist, it did nothing to alter his depression.

On 15 November 1991 Borneman received the Cross of Honour, First Class from the Republic of Austria for his work in the field of sexology, an event that brought him particular pleasure, as it meant that "sexual science achieved recognition and honor for the first time in Austria."[437] Yet it could not help the fact, which emerged more clearly than ever before during the weeks surrounding the prize's conferral, that he was disputed within his field. Since the early 1990s it had become noticeably more difficult for him to place manuscripts, nor did anybody show an interest in a new column. He must also have taken note of the fact that stars—even researchers and academics—were subject to the mechanisms of media exploitation and judged according to their novelty value. In 1993 the chief editor of *Penthouse* replied to the Austrian writer Georg Biron, who interceded on Borneman's behalf, that Borneman "is nothing to us. He declares his views on any number of talk shows, seen in this way he is old hat."[438] Spurned, Borneman answered such hostility and rejection—or what he considered to be as such—with increasing indignity, suspecting censorship and mistrust even in cases of inquiries from editors. Nor did he have much patience for the slightest critique from friends. In one case Rolf Gindorf, one of his truly reliable allies, defended himself against Borneman's accusation that Gindorf was constantly attacking him, writing:

> Since we've known each other I have supported and defended you: against the 'leftist' gays who called you a 'hetero-terrorist' . . . ; against Kentler and later Sigusch with their personal animosities and offensive agitations (I organized voices and letters in your support, and spoke out and wrote myself); I brought you onto the GFSS board, edited a commemorative volume for you, gave you encouragement and suggested you for the first chairmanship in the new DGSS; I wanted you as an honorary chairman and proposed you for the Magnus Hirschfeld Award. And recently I've defended you in numerous talks from the particularly unfriendly press against you.

Why was Borneman reacting by attacking his friends? Gindorf asked, continuing, "I cannot prevent aging, but I would like to spare you the feeling of being left in the lurch."[439] In his reply Borneman conceded that aging and the "total loneliness in which I live has made me enormously sensitive."[440] When one further considers the loss in legitimacy of his leading ideas, the outline of a severe life crisis emerges—one that did not recede.

Borneman had also witnessed the object of his research efforts decline over the last three decades, leaving him uncertain as to whether he would still complete a final three-volume work documenting sexuality's position and current prospects: first, a sociological assessment of the status of sexuality in the present day entitled *Sex 2000*; second, a speculative piece of futurology with the working title *Zukunft der Liebe* (The Future of Sexuality); and finally, an analysis of the "end of heterosexuality" under the title *Aus!* (*Finis!*). Borneman ideally would have published the entire series with the same publisher; a few showed interest but then got cold feet due to the scope of the project. *Aus!* alone, intended for publication in mid-1995, was set to reach 650 pages. To then publish two other books—it was too much for Lutz Kroth from Zweitausendeins Verlag, who otherwise wanted to work with Borneman.[441] Borneman had placed *Die Zukunft der Liebe* years earlier at Kindler, but the tone between the publisher and author had grown chillier when the delivery of the manuscript, intended for publication in 1987, dragged on. Other projects were not conceivable under such circumstances; the fragment was recovered only after his death and published by another press. Nor could Suhrkamp Verlag, the publisher of *Psychoanalyse des Geldes*, make up its mind to publish Borneman's late work. Siegfried Unseld wrote to him that *Aus!* was too broad in scope, and as far as *Die Zukunft der Liebe* was concerned, "It's not an easy decision by any means. In this case too there is an imposing profusion of individual insights, borne in equal part by a tempered sagacity and—all the gloom in your description of missteps in social development and portrayal of catastrophic scenarios notwithstanding—a refreshing will to optimism." Unseld criticized, however, the "somewhat straightforward, direct analogy and connection drawn between developmental processes in society and those in sexuality, and more precisely the relationship between the sexes (i.e., a classless society = sexless society)," as well as a certain "scholasticism."[442]

In truth *Die Zukunft der Liebe*, "an expansion" of the final part of *Das Patriarchat*, contained a number of the same weaknesses that had characterized his "magnum opus."[443] It was speculative to the extent that it not only made sexuality's mutability dependent on social relations, but sought to use it as a model for considering the future. In this regard Borneman aligned himself with Ossip K. Flechtheim and Robert Jungk, both of whom pursued futurology not in terms of economic or political goals, but as socially and ecologically minded research. The book was not intended to provide "the reader with any prophecies, but only models of thought. They should awaken his fantasies and stimulate his thinking, but also challenge his critical capacity." "If in the euphoria of my writing I should have forgotten," he continued, obliged by experiences with overstated theories, "to limit prognoses that are overly bold, and overlooked changing sentences like "it will happen" to "it may happen" in the editing of the text, I ask the reader's forgiveness. At times the pen moves more quickly than the hand."[444] Borneman had written on sexual futurology before, not only in *Das Patriarchat* but also in numerous articles—first in 1975 for *Playboy*, then in the 1978 *Enzyklopädie der Zukunft* (Encyclopedia of the Future) edited by Robert Jungk—and now maintained that many of his prognoses, initially greeted with annoyance or even hostility, had now shown themselves to be accurate, as in the fields of genetic technology and reproductive medicine, while others hadn't.[445]

He judged his thesis of the constant increase in the use of state pressure against sexual minorities to be correct, devoting a large part of his further considerations to it. He also found many of his historical assessments convincing, including of love as the "story of utopia," which reconstructed on a large scale the emergence and transformation in what he termed the "ideologization of sexuality."[446] The very fact that love was placed under the care of the state through marriage and the family meant it was brought to bear "as a whip against forms of eroticism and sexuality that were not partner fixated or 'socially acceptable.'"[447] At the same time, the commodification of sex had made it a new opium of the masses that the state employed to divert citizens' discontent into nonthreatening channels. Still, "remnants of old sexually repressive strategies" were preserved throughout this "new liberal technique of mass control."[448] One of the "latent possibilities"[449] contained within the welfare state was to help prevent or reduce not only social but also sexual tensions in order to avoid protests.

In his statements on a classless and therefore sexless society, as Siegfried Unseld had criticized them, Borneman employed an analogy that played a consistent role in his writings. Just as Marx viewed primitive society as a harmonious but undeveloped form whose basic features—equality and community instead of hierarchy and individualism—would return once again at a higher level to define society in communism, Borneman considered the properties ascribed to the initial pre-genital stage or "polymorphous" phase—a "tactile pleasure spread over the entire surface of the skin"—to be the ideal form of human sexuality. The continued evidence of efforts at harmony and a vague memory "manifestly connects to the feeling of total security one can only find in a community that has not yet completed a breakthrough to individual consciousness, that of being different, separate, and therefore alone. This is reflected in a form of sexuality that is not yet fixated on the polarity of the sexes but which seeks out in other people, independently of their sex, a warming, comforting creature."[450]

The book closes with a number of reflections on the artificial manufacture of ideal sexual partners, that is, through planned mutation or in the form of a cyborg, a mixture of man and machine. Borneman was skeptical of such scenarios and in the end oscillated between pessimism and optimism. He agreed with Günter Anders—"What can be done is being done"—but this recognition shouldn't lead to resignation. "Progress, which according to postmodernism does not and even cannot exist, rests on the notion that a tiny minority attempts the impossible against the advice of the vast majority—and succeeds!"[451]

While *Die Zukunft der Liebe* glimpsed the light of day after Borneman's death, the other two books did not move past preliminary research. Detailed conceptual notes do exist for Borneman's most interesting work in terms of his views on the future development of sexuality. *Aus! Nachruf auf die Heterosexualität* (*Finis*! An Obituary for Heterosexuality) contains only 111 pages of text from two out of a planned total of nine chapters—a mere fraction of the intended length. Borneman gave a more thorough description of the work's expected content in the form of an exposé:[452] he saw the reason for a growing lack of enthusiasm about sex not only in the rise of HIV/AIDS (which from a longer historical perspective led de facto to a stronger acceptance of homosexual lifestyles), but also in an increasing "rage toward the other sex"—women who regarded men as representatives of the patriarchy, and men who saw women as the "soldiers of a hostile army bent on taking power." The thesis of a sharpening polarity between the sexes culminating in a "sex war" was a central assumption. In the 1990s there was "less coitus occurring than at any other point in human history." This stood in contrast to another phenomenon that he discussed in some detail shortly before: the commercialization of sex in the form of soft-core porn on television, hard-core videos, and a flourishing mail-order business in vibrators, erotic lingerie, and other aids.[453] None of this, Borneman wrote, was evidence of a satisfying sexual life but showed only that the economy was putting "substitutes for intercourse" up for sale on the market "in order to fill the growing demand for sex surrogates." He was convinced that this turn from sexuality was in truth a turn from heterosexuality, whereas signs of fatigue among homosexual minorities were not to be observed. The crisis in heterosexuality proceeded hand in hand with a "splitting up of erstwhile sexual majorities into smaller and increasingly numerous sexual minorities." Borneman cited survey results from 1960, 1970, 1980, and 1990 as empirical evidence for his conclusions. The results were themselves noteworthy; when respondents were asked about the frequency of intercourse, it turned out that coitus had declined overall, and the number of those who specifically stated they rarely or never had sexual intercourse rose sharply. The source of the figures, however, remained a secret—occasionally Borneman referred to questionnaires that he sent out while working as a sex columnist. This was in reference only to figures for the 1990s, however; he hadn't been employed in the previous decades as such.

Borneman interpreted the notion of a diminishing generational conflict (in contrast to findings from family research) as a growing mutual disinterest between parents and children:

> The result is today's sons, who do not undergo sexual socialization via passionate clashes with their parents but with the help of distant, never personally experienced display of onanism . . . are in no way prepared for the reciprocity of a sexual relationship, and fall into depression when their first living sexual partner exhibits human weaknesses and is not as pretty as the nudes dolled up in sticking plaster in *Penthouse*, *Playboy* or *Lui*, whose breath smells, has a period, states her own views, isn't in the mood today or even loves somebody else.[454]

In the "age of sexual counterrevolution," this was compounded by the fact that fathers had to live with the fear "of being denounced as incestuous corrupters of youth. Today a father can scarcely establish a normal, affectionate relationship with his daughter without having to fear that organizations hostile to sex and which have taken up the mantle of child protection will accuse them of sexual abuse. As a result, there is hardly any young girl who can look a boy in the eyes without seeing the embodiment of the rapist patriarch. With it, impotence and frigidity are pre-programmed for an entire generation" came the conclusion—which along with Unseld one might actually deem scholastic. This collapse in desire was redoubled by postmodern trends. "The apologists of postmodernism, the New Age and the ethos of the era attempt to make a virtue of necessity by representing the fragmented self as the only correct path for our fragmentary society" and in doing so drive forward the "counterreformation in sex education":

> People who have been socialized pluralistically are less sensual than even the most deadened victims of the age of authoritarianism. At least these latter victims were at least one time in their lives consumed by a longing for the forbidden. Those who have been socialized under pluralism have not felt a great longing for somebody or something, but only wax melancholic about their fate as victims of society. They do nothing to change society.

Borneman's theories were those of a radical critic of society and advocate of sexual education. Within the context of the "new obscurity" of postmodernism and the erosion of Marxism and psychoanalysis, not to mention the political collapse of "real" socialism, such ideas could only come across as outdated or at times pigheaded, mistaken in many a detail and in any event obstinate. One part of the professional world was more than skeptical when it came to findings as categorical as an increasing hostility between sexes or the debate around abuse causing frigidity. In 1993 Gerti Senger, an Austrian ally of Borneman's, published the results of a questionnaire handed out to seventy thousand readers of *Krone*, which gave a more differentiated picture, ascribing, for example, an "almost sensational sexual self-consciousness" to Austrian women and concluding that sexual desire among adolescents was in no way on the retreat.[455] When consulted by a magazine as an authority on the subject, Borneman called the validity of the data into question.[456] GDR sexologist Kurt Starke was less pessimistic than Borneman but found any number of the latter's findings valid—emotional alienation between the sexes, for example, or uncertainties in sex education arising from suspicious parents in the face of a simultaneous commodification of sexuality. Yet for Starke, love among young people remained as effusive as ever, and intercourse was certainly not occurring any less frequently. Asked about the accuracy of Borneman's "apocalyptic scenario" of a human race on the road to ruin due to a loss in sexual desire, Starke replied, "I don't share his conclusion, although I follow Ernest Borneman in many respects. For decades he has been a critical, able and realistic observer of lifestyles in modern Western industrial societies."[457] Starke's statement indicates that Borneman was not alone in his general diagnosis of increasing problems in partnership; developments in other countries, the United States in particular, hinted at a return to the ideal of abstinence. Late in 1993 *Der Spiegel* led with an article entitled "Sex with Marilyn": "zero connection, a loss in libido, a trend toward self-satisfaction and pornography—social researchers have observed an 'onanization' of human sexual drives. While marriage crumbles away as a form of life, the high-tech industry is working on surrogates for partnerless happiness: cybersex, or virtual eroticism with a computer."[458] It set Borneman's findings alongside statements from many other experts and surveys from Germany, France, and England. As Volkmar Sigusch summarized, "Overall sexuality has declined in importance over the past two decades."[459] Borneman's rigorism was "too dramatic" for Gunter Schmidt, but the latter similarly detected "a large discrepancy between people's ideas about what is or should be happening and what is actually happening."[460] Media outlets, interested as always in sex and hyperbolic statements, took up with Borneman's theses, landing him once again in newspaper columns and on people's screens.[461] He was invited to speak on the popular RTL TV show *Explosiv—der heiße Stuhl* (Explosive—The Hot Seat) on the topic "No Action in Bed—There's Never Been So Little Sex as Today!" in order to defend his theories against a chorus of dissenting voices.

Yet media presence was not to be equated with recognition. On his eightieth birthday of all days—a moment Sigrid Standow had tried to make the most of—it

Figure 4.4. With Sigrid Standow in Scharten, 1990. Courtesy AdK.

became clear that it had grown much lonelier around the "trusty steed of Communist sex theory," as the *FAZ* had recently described him.[462] The calendar Standow sent out to the press included thirteen events between March and May 1995, ranging from a jazz concert and television appearances to lectures and a press conference for the inauguration of the "Ernest Borneman Archive" at the Berlin Academy of Arts.[463] The festivities culminated in a party at Vienna's Literaturhaus featuring a congratulatory address by Rolf Schwendter, speeches, and a buffet meal that had been organized by the authors' guild in Graz and was advertised as a public reading. The unedited material filmed by Eva Brenner in preparation for a documentary film about Borneman shows a happy anniversary spent together with his girlfriend while interviewed by Brenner and a handful of journalists, a large crowd of people, and Borneman greeting acquaintances who congratulate the birthday boy, among them a heartfelt encounter with Gerti Senger. Seen flipping through the freshly printed commemorative volume organized by Sigrid Standow, Borneman is visibly touched by the thick volume containing sixty-nine articles by friends and colleagues from every period in his life. But in interviews with guests it also becomes clear that many former collaborators did not come, not to mention official representatives from the state, city, or political parties. "At the moment he is not especially well respected," a journalist friend is filmed saying; another opined that Rotraud Perner's critique had cost Borneman his prominent status. At the edge of conversation one can hear Gerti Senger ask another attendee where all the notable figures are. They hadn't come, replied her counterpart, "you're the best-known person here." The public was primarily composed of people who had come off the street.

Borneman addressed the issue himself in a long speech; the accolades pleased him, but he explained that there were three things with which he was actually concerned: the decline of socialism, the decline of psychoanalysis, and the decline of sexuality. Nor did he mince words about his bitterness towards the SPÖ, which at some point had suddenly stopped inviting him to their sessions. "They don't want any radicals there." In practice, his "open marriage" with Eva hadn't worked well—"We were often jealous of one another." And as he had said once before to the camera with his girlfriend present, he found the notion "very difficult . . . that here and there Sigrid is in need of someone younger." It was also a question of age—it was "very difficult" that younger men who could still get a proper erection were given preference.

On Whit Sunday, 4 June 1995, several days after all the birthday celebrations had finished, Ernest Borneman put an end to his life. The cause was a recently renewed confrontation with the fact that his girlfriend was involved in a sadomasochistic relationship with another man in Cologne. Borneman spoke of a sexual dependence to her that he could only escape through suicide. He describes the details of the saga in a farewell note and a tape recording of just under ten minutes that he sent to his girlfriend. Once they gained possession of the source, the entire affair was gleefully spread by the Austrian news magazine *News* and the *Bild* newspaper, among other outlets. Borneman made the headlines in *Bild* for two days running: "Young Lover Runs Away: Sex Pope Professor Dr. Borneman Poisons Himself" and "The Poisoned Death of Professor Borneman: Sexual Depths Recorded on Tape. Spanking Orgasms, Dependency, Despair."[464] Further reports and readers' letters appeared in the days to come. In order to raise the profile of the story, the newspaper made its protagonists out to be larger than life: "tireless prophet of eroticism," "the German sex pope," "sex obsessed," but also "thoughtful academic" and "very wise"—the title "professor" was constantly mentioned in order to accentuate more sharply its contradiction to the seemingly irrational field of love. The commentary from the chief editor struck a similar tone, suggesting sympathy while also circulating banalities: "The odd thing is that one can teach, but not learn love. One can describe, but not suppress feelings. The one left is always the loser." In days the maudlin had given way to an unrestrained aggression, with long quotations from Borneman's farewell note and tape recording sending his lover to the pillory. Borneman's suicide was the "desperate plea of a deeply humiliated man," readers learned on page one. In terms such as "a desperate legacy," "bitter reckoning," etc., Sigrid Standow was disparaged as false and egocentric, while Borneman appeared as a poor old man who had run up against his own notions of sexual liberality. In the German press, *Focus* used the suicide as a pretext for a general attack on the entire field of sexology, seeing the "credibility of the lust experts" that had already elicited murmurs of discontent during many a barroom conversation shaken once again. "They give no intelligent advice and fail on their own terms."[465]

Borneman's suicide was not a spontaneous decision; it was carefully prepared. He used a combination of alcohol and tablets, following instruction. As a longer letter to Eva from his time in Canada showed early on, Borneman considered suicide a legitimate way of maintaining power over one's life until the end. "Death is my redeemer."[466] He made no secret of this but spoke about it continuously. Shortly after Eva's death he had bought a handgun, as he wrote to a friend from youth. "When life simply becomes too unbearable, I can take matters into my own hands." He had also filled out a "suicide order" issued by the German Society for Humane Death (Deutsche Gesellschaft für Humanes Sterben), of which he had become a member. At the site of his suicide, written in large red letters were the words "No resuscitation please, no emergency room please!"

Notes

1. See Herzog, *Die Politisierung der Lust*; Silies, *Liebe, Lust und Last*.
2. See Schildt, "Die Kräfte der Gegenreform sind auf breiter Front angetreten."
3. Borneman, "Sexualität und Sprache," 140–41.
4. Sigusch, *Geschichte der Sexualwissenschaft*, 430–58. For a historiographical perspective, see Herzog, "Where They Desire They Cannot Love."
5. Ferle, "Bornemans erstes Buch in deutscher Sprache."
6. Borneman, *Lexikon der Liebe*, 29.
7. Ibid., 25.
8. *SZ*, 15 and 16 February 1969.
9. *Pardon*, March 1969, no pagination.
10. Henryk M. Broder, discussion of *Lexikon der Liebe*, broadcast on WDR 2, 2 September 1969.
11. Borneman, *Die Ur-Szene*, 314.
12. *St. Pauli Nachrichten*, 22 May 1970.
13. *Der Spiegel* 22 (1971): 165; *Der Sprachdienst* 6 (1971); H. Hunger, in *Sexualpädagogik* 4 (1971).
14. *Darmstädter Echo*, 21 June 1971.
15. *Die Zeit*, 2 July 1971.
16. *Münchner Merkur*, 30 July 1971.
17. E.g., *Wochenpresse*, 23 June 1971.
18. Borneman, *Die Ur-Szene*, 331; Borneman, "Sexualität und Semantik," 58.

19. Ibid., 64; Borneman, *Die Ur-Szene*, 336–37.

20. Borneman, *Lexikon der Liebe*, 1:7.

21. *Underground* 3 (1970): 23–26, 42.

22. Borneman, "When Dogma Bites Dogma, or the Difficult Marriage of Marx and Freud."

23. Borneman to Herbert [Steinthal], 7 August 1971.

24. Peglau, *Unpolitische Wissenschaft?*, 107, fn. 186.

25. Borneman, "Aufstieg und Fall des Wilhelm Reich"; Rackelmann, "Was war die Sexpol," 93, fn. 22.

26. Peglau, *Unpolitische Wissenschaft?*, 108.

27. Borneman, "Aufstieg und Fall des Wilhelm Reich," 26.

28. Borneman to stepmother Erna, 29 May 1967.

29. Borneman to father, 15 April 1946.

30. Borneman himself mentions 40,000 volumes, while Franz Altrichter, the librarian for the Chamber of Labor in Vienna, which accepted 7,000 volumes in 1988, estimates the total collection to be between 10,000 and 11,000.

31. Borneman to father, 13 December 1970.

32. Short for "kaiserlich und könglich" or "imperial and royal," a shorthand reference to the Austrian Habsburg court that came to imply a bureaucratic or stratified society with a narrow mind-set, as described in Robert Musil's *The Man Without Qualities* —Trans.

33. *Medien Kritik*, manuscript, n.d.

34. Bilstein, "Die Wieder-Entdeckung der Psychoanalyse," 222.

35. See Borneman, "Autobiographisches zur Methodologie der Kinderliedforschung."

36. The issue is raised in the *Jahrbuch für Volksliedforschung* 1974, 1976, and 1977 by Gerda Grober-Glück, Ingrid Kroner, and Annegret von Wedel.

37. *Der Spiegel* 27 (1973): 102.

38. Borneman to Thomas von der Vring, 12 February 1974.

39. Preface to Borneman, *Studien zur Befreiung des Kindes*, 1:9–10.

40. *FR*, 14 August 1971.

41. Borneman, *Die Ur-Szene*, 181.

42. Borneman, *Studien zur Befreiung des Kindes*, 1:13.

43. On the work's origins in Róheim, see ibid., 1:29; Borneman, *Die Ur-Szene*, 174–75, 179.

44. This is Ingrid Kroner's conclusion in her review of the second volume for the *Jahrbuch für Volksliedforschung* 21 (1976): 204–5.

45. Borneman's full description in *Die Ur-Szene*, 210–25.

46. Borneman, *Studien zur Befreiung des Kindes*, 1:16.

47. This and the following in Borneman, *Studien zur Befreiung des Kindes*, 3:18.

48. Preface to ibid., 3:12.

49. Borneman, *Studien zur Befreiung des Kindes*, 2:39. The following on 41.

50. Borneman, *Die Ur-Szene*, 225.

51. Borneman, *Studien zur Befreiung des Kindes*, 2:47.

52. Borneman, *Studien zur Befreiung des Kindes*, 1:26.

53. Ibid., 1:21. The following on 1:23.

54. *Der Spiegel* 23 (1967): 140–41.

55. Borneman, *Die Ur-Szene*, 195.

56. Borneman, *Studien zur Befreiung des Kindes*, 3:203.

57. Aside from his three-volume *Studien zur Befreiung des Kindes*, see Borneman, "Erziehung und Sexualerziehung"; Borneman, "Wer nicht frei ist, kann auch nicht befreien."

58. The critique cited here is in Mechler, "Für Sexualerziehung in der Schule," 134, 130. The following on 134.

59. Borneman, "Sexualität und Lernen im Kindesalter," 104.

60. Borneman, *Reifungsphasen der Kindheit*.

61. Ibid., 10.

62. Ibid., 9.

63. Borneman, "Progress in Empirical Research on Children's Sexuality"; Borneman, *Childhood Phases of Maturity.*

64. Okami, Olmstead, and Abrahamson, "Sexual Experiences in Early Childhood," 339.

65. German translation by Eva Geisel: Borneman, *Am Apparat.*

66. Borneman, *Tremolo*, 210.

67. Sigusch, *Geschichte der Sexualwissenschaft*, 511.

68. Ernest to Eva, 7 January [no year]; Eva to Ernest, 25 August 1941.

69. Borneman to Katharina Friedrich, 21 September 1989, Novak Collection.

70. Borneman, *Die Ur-Szene*, 10; interview with Eckart Frahm, 15.

71. Borneman, "Zwei Schwestern"; Borneman, *Die Ur-Szene*, 147–48 and elsewhere.

72. Borneman to U.P., 4 December 1971.

73. In an interview from 1991 with Martin Giese; a copy without information on the place of publication is in AdK, EBA.

74. Complete transcript of the Ernest Borneman interview in the *Marburger Zeitung*, July 1979.

75. The traits of the new feminism as described in Schulz, *Der lange Atem der Provokation*, 74–75.

76. Ibid., 204.

77. Borneman, *Das Patriarchat*, 11.

78. Borneman to his father, 25 February 1976.

79. Borneman, *Das Patriarchat*, 23.

80. Ibid., 26.

81. Ibid., 107.

82. Ibid., 123.

83. Ibid., 10.

84. Ibid.

85. This and the following according to Herzog, *Die Politisierung der Lust*, 269–310; Heider, *Vögeln ist schön*, 137–51.

86. Janssen-Jurreit, *Sexismus*, 711.

87. Complete transcript of the Ernest Borneman interview in the *Marburger Zeitung*, July 1979.

88. *Der Spiegel*, 12 December 1983, 189.

89. Krechel, *Selbsterfahrung und Fremdbestimmung*, 50.

90. Heider, *Vögeln ist schön*, 138.

91. *Petra*, June 1977, 220–24.

92. Borneman, *Das Patriarchat*, 61.

93. Ibid., 531.

94. Ibid., 531.

95. Ibid., 533.

96. Heider, *Vögeln ist schön*, 120–21.

97. Schulz, *Der lange Atem der Provokation*, 47–48.

98. Janssen-Jurreit, *Sexismus*, 711, 558.

99. Heider, *Vögeln ist schön*, 140–41.

100. Gremliza, *Sexualität konkret* 1:8.

101. *Der Spiegel* 21 (1979): 204.

102. Herzog, *Die Politisierung der Lust*, 287.

103. Reichardt, *Authentizität und Gemeinschaft*, 657.

104. Ibid., 658.

105. Borneman, *Das Patriarchat*, 542.

106. Ibid., 534–35.

107. Schwarzer, *So fing es an!*, 92.

108. Borneman, *Das Patriarchat*, 537–40.

109. Ibid., 543.

110. Borneman, *Die Ur-Szene*, 118.

111. Ibid., 124.

112. Borneman, *Das Patriarchat*, 545.

113. Borneman to his father and Erna, 17 September 1965.

114. Borneman to Peter von Zahn, 29 September 1967; Heinz Klüter, exposé "Die Sitten der Menschheit," 5 August 1966.

115. Borneman to Kamnitzer, 19 July 1971, StBB, 375/852.

116. See the foreword in Borneman, *Das Patriarchat*, 9.

117. Borneman to his father, 21 September 1972.

118. Udo Reiter's conclusion on SFB, *Das Thema*, manuscript by Udo Reiter: "Bornemans Frauenlob: Interessante Beobachtungen und kuriose Folgerungen über Ursprung und Zukunft unsere Gesellschaftssystems," broadcast 9 April 1976. See also Hans Krieger in *Die Zeit*, 24 October 1975.

119. Göttner-Abendroth, *Das Matriarchat I*, 172 and 175.

120. Borneman, *Die Ur-Szene*, 124.

121. Ernest to Curt, 25 March 1975.

122. Ernest to Curt, 25 March 1974.

123. Ernest to Curt, 25 March 1975.

124. Ibid.

125. Borneman to Wilmont Haacke, 30 January 1974.

126. Borneman to Martin Humer, 20 January 1983.

127. Leopoldine Boxrucker to Borneman, 4 February 1983, and the latter's reply from 8 February 1983.

128. Borneman to von der Vring, 12 February 1974.

129. Doctoral Committee "Dr. phil." to Borneman, 1 September 1975; Borneman to Leithäuser, 20 July 1982.

130. Borneman to the leadership of the Doctoral Committee "Dr. phil," 5 September 1975.

131. Ernest Borneman, "Abriss des Lebens- und Bildungsganges," 4 September 1975.

132. Borneman to Michel Walter, 25 July 1991.

133. Ernest Borneman, "Thesen zu meinem als Dissertation eingereichten Buch 'Das Patriarchat' für das öffentliche Kolloquium vom 4. Mai 1976."

134. *Die Presse*, 5 September 2008; Aigner, "Die 'Wahrheit' liegt nicht in der Mitte, sondern in der Übertreibung," 159. See Axel Krefting's foreword in Engert, *Die Verarmung der Psyche*.

135. Listed in Engert, *Die Verarmung der Psyche*, 216–17.

136. Borneman, *Lexikon der Liebe*, 1:7–9; Borneman, *Studien zur Befreiung des Kindes*, 1:29.

137. "Wissenschaftlicher Werdegang in tabellarischer Form," n.d. [1985]; Borneman, *Die Ur-Szene*, 122 and 174.

138. Aigner, "Die 'Wahrheit' liegt nicht in der Mitte, sondern in der Übertreibung," 158; Aigner, "Ohne Liebe kein Leben," 8; ibid., 7.

139. Hartinger, "Als Student bei E.B."

140. Trübswasser, "Ernest Borneman."

141. Aigner, "Die 'Wahrheit' liegt nicht in der Mitte, sondern in der Übertreibung," 160.

142. Aigner, "Ohne Liebe kein Leben," 7.

143. Interview with Eckart Frahm, 28 January 1984; reprint of obituary in Borneman, *Rot-weiß-rote Herzen*, 241–42.

144. *Forum* 344/346 (1982): 57–58.

145. Trübswasser, "Ernest Borneman," 5; Borneman, "Tabu Freud," 53.

146. Borneman to Michel Walter, 25 July 1991. The quoted reply from 14 December 1982 is reprinted in one of Humer's pamphlets, "Nachrichten der europäischen Bürgerinitiativen zum Schutze der Menschenwürde," no. 9, 1983.

147. "Wissenschaftlicher Werdegang in tabellarischer Form" [1990].

148. Tändler, "'Psychoboom,'" quote on 60.

149. Mattes, "Die Psychologiekritik der Studentenbewegung"; Krovoza, "Zur Rolle von Psychologie und Psychoanalyse in der anti-autoritären Protestbewegung"; Kersting, "Juvenile Left-Wing Radicalism, Fringe Groups and Anti-psychiatry in West Germany."

150. As quoted in Eitler, "'Alternative' Religion," 341.

151. Manuscript, n.d.

152. Borneman, "When Dogma Bites Dogma, or the Difficult Marriage of Marx and Freud."

153. Bach and Molter, *Psychoboom: Wege und Abwege moderner Psychotherapie.*

154. This and the following in *Konkret* 9 (1976): 56; *Konkret* 2 (1977): 41.

155. Tändler, "'Psychoboom,'" 78.

156. *Konkret* 1 (1977).

157. Foucault, "Technologies of the Self"; Bröckling, Krasmann, and Lemke, *Gouvernementalität der Gegenwart*; Krasmann and Volkmer, "Einleitung" (the following quote on 11).

158. Maasen, *Das beratene Selbst*, 8.

159. Ibid., 11.

160. *Stern* 43 (1975): 70–80; *Petra* 11 (1975), no pagination; *Spontan* 2 (1976), no pagination.

161. *Neue Zürcher Zeitung*, 13 May 1976; *Deutsche Zeitung*, 10 October 1975; *Bayernkurier*, 10 July 1976.

162. *SZ*, 13 November 1975. Also see Kaufmann's discussion in the *Kölner Stadt-Anzeiger*, 11 September 1975.

163. *Die Welt*, 9 October 1975.

164. Ivo Frenzel, "Generalangriff auf das Patriarchat," *Merkur* 2 (1976).

165. *Nürnberger Nachrichten*, n.d., AdK, EBA; *Münchner Merkur*, 18 and 19 October 1975.

166. *Die Zeit*, 24 October 1975.

167. *FAZ*, 7 October 1975.

168. *Der Spiegel* 38 (1975): 154–55.

169. SFB, *Das Thema*, manuscript by Udo Reiter: "Bornemans Frauenlob: Interessante Beobachtungen und kuriose Folgerungen über Ursprung und Zukunft unseres Gesellschaftssystems," broadcast 9 April 1976.

170. *Konkret* 8 (1976): 48; *Weg und Ziel* 2 (1976): 90–91; *Päd. extra* 16 (1976): 13–17.

171. *Psyche* 4 (1977), no pagination.

172. Ottomeyer, "Zur Diskussion um das Patriarchat," quote on 484.

173. Letter to the editor on the article in *Stern* 43 (1975), n.p.

174. Hans Paeschke to Ivo Frenzel, 18 November 1975, in Deutsche Literaturarchiv, Marbach, D: Merkur, Briefe von Merkur an WDR, Mappe 2. I would like to thank Axel Schildt for referring me to this source.

175. WDR, *Kulturelles Wort*, manuscript by Caroline Neubaur, "Buchbesprechung Ernest Borneman: Das Patriarchat," broadcast on 8 April 1976.

176. Borneman, "Emanzipation der Geschlechter."

177. Thus in the afterword to the paperback edition, 681.

178. Compare p. 531 in the hardcover edition with the paperback editions from 1975 and 1979.

179. As noted at a conference in Königswinter by a participant, Bleibtreu-Ehrenberg, "Matriarchat und Patriarchat bei Ernest Borneman," 250.

180. Joan Daves, assessment of "Das Patriarchat," 1 May 1976.

181. Gerhard, "Frauenbewegung," 201.

182. Gerhard, *Unerhört*, 83–110; Meyer, "Frauenbewegung und politische Kultur in den 80er Jahren"; Notz, "Die autonomen Frauenbewegungen der Siebzigerjahre"; Lenz, *Die Neue Frauenbewegung in Deutschland*, 97–144.

183. *FR*, 26 January 1976; Standow, *Ein lüderliches Leben*, 143.

184. *Konkret* 2 (1984): 96.

185. *Korrespondenz Die Frau* 10 (1975): 17–21.

186. *FR*, 17 January 1976.

187. Radio Bremen/HA Kultur, manuscript by Vera Gaserow/Rüdiger Krohn, "Bücher für junge Leute," broadcast 2 March 1976.

188. Manuscript by Erika Wisselinck, "Über die Abtreibung der Frauenfrage: Borneman contra Janssen-Jureit," broadcast on HR 2, 8 May 1977.

189. *Vorwärts*, 9 October 1975.

190. Janssen-Jurreit, *Sexismus*, 702.

191. Ibid., 467.

192. Ibid., 699.

193. Ibid., 701.

194. Ibid., 714.

195. Ibid., 712.

196. Ibid., 713.

197. *Konkret* 1 (1977): 36–37.

198. *Die Weltwoche*, 16 February 1977; *Warum!*, February 1977, 35–37.

199. *Konkret* 2 (1977): 42.

200. *Vorgänge* 2 (1977): 102–4.

201. *Courage* 4 (1977): 53.

202. *Korrespondenz die Frau* 3 (1977).

203. *Konkret* 3 (1977).

204. Manuscript by Erika Wisselinck, "Über die Abtreibung der Frauenfrage: Borneman contra Janssen-Jureit," broadcast on HR 2, 8 May 1977.

205. *FR*, 5 February 1977.

206. *Vorwärts*, 11 and 25 December 1975.

207. Borneman, *Das Patriarchat* (paperback edition), 683.

208. *Express*, 30 March 1976; *Nürnberger Nachrichten*, 17 January 1977.

209. Ernest to Eva, 18 February 1942.

210. Borneman to his father, 16 December 1970.

211. Borneman, *Die Ur-Szene*, 49.

212. Ibid., 53.

213. *Die Zeit*, 11 November 1977.

214. *Konkret* 2 (1978): 44.

215. *Basler Zeitung*, 31 December 1977.

216. Weiss in conversation with Rolf Michaelis for *Die Zeit*, 10 October 1975.

217. Borneman, *Die Ur-Szene*, 22, 372.

218. *Warum!*, October 1981, 26.

219. *Die Zeit*, 10 October 1975.

220. Thus in "Wege und Ziele der Emanzipation," an undated article without a specified place of publication.

221. Borneman, *Das Patriarchat* (paperback edition), 682.

222. Janssen-Jurreit, *Sexismus*, 706–7.

223. Borneman, *Das Patriarchat* (paperback edition), 683.

224. Borneman to his father, 24 March 1976.

225. Oral communication N.N.

226. Trübswasser, "Ernest Borneman," 4.

227. Scheub, *Heldendämmerung*, 112.

228. Herzog, *Die Politisierung der Lust*, 286.

229. Ibid., 289.

230. *FAZ*, 2 October 1984.

231. Hausen, *Patriarchat*, 365.

232. Menschik, *Feminismus*; Wesel, *Der Mythos vom Matriarchat*; Müller, *Die bessere und die schlechtere Hälfte*.

233. Distler, *Mütter, Amazonen & dreifältige Göttinnen*.

234. Laugsch, *Der Matriarchats-Diskurs (in) der Zweiten Deutschen Frauenbewegung*, 108.

235. Göttner-Abendroth, *Das Matriarchat I*, 165, 151. The following on 171.

236. Sigusch, *Geschichte der Sexualwissenschaft*, 448; *Sexualität Konkret*, 1985, 22.

237. Borneman, "Sex im Jahr 2075"; Borneman, "Sex-2 auf Empfang"; Borneman, "Paradies der neuen Liebe"; Borneman, "Das Tabu".

238. Ernest to Curt, 25 March 1975.

239. *Konkret* 2 (1977): 42.

240. *Konkret* 3 (1977).

241. As quoted in Kaupp, *Die schlimmen Illustrierten*, 59. A similar account in *Der Spiegel* 44 (1971): 89.

242. *Der Spiegel*, 19 June 2008.

243. Kaupp, *Die schlimmen Illustrierten*, 57.

244. Tieben-Heibert, *Das Bild von Partnerschaft und Ehe in deutschen Illustrierten*, 226 (the following on 565).

245. Kaupp, *Die schlimmen Illustrierten*, 24, 27.

246. Tieben-Heibert, *Das Bild von Partnerschaft und Ehe in deutschen Illustrierten*, 565.

247. Noted in Merscheim, *Medizin in Illustrierten*.

248. Heinrich Bauer Verlag, *Neue Revue*.

249. *Der Spiegel*, 19 June 2008; Sigusch, *Geschichte der Sexualwissenschaft*, 445.

250. *NR* 51 (1982): 13.

251. Borneman to Klaus Wolfram, 28 December 1990.

252. *NR*, 5 February 1983, 13.

253. Borneman to N.N., 24 August 1989.

254. Borneman to Antje Kunstmann, 8 September 1985.

255. Eckart Frahm, "Erfahrungen eines Sexualberaters," broadcast on SWF 1, 25 March 1984.

256. Borneman, "Grenzen und Chancen sexualwissenschaftlicher Ratgeberkolumnen in populären Zeitschriften." In this volume also see the report from the "Zeitschrift (Beratung)" working group on p. 45–46, as well as the draft of a letter that was apparently unsent: "Borneman an Redaktion Pro Familia Magazin, 15.1.1987."

257. Maasen, "Sexualberatung auf dem Boulevard," 331.

258. Borneman to Antje Kunstmann, 8 September 1985.

259. *Die Zeit*, 22 March 1985; Borneman, "Grenzen und Chancen sexualwissenschaftlicher Ratgeberkolumnen in populären Zeitschriften."

260. Oral communication from Franz Altrichter.

261. Borneman to N.N., 24 August 1989.

262. Borneman to N.N., n.d.

263. Bänziger, *Fragen Sie Dr. Sex!*; Bänziger, *Sex als Problem*; Wellmann, *Beziehungssex.*

264. *Wochenpresse*, 21 October 1988.

265. Gruppe 5., "Zeitschrift (Beratung)."

266. The findings for the *Blick* column in Wellmann, *Beziehungssex*, 136–60.

267. Perner, *Zeugin der Lüste*, 17.

268. *NR* 38 (1984): 45.

269. *NR* 11 (1984): 49.

270. Borneman to N.N., 18 July 1987.

271. Quote in Borneman, *Lexikon der Liebe*, 1:462.

272. Borneman, "Der Patriarch als Dorian Gray," 38.

273. Lindau, *Lebenshilfe in Ratgeberrubriken*, 176.

274. *NR* 40 (1984): 45.

275. Certificate, 14 July 1990.

276. Sigusch, "Der Ratschläger."

277. "Schwerpunktthema: Sexualität und Medien," *Pro Familia Magazin* 1 (1987). See Maase, *Die Kinder der Massenkultur.*

278. This and the following in Sigusch, "Der Ratschläger," 13–14.

279. The above quotes, in order of appearance: Borneman to Oskar Ausserer, 1 February 1987; to Axel Thiel, 1 February 1987; handwritten note, n.d.

280. Borneman to the editors of *Pro Familia Magazin*, 15 January 1987. Later he would offer a different, equally unconvincing reason: "Back when he was still young and ill-fed, Eva had invited him and

his lover over to Scharten multiple times and fed him. It was something he never forgave us for."
(His version of events in an interview for Standow, *Ein lüderliches Leben*, 388.)

281. Borneman to N.N., 3 February 1987; Sigusch, "Ernest Borneman," 75.

282. This and the following in Borneman, "Was will Sigusch eigentlich?," 53. The skirmish carried over into the letters column of *Pro Familia Magazin* 3 (1987): 24–26.

283. *Pro Familia Magazin* 2 (1987): 55–56.

284. This and the following in Sigusch, *Geschichte der Sexualwissenschaft*, 443–45.

285. Ibid., 425–26.

286. Transcript of the DGSS executive board meeting, 14 August 1982.

287. Gindorf to Borneman, 29 April 1983.

288. Borneman to Gindorf, 4 May 1983.

289. Gindorf to Borneman, 6 September 1982.

290. Sigusch, *Geschichte der Sexualwissenschaft*, 445.

291. Borneman to N.N., 3 February 1987.

292. Manuscript in AdK, EBA. I have not found a printed version.

293. From the foreword in Borneman, *Sexualität: Materialien zur Sexualforschung*, 5.

294. Sigusch, *Geschichte der Sexualwissenschaft*, 445.

295. *FAZ*, 13 February 1997.

296. Eva Borneman, "Leichen am Legendenwegrand," 264.

297. Quoted in Heider, *Vögeln ist schön*, 158.

298. *Der Spiegel* 21 (1979): 204.

299. Borneman viewed this as the "main concern" of "today's sexual sciences"; foreword in Borneman, *Sexualität: Materialien zur Sexualforschung*, 5.

300. Ernest Borneman, review of Sigusch's *Die sexuelle Frage*, n.d.

301. Complete transcript of the Ernest Borneman interview in the *Marburger Zeitung*, July 1979.

302. *taz*, 9 May 1983.

303. A reference to Heinrich Mann's 1905 novel *Professor Garbage* (*Professor Unrat*) about a stuffy, hapless professor who loses himself to the world of cabaret. The novel provided the basis for the 1930 German film *The Blue Angel* (*Der Blaue Engel*, dir. Josef von Sternberg) starring Emil Jannings and Marlene Dietrich. –Trans.

304. Jäger, "Erfahrungen mit Aggressionen," 221, 223.

305. *Der Spiegel* 24 (1977): 191 (there the following quote as well). The first quote in *Berliner Zeitung*, 29 January 1999.

306. Eppendorfer, *Der Ledermann spricht mit Hubert Fichte*; *Die Zeit*, 24 December 1976.

307. Herzog, *Sexuality in Europe*, 172–74.

308. Perinelli, "Lust, Gewalt, Befreiung," 98.

309. Eitler, "Das 'Reich der Sinne'?," 262 (the following quote on 271).

310. The first quote from Herzog, *Die Politisierung der Lust*, 289; the second in Magenau, *Die taz*, 83. See Reichardt, *Authentizität und Gemeinschaft*, 711–18.

311. Heider, *Vögeln ist schön*, 154.

312. *Der Spiegel* 24 (1977): 189.

313. Complete transcript of the Ernest Borneman interview in the *Marburger Zeitung*, July 1979.

314. Borneman, "Vom Kismet der Zwei," 72.

315. Sigusch, "Der Ratschläger," 14.

316. As quoted in Sigusch, *Geschichte der Sexualwissenschaft*, 432.

317. Igor Caruso quoting from the invitation of the editor in chief: Caruso, in Gehrke, *Mein heimliches Auge*, 123.

318. This and the following in Gehrke, *Mein heimliches Auge*, 10–13.

319. Ulrich Greiner, in ibid., 100.

320. Complete transcript of the Ernest Borneman interview in *Marburger Zeitung*, July 1979.

321. Borneman to Fritz J. Raddatz, 25 April 1985. Borneman had already been made such a view public in his review of Sigusch's book *Vom Trieb und von der Liebe*, in Borneman, "Lehrstuhl und Leidenschaft."

322. Overview in Sigusch, *Geschichte der Sexualwissenschaft*, 415–45.

323. Quote in Sigusch, "Thesen über Natur und Sexualität," 123.

324. *FAZ*, 2 October 1984.

325. Sigusch, "Über den Versuch, das Sexuelle zu definieren," 567.

326. Sigusch, "Lob des Triebes." Another version, as well as Schmidt's retort to Sigusch's critique can be found in Dannecker and Sigusch, *Sexualtheorie und Sexualpolitik*, 3–16, 17–19 (Schmidt); quote on 17. On this conflict, see Herzog's brief sketch in Herzog, "Where They Desire They Cannot Love," 251–52.

327. Schmidt, "Drang und Lust."

328. Sigusch, "Lob des Triebes," 38. The following on 41.

329. Schmidt, "Entgegnung," 19.

330. Schmidt, "Drang und Lust," 316–17.

331. Schmidt, "Entgegnung," 17.

332. Sigusch, "Über den Versuch, das Sexuelle zu definieren," 563–64.

333. Borneman, "Lehrstuhl und Leidenschaft."

334. Heider, *Sadomasochisten, Keusche und Romantiker*.

335. Borneman, "Vom Kismet der Zwei," 70–71. Reprinted under the title "Zur Sexualsoziologie," in Borneman, *Ausgewählte Texte*.

336. As Borneman quotes from the foreword in Sigusch, *Vom Trieb und von der Liebe*, 9–10.

337. Sigusch, "Lob des Triebes," 31.

338. Borneman to Norbert Mappes (*Vorwärts*), 28 February 1987.

339. *FAZ*, 13 October 1986.

340. At issue is Sigusch's text from 1979 "Das gemeine Lied der Liebe," 11. The text was reprinted on multiple occasions, e.g., in *Das Argument* 121 (1980): 403–7; and in Sigusch, *Vom Trieb und von der Liebe*, 12–19.

341. Sigusch, *Neosexualitäten*, 54, 80.

342. Borneman to Sigrid Standow, 4 March 1986.

343. *Der Spiegel* 22 (1986): 180–81.

344. See Gremliza's commentary in *Konkret* 7 (1986): 28.

345. Borneman is discussing a text from the first issue of *Sexualität konkret*: Sigusch, "Das gemeine Lied der Liebe."

346. Borneman, "Protest!," 108; Sigusch's correction under the title "Ruchlose Behauptung," ibid.

347. Sigusch, "Liebe Kollegen!"

348. *Emma*, March 1986.

349. Rolf Gindorf to board members, 13 January 1987.

350. Sigusch, "Der Ratschläger" (1990); Sigusch, *Geschichte der Sexualwissenschaft*, 443–48; Sigusch, "Ernest Borneman."

351. Sigusch, "Ernest Borneman," 75.

352. Schmidt, *Kinder der sexuellen Revolution*, 13.

353. Sigusch, *Geschichte der Sexualwissenschaft*, 442.

354. Schmidt, *Kinder der sexuellen Revolution*, 14.

355. On the import of psychoanalysis in the field of the West German sexual sciences, see Herzog, "Where They Desire They Cannot Love."

356. Habermas, *Die neue Unübersichtlichkeit*, 160–62. The following quote on 154.

357. *Die Zeit*, 22 March 1985.

358. This and the following in Heider, *Vögeln ist schön*, 156–57, 163, 174. Also see Eitler, "Das 'Reich der Sinne'?," 269.

359. See also a less skeptical position on Foucault in Herzog, "Tomorrow Sex Will be Good Again."

360. Mohr, *Zaungäste*, 108.

361. As quoted in Bremme, *Sexualität im Zerrspiegel*, 105.

362. As quoted in Mohr, *Zaungäste*, 117.

363. See Eitler, "Das 'Reich der Sinne'?," 290–96; quote from Alice Schwarzer on 291. In addition, see Bremme, *Sexualität im Zerrspiegel*, 117–25.

364. Thus in his comments at a hearing of the SPD Bundestag party faction, documented in *Konkret* 10 (1988): 14. "Begleiterscheinung" in *Konkret-Sexualität* 1986, 22. On the campaign, see Heineman, *Before Porn Was Legal*, 167, 177.

365. Tümmers, "Aidspolitik"; on European trends, see Herzog, *Sexuality in Europe*, 176–83.

366. Reiche, "Sexuelle Revolution—Erinnerung an einen Mythos," 69; Siegfried, "Die Entpolitisierung des Privaten."

367. Borneman to Heino Held, 21 November 1991.

368. Borneman to Jean-Jacques Kroeber, 22 October 1990.

369. Borneman to Klaus Wolfram, 26 November 1990.

370. Borneman to Kroebner, 24 December 1990.

371. *Westdeutsche Zeitung*, 20 September 2007.

372. Foltin, "Die Talkshow."

373. Bonfadelli, "Talkshows und ihre Zuschauer," 212, 220.

374. Bublitz, *Im Beichtstuhl der Medien*, 199–218.

375. Herbert Trautwein to Borneman, 21 April 1994.

376. *Der Spiegel* 51 (1975): 125; epd "Kirche und Rundfunk," no. 91 from 13 December 1975.

377. *FAZ*, 9 September 1982.

378. *Der Spiegel*, 37 (1982): 250.

379. https://www.youtube.com/watch?v=OfD6FmccGXs, accessed 10 July 2014.

380. GKK/Kundendienst/RE, 23 and 25 April 1981.

381. *Kurier*, 15 January 1985.

382. See, e.g., *Die Arbeiter Zeitung*, 14 February 1985.

383. Reactions by telephone, 12 and 13 February 1985.

384. Program information for SDR (Süddeutscher Rundfunk) Fernsehen, n.d. (1989); broadcast manuscript for "Die wilden Alten," concept by Karo Wolm and Peter Resetarits, 31 October 1986.

385. *Arbeiter-Zeitung*, 6 June 1988.

386. *Wochenpresse*, 21 October 1988. In detail see Perner, *Zeugin der Lüste*.

387. Quote in *Falter*, 11 December 2002, 13.

388. Aigner, "Die 'Wahrheit' liegt nicht in der Mitte, sondern in der Übertreibung," 164.

389. "Nachrichten der europäischen Bürgerinitiativen zum Schutze der Menschenwürde," no. 53, 1981.

390. On the dénouement, see, e.g., *Kronenzeitung*, 6 July 1983; *Oberösterreichisches Tagblatt*, 23 December 1983.

391. Borneman to Hans Perner, 1 February 1988.

392. *Der Spiegel* 30 (1980): 149.

393. Adorno, "Sexualtabus und Recht heute," 311. Regarding Adorno's critical works on sexuality, see Herzog, "Where They Desire They Cannot Love," 243–52.

394. Borneman, "Sexualität."

395. This and the following in ibid., 298.

396. Ibid., 304.

397. "Zum Inzest," n.d. Evidently this is intended as a section for a book manuscript, paginated from 152 to 170.

398. See the contemporary report in *Der Spiegel* 30 (1980): 148–54.

399. See Heider, *Vögeln ist schön*, 282–309. The following quote on 285.

400. Reichardt, *Authentizität und Gemeinschaft*, 762–77.

401. *Der Spiegel* 30 (1980): 150–51, 153; *Konkret* 5 (1980): 26; *Der Spiegel*, 21 June 2010, 45.

402. Amendt, "Sexueller Missbrauch von Kindern."

403. Thus in the foreword to Borneman, *Rot-weiß-rote Herzen*, 9–11.

404. *Emma*, September/October 1993.

405. Becker, "Pädophilie zwischen Dämonisierung und Verharmlosung."

406. Dannecker, "Sexueller Missbrauch und Pädosexualität," 265.

407. Ernest Borneman, "Kurze Beschreibung meiner Beziehung zu Frau Dr. Perner," n.d.

408. Borneman, "Rotraud: Persönliches," n.d. See also his interview in Standow, *Ein lüderliches Leben*, 387–88.

409. *Basta* 10 (1991): 24.

410. *Stimme der Frau*, 7 (August 1991): 19; *Salto*, 17 May 1991, 23.

411. This and the following in *Salto*, 17 May 1991, 23; *Stimme der Frau* 7/8 (1991): 19, 22; *Kirche intern* 9 (1991), no pagination.

412. *Basta* 10 (1991): 23–24; *Quick* 46 (1991): 18–20.

413. Borneman to Angelika Gödde, 18 June 1989.

414. Borneman, "Kindersexualität, Kindesmissbrauch, Kinderprostitution, Pädophilie," 122. The essence of these theses is repeated in Borneman, "Wenn der Versuch der Verhinderung Schaden erzeugt."

415. This and the following in Borneman, "Kindersexualität, Kindesmissbrauch, Kinderprostitution, Pädophilie," 124–25.

416. Ibid., 127.

417. Borneman to Gindorf, 25 August 1991.

418. Perner, "Zuliebe zu Leibe," 28.

419. Manuscript draft, n.d.

420. This is also the accusation of feminist political scientist Gudrun Hauer, a former student of Borneman's and the first chair of the Austrian Society for Sexual Research at the time, who contradicted leftist historian Fritz Keller: Fritz Keller to the editors of *Linken*, 29 April 1993.

421. Borneman to Franz Gruber, 13 March 1993.

422. Ernest Borneman, "Kurze Beschreibung meiner Beziehung zu Frau Dr. Perner," n.d.

423. This and the following in *Hamburger Morgenpost*, 19 May 1992.

424. *SZ*, 12 June 1992.

425. *Emma*, September/October 1993.

426. Rutschky, *Erregte Aufklärung*, 107. The following on 97.

427. Borneman to Ralph Schilling, 16 August 1992.

428. Quotes from Rutschky's foreword in Rutschky, *Handbuch Sexueller Missbrauch*, 10.

429. Herzog, "Tomorrow Sex Will be Good Again," 286.

430. *taz*, 12 April 1990.

431. Standow, *Ein lüderliches Leben*, 343–44.

432. *Stimme der Frau* 7/8 (1991): 20.

433. Aigner, "Die 'Wahrheit' liegt nicht in der Mitte, sondern in der Übertreibung," 161.

434. *Stuttgarter Zeitung*, 20 March 1992.

435. Interview in *Engel Luzifer*, December 1979, no pagination.

436. Schwendter, "Laudatio zum Fünfundsiebzigsten," 14.

437. Borneman to Bernd Lohse, 13 November 1991.

438. Paul Sahner to Biron, 10 February 1993.

439. Gindorf to Borneman, 26 November 1992.

440. Borneman to Gindorf, 3 November 1992.

441. Borneman to Kroth, 1 November 1994.

442. Unseld to Borneman, 21 November 1994.

443. Borneman to Heinz Liehr and Johannes Werres, 9 January 1991. Borneman, *Die Zukunft der Liebe*.

444. Borneman, *Die Zukunft der Liebe*, 19.

445. Ibid., 21.

446. Ibid., 36.

447. Ibid., 41.

448. Ibid., 43.

449. Ibid., 69.

450. Ibid., 82.

451. Ibid., 122.

452. Ernest Borneman, "Aus! Bericht über ein kommendes Buch," n.d. A summary of the most important findings can be found in Borneman, "Der Verfall des sexuellen Begehrens."

453. Borneman, *Sexuelle Marktwirtschaft.*
454. This and the following in *Sexuelle Marktwirtschaft.*
455. Senger and Hoffmann, Österreich intim.
456. *News* 38 (1993): 140–44.
457. *Junge Welt,* 25 March 1993.
458. *Der Spiegel* 46 (1993): 222–37.
459. *Die Zeit,* 16 August 1996.
460. *taz,* 14 August 1995.
461. For a sample of the many reports on his theses, see *Berliner Zeitung,* 26 September 1993; *Falter* 15 (1993): 15–16; *News* 8 (1993): 108–22; *Tango* 45 (1994): 74–77; *P.M. Perspektive,* n.d.
462. *FAZ,* 8 December 1992.
463. Standow to Hans Haider (*Die Presse*), n.d.
464. *Bild Hamburg,* 7 and 8 June 1995.
465. *Focus,* 12 June 1995, 38.
466. Ernest to Eva, 5 May 1942.

CONCLUSION
BODIES ALONG THE ROADSIDE

In an article for the second commemorative volume assembled in honor of her spouse, Eva Borneman quoted a friend who initially wanted to review Borneman's autobiography but then decided against it. "Dear Ernest, unfortunately I have to pass. I don't want to tear it to pieces. It's all well and good what you write, but there's nothing but high points. Where are the bodies along the roadside?"[1] If one takes "bodies" in a nonliteral sense to mean defeats, weaknesses, ambivalence, as well as others' sacrifices, another image of Borneman's life emerges, one that while more uneven also makes him more human. Even during the attacks of the 1980s and 1990s that followed in the wake of *Die Ur-Szene*, published at the high point of his career, to many Borneman's biography and accomplishments made him seem a giant. "What a Life" *Die Zeit* titled its obituary.[2] That there was a flip side to all of this, of course, became clearer in the final years of his life, in his weakness and despair.

Bourneman's own private assessments were always ambivalent and often depressive; it was just that the public found out little about them. He wrote about a lack of recognition for his achievements and the persistent feeling of not having truly accomplished anything until the late 1960s, but also about his failures with regard to those closest to him and their fate during the Third Reich—his relationship to Eva, who felt neglected not only because of his countless affairs, and what was at times a difficult relationship with his son, Stephen. In this regard he was also more communicative than many authors; it is one of the recurring themes of his work that he would always bring his own experiences to bear, incorporating personal events of a more or less private nature even in his academic writing. As a sexologist operating in the public sphere, this role was also foisted upon him, an expectation he saw no reason to sidestep but chose instead to meet with an unusual degree of candor. Nevertheless, a tendency to exaggerate, to present himself as an important figure on the scene, and to state his convictions forcibly cannot be overlooked. The fact that he felt himself compelled to underscore this by inventing stories about his life, if need be, makes it difficult to come to a realistic appraisal. Ultimately however, the biographical sketch attempted here still speaks to a tremendous life accomplishment.

This accomplishment impresses first and foremost for the fact that Borneman engaged profoundly—and achieved a considerable amount—in three major fields of knowledge as an autodidact. He was driven in this pursuit by a fundamental curiosity that aimed, generally speaking, at contemporary cultural phenomena. "The important thing is to be creative, whatever field it is in" was one of his maxims.[3] Even if it was guided by set baseline convictions, this inquisitive form of creativity had an unreserved quality to it; he paid no mind to learned opinion or "common sense." Ingrid Zwerenz correctly observed in Borneman "a considerable gift for moving freely through gray areas with total innocence."[4] To others he did not seem of this world— as one student expressed, "For me, Borneman is a dreamer."[5]

The impression Borneman gave of being a "dreamer" can be found in as many words throughout contemporaries' descriptions. Ulrike Heider, for example, writes that "Borneman was a romantic. A romantic of love, who actually viewed through the whole affair in unromantic fashion, but wanted to preserve its integrity for the same reason."[6] Barbara Bronnen finds that he was "fascinated by deviation and aberration, they are what make up people. Eroticism, pornography and popular language were the raw materials of Borneman's research, work and life—and of his art. Yet in truth his collections are novels and fairytales, outgrowths of a man filled with an erotic aptitude for writing and fantasy."[7] Novels and fairy tales—it is a description Borneman may not have been thrilled to hear. Yet there is in fact a dreamlike element not only in his autobiographical anecdotes but also in many of his factual texts, which, while concrete in detail, were essentially conceived of from the future, or an ideal point of view. The material was empirically verifiable, in film as in jazz or sex, but in the end it wasn't necessary to take the claim to reality all that seriously. Rather, the empirical record was arranged and interpreted, and invented where necessary, according to defined, guiding ideas that could be of an aesthetic nature but more often took their cue from social aims, or dreams from which there also grew resistance to what was currently there for concealing within themselves the idea of something better. Taking this as Borneman's point of departure, his musing on the world appears all the less as "objective science"—something that could anyway not be fully accomplished—and all the more as the viewpoints of an unremitting researcher and reflective individual of his time. More than any kind of academic discipline, such viewpoints are able to point to the type of arguments, triumphs, and "bodies along the roadside" that resulted from the fight for the interpretation and legitimation of desire and the senses in the twentieth century.

This is borne out in part by Borneman's intensive engagement with the future, which for him carried an element of reality within it; it is contradicted in part by his constant references to contemporary movements in art and politics, leading one commentator to remark in 1980 that "with someone like Borneman one always has a slight feeling that he is also and not least concerned with playing the role of the intellectual expert and figurehead for popular, fashionable movements."[8] Peeling back the apparent layer of resentment, one finds a large degree of truth to the comment. Borneman's constant referral to the present, which in principle also served his utopian visions, is precisely what makes his analysis so rewarding at a more removed level: he opens up a perspective on a number of "fashionable movements" in modernity.

From the perspective of a history of the senses, Borneman's work represents an enormous trove of significant insights into and interpretations of modernity in the twentieth century, one only partially mined in this book. His views are characterized by five features. First, for Borneman sensuality was an all-encompassing phenomenon; individual senses should not be separated individually but apprehended in their "multi-sensorial complexity" (Leigh Eric Schmidt). There existed no hierarchy in the senses, as is commonly noted with reference to the "visual primacy" of modernity, that is, privileging the sense of sight in lopsided fashion as the alleged sensory bearer of truth and reason. Nor can one speak of an auditory or tactile primacy.[9] Rather, his oeuvre represents a common tendency in the twentieth century toward setting different sensory impressions on equal footing, and at times fusing them into the multiple-sense perceptions that developed in response to a growing need for authenticity, and which led to a revaluation of senses previously regarded as less valuable than sight. A purely visual perspective was considered superficial; this explains the increased interest in oral and auditory cultures. In Borneman's case, the fusion of heterogeneous sense impressions became particularly clear within film, especially musical films. In the realm of sexuality, too, he considered the boundaries drawn around the partial drives to be much too narrow. Rather, as a sensitive resonant chamber for touch, the entire body became a sexual organ, including the "wonderful smells of my loved ones," as he had occasion to remark.[10] While historically there had been an effort to control the lusts and their "close relatives" the senses (Thomas Wright) through will of effort and reason, the modern self, Borneman thought, was defined to a remarkable degree by individual sensual needs. Music may trigger strong emotions, but the words spoken in listening and discussion groups also played an important role in constituting the self-definition of jazz. Left completely to their own devices, desires would not develop. Equality and reciprocity remained his key moral criteria throughout.[11] Jazz not only brought listening pleasure, it also meant observing artist and audience and discussing music's place in community, clothing, and dance—it all belonged to the "jazz cult" as a part of modern life. In documentary film it was the connection between sound and vision that particularly interested him. During editing, how did sound and image have to be matched to one another to produce the desired effect? While separate acoustic, visual, and tactile regimes thus existed in modernity for Borneman, in principle they shouldn't be separated, and they acquired their specifically contemporary form above all in combination with one another. One essential feature was that they weren't to be limited by their reception; rather, the criteria of truth lay in praxis. This was especially evident from his jazz criticism, in his skepticism toward styles of the art form that were primarily enjoyed as a form of contemplation, and in his praise for jazz when it was danceable. This also had a social component, as the cultural preferences of social underclasses were traditionally seen, in a classic Western dichotomy, as close to the body and those of the upper classes as rational and distanced—the very schism that Borneman looked to overcome.[12]

Second, Borneman systematically developed this socially inclusive approach from an ethnological perspective. He was interested in the "popular culture," or the music, language, and physicality of "ordinary people," particularly of groups that were looked down upon—women, children, African Americans, and outcasts of all types. He saw them as models who must be supported and in case of doubt had the right to interpret their own preferences—even in contradiction of his own. This type of identifying with the oppressed was not unproblematic to the extent that it involved idealization and essentialization, that is, women or blacks having definite properties ascribed to them. On the other hand, as his crime novel *The Face on the Cutting-Room Floor* unmistakably shows, he harbored no illusions whatsoever about the futility of any attempt at authenticity or about the constructed nature of any art form. His novels and the films that were anything but "purely" documentary films, at any rate, were at heart experimental. He held no faith in the assertion that documentary film would enable one to represent and visualize the world objectively, in a distanced, rational manner, as it were. Although he wrote books himself, made films, painted in his free time, and thus showed a decided interest in questions of form, he rejected what was defined as "high culture," in particular the excessively philosophical interpretation of social relationships so highly prized in Germany. What is more, Borneman's interest in popular culture was not accompanied by a fundamental rejection of the culture industry, as prominently represented by the Frankfurt School; in this case he remained ambivalent. He rejected the "commercialization" of jazz—anyone who gave himself up to the machinations of the powerful not only betrayed the roots of jazz but also lost his audience—instead promoting thoroughly popular styles and from time to time working on the front lines of the culture industry as a journalist, television manager, and advertising consultant.

Third, technical questions consistently played an important role for Borneman. Whether it was differences between "African" and "European" phrasing in jazz, pairing image and sound to one another in film, or reproductive medicine in sexuality, technological aspects and/or new technologies that changed the production of sound, image, or sexual sensation were key. Questions of technique and form generally played an important role within the sensual regimes of the twentieth century, but there were other positions, too, against which Borneman had to assert himself, for example Grierson's anti-aesthetic and content-related policies, as well as the cult of authenticity and technological skepticism in both jazz and German feminism.

Fourth, hearing, seeing, and touching were always embedded in a political context. If Walter Benjamin had claimed a "politicization of art" for communism, this was precisely what Borneman actively pursued in most phases of his life, through his propaganda films, his defense of jazz as the property of African Americans, and his idea of the "sexual revolution." In less political settings he would subsequently assert a political intent, as when assigning himself the role of a "Socialist Goebbels" in his television work. He viewed the development of the senses fundamentally as a method of liberation, a position that by the 1980s ran up against the boundaries of acceptance even within leftist circles, best shown in the debate around children's sexuality. At this point the limits of this postulate, moreover, also became more clear in Borneman's private life. Another, somewhat more productive contradiction arose from his initial Marxist position, which demanded scientific rigor or comprehensibility, and the often-blurred definitions surrounding the objects of his interest. Practically without exception, they were traditionally considered as emotional and subjective: mass culture, blacks, African American music, musicals, women, psychology, and sexuality. At issue here was legitimizing groups and styles that were considered irrational and kept from holding positions of power to reconsider their social and political significance.

Fifth, all of this occurred set against an international horizon, an essential feature of Borneman's productive streak that at the same time made him a set target for a wide range of attacks as a returning emigrant. Even in retrospect, many of his positions still come across as fresh and original—his idea of enlisting a new type of film in the service of an allegedly increasingly international culture, for example, one that would be understandable across borders by operating without language and would instead communicate nonverbally, through music and dance. In this case, the central auditory medium was not a nationally determined language but music.

What a life, indeed. More than enough for a single person, even without the inventions. But it is precisely these strategies of deception and camouflage, with their conceptual grounding in dangerous time where truthfulness could be lethal—or was at least rarely beneficial, if not simply impossible—that give Borneman's biography an additional shade of complexity. He was vulnerable not only for this reason alone, but also because he consistently represented obstinate positions. One need not aim as high as Ernst Alexander Rauter once did, stating that Borneman "should have won the Nobel Prize for lessening people's fear."[13] Still, his accomplishments in researching African American music, in documentary film, in the television studio, and in spreading the idea of liberated sexuality were sustained by an awareness that there must be something better than what currently exists—not a cold utopia to be reached by any means necessary, but one accomplished with empathy. Ernst Bloch would have attributed such a position to the "warm stream" of Marxism, which contains human wishes and hopes. Such a bearing carried high risks—it is little wonder in this case that at the end of the twentieth century Borneman viewed himself as a "failed optimist."[14] How could it have been otherwise?

Notes

1. Eva Borneman, "Leichen am Legendenwegrand," 263.
2. *Die Zeit*, no. 25 (1995). Aside from many other German-language obituaries, the British press discusses in a similar vein in *Guardian*, 9 June 1995; *Independent*, 14 June 1995.
3. Quoted in Andreas Marck to Borneman, 30 August 1978, reprinted in Standow, *Ein lüderliches Leben*, 333.

4. In her review of *Die Ur-Szene* from 1977, newspaper clipping without source citation in AdK, EBA.

5. As quoted in Standow, *Ein lüderliches Leben*, 77.

6. From a personal conversation with Heider.

7. Standow, *Ein lüderliches Leben*, 171.

8. *Neues Volksblatt*, 12 July 1980.

9. Jay, "In the Realm of the Senses," 310.

10. Interview with Manfred Lechner in *Der Standard*, n.d. AdK, Borneman.

11. Harvey, "The Portal of Touch," 387.

12. Classen, "The Senses," 358.

13. Standow, *Ein lüderliches Leben*, 204.

14. Ibid., 100.

BIBLIOGRAPHY

Archives

Archiv der Akademie der Künste, Berlin (Archive of the Academy of Arts)
  – Bertolt Brecht Archiv
  – Elisabeth Hauptmann Archive
  – Ernest Borneman Archive
  – Helene Weigel Archive
Bundesarchiv Koblenz (German Federal Archives, Koblenz)
Jazzinstitut Darmstadt
Library and Archives Canada, Ottawa
Lippmann+Rau-Musikarchiv, Eisenach
The National Archives, London
National Film Board of Canada, Montreal
Northwestern University Library, Evanston, IL
Radio Bremen
Sammlung Irmi Novak, Wien (Irmi Novak Collection, Vienna)
Staatsbibliothek zu Berlin (Berlin State Library)
Stiftung Deutsche Kinemathek, Berlin
UNESCO Archives, Paris
University of Stirling
Yale University, Beinecke Library

Literature

Adelt, Ulrich. *Blues Music in the Sixties: A Story in Black and White*. New Brunswick, NJ: Rutgers University Press, 2010.

Adorno, Theodor W. "Sexualtabus und Recht heute." In *Sexualität und Verbrechen: Beiträge zur Strafrechtsreform*, edited by Fritz Bauer, 299–317. Frankurt: Fischer Bücherei, 1963.

Aigner, Josef Christian. "Die 'Wahrheit' liegt nicht in der Mitte, sondern in der Übertreibung." In *Ein Lüderliches Leben*, edited by Sigrid Standow, 158–66. Löhrbach: Pieper's MedienXperimente, 1995.

————. "Ohne Liebe kein Leben: Zum Tod Ernest Bornemans." *Werkblatt: Zeitschrift für Psychoanalyse und Gesellschaftskritik* 33, no. 2 (1994): 7–13.

Aigner, Josef Christian, and Rolf Gindorf, eds. *Von der Last der Lust: Sexualität zwischen Liberalisierung und Entfremdung.* Vienna: Verlag für Gesellschaftskritik, 1986.

Aitken, Ian. *Film and Reform: John Grierson and the Documentary Film Movement.* New York: Routledge, 2014.

Amendt, Günter. *Sexfront.* Frankfurt: März Verlag, 1970.

————. "Sexueller Missbrauch von Kindern: Zur Pädophiliediskussion von 1980 bis heute." *Merkur* 64, no. 12 (2010): 1161–72.

Andresen, Knud. "Kommunistische Politik an höheren Schulen: Der Sozialistische Schülerbund 1926–1932." *Internationale Wissenschaftliche Korrespondenz zur Geschichte der deutschen Arbeiterbewegung* 42, no. 2/3 (2006): 237–55.

Arendt, Hannah. "The Aftermath of Nazi Rule: Report from Germany." *Commentary* 10 (1950): 342–53.

Armstrong, Derick. "Cuban Music—A Reply." *Jazz Monthly*, December 1959, 9–10.

Bach, George R., and Haja Molter. *Psychoboom: Wege und Abwege moderner Psychotherapie.* Düsseldorf: E. Diederichs, 1976.

Bänziger, Peter-Paul, ed. *Fragen Sie Dr. Sex! Ratgeberkommunikation und die mediale Konstruktion des Sexuellen.* Frankfurt: Suhrkamp Verlag, 2010.

————. *Sex als Problem: Körper und Intimbeziehungen in Briefen an die "Liebe Marta."* Frankfurt: Campus Verlag, 2010.

Bausch, Hans. *Rundfunkpolitik nach 1945.* Vol. 3. Munich: Deutscher Taschenbuch Verlag, 1980.

Becker, Sophinette. *"Pädophilie zwischen Dämonisierung und Verharmlosung."* Accessed 13 October 2014 from http://www.itp-arcados.net/wissenschaft/023.html.

Berendt, Joachim-Ernst. *Blues.* Cologne: Grieg, 1970.

————. "'The Blues got white—got he?': Das Für und Wider eines aktuellen Themas." *Jazz Podium* 10 (1968): 316–17.

————. *Das große Jazzbuch: Von New Orleans bis Salsa und Jazz Rock.* Frankfurt: Büchergilde Gutenberg, 1981.

————. *Ein Fenster aus Jazz: Portraits, Reflexionen.* Frankfurt: Fischer Taschenbuch Verlag, 1980.

————. "Ernest Borneman und die weiblichen Stimmen." In *Ein Lüderliches Leben*, edited by Sigrid Standow, 116–23. Löhrbach: Pieper's MedienXperimente, 1995.

Bernhard, Henry. "Die Geschichte der FDJ in Großbritannien 1939–1946." *Deutschland-Archiv* 38, no. 1 (2005): 33–43.

Berrett, Joshua, ed. *The Louis Armstrong Companion: Eight Decades of Commentary.* New York: Schirmer, 1999.

Beveridge, James. *John Grierson, Film Master.* New York: Macmillan, 1978.

Bignell, Johnathan, and Andreas Fickers. "Introduction: Comparative European Perspectives on Television History." In *A European Television History*, edited by Jonathan Bignell and Andreas Fickers, 1–54. Oxford: Wiley-Blackwell, 2008.

Bilstein, Johannes. "Die Wieder-Entdeckung der Psychoanalyse." In *"Seid realistisch, verlangt das Unmögliche!": Wie 1968 die Pädagogik bewegte*, edited by Meike Sophia Baader, 212–26. Weinheim: Beltz, 2008.

Bleibtreu-Ehrenberg, Gisela. "Matriarchat und Patriarchat bei Ernest Borneman." *Anthropos* 75, no. 1/2 (1980): 250–57.

Boatfield, Graham. "From the Sidelines." In *Just Jazz 3*, edited by Sinclair Traill and Gerald Lascelles, 60–69. London: Peter Davies, 1959.

Bonfadelli, Heinz. "Talkshows und ihre Zuschauer: Zwischen Beratung, Orientierung und Sensationssuche." In *Fragen Sie Dr. Sex!: Ratgeberkommunikation und die mediale Konstruktion des Sexuellen*, edited by Peter Paul Bänziger, 208–31. Frankfurt: Suhrkamp Verlag, 2010.

Borneman, Ernest. *Am Apparat: Das Jenseits*. Translated by Eva Geisel. Bern and Munich: Scherz, 1968.

———. "The Anthropologist Looks Back." *The Record Changer*, August 1947, 6ff., 14.

———. "Ashamed of Race." *Jazz Monthly*, April 1958, 6–7.

———. "Ashamed of Race II." *Jazz Monthly*, January 1959, 28.

———. "Aufstieg und Fall des Wilhelm Reich." *Warum!*, October 1981, 26–30.

———. *Ausgewählte Texte*. Munich: Goldmann, 1990.

———. "Autobiographisches zur Geschichte des Films und Fernsehens." *Kürbiskern*, no. 2 (1977): 41–49.

———. "Autobiographisches zur Methodologie der Kinderliedforschung." *Jahrbuch für Volksliedforschung* 22 (1977): 102–12.

———. "Back to Berlin: The Diary of a Native's Return." *Harper's Magazine*, August 1948, 58–66.

———. "Black Light and White Shadow: After Black Power, What?" *Jazzforschung/Jazz Research* no. 3/4 (1971–72): 11–34.

———. "Black Light and White Shadow: Notes for a History of American Negro Music." *Jazzforschung/Jazz Research* 2 (1970): 24–93.

———. "The Black Mask." *GO*, February/March 1952, 63–66.

———. "The Blues: A Study in Ambiguity." In *Just Jazz 3*, edited by Sinclair Traill and Gerald Lascelles, 75–91. London: Peter Davies, 1959.

———. "Boogie Woogie." In *Just Jazz*, edited by Sinclair Traill and Gerald Lascelles, 13–40. London: Peter Davies, 1957.

———. "Canada, Unesco and the Movies." *Evening Citizen*, 10 September 1948.

———. *Childhood Phases of Maturity: Sexual Developmental Psychology*. Amherst, NY: Prometheus Books, 1994.

———. *The Compromisers*. London: Sphere Book, 1962.

———. "Credo Quia Absurdum: An Epitaph for Bertolt Brecht." *Kenyon Review* 21, no. 2 (1959): 169–98.

———. "Creole Echoes." In *Just Jazz 2*, edited by Sinclair Traill and Gerald Lascelles, 25–52. London: Peter Davies, 1958.

————. "Creole Echoes." *Jazz Review*, September 1959, 13–15, and November 1959, 26–27.

————. *A Critic Looks at Jazz*. London: Jazz Music Books, 1946.

————. *Das Geschlechtsleben des Kindes: Beiträge zur Kinderanalyse und Sexualpädologie*. Munich: Deutscher Taschenbuch Verlag, 1988.

————. *Das Patriarchat: Ursprung und Zukunft unseres Gesellschaftssystems*. Frankfurt: S. Fischer, 1975.

————. *Der Neanderberg: Beiträge zur Emanzipationsgeschichte des 19. und 20. Jahrhunderts*. Frankfurt: Ullstein, 1983.

————. "Das Tabu." *Playboy*, no. 12 (1976), and nos. 1–3 (1977).

————. "D-Day: Oder wie ich den Zweiten Weltkrieg gewann und den Frieden verlor." *Exil: Forschung, Erkenntnisse, Ergebnisse*, no. 1 (1994): 5–6.

————. "Der Patriarch als Dorian Gray." In *Der Mann: Ansätze für ein neues Bewusstsein*, edited by Dieter Lamping and Hermann Schulz, 28–38. Wuppertal: Hammer, 1977.

————. "Der Verfall des sexuellen Begehrens: Notizen zur pluralistischen Sozialisation." *Sexualmedizin*, no. 12 (1994): 353–59.

————. "Die kreolische Tradition: Zur Rolle des Jazz in der amerikanischen Volksmusik." *Der Monat* 18, no. 214 (1966): 60–70.

————. *Die Ur-Szene: Das prägende Kindheitserlebnis und seine Folgen*. Frankfurt: Fischer Taschenbuch, 1980.

————. *Die Zukunft der Liebe*. Frankfurt: Fischer Taschenbuch Verlag, 1997.

————. "Documentary Films: World War II." In *Canadian Film Reader*, edited by Seth Feldman and Joyce Nelson, 48–58. Toronto: Peter Martin Associates, 1977.

————. "Eight Points on American TV." *British Screen and Television Writers Association Bulletin*, October 1955, 3–6.

————. "Ein Epitaph für Bertolt Brecht." *Sinn und Form, 2: Sonderheft Bertolt Brecht*, 142–58. Berlin: Rütten und Loening, 1957.

————. "Emanzipation der Geschlechter: Ein Gespräch." *Vorgänge*, no. 1 (1976): 53–59.

————. "Erziehung und Sexualerziehung." *betrifft: erziehung*, no. 4 (1977): 32–37.

————. *The Face on the Cutting-Room Floor*. Harmondsworth: Penguin, 1986. [First published in 1937 under the pseudonym Cameron McCabe.]

————. "Films for International Understanding: The UNESCO Story." *The Penguin Film Review*, no. 7 (1948): 96–106.

————. "Form and Content in Jazz." *Jazz*, December 1965, 22 and 30.

————. "Geheimtipps für den Tänzer." In *In der Ferne das Glück: Geschichten für Hollywood von Vicky Baum u.a.*, edited by Wolfgang Jacobsen and Heike Klapdor, 406–9. Berlin: Aufbau, 2013.

————. "Grenzen und Chancen sexualwissenschaftlicher Ratgeberkolumnen in populären Zeitschriften." In *Medien als Sexualaufklärer*, edited by Norbert Kluge, 31–32. Frankfurt: dipa Verlag, 1988

———. "Jazz and the Creole Tradition." *Jazzforschung/Jazz Research* 1 (1969): 99–112.

———. "The Jazz Cult, I: Intimate Memoirs of an Acolyte." *Harper's Magazine*, February 1947, 141–47.

———. "The Jazz Cult, II: War among Critics." *Harper's Magazine*, March 1947, 261–73.

———. "Kindersexualität, Kindesmissbrauch, Kinderprostitution, Pädophilie: Ein Beitrag zur Klärung der Begriffe." In *Gestörte Sexualentwicklung bei Kindern und Jugendlichen: Begutachtung, Straffälligkeit, Therapie*, edited by Christian König, 120–28. Munich: Reinhardt, 1989.

———. "King Jazz." *Record Changer*, January 1946, 8–10.

———. "Korrupte SPÖ, Gott-Vater Kreisky & sexfeindliche Eminenzen: Interview mit Ernest Borneman." *Panorama: Studentenzeitschrift für Politik, Wirtschaft und Kultur*, no. 8 (June 1981): 8–11.

———. *Landschaft mit Figuren*. Gütersloh: Bertelsmann, 1971.

———. "Lehrstuhl und Leidenschaft." *Psychologie heute*, September 1984, 75–76.

———. "Les racines de la musique Américaine Noir." *Présence Africaine*, no. 4 (Summer 1948): 576–89.

———. *Lexikon der Liebe*. 2 vols. Munich: List, 1968.

———. *Love Story*. Jarrolds: London, 1941.

———. "Macht und Sprache: Wie schreibt man im Exil." *Wespennest*, no. 52 (1983): 25–31.

———. "Mann kaputt?" In *Männertraum(a): Ein Lesebuch für Erwachsene*, edited by Heinz Körner and Roland Kübler, 17–24. Fellbach: Körner, 1984.

———. *The Man Who Loved Women: A Landscape with Nudes*. New York: New American Library, 1968.

———. "Ninth German Jazz Festival." *Jazz*, September 1964, 26.

———. "Paradies der neuen Liebe." *Playboy*, no. 8 (1975): 64ff.

———. "Progress in Empirical Research on Children's Sexuality." In *Handbook of Sexology*, vol. 7, *Childhood and Adolescence Sexology*, edited by M. E. Perry, 201–7. Amsterdam: Elsevier, 1990.

———. "Protest!" *Sexualmedizin*, no. 3 (1987): 108.

———. "Psychoanalyse: Die verdrängte Wissenschaft." *Merian*, December 1980.

———. *Psychoanalyse des Geldes: Eine kritische Untersuchung psychoanalytischer Geldtheorien*. Frankfurt: Suhrkamp, 1977.

———. "The Real Brecht." *Encore: The Voice of Vital Theatre* 5, no. 2 (1958): 20–33.

———. "The Record Companies, 'The Melody Maker' and The Cha Cha Chá." *Jazz Monthly*, April 1959, 26–27.

———. *Reifungsphasen der Kindheit*. Vol. 1. Sexuelle Entwicklungspsychologie. Wien: Jugend und Volk, 1981.

———. "Remembered Faces." *Bandwagon* 13, no. 3 (1962): 26–28.

———. "Replik auf Klaus Ottomeyer." *Das Argument*, no. 99 (1976): 828–35.

———. "Rezension von Horst E. Richter, Flüchten oder standhalten, Reinbek 1976." *Psychologie heute*, no. 2 (June 1976): 73–75.

———. "Rezension von John F. Sweed (Hrsg.), Black America, New York/London 1970." *Jazzforschung/Jazz Research* 5 (1973): 165.

———. "The Roots of Jazz." In *Jazz: New Perspectives on the History of Jazz by Twelve of the World's Foremost Jazz Critics and Scholars*, edited by Nat Hentoff and Albert J. McCarthy, 1–20. New York: Da Capo Press, 1959.

———. *Rot-weiß-rote Herzen: Das Liebes-, Ehe- und Geschlechtsleben der Alpenrepublik*. Wien: Hannibal Verlag, 1984.

———. "Sex im Jahr 2075." *Playboy*, no. 7 (1975): 58ff.

———. "Sex-2 auf Empfang." *Playboy*, no. 9 (1975): 72ff.

———. "Sexualität." In *Kritische Stichwörter zur Kinderkultur*, edited by Karl W. Bauer and Heinz Hengst, 292–305. Munich: W. Fink, 1978.

———, ed. *Sexualität: Materialien zur Sexualforschung*. Weinheim: Beltz, 1979.

———. "Sexualität und Lernen im Kindesalter." In *Sexualerziehung zwischen Elternhaus und Grundschule*, edited by Petra Millhoffer and Brigitte Maier, 100–104. Frankfurt: Arbeitskreis Grundschule, 1988.

———. "Sexualität und Politik im heutigen Deutschland." *Aufrisse*, no. 2 (1991): 3–7.

———. "Sexualität und Semantik: Das Sexualsymbol im Sprachgebrauch." In *Sexualität: Materialien zur Sexualforschung*, edited by Ernest Borneman, 51–66. Weinheim: Beltz, 1979.

———. "Sexualität und Sprache." In *Handbuch der Sexualpädagogik*, vol. 1, edited by Norbert Kluge, 139–50. Düsseldorf: Schwann, 1984.

———. *Sexuelle Marktwirtschaft: Vom Waren- und Geschlechtsverkehr in der bürgerlichen Gesellschaft*. Wien: Promedia Verlag, 1992.

———. "Some Jazz Myths Questioned." *Jazz*, January 1963, 6–13.

———. "Sound Rhythm and the Film." *Sight and Sound*, Summer 1934, 65–67.

———. *Studien zur Befreiung des Kindes*. Vol. 1, *Unsere Kinder im Spiegel ihrer Lieder, Reime, Verse und Rätsel*. Frankfurt: Ullstein, 1980.

———. *Studien zur Befreiung des Kindes*. Vol. 2, *Die Umwelt des Kindes im Spiegel seiner "verbotenen" Lieder, Reime, Verse und Rätsel*. Frankfurt: Ullstein, 1980.

———. *Studien zur Befreiung des Kindes*. Vol. 3, *Die Welt der Erwachsenen in den "verbotenen" Reimen deutschsprachiger Stadtkinder*. Frankfurt: Ullstein, 1981.

———. *Stumme Zeugen lügen nicht*. Bern and Munich: Scherz, 1969.

———. "Tabu Freud." *Profil*, 4 May 1981, 52–56.

———. *Tomorrow Is Now*. London: Neville Spearman, 1959.

———. *Tremolo*. London: Jarrolds, 1948.

———. "Two Brechtians." *Kenyon Review* 22, no. 3 (1960): 465–92.

———. "Vom freiwilligen Exil." In *Literatur des Exils*, edited by Bernt Engelmann, 49–60. Munich: Goldmann, 1981.

———. "Vom Kismet der Zwei: Entstehung der Liebe und Rückkehr der Zeitgenossen zu Liebesidealen der Vergangenheit." In *Sadomasochisten, Keusche und Romantik*, edited by Ulrike Heider, 55–72. Reinbek: Rowohlt Verlag, 1986

———. "Von der schwindenden Möglichkeit, mit dem Vater zu streiten." In *Neue Väterlichkeit: Von Möglichkeiten und Unmöglichkeiten des Mannes*, edited by Siegfried Rudolf Dunde, 12–22. Gütersloh: Gütersloher Verlagshaus Mohn, 1986.

———. "'Was will Sigusch eigentlich?'" *Pro Familia Magazin*, no. 2 (1987): 53–56.

———. "Wenn der Versuch der Verhinderung Schaden erzeugt: Sexualfreundlichkeit und sexuelle Gewalt." In *Jugendsexualität: Zwischen Lust und Gewalt*, edited by Frank Herrath and Uwe Sielert, 81–90. Wuppertal: Hammer, 1990.

———. "Wer nicht frei ist, kann auch nicht befreien." In *Kinder, Kinder! Lust und Last der linken Eltern*, edited by Helga Häsing and Volkhard Brandes, 138–45. Frankfurt: Extrabuch, 1983.

———. "When Dogma Bites Dogma, or the Difficult Marriage of Marx and Freud." *The Times Literary Supplement*, 8 January 1971, 1–2.

———. "Wie es war und wie es ist: Korrupte Mittel für die korrumpierte Nation." *Medium* 9 (March 1979): 18.

———. "Wie frei war das 'Freie Fernsehen'?" *Der Monat* 155 (August 1961): 94–96.

———. "'Will Jazz Survive the Century?'" *Jazz*, March 1963, 22.

———. "Zur Frage einer wertfreien Jazzforschung." *Saalfelder Jazztage*, 1979, 30–37.

———. "Zur Klassenstruktur des deutschen Fernsehens." *Vorgänge*, no. 6 (1973): 123–26.

———. "Zur Sexualsoziologie." In *Ausgewählte Texte*, 65–93. Munich: Goldmann, 1990.

———. "Zwei Schwestern: Erinnerungen." *Eros & Psyche*, no. 4 (1989): 6–15.

Borneman, Eva. "Leichen am Legendenwegrand . . . Sehr persönliche Bemerkungen zum innerehelichen Verhältnis von Licht, Identität und Schatten." In *Von der Last der Lust: Sexualität zwischen Liberalisierung und Entfremdung*, edited by Josef Christian Aigner and Rolf Gindorf, 261–64. Vienna: Verlag für Gesellschaftskritik, 1986.

Brady, Frank. *Citizen Welles: A Biography of Orson Welles*. London: Hodder & Stoughton, 1990.

Brandt, George W. "Internment and After." In *Ein Lüderliches Leben*, edited by Sigrid Standow, 71–2. Löhrbach: Pieper's MedienXperimente, 1995.

Brecht, Bertolt. *Bertolt Brecht Werke: Stücke 3*. Edited by Manfred Nössig. Vol. 3. Berlin: Aufbau Verlag, 1988.

———. *Collected Plays*. Vol. 1, *1918–1923*. Edited by John Willett and Ralph Manheim. London: Methuen, 1970.

———. *Versuche 1–12*. Frankfurt: Suhrkamp, 1959.

Bremme, Bettina. *Sexualität im Zerrspiegel: Die Debatte um Pornographie*. Münster: Waxmann, 1990.

Brigl, Kathrin, and Siegfried Schmidt-Joos. *Fritz Rau, Buchhalter der Träume*. Berlin: Quadriga, 1985.

Bröckling, Ulrich, Susanne Krasmann, and Thomas Lemke, eds. *Gouvernementalität der Gegenwart: Studien zur Ökonomisierung des Sozialen*. Frankfurt: Suhrkamp, 2000.

Brunnhuber, Nicole. "After the Prison Ships: Internment Narratives in Canada." In *"Totally Un-English"? Britain's Internment of "Enemy Aliens" in Two World Wars*, edited by Richard Dove, 165–78. Amsterdam: Rodopi, 2005.

———. *The Faces of Janus: English-Language Fiction by German-Speaking Exiles in Great Britain, 1933–45*. Oxford: Peter Lang, 2005.

Bublitz, Hannelore. *Im Beichtstuhl der Medien: Die Produktion des Selbst im öffentlichen Bekenntnis*. Bielefeld: Transcript, 2010.

Buhle, Paul M. *C. L. R. James: The Artist as Revolutionary*. London: Verso, 1988.

Campbell, James. *Exiled in Paris: Richard Wright, James Baldwin, Samuel Beckett, and Others on the Left Bank*. New York: Scribner, 1995.

Classen, Constance. "The Senses." In *Encyclopedia of European Social History*, vol. 4, edited by Peter N. Stearns, 355–64. New York: Scribner, 2001.

Condon, Eddie, and Richard Gehman. *Eddie Condon's Treasury of Jazz*. New York: Dial Press, 1956.

Dannecker, Martin. "Bemerkungen zur strafrechtlichen Behandlung der Pädosexualität." In *Sexualwissenschaft und Strafrecht*, edited by Herbert Jäger and Eberhard Schorsch, 71–83. Stuttgart: F. Enke, 1987.

———. "Sexueller Missbrauch und Pädosexualität." In *Sexuelle Störungen und ihre Behandlung* edited by Volkmar Sigusch, 265–75. Stuttgart: Thieme, 2007.

Dannecker, Martin, and Sigusch Volkmar, eds. *Sexualtheorie und Sexualpolitik: Ergebnisse einer Tagung*. Stuttgart: Enke, 1984.

Dauer, Alfons Michael. *Jazz, die Magische Musik: Ein Leitfaden durch den Jazz*. Bremen: Carl Schünemann Verlag, 1961.

Dhondy, Farrukh. *C. L. R. James: A Life*. London: Weidenfeld & Nicolson, 2001.

Distler, Sonja. *Mütter, Amazonen & dreifältige Göttinnen: Eine psychologische Analyse der feministischen Matriarchatsdebatte*. Vienna: Picus Verlag, 1989.

Dobson, Terence. *The Film Work of Norman McLaren*. London: Libbey, 2006.

Dodge, Roger Pryor. *Hot Jazz and Jazz Dance: Collected Writings 1929–1964*. New York: Oxford University Press, 1995.

Drazin, Charles. *In Search of the Third Man*. London: Methuen, 2000.

Druick, Zoë. *Projecting Canada: Government Policy and Documentary Film at the National Film Board of Canada*. Montreal: McGill-Queen's University Press, 2007.

Eckert, Gerhard. *Das Fernsehen in den Ländern Westeuropas: Entwicklung und gegenwärtiger Stand*. Gütersloh: C. Bertelsmann, 1965.

Eckert, Gerhard, and Fritz Niehus, eds. *Zehn Jahre Fernsehen in Deutschland: Dokumentation—Analyse—Kritik*. Frankfurt: Verlag für Funk- und Fernsehpublizistik, 1963.

Ege, Moritz. *Schwarz werden: "Afroamerikanophilie" in den 1960er und 1970er Jahren*. Bielefeld: Transcript, 2007.

Eitler, Pascal. "'Alternative' Religion: Subjektivierungspraktiken und Politisierungsstrategien im 'New Age' (Westdeutschland 1970–1990)." In *Das alternative Milieu: Antibürgerlicher Lebensstil und linke Politik in der Bundesrepublik Deutschland und Europa 1968–1983*, edited by Sven Reichardt and Detlef Siegfried, 335–52. Göttingen: Wallstein, 2010.

———. "Das 'Reich der Sinne'? Pornographie, Philosophie und die Brutalisierung der Sexualität (Westdeutschland 1968–1988)." *Body Politics* 1, no. 2 (2013): 259–96.

Ellis, Jack C. *John Grierson: Life, Contributions, Influence*. Carbondale, IL: Southern Illinois University Press, 2000.

Engert, Ewald H., ed. *Die Verarmung der Psyche: Igor A. Caruso zum 65. Geburtstag*. Frankfurt: Campus, 1979.

Eppendorfer, Hans. *Der Ledermann spricht mit Hubert Fichte*. Frankfurt: Suhrkamp Verlag, 1977.

Evans, Gary. *John Grierson and the National Film Board: The Politics of Wartime Propaganda, 1939–1945*. Toronto: University of Toronto Press, 1984.

Feather, Leonard. "Not Ashamed of the Blues." *Jazz Monthly*, February 1958, 9–10.

Ferle, Horst. "Bornemans erstes Buch in deutscher Sprache." In *Ein Lüderliches Leben*, edited by Sigrid Standow, 103–4. Löhrbach: Pieper's MedienXperimente, 1995.

Floyd, Samuel A., Jr. *The Power of Black Music: Interpreting Its History from Africa to the United States*. New York: Oxford University Press, 1995.

Foltin, Hans-Friedrich. "Die Talkshow: Geschichte eines schillernden Genres." In *Unterhaltung, Werbung und Zielgruppenprogramme*, edited by Hans Dieter Erlinger and Hans-Friedrich Foltin, 69–112. Munich: W. Fink, 1994.

Forman, Denis. *Persona Granada: Some Memories of Sidney Bernstein and the Early Days of Independent Television*. London: Andre Deutsch, 1997.

Foucault, Michel. *Technologies of the Self: A Seminar with Michel Foucault*. Edited by Luther H Martin. Amherst: University of Massachusetts Press, 1988.

Fryer, Peter. *Staying Power: The History of Black People in Britain*. London: Pluto Press, 1984.

Gabbard, Karin, ed. *Representing Jazz*. Durham: Duke University Press, 1995.

Garon, Paul. *Blues and the Poetic Spirit*. London: Eddison, 1975.

Gehrke, Claudia, ed. *Mein heimliches Auge*. Tübingen: konkursbuch Verlag, 1982.

Geiss, Imanuel. *Panafrikanismus: Zur Geschichte der Dekolonisation*. Frankfurt: Europäische Verlagsanstalt, 1968.

Gendron, Bernard. *Between Montmartre and the Mudd Club: Popular Music and the Avant-Garde*. Chicago: University of Chicago Press, 2002.

Gennari, John. *Blowin' Hot and Cool: Jazz and Its Critics*. Chicago: University of Chicago Press, 2016.

Gerhard, Ute. "Frauenbewegung." In *Die sozialen Bewegungen in Deutschland seit 1945: Ein Handbuch*, edited by Roland Roth and Dieter Rucht, 187–217. Frankfurt: Campus Verlag, 2008.

———. *Unerhört: Die Geschichte der deutschen Frauenbewegung*. Reinbek: Rowohlt Verlag, 1990.

Gershenhorn, Jerry. *Melville J. Herskovits and the Racial Politics of Knowledge*. Lincoln: University of Nebraska Press, 2007.

Gilroy, Paul. *The Black Atlantic: Modernity and Double Consciousness*. Cambridge, MA: Harvard University Press, 1993.

Gittings, Christopher E. *Canadian National Cinema: Ideology, Difference and Representation*. London: Routledge, 2013.

Göttner-Abendroth, Heide. *Das Matriarchat I: Geschichte seiner Erforschung*. Stuttgart: Kohlhammer, 1995.

Graves, James. "Zur Geschichte des Blues." In *Die Könige des Blues*, edited by James Graves, 7–17. Zurich: Sanssouci, 1961.

Gremliza, Hermann L., ed. *Sexualität konkret*. Vol. 1. Frankfurt: Zweitausendeins, 1980.

Grierson, John. "The Documentary Idea: 1942." In *Grierson on Documentary*, edited by Forsyth Hardy, 248–59. New York: Harcourt, Brace, 1947.

Groom, Bob. *The Blues Revival*. London: Studio Vista, 1971.

Grünzweig, Werner. "Not Just a 'One Night Stand': Zur Einrichtung eines Ernest Borneman Archivs an der Stiftung der Akademie der Künste." In *Ein Lüderliches Leben*, edited by Sigrid Standow, 111–15. Löhrbach: Pieper's MedienXperimente, 1995.

Gruppe 5. "Zeitschrift (Beratung)." In *Medien als Sexualaufklärer*, edited by Norbert Kluge, 45-46. Frankfurt: dipa Verlag, 1988.

Habermas, Jürgen. *Die neue Unübersichtlichkeit*. Frankfurt: Suhrkamp, 1985.

Hardy, Forsyth, ed. *Grierson on Documentary*. New York: Harcourt, Brace, 1947.

———. *John Grierson: A Documentary Biography*. London: Faber, 1979.

Hartinger, Ingram. "Als Student bei E.B." In *Ein Lüderliches Leben*, edited by Sigrid Standow, 75–77. Löhrbach: Pieper's MedienXperimente, 1995.

Harvey, Elizabeth D. "The Portal of Touch." *American History Review* 116, no. 2 (April 2011): 385–400.

Hausen, Karin. "Patriarchat: Vom Nutzen und Nachteil eines Konzepts für Frauenpolitik und Frauengeschichte." In *Geschlechtergeschichte als Gesellschaftsgeschichte*, 359–70. Göttingen: Vandenhoeck & Ruprecht, 2013.

Heider, Ulrike. *Sadomasochisten, Keusche und Romantiker: Vom Mythos neuer Sinnlichkeit*. Reinbek: Rowohlt Verlag, 1986.

———. *Vögeln ist schön: Die Sexrevolte von 1968 und was von ihr bleibt*. Berlin: BEBUG, 2014.

Heineman, Elizabeth D. *Before Porn Was Legal: The Erotica Empire of Beate Uhse*. Chicago: University of Chicago Press, 2011.

Held, Heino. "Geschichte einer Freundschaft." In *Ein Lüderliches Leben*, edited by Sigrid Standow, 57–60. Löhrbach: Pieper's MedienXperimente, 1995.

Hentoff, Nat, and Albert J. McCarthy, eds. *Jazz: New Perspectives on the History of Jazz by Twelve of the World's Foremost Jazz Critics and Scholars*. New York: Da Capo Press, 1959.

Herbert, Ulrich. *Geschichte Deutschlands im 20. Jahrhundert*. Munich: C. H. Beck, 2014.

Herskovits, Melville Jean. *The Myth of the Negro Past*. New York: Harper, 1941.

Herzog, Dagmar. *Die Politisierung der Lust: Sexualität in der deutschen Geschichte des zwanzigsten Jahrhunderts*. Munich: Siedler, 2005.

———. *Sexuality in Europe: A Twentieth-Century History*. Cambridge: Cambridge University Press, 2011.

———. "Tomorrow Sex Will Be Good Again." In *After the History of Sexuality: German Genealogies with and beyond Foucault*, edited by Scott Spector, Helmut Puff, and Dagmar Herzog, 282–86. New York: Berghahn, 2012.

———. "Where They Desire They Cannot Love: Recovering Radical Freudianism in West German Sexology (1960s–1980s)." *Psychoanalysis and History* 16, no. 2 (2014): 237–61.

Hickethier, Knut. *Das Fernsehspiel der Bundesrepublik: Themen, Form, Struktur, Theorie und Geschichte 1951–1977*. Stuttgart: J. B. Metzler, 1980.

———. *Geschichte des deutschen Fernsehens*. Stuttgart: J. B. Metzler, 1998.

Hill, John. "Television and Pop: The Case of the 1950s." In *Popular Television in Britain: Studies in Cultural History*, edited by John Corner, 90–107. London: BFI, 1991.

Hobsbawm, E. J. *The Jazz Scene*. London: Weidenfeld and Nicolson, 1989.

Hodenberg, Christina von. *Konsens und Krise: Eine Geschichte der westdeutschen Medienöffentlichkeit, 1945–1973*. Vol. 12. Moderne Zeit. Wallstein Verlag, 2006.

Hurley, Andrew W. *The Return of Jazz: Joachim-Ernst Berendt and West German Cultural Change*. New York: Berghahn, 2009.

Jäger, Herbert. "Erfahrungen mit Aggressionen: Ein Nachwort." In *Der Ledermann spricht mit Hubert Fichte* by Hans Eppendorfer, 217–24. Frankfurt: Suhrkamp Verlag, 1977.

James, C. Rodney. *Film as a National Art: NFB of Canada and the Film Board Idea*. New York: Arno P., 1977.

Janssen-Jurreit, Marielouise. *Sexismus: Über die Abtreibung der Frauenfrage*. Frankfurt: Fischer Taschenbuch Verlag, 1987.

Jay, Martin. "In the Realm of the Senses: An Introduction." *American Historical Review* 116, no. 2 (April 2011): 307–15.

Jones, David Barker. *Movies and Memoranda: An Interpretative History of the National Film Board of Canada*. Ottawa: Canadian Film Institute, 1981.

Jones, LeRoi. *Blues People: Negro Music in White America*. New York: Morrow, 1971.

Jones, Max. "On Blues." In *The PL Yearbook of Jazz 1946*, edited by Albert McCarthy, 71–107. London: Editions Poetry, 1946.

Jütte, Robert. *Geschichte der Sinne: Von der Antike bis zum Cyberspace*. Munich: C. H. Beck, 2000.

Kaupp, Peter. *Die schlimmen Illustrierten: Leserschaft, Inhalt und Wirkung der Neuen Revue: Massenmedien und die Kritik ihrer Kritiker*. Düsseldorf: Econ Verlag, 1971.

Keil, Charles. *Urban Blues*. Chicago: University of Chicago Press, 1966.

Kersting, Franz-Werner. "Juvenile Left-Wing Radicalism, Fringe Groups and Anti-psychiatry in West Germany." In *Between Marx and Coca-Cola: Youth Cultures in Changing European Societies, 1960–1980*, edited by Axel Schildt and Detlef Siegfried, 353–75. New York: Berghahn, 2006.

Khouri, Malek. *Filming Politics: Communism and the Portrayal of the Working Class at the National Film Board of Canada, 1939–46*. Calgary: University of Calgary Press, 2007.

Kluge, Norbert, ed. *Medien als Sexualaufklärer—Projekte, Probleme, Prognosen: Bericht über die 2. Arbeitstagung der "Arbeitsgemeinschaft Sexualpädagogische Forschung" vom 22. bis 23. Oktober 1987 in Landau/Pfalz*. Frankfurt: dipa Verlag, 1988.

Knight, Arthur. "Jammin' the Blues, or the Sight of Jazz, 1944." In *Representing Jazz*, edited by Karin Gabbard, 11–53. Durham: Duke University Press, 1995.

Knopf, Jan. *Brecht-Handbuch Theater: Eine Ästhetik der Widerspüche*. Stuttgart: J. B. Metzlersche Verlagsbuchhandlung, 1986.

Koch, Eric. *Deemed Suspect: A Wartime Blunder*. Halifax, NS: Goodread Biographies, 1985.

Kofsky, Frank. *Black Nationalism and the Revolution in Music*. New York: Pathfinder Press, 2013.

Krasmann, Susanne, and Michael Volkmer. "Einleitung." In *Michel Foucaults "Geschichte der Gouvernementalität" in den Sozialwissenschaften: Internationale Beiträge*, edited by Susanne Krasmann and Michel Volkmer, 7–22. Bielefeld: Transcript Verlag, 2007.

Krechel, Ursula. *Selbsterfahrung und Fremdbestimmung: Bericht aus der Neuen Frauenbewegung*. Darmstadt: Luchterhand, 1983.

Krovoza, Alfred. "Zur Rolle von Psychologie und Psychoanalyse in der anti-autoritären Protestbewegung." In *Die Phantasie an die Macht? 1968—Versuch einer Bilanz*, edited by Richard Faber and Erhard Stölting, 159–72. Berlin: Philo, 2002.

Kübler, Hans-Dieter. "Von der Vorführstunde zur Agentur für Medienwaren: Zur Entwicklung des Kinderfernsehens zum Inbegriff kommerzieller Kinderkultur." In *Unterhaltung, Werbung und Zielgruppenprogramme. Geschichte des Fernsehens in der Bundesrepublik Deutschland*, vol. 4, edited by Hans Dieter Erlinger and Hans-Friedrich Foltin, 327–370. München: Fink, 1994.

Lang, Iain. *The Background of the Blues*. London: Hutchinson, 1947.

Laugsch, Helga. *Der Matriarchats-Diskurs (in) der zweiten deutschen Frauenbewegung: Die (Wider)Rede von der "anderen" Gesellschaft und vom "anderen" Geschlecht : Genese, Geschichte, Positionen, Implikationen, Ideologien*. Munich: H. Utz, 1995.

Lenz, Ilse. *Die neue Frauenbewegung in Deutschland: Abschied vom kleinen Unterschied, Eine Quellensammlung.* Wiesbaden: VS Verlag, 2008.

Lethen, Helmut. *Cool Conduct: The Culture of Distance in Weimar Germany.* Translated by Don Reneau. Berkeley: University of California Press, 2002.

———. *Verhaltenslehren der Kälte: Lebensversuche zwischen den Kriegen.* Frankfurt: Suhrkamp Verlag, 1994.

Lindau, Susanne. *Lebenshilfe in Ratgeberrubriken: Analyse unterhaltender Wochenzeitschriften der Jahre 1962 und 1992.* Wiesbaden: Deutscher Universitäts -Verlag, 1998.

Lindegk, Lutz (i.e., Gerhard Eckert). "Warum erst nach zehn Jahren? Ein kleiner Streifzug durch Gründe und Abgründe der bundesdeutschen Fernsehpolitik." In *Zehn Jahre Fernsehen in Deutschland: Dokumentation—Analyse—Kritik*, edited by Gerhard Eckert and Fritz Niehus, 81–96. Frankfurt: Verlag für Funk- und Fernsehpublizistik, 1963.

Maase, Kaspar. *Die Kinder der Massenkultur: Kontroversen um Schmutz und Schund seit dem Kaiserreich.* Frankfurt: Campus Verlag, 2012.

Maasen, Sabine. *Das beratene Selbst: Zur Genealogie der Therapeutisierung in den "langen" Siebzigern.* Bielefeld: Transcript, 2011.

———. "Sexualberatung auf dem Boulevard: Ein Beitrag zur Genealogie normal/istisch/er Selbstführungskompetenz." In *Fragen Sie Dr. Sex!: Ratgeberkommunikation und die mediale Konstruktion des Sexuellen*, edited by Peter Paul Bänziger, 317–46. Frankfurt: Suhrkamp Verlag, 2010.

Magenau, Jörg. *Die taz: Eine Zeitung als Lebensform.* Munich: Hanser, 2007.

Mailer, Norman. "The White Negro: Superficial Reflections on the Hipster." *Dissent Magazine*, Fall 1957.

Marwick, Arthur. *The Sixties: Cultural Revolution in Britain, France, Italy, and the United States, 1958–1974.* Oxford: Oxford University Press, 1998.

Marx, Gary T. "The White Negro and the Negro White." *Phylon* 28, no. 2 (Summer 1967): 168–77. Accessed 2 October 2006 from https://web.mit.edu/gtmarx/www/whitenegro.html.

Mattes, Peter. "Die Psychologiekritik der Studentenbewegung." In *Geschichte der deutschen Psychologie im 20. Jahrhundert*, edited by Mitchell G. Ash and Ulfried Geuter, 286–313. Opladen: Westdeutscher Verlag, 1985.

McCarthy, Albert. "The Literature of Jazz." In *The PL Yearbook of Jazz 1946*, edited by Albert McCarthy, 169–78. London: Editions Poetry, 1946.

———, ed. *The PL Yearbook of Jazz 1946.* London: Editions Poetry, 1946.

McInnes, Graham. *One Man's Documentary: A Memoir of the Early Years of the National Film Board.* Winnipeg: University of Manitoba Press, 2008.

McKay, Marjorie. *History of the National Film Board of Canada.* N.p.: National Film Board of Canada, 1977.

Mechler, Hans-Jürgen. "Für Sexualerziehung in der Schule: Ein Plädoyer." In *Sexualität: Materialien zur Sexualforschung*, edited VS Ernest Borneman, 125–36. Weinheim: Beltz, 1979.

Menschik, Jutta. *Feminismus: Geschichte, Theorie, Praxis.* Cologne: Pahl-Rugenstein, 1977.

Merscheim, Horst. *Medizin in Illustrierten: Berichterstattungs-Analyse von "Bunte," "Neue Revue" "Quick" und "Stern."* Bochum: Studienverlag Brockmeyer, 1978.

Meyer, Brigit. "Frauenbewegung und politische Kultur in den 80er Jahren." In *Die Bundesrepublik in den 80er Jahren: Innenpolitik, Politische Kultur, Außenpolitik,* edited by Werner Süß, 219–34. Opladen: Leske + Budrich, 1991.

Mezzrow, Mezz, and Bernard Wolfe. *Really the Blues.* New York: Random House, 1946.

Miller, Manfred. "Vorwort." In *Blues People: Negro Music in White America,* by Leroi Jones (German translation). Wiesbaden: Fourier, 1981.

Mohr, Reinhard. *Zaungäste: Die Generation, die nach der Revolte kam.* Frankfurt: S. Fischer, 1992.

Monod, David. *Settling Scores: German Music, Denazification, & The Americans, 1945–1953.* Chapel Hill: University of North Carolina Press, 2005.

Monson, Ingrid T. *Freedom Sounds: Civil Rights Call Out to Jazz and Africa.* Oxford: Oxford University Press, 2007.

———. *Saying Something: Jazz Improvisation and Interaction.* Chicago: University of Chicago Press, 1996.

Moore, Hilary. *Inside British Jazz: Crossing Borders of Race, Nation and Class.* Aldershot: Ashgate, 2007.

Morat, Daniel. "Die Stadt und die Sinne: Sinnesgeschichtliche Perspektiven auf Urbanisierung und Großstadterfahrung." *Informationen zur modernen Stadtgeschichte* 43, no. 2 (2012): 23–28.

Morley, David, and Kevin Robins. *Spaces of Identity: Global Media, Electronic Landscapes and Cultural Boundaries.* London: Routledge, 1995.

Müller, Klaus-Detlef. *Die Funktion der Geschichte im Werk Bertolt Brechts: Studien zum Verhältnis von Marxismus und Ästhetik.* Tübingen: Niemeyer, 1972.

Müller, Klaus E. *"Die bessere und die schlechtere Hälfte": Ethnologie des Geschlechterkonflikts.* Frankfurt: Campus, 1984.

National Film Board of Canada. *The NFB Film Guide: The Productions of the National Film Board of Canada from 1939 to 1989.* Montreal: The Board, 1991.

Nelson, Joyce. *The Colonized Eye: Rethinking the Grierson Legend.* Toronto: Between the Lines, 1988.

Noble, Peter. *The Fabulous Orson Welles.* London: Hutchinson, 1956.

Notz, Gisela. "Die autonomen Frauenbewegungen der Siebzigerjahre: Entstehungsgeschichte—Organisationsformen—politische Konzepte." *Archiv für Sozialgeschichte* 44 (2004): 123–48.

Okami, Paul, Richard Olmstead, and Paul R. Abrahamson. "Sexual Experiences in Early Childhood: 18-Year Longitudinal Data from the UCLA Family Lifestyles Project." *Journal of Sex Research* 34, no. 4 (1997): 339–47.

Oliver, Paul. "Blue-Eyed Blues: The Impact of Blues on European Popular Culture." In *Approaches to Popular Culture*, edited by C. W. E. Bigsby, 227–39. London: Edward Arnold, 1976.

———. *Savannah Syncopators: African Retentions in the Blues*. New York: Stein and Day, 1970.

———. *Songsters and Saints: Vocal Traditions on Race Records*. Cambridge: Cambridge University Press, 1984.

———. "Taking the Measure of the Blues." In *Cross the Water Blues: African American Music in Europe*, edited by Neil A. Wynn, 23–38. Jackson: University Press of Mississippi, 2007.

———. "That Certain Feeling: Blues and Jazz . . . in 1890?" *Popular Music* 10, no. 1 (January 1991): 11–19.

Osgerby, Bill. *Youth in Britain since 1945*. Oxford: Blackwell, 1998.

Ottomeyer, Klaus. "Zur Diskussion um das Patriarchat." *Das Argument* 97 (1976): 466–84.

Peglau, Andreas. *Unpolitische Wissenschaft?: Wilhelm Reich und die Psychoanalyse im Nationalsozialismus*. Giessen: Psychosozial Verlag, 2013.

Perinelli, Massimo. "Lust, Gewalt, Befreiung, Sexualitätsdiskurse." In *agit 883: Bewegung Revolte, Underground in Westberlin 1969–1972*, edited by rotaprint 25, 85–100. Berlin: Assoziation A, 2006.

Perner, Rotraud A. *Zeugin der Lüste: Lust und Frust der Rundfunksexualberatung*. Bad Sauerbrunn: Edition Tau, 1991.

———. "Zuliebe zu Leibe." In *Zuliebe zu Leibe: Über die Möglichkeit und Unmöglichkeit kindlicher Erotik*, edited by Rotraud A. Perner, 9–34. Bad Sauerbrunn: Edition Tau, 1991.

Porter, Eric C. *What Is This Thing Called Jazz? African American Musicians as Artists, Critics, and Activists*. Berkeley: University of California Press, 2002.

Rackelmann, Marc. "Was war die Sexpol? Wilhelm Reich und der Einheitsverband für Proletarische Sexualreform und Mutterschutz." *Emotion: Beitrage zum Werk von Wilhelm Reich* 11 (1993): 56–93.

Radano, Ronald Michael. *New Musical Figurations: Anthony Braxton's Cultural Critique*. Chicago: University of Chicago Press, 1993.

Raeburn, Bruce Boyd. "Beyond the 'Spanish Tinge': Hispanics and Latinos in Early New Orleans Jazz." In *Eurojazzland: Jazz and European Sources, Dynamics, and Contexts*, edited by Luca Cerciari, 21–46. Boston: Northeastern University Press, 2012.

Rebhandl, Bert. *Orson Welles: Genie im Labyrinth*. Vienna: Zsolnay, 2005.

Reichardt, Sven. *Authentizität und Gemeinschaft: Linksalternatives Leben in den siebziger und frühen achtziger Jahren*. Berlin: Suhrkamp Verlag, 2014.

Reiche, Reimut. "Sexuelle Revolution—Erinnerung an einen Mythos." In *Die Früchte der Revolte: Über die Veränderung der politischen Kultur durch die Studentenbewegung*, edited by Lothar Baier et al., 45–71. Berlin: K. Wagenbach, 1988.

Reinfrank, Arno. "The Windows of Heaven." In *Ein Lüderliches Leben*, edited by Sigrid Standow, 101ff. Löhrbach: Pieper's MedienXperimente, 1995.

Richard, Valliere T. *Norman McLaren, Manipulator of Movement: The National Film Board Years, 1947–1967*. London: Associated University Presses, 1982.

Ritchie, James M., ed. *German Exiles: British Perspectives*. New York: Peter Lang, 1997.

Roberts, John Storm. *Black Music of Two Worlds: African, Caribbean, Latin and African-American Traditions*. New York: Schirmer, 1998.

Robinson, Cedric J. *Black Marxism: The Making of the Black Radical Tradition*. N.p: University of North Carolina, 1983.

Rotha, Paul. *Documentary Film*. London: Faber and Faber, 1936.

Rowley, Hazel. *Richard Wright: The Life and Times*. New York: Henry Holt, 2001.

Rutschky, Katharina. *Erregte Aufklärung: Kindesmissbrauch; Fakten & Fiktionen*. Hamburg: Klein Verlag, 1992.

Rutschky, Katharina, and Reinhart Wolff, eds. *Handbuch Sexueller Missbrauch*. Hamburg: Klein, 1994.

Salzinger, Helmut. *Rock Power oder Wie musikalisch ist die Revolution?* Frankfurt: Fischer Taschenbuch Verlag, 1972.

Schall, Hans-Jürgen. "Der vergessene Jazzkritiker: Sexualforscher Ernest Borneman." *JazzZeitung*, December 2003 and January 2004, 22–23.

Scheub, Ute. *Heldendämmerung: Die Krise der Männer und warum sie auch für Frauen gefährlich ist*. Munich: Pantheon, 2010.

Schildt, Axel. "Die Kräfte der Gegenreform sind auf breiter Front angetreten: Zur konservativen Tendenzwende in den Siebzigerjahren." *Archiv für Sozialgeschichte* 44 (2004): 449–78.

———. *Moderne Zeiten: Freizeit, Massenmedien und "Zeitgeist" in der Bundesrepublik der 50er Jahre*. Vol. 31. Hamburger Beiträge zur Sozial- und Zeitgeschichte. Hamburg: Christians, 1995.

Schmidt, Gunter. "Drang und Lust." In *Sexualwesen Mensch: Texte zur Erforschung der Sexualität*, edited by Helmut Kentler, 300–317. Hamburg: Hoffmann und Campe, 1984.

———. "Entgegnung." In *Sexualtheorie und Sexualpolitik: Ergebnisse einer Tagung*, edited by Martin Dannecker and Volkmar Sigusch, 17–19. Stuttgart: Enke, 1984.

———, ed. *Kinder der sexuellen Revolution: Kontinuität und Wandel studentischer Sexualität 1966–1999*. Giessen: Psychosozial Verlag, 2000.

Schmidt-Joos, Siegfried. *My Back Pages: Idole und Freaks, Tod und Legende in der Popmusik*. Berlin: Lukas Verlag, 2004.

Schuller, Gunther. *Early Jazz: Its Roots and Musical Development*. New York: Oxford University Press, 1968.

Schulz, Kristina. *Der lange Atem der Provokation: Die Frauenbewegung in der Bundesrepublik und in Frankreich 1968–1976*. Frankfurt: Campus Verlag, 2002.

Schwartz, Roberta Freund. *How Britain Got the Blues: The Transmission and Reception of American Blues Style in the United Kingdom.* Aldershot: Ashgate, 2007.

————. "Preaching the Gospel of the Blues: Blues Evangelists in Britain." In *Cross the Water Blues: African American Music in Europe,* edited by Neil A. Wynn, 145–66. Jackson: University Press of Mississippi, 2007.

Schwarzer, Alice. *So fing es an! 10 Jahre Frauenbewegung.* Cologne: Emma Frauenverlag, 1981.

Schwendter, Rolf. "Laudatio zum Fünfundsiebzigsten." In *Ein Lüderliches Leben,* edited by Sigrid Standow, 11–15. Löhrbach: Pieper's MedienXperimente, 1995.

Sendall, Bernard. *Independent Television in Britain: Origin and Foundation 1946–62.* Vol. 1. London: Macmillan, 1982.

Senger, Gerti, and Walter Hoffmann. Österreich intim: Der Senger-Report über Seele, Sex und Sinnlichkeit. Vienna: Amalthea, 1993.

Sessler, Thomas. "Parallele Lebensstränge" In *Ein Lüderliches Leben,* edited by Sigrid Standow, 66ff. Löhrbach: Pieper's MedienXperimente, 1995.

Seyfert, Michael. "'His Majesty's Most Loyal Internees': Die Internierung und Deportation deutscher und österreichischer Flüchtlinge als 'enemy aliens'. Historische, kulturelle und literarische Aspekte." In *Exil in Großbritannien: Zur Emigration aus dem nationalsozialistischen Deutschland,* edited by Gerhard Hirschfeld, 155–182. Stuttgart: Klett-Cotta, 1983.

Siegfried, Detlef. "Die Entpolitisierung des Privaten: Subjektkonstruktionen im alternativen Milieu." In *Privatisierung: Idee und Praxis seit den 1970er Jahren* edited by Norbert Frei and Dietmar Süß, 124–39. Göttingen: Wallstein Verlag, 2012.

————. *Time is on my Side: Konsum und Politik in der westdeutschen Jugendkultur der 60er Jahre.* Göttingen: Wallstein, 2006.

Sigusch, Volkmar. "Das gemeine Lied der Liebe." In *Sexualität konkret,* vol. 1, edited by Hermann Gremliza, 11–20. Frankfurt: Zweitausendeins, 1980.

————. "Der Ratschläger: Sexualität als Phrase." *Pro Familia Magazin* 1 (1987): 12–16.

————. "Der Ratschläger oder Sexologie als Phrase." In *Anti-Moralia, Sexualpolitische Kommentare,* 84–94. Frankfurt: Campus, 1990.

————. "Ernest Borneman." In *Personenlexikon der Sexualforschung,* edited by Volkmar Sigusch and Günter Grau, 73–78. Frankfurt: Campus, 2009.

————. *Geschichte der Sexualwissenschaft.* Frankfurt: Campus Verlag, 2008.

————. "Liebe Kollegen!" *Sexualmedizin* 10 (1986): 475.

————. "Lob des Triebes." In *Vom Trieb und von der Liebe,* 27–42. Frankfurt: Campus Verlag, 1984.

————. *Neosexualitäten: Über den kulturellen Wandel von Liebe und Perversion* Frankfurt: Campus Verlag, 2005.

————. "Thesen über Natur und Sexualität." In *Sexualität konkret,* vol. 1, edited by Hermann Gremliza, 118–23. Frankfurt: Zweitausendeins, 1980.

———. "Über den Versuch, das Sexuelle zu definieren." In *Sexualität konkret: Sammelband 2*, edited by Volkmar Sigusch, Ingrid Klein, and Hermann Gremliza, 563–69. Frankfurt: Zweitausendeins, 1984.

———. *Vom Trieb und von der Liebe*. Frankfurt: Campus Verlag, 1984.

Silies, Eva-Maria. *Liebe, Lust und Last: Die Pille als weibliche Generationserfahrung in der Bundesrepublik 1960–1980*. Göttingen: Wallstein, 2010.

Smith, Mark M. *Sensory History*. Oxford: Berg, 2007.

Sollors, Werner. *Amiri Baraka/LeRoi Jones: The Quest for a "Populist Modernism."* New York: Columbia University Press, 1978.

Sollors, Werner, and Bernd Weyergraf. "Nachwort (1969)." In *Blues People: Negro Music in White America*, by Leroi Jones (German translation). Darmstadt: Melzer, 1969.

Standow, Sigrid, ed. *Ein lüderliches Leben: Portrait eines Unangepassten; Festschrift für Ernest Borneman zum achtzigsten Geburtstag*. Löhrbach: Pieper's MedienXperimente, 1995.

Steinmetz, Rüdiger. *Freies Fernsehen: Das erste privat-kommerzielle Fernsehprogramm in Deutschland*. Konstanz: UVK Medien, 1996.

Sternfeld, Wilhelm, and Eva Tiedemann, eds. *Deutsche Exil-Literatur, 1933–1945: Eine Bio-Bibliographie*. 2nd ed. Heidelberg: Lambert Schneider, 1970.

Strickhausen, Waltraud. "Englische Romane von Exilautoren: Ernest Borneman und Anna Sebastian." In *"England? Aber wo liegt es?" Deutsche und österreichische Emigranten in Großbritannien 1933–1945*, edited by Charmian Brinson, 207–19. Munich: ludicium, 1996.

Sundquist, Eric J. *To Wake the Nations: Race in the Making of American Literature*. Cambridge, MA: Harvard University Press, 1993.

Symons, Julian. *Bloody Murder: From the Detective Story to the Crime Novel; A History*. Harmondsworth: Penguin Books, 1974.

Tändler, Maik. "'Psychoboom': Therapeutisierungsprozesse in Westdeutschland in den späten 1960er und 1970er Jahren." In *Das beratene Selbst: Zur Genealogie der Therapeutisierung in den "langen" Siebzigern*, edited by Sabine Maasen, 59–94. Bielefeld: Transcript, 2011.

Tavares, Frank. "Orson Welles, Harry Allan Towers, and the Many Lives of Harry Lime." *Journal of Radio & Audio Media* 17, no. 2 (2010): 167–81.

Thomson, David. *Rosebud: The Story of Orson Welles*. New York: Knopf, 1996.

Tieben-Heibert, Annette. *Das Bild von Partnerschaft und Ehe in deutschen Illustrierten: Inhaltsnalytische Untersuchung der Zeitschriften "Bunte", "Neue Revue" und "Stern" auf der Grundlage psychologischer Theorien über intime zwischenmenschliche Beziehungen*. Münster, n.p., 1976.

Traill, Sinclair, and Gerald Lascelles, eds. *Just Jazz*. London: Peter Davies, 1957.

———, eds. *Just Jazz 2*. London: Peter Davies, 1958.

———, eds. *Just Jazz 3*. London: Peter Davies, 1959.

Trübswasser, Gerhild. "Ernest Borneman." *Werkblatt: Zeitschrift für Psychoanalyse und Gesellschaftskritik* 33, no. 2 (1994): 4–5.

Tümmers, Henning. "Aidspolitik: Bonn und der Umgang mit einer neuen Bedrohung." *Archiv für Sozialgeschichte* 52 (2012): 231–52.

UNESCO. *Report of the Director General on the Activities of the Organisation in 1947.* Paris: UNESCO, 1947.

———. *Report of the Director General on the Activities of the Organisation in 1948.* Paris: UNESCO, 1948.

Vian, Boris. *Oeuvres.* Vol. 6. Edited by Ursula Kübler. Paris: Fayard, 1999.

Wellmann, Annika. *Beziehungssex: Medien und Beratung im 20. Jahrhundert.* Cologne: Böhlau, 2012.

Wesel, Uwe. *Der Mythos vom Matriarchat.* Frankfurt: Suhrkamp, 1985.

Wiemann, Dirk. *Exilliteratur in Großbritannien 1933–1945.* Opladen: Westdeutscher Verlag, 1998.

Winston, Brian. *Claiming the Real: The Griersonian Documentary and Its Legitimations.* London: British Film Institute, 1995.

———. "John Grierson Versus Ethnography." In *Memories of the Origins of Ethnographic Film*, edited by Beate Engelbrecht, 49–55. Frankfurt: Peter Lang, 2007.

Worcester, Kent. *C. L. R. James: A Political Biography.* Albany: State University of New York Press, 1996.

Wynn, Neil A. *Cross the Water Blues: African American Music in Europe.* Jackson: University Press of Mississippi, 2007.

Zimmer, Dieter. "Der Blues ist überall: Gedanken zum American Folk Blues Festival 1963." *Jazz Podium*, no. 11 (1963): 232–33.

Zwerin, Mike, ed. *Round About Close to Midnight: The Jazz Writings of Boris Vian.* London: Quartet Books, 1988.

INDEX